To Uncle Alwyn
Xmas 202?
From Archie Mic...
+ Carly
+

Special Transfer
To

John Crosby

Hospital Friend

From:
Q & S. Cardwell
Tarbolton

BURNS
for
EVERY
DAY
of the
YEAR

BURNS

for

EVERY

DAY

of the

YEAR

PAULINE
MACKAY

BLACK & WHITE PUBLISHING

First published 2021
by Black & White Publishing Ltd
Nautical House, 104 Commercial Street, Edinburgh, EH6 6NF

1 3 5 7 9 10 8 6 4 2   21 22 23 24

ISBN: 978 1 78530 298 5

A CIP catalogue record for this book is available from the British Library.

Typeset by Iolaire, Newtonmore
Printed and bound by CPI Group (UK) Ltd Croydon, CR0 4YY

MIX
Paper from
responsible sources
FSC® C020471

for Dòmhnall, Eimhir and Calum Peter

Contents

'Welcome and welcome again!'

ROBERT BURNS IS THE Scottish National Bard and one of the world's most famous poets and songwriters. He was born in Alloway, Ayrshire, on the 25th of January 1759 and, since his death in Dumfries on the 21st of July 1796, he has become the most commemorated of all authors. After all, what other cultural figure has a night every year dedicated to the celebration of their life and works? In a ritual that began early in the nineteenth century, on the 25th of January, the bard is exuberantly toasted at Burns Suppers in every corner of the globe, from Scotland to Australia, from China to the United States.

Burns for Every Day of the Year offers daily glimpses into the bard's life and works. The combination of Burns's intellect, imagination and sheer ability with language (in both English and Scots) makes for compelling reading. Not only this, but Burns led a colourful, if tragically short, life. Ultimately, Burns was a lover – and a 'leaver'; a brother and a friend; a husband and a father; a pleasure-seeker and a labourer. He was a sincerely religious man, albeit one with a scathing satirical bent and an intolerance for religious hypocrisy. From his writing we might derive his broad support for Jacobitism and Republicanism, if reined in at times owing to his employment as a government excise officer in the last seven years of his life. As a ploughman Burns was no stranger to the earthly turning of the seasons, hard labour or financial penury, but he also enjoyed a taste of the finer things in life when, following the success of the 'Kilmarnock edition' of *Poems, Chiefly in the Scottish Dialect* (1786), he spent a short time as the toast of Edinburgh high society and made several tours, or 'pilgrimages', across Scotland and the north of England. The eminently clubbable bard revelled in the company of his male cronies – in particular, in the fraternity of the Freemasons, the enlightened debate of the Tarbolton Bachelors' Club, and in the composition of bawdy verse for the entertainment of his convivial 'comrades', the Crochallan Fencibles. A remarkable poet and a herald of the Romantic era, he was also, perhaps, the world's best composer of love songs, and it is to Burns that we owe the exquisite lyrics of 'Ae Fond Kiss' and 'O, My Luve's Like a Red, Red, Rose'.

Burns for Every Day of the Year embraces, celebrates and explores this complexity through a series of carefully curated extracts from the bard's poetry, song and prose. Thematic 'pockets' of texts are punctuated with works inspired by the seasons and pleasingly apposite references to key dates in Burns's life, Scottish history and modern observances.

In January, the celebrations of New Year and the Burns Supper season are set against the backdrop of the harsh Scottish winter. February explores the theme of love with reference to Burns's many intrigues with the opposite sex, not least his fraught courtship of the woman who would become his wife, Jean Armour, and his sentimental – at times passionate – correspondence with Agnes McLehose, or 'Clarinda'. March offers a rich diversity of topics, among which you will encounter a selection of Burns's writing inspired by our 'fellow mortals' in the animal kingdom, and in April we discover more about his thoughts on Jacobitism. Spring is fully sprung by May, when we accompany Burns on a leg of his 1787 tour of the Scottish Borders and encounter writing inspired by the elusive 'Highland Mary'. In June we turn our attention to Burns's agricultural endeavours and, at a time of year when the 'wedding season' is underway, we discover his thoughts on marriage. July presents works inspired by the bard's association with freemasonry, his engagement with contemporary politics (particularly the American and French Revolutions), and an account of his untimely death at the age of thirty-seven. August surveys his independent and shrewd observations on matters religious, and then we join the bard on several stops from his 1787 Highland Tour, taking us into September and that vital season for any farmer: harvest time. October's atmosphere turns eerie with a selection of Burns's supernatural writings, November takes on a more explicitly Scottish flavour around St Andrew's Night, while December provides a contrast between the gloom that Burns clearly felt in the bleak depths of winter and the warm conviviality that many of us seek out during the festive season.

Ultimately, this book offers 366 glimpses into the many layers of Burns's complicated and brilliant mind, his fascinating life, and his remarkable literary legacy, encompassing the variety that has helped to sustain the bard's timeless and universal appeal. I hope you enjoy reading it as much as I have enjoyed curating it – and that you welcome Burns's 'gude fellowship' on your journey throughout the year ...

Note on the text

Texts are based, as far as possible, upon first printed edition, with consultation of manuscript or later printed editions in a very few cases where this has been superseded by a substantially different version. Where a song has been set to a well-known and easily identifiable air, this has been indicated. Titles, or topics, provided for letter extracts are the editor's own.

JANUARY

'All hail! my own inspired Bard!'

from The Vision

1st JANUARY

from Sketch. New Year's Day. To Mrs Dunlop

O N NEW YEAR'S DAY IN 1789, Burns sent the following verses to a valued and trusted friend, Mrs Frances Anna Dunlop (1730–1815). Many of us reach out to a particular friend or family member at the turn of the year and, for Burns, Frances Dunlop, his 'honor'd first of friends', was that person.

Burns wrote more letters to Frances Dunlop than to any other correspondent. She was significantly older than the poet and the source of much advice, both solicited and unsolicited. In fact, Frances thought her age and status qualified her to comment on everything from Burns's poetry to his love-life. She wrote to Burns: 'I have been told that Voltaire read all his manuscripts to an old woman and printed nothing but what she would have approved. I wish you would name me to her office.' Although Burns sincerely respected Frances, he did not always take her advice or humour her suggestions, sometimes to her obvious displeasure.

In the poem Burns recognises that time is both fixed and inescapable. He invites his friend to pause with him for a moment; to take some time away from the daily goings-on of family life and consider the value of reflecting upon the past year. Burns ponders the uncertainty of the future, in life and beyond, and encourages his friend to embrace the present and 'live as those who never die'. In casting his mind back and forward Burns captures the essence of the month of January, so named after Janus; the two-faced Roman god of beginnings and endings.—

First, what did yesternight deliver?
"Another year is gone for ever."
And what is this day's strong suggestion?
"The passing moment's all we rest on!"
Rest on — for what? what do we here?
Or why regard the passing year?
Will time, amus'd with proverb'd lore,
Add to our date one minute more?
A few days may — a few years must —
Repose us in the silent dust.

Then is it wise to damp our bliss?
Yes — all such reasonings are amiss!
The voice of nature loudly cries,
And many a message from the skies,
That something in us never dies:
That on his frail, uncertain state,
Hang matters of eternal weight:
That future life in worlds unknown
Must take its hue from this alone;
Whether as heavenly glory bright,
Or dark as misery's woeful night.—

Since then, my honor'd, first of friends,
On this poor being all depends;
Let us th' important *now* employ,
And live as those who never die.
Tho' you, with days and honors crown'd,
Witness that filial circle round,
(A sight life's sorrows to repulse,
A sight pale envy to convulse)
Others now claim your chief regard;
Yourself, you wait your bright reward.

2ND JANUARY

On New Year
from a letter to Frances Dunlop, New Year's Day morning, 1789

THE 'SKETCH' TO FRANCES DUNLOP accompanied a letter in which Burns refers to New Year as a time to be hopeful: it is 'a morning of wishes'. The bard goes on to explain the importance he places upon annual celebrations and the changing seasons. For him, they frame human existence and break the monotony of everyday life.

I own myself so little Presbyterian that I approve of set times & seasons of more than ordinary acts of Devotion; for breaking in on that habituated routine of life & thought which is so apt to reduce our existence to a kind of Instinct; or even sometimes & with some minds to a state very little superior to mere Machinery.— This Day; the first Sunday of May; a breezy, blue-skyed noon some time about the beginning, & a hoary morning & calm sunny day about the end, of Autumn; these, time out of mind, have been with me a kind of Holidays.— Not like the Sacramental, Executioner-face of a Kilmarnock Communion; but to laugh or cry, be cheerful or pensive, moral or devout, according to the mood & tense of the Season & Myself.—

from The Auld Farmer's New-Year Morning Salutation to His Auld Mare, Maggie, on Giving Her the Accustomed Ripp of Corn to Hansel in the New-Year

BURNS MADE POWERFUL USE of language whether writing in English or Scots and this poem is a strong performance in the latter. Burns's 'Auld Farmer' reflects upon times past, age and loyalty. The title refers to the tradition of 'Auld Handsel Monday' whereby, on the first Monday of the year, labourers and servants were presented with a token of thanks from their employers and given a day's holiday to celebrate the season. Likewise, farm animals would be treated to an extra special feed. As a farmer himself, Burns greatly valued his creature companions, composing several poems in their honour.

A *Guid New-year* I wish you, Maggie!
Hae, there's a ripp to thy auld baggie:
Tho' thou's howe-backit, now, an' knaggie,
                    I've seen the day,
Thou could hae gaen like ony staggie
                    Out owre the lay.

Tho' now thou's dowie, stiff an' crazy,
An' thy auld hide as white's a daisie,
I've seen thee dappl't, sleek an' glaizie,
                    A bonie gray:
He should been tight that daur't to *raize* thee,
                    Ance in a day.

Thou ance was i' the foremost rank,
A *silly* buirdly, steeve an' swank,
An' set weel down a shapely shank,
                    As e'er tread yird;
An' could hae flown out owre a stank,
                    Like onie bird.

[...]

Mony a sair daurk we twa hae wrought,
An' wi' the weary warl' fought!
An' mony an *anxious day*, I thought
                    We wad be beat!
Yet here to *crazy Age* we're brought,
                    Wi' something yet.

An' think na, my auld, trusty *Servan'*,
That now perhaps thou's less deservin,
An' thy *auld days* may end in starvin';
                    For my last fow,
A heapit *Stimpart*, I'll reserve ane
                    Laid by for you.

We've worn to crazy years thegither;
We'll toyte about wi' ane anither;
Wi' tentie care I'll flit thy tether
                    To some hain'd rig,
Whare ye may nobly rax your leather,
                    Wi' sma' fatigue.

4TH JANUARY

To Miss Logan
with Beattie's Poems for a *New–Year's Gift,* 1st January 1787

O N NEW YEAR'S DAY in 1787, Burns sent Susan Logan – the sister of his acquaintance, William Logan of Park – a copy of James Beattie's *The Minstrel; or, The Progress of Genius* (1771; 1774). A poem about poetic growth and inspiration, *The Minstrel* tells the story of Edwin, another bard born into 'the lowly vale of shepherd life'. *The Minstrel* was profoundly influential for Burns and for many significant authors of the Romantic period, among them William Wordsworth and Lord Byron. Here Burns playfully warns Miss Logan of the cunning and inconstancy of some men, wishing her lovers who are as honest, gentle and sentimental as Beattie's bard, Edwin. Not, presumably, Burns himself whose womanising is well documented and who was only too aware of his own proclivities in that respect.

Again the silent wheels of time
Their annual round have driv'n,
And you, tho' scarce in maiden prime,
Are so much nearer Heav'n.

No gifts have I from Indian coasts
The infant year to hail;
I send you more than India boasts,
In *Edwin's* simple tale.

Our Sex with guile and faithless love,
Is charg'd, perhaps too true;
But may, dear Maid, each Lover prove
An *Edwin* still to you.

5TH JANUARY

On New Year
from a letter to Frances Dunlop, 1st January 1795

I N ANOTHER NEW YEAR MESSAGE to Frances Dunlop, Burns's mood is again one of profound reflection. Here we see something of the poet's own creed; an inclusive outlook that is emphasised and restated throughout his verse and correspondence. Burns's universal sentiments are in many ways ahead of their time and resonate as keenly in the twenty-first century as they did in January 1795.

What a transient business is life!— Very lately I was a boy; but t'other day I was a young man; and I already begin to feel the rigid fibre and stiffening joints of Old Age coming fast o'er my frame.— With all my follies of youth, and I fear, a few vices of manhood, still I congratulate myself on having had in early days religion strongly impressed on my mind.— I have nothing to say to any body as to which Sect they belong, or what Creed they believe; but I look on the Man who is firmly persuaded of Infinite Wisdom and Goodness superintending and directing every circumstance that can happen in his lot— I felicitate such a man as having a solid foundation for his mental enjoyment; a firm prop and sure stay in the hour of difficulty, trouble and distress: and a never-failing anchor of hope when he looks beyond the grave.—

6TH JANUARY

My Father Was a Farmer

THIS REPRESENTS ONE of Burns's earliest attempts at song-writing. He was unhappy with this song, describing it in his 'First Commonplace Book' as 'a wild Rhapsody, miserably deficient in Versification, but as the sentiments are the genuine feelings of my heart, for that reason I have a particular pleasure in conning it over'. If not Burns's most elegant work, it is interesting for the perspective it offers on his background and upbringing.

Burns's father William Burnes (1721–1784) grew up in Kincardineshire in the north-east of Scotland. He moved to Ayrshire via Edinburgh in search of agricultural work and it was here that he met Burns's mother, Agnes Broun (1732–1820) from Culzean. The couple married on the 15th of December 1757 and had seven children, of whom Robert was the eldest. While the family name was originally the north-eastern 'Burnes', both Robert and his brother Gilbert changed their surname to the southern variant, 'Burns', in adulthood.

William Burnes was unfortunate in his farming endeavours. Each of the Ayrshire farms that he leased, Mount Oliphant and then Lochlea, proved difficult to cultivate and the family endured periods of significant hardship. According to an account by his brother Gilbert, Burns was assisting his father on the farm at the age of thirteen and by the age of fifteen he was the principal labourer. Despite the family's financial troubles, William Burnes remained committed to his children's education and religious understanding, providing Robert and Gilbert with a private tutor and opportunities to attend school, and even composing his own *Manual of Religious Belief* for their religious and moral instruction.

My father was a farmer upon the Carrick border O
And carefully he bred me, in decency and order O
He bade me act a manly part, though I had ne'er a farthing O
For without an honest manly heart, no man was worth regarding O

Chorus Row de Dow &c.

Then out into the world my course I did determine. O
Tho' to be rich was not my wish, yet to be great was charming. O
My talents they were not the worst; nor yet my education: O
Resolv'd was I, at least to try, to mend my situation. O

In many a way, and vain essay, I courted fortune's favour; O
Some cause unseen, still stept between, and frustrate each endeavour; O
Some times by foes I was o'erpower'd; sometimes by friends forsaken; O
And when my hope was at the top, I still was worst mistaken. O

Then sore harass'd, and tir'd at last, with fortune's vain delusion; O
I dropt my schemes, like idle dreams, and came to this conclusion; O
The past was bad, and the future hid; its good or ill untryd; O
But the present hour was in my pow'r, and so I would enjoy it. O

No help, nor hope, nor view had I; nor person to befriend me; O
So I must toil, and sweat and moil, and labor to sustain me. O
To plough and sow, to reap and mow, my father bred me early, O
For one, he said, to labour bred, was a match for fortune fairly. O

Thus all obscure, unknown and poor, thro' life I'm doom'd to wander, O
Till down my weary bones I lay in everlasting slumber: O
No view nor care, but shun whate'er might breed me pain or sorrow; O
I live today as well's I may, regardless of tomorrow. O

But chearful still, I am as well as a Monarch in a palace; O
Tho' fortune's frown still hunts me down with all her wonted malice: O
I make indeed, my daily bread, but ne'er can make it farther; O
But as daily bread is all I heed, I do not much regard her. O

When sometimes by my labour I earn a little money, O
Some unforeseen misfortune comes generally upon me; O
Mischance, mistake, or by neglect, or my good-natur'd folly; O
But come what will I've sworn it still, I'll ne'er be melancholy. O

All you who follow wealth and power with unremitting ardor, O
The more in this you look for bliss, you leave your view the farther; O
Had you the wealth Potosi boasts, or nations to adore you, O
A cheerful honest hearted clown I will prefer before you. O

7TH JANUARY

from Epistle to John Lapraik, An Old Scotch Bard

THE GREAT SCOTTISH POET Allan Ramsay, one of Burns's most significant poetic influences, died in Edinburgh on this day in 1758. Burns makes several mentions of Ramsay in his poetry, often alongside the poet Robert Fergusson. The trio's work is now considered to represent the best of eighteenth-century Scottish vernacular poetry.

In this extract from an epistle to another Scottish bard, John Lapraik, Burns wishes for 'a spunk o' ALLAN's glee'. He emphasises that inspiration is paramount and true talent cannot be 'learned', leading him to the famously irresistible line: 'Gie me a spark o' Nature's fire.' However, Burns's own education and extensive reading belies the poem where he names several prominent writers. In doing so, the poet makes clear that he 'kens' perfectly well his *'verse frae prose'*, highlights the richness of the Scottish poetic tradition, and cleverly positions himself within it. Fittingly, the poem is written in the distinctively Scottish 'Standard Habbie' verse form, adopted by Burns in the wake of Ramsay and Fergusson.

I am nae *Poet*, in a sense,
But just a *Rhymer* like by chance,
An' hae to Learning nae pretence,
             Yet, what the matter?
Whene'er my Muse does on me glance,
             I jingle at her.

Your Critic-folk may cock their nose,
And say, 'How can you e'er propose,
'You wha ken hardly *verse* frae *prose*,
             To mak a *sang*?'
But by your leaves, my learned foes,
             Ye're maybe wrang.

What's a' your jargon o' your Schools,
Your Latin names for horns an' stools;
If honest Nature made you *fools*,
             What sairs your Grammars?
Ye'd better taen up *spades* and *shools*,
             Or *knappin-hammers*.

A set o' dull, conceited Hashes,
Confuse their brains in *College-classes!*
They *gang in* stirks, and *come out* asses,
             Plain truth to speak;
An' syne they think to climb Parnassus
             By dint o' Greek!

Gie me ae spark o' Nature's fire,
That's a' the learning I desire;
Then tho' I drudge thro' dub an' mire
             At pleugh or cart,
My muse, tho' hamely in attire,
             May touch the heart.

O for a spunk o' ALLAN's glee,
Or FERGUSON's, the bauld an' slee,
Or bright LAPRAIK's, my friend to be,
　　　　If I can hit it!
That would be *lear* eneugh for me,
　　　　If I could get it.

8TH JANUARY

from The Vision

I N 'THE VISION', Burns cements his status as a bard native to
Scotland yet writing as part of a tradition of esteemed poets both
north and south of the border. In this excerpt from 'Duan First' of
the poem, Burns, at the end of a cold winter's day, ponders the value
of time spent composing verse rather than pursuing a more lucrative
occupation. He vows never to rhyme again, but in doing so summons
his 'SCOTTISH muse', the ethereal Coila.

The sun had clos'd the *winter-day*,
The Curlers quat their roaring play,
And hunger'd Maukin taen her way
　　　　To kail-yards green,
While faithless snaws ilk step betray
　　　　Whare she has been.

The Thresher's weary *flingin-tree*,
The lee-lang day had tir'd me;
And when the Day had clos'd his e'e,
　　　　Far i' the West,
Ben i' the *spence*, right pensivelie,
　　　　I gaed to rest.

There, lanely, by the ingle-cheek,
I sat and ey'd the spewing reek,
That fill'd, wi' hoast-provoking smeek,
      The auld, clay biggin;
And heard the restless rattons squeak
      About the riggin.

All in this mottie, misty clime,
I backward mus'd on wasted time,
How I had spent my youthfu' prime,
      An' done nae-thing,
But stringing blethers up in rhyme
      For fools to sing.

Had I to guid advice but harkit,
I might, by this, hae led a market,
Or strutted in a Bank and clarkit
      My *Cash-Account*;
While here, half-mad, half-fed, half-sarket.
      Is a' th' amount.

I started, mutt'ring, blockhead! coof!
And heav'd on high my wauket loof,
To swear by a' yon starry roof,
      Or some rash aith,
That I, henceforth, wad be *rhyme-proof*
      Till my last breath—

When click! the *string* the *snick* did draw;
And jee! the door gaed to the wa';
And by my ingle-lowe I saw,
      Now bleezan bright,
A tight, outlandish *Hizzie*, braw,
      Come full in sight.

[…]

Green, slender, leaf-clad *Holly-boughs*
Were twisted, gracefu', round her brows,
I took her for some SCOTTISH MUSE,
   By that same token;
And come to stop those reckless vows,
   Would soon been broken.

9TH JANUARY

On Poets and Beggars
from a letter to John McMurdo of Drumlanrig, 9th January 1789

W ITH HIS TONGUE FIRMLY in his cheek, Burns again gestures towards the unprofitable business of poetry in a letter to his friend and patron, John McMurdo of Drumlanrig (1743–1803). McMurdo helped Burns to more than 'a mug of ale' and is known to have come to his financial aid on at least one occasion. We might consider it remarkable that, despite the success of the Kilmarnock (1786) and Edinburgh (1787) editions of *Poems, Chiefly in the Scottish Dialect*, the poet who would become the Scottish national bard and who, in the twenty-first century, generates upwards of £300 million annually for the Scottish economy, never quite escaped the grip of financial hardship during his lifetime.

Sir,

 A Poet and a Beggar are in so many points of view alike, that one might take them for the same individual character under different designations; were it not that though, with a trifling Poetic license, most Poets may be styled Beggars, yet the converse of the proposition does not hold, that every Beggar is a Poet.— In one particular, however, they remarkably agree; if you help either the one or the other to a mug of ale or the picking of a bone, they will very willingly repay you with a Song.—

10TH JANUARY

I Am a Bard of No Regard
from Love and Liberty – A Cantata
to the tune of For a' That an' a' That

BURNS GIVES A 'POET BEGGAR' full voice in the following song from 'Love and Liberty: A Cantata', also commonly known as 'The Jolly Beggars'. In January 1787 Burns quoted from the song in a letter to Gavin Hamilton referring to a recent disappointment in love. Although Burns was a 'ladies' man', it was Jean Armour (1765–1834) who would become his most constant romantic interest and, eventually, his wife. He met Jean in spring of 1785 and they began courting in the autumn of that year. Soon Jean was pregnant and it is thought that Burns presented her with a written promise or declaration of marriage. This 'unlucky paper', as Burns later referred to it, would likely have been a satisfactory, if irregular, contract of marriage according to eighteenth-century Scottish law. However, Jean's father, furious that his daughter had taken up with a man of whom he expressly disapproved, set out to annul the marriage. He reportedly presented the document to the lawyer Robert Aiken, demanding that he deface it by cutting out the couple's names.

Jean was sent to Paisley to reside with relatives for the duration of her pregnancy, leaving Burns so dejected that he contemplated emigration to the West Indies. Despite dalliances with several other women in Ayrshire and Edinburgh, Burns wrote to Hamilton, 'To tell the truth among friends, I feel a miserable blank in my heart, with want of her, and I don't think I shall ever meet with so delicious an armful again. She has her faults; and so have you and I; and so has every body.' Burns's affection for Jean endured and,

21

following the birth of two sets of twins and much controversy, they married – probably in Mauchline, Ayrshire – in the spring of 1788.

Steeped in humour and double entendre, Burns's sexually promiscuous bard professes his love of women despite 'their tricks an' craft'. This is one of the poet's bawdier productions.

I am a Bard of no regard,
　　Wi' gentle folks an' a' that;
But Homer-like, the glowran byke,
　　Frae town to town I draw that.

For a' that an' a' that,
　　An' twice as muckle's a' that,
I've lost but ane, I've twa behin',
　　I've wife eneugh for a' that.

I never drank the Muses' stank,
　　Castalia's burn, an' a' that,
But there it streams, an' richly reams,
　　My Helicon I ca' that.
　　　　For a' that, &c.

Great love I bear to a' the fair,
　　Their humble slave, an' a' that;
But lordly Will, I hold it still
　　A mortal sin to thraw that.
　　　　For a' that, &c.

In rapture sweet, this hour we meet,
　　Wi' mutual love, an' a' that;
But for how lang the flie may stang,
　　Let Inclination law that.
　　　　For a' that, &c.

Their tricks an' craft hae put me daft,
    They've ta'en me in, an' a' that,
But clear the decks, an' here's the sex!
    I like the jads for a' that.
        For a' that, &c.

For a' that, an' a' that;
    An' twice as muckle's a' that;
My dearest bluid, to do them guid,
    They're welcome till 't for a' that.

11TH JANUARY

On Burn's First Poetic Composition
from Burns's autobiographical letter to Dr John Moore

D R JOHN MOORE (1729–1802) was a medic and the author of *Zeluco* (1786), a novel admired by Burns. Burns's letter to Moore (sent in August of 1787) is the most extensive and explicit account of the poet's life in his own words. In the extract below Burns provides an account of the first occasion that inspired him to 'commit the sin of RHYME'. Perhaps unsurprisingly, this anecdote goes hand-in-hand with Burns's description of his first love.

You know our country custom of coupling a man and woman together as Partners in the labors of Harvest.— In my fifteenth autumn, my Partner was a bewitching creature who just counted an autumn less.— My scarcity of English denies me the power of doing her justice in that language; but you know the Scotch idiom.

She was a bonie, sweet, sonsie lass.— In short, she altogether unwittingly to herself, initiated me in a certain delicious Passion, which in spite of acid Disappointment, gin-horse Prudence and bookworm Philosophy, I hold to be the first of human joys, our dearest pleasure here below.— How she caught the contagion I can't say; you medical folks talk much of infection by breathing the same air, the touch, &c. but I never expressly told her that I loved her.— Indeed I did not well know myself, why I liked so much to loiter behind with her, when returning in the evening from our labors; why the tones of her voice made my heartstrings thrill like an Eolian harp; and particularly, why my pulse beat such a furious ratann when I looked and fingered over her hand, to pick out the nettle-stings and thistles.— Among her other love-inspiring qualifications, she sung sweetly; and 'twas her favorite reel to which I attempted giving an embodied vehicle in rhyme.— I was not so presumptive as to imagine that I could make verses like printed ones, composed by men who had Greek and Latin; but my girl sung a song which was said to be composed by a small country laird's son, on one of his father's maids, with whom he was in love; and I saw no reason why I might not rhyme as well as he, for excepting smearing sheep and casting peats, his father living in the moors, he had no more Scholarcraft than I had.—

Thus with me began Love and Poesy; which at times have been my only, and till within this last twelvemonth have been my highest enjoyment.—

12TH JANUARY

O Once I Lov'd
to the tune of I Am a Man Unmarried

I**N HIS AUTOBIOGRAPHICAL LETTER** to Dr John Moore, Burns claimed to have written his first poetic composition, 'O Once I Lov'd', at the age of just fifteen. The first of a great many love songs composed by Burns, it is thought that the song was inspired by a farm servant named Nellie Kilpatrick and set to her favourite tune, 'I Am a Man Unmarried'. In the song, Burns suggests that female grace and virtue are more desirable 'qualities' than beauty alone.

O Once I lov'd a bonnie lass,
    An' aye I love her still,
An' whilst that virtue warms my breast,
    I'll love my handsome Nell.

As bonnie lasses I hae seen,
    And mony full as braw,
But for a modest gracefu' mein,
    The like I never saw.

A bonny lass I will confess,
    Is pleasant to the e'e,
But without some better qualities,
    She's no a lass for me.

But Nelly's looks are blythe and sweet,
    And what is best of a',
Her reputation is compleat,
    And fair without a flaw;

She dresses ay sae clean and neat,
　　Both decent and genteel;
And then there's something in her gait
　　Gars ony dress look weel.

A gaudy dress and gentle air
　　May slightly touch the heart,
But it's innocence and modesty
　　That polishes the dart.

'Tis this in Nelly pleases me,
　　'Tis this enchants my soul;
For absolutely in my breast
　　She reigns without controul.

13TH JANUARY

from The Vision

I N THIS EXTRACT FROM 'Duan Second' of 'The Vision', Burns's
muse Coila narrates the development of his poetic disposition from
childhood. Burns emphasises the inspirational qualities of nature
and passion upon his writing; recurring themes in his poetry and
song. Burns suggests that his poetic talent and penchant for passion
and pleasure are heaven-inspired, innate – and therefore outwith his
control. In doing so, he alludes to his tumultuous personal life and
many romantic entanglements, and introduces another important
preoccupation of his work: the acceptance of inescapable humanity.

'All hail! *my own* inspired Bard!
'In me thy native Muse regard!
'Nor longer mourn thy fate is hard,
   'Thus poorly low!
'I come to give thee such *reward*,
   'As *we* bestow.

[...]

'With future hope, I oft would gaze,
'Fond, on thy little, early ways,
'Thy rudely-caroll'd, chiming phrase,
   'In uncouth rhymes,
'Fir'd at the simple, artless lays
   'Of other times.

'I saw thee seek the sounding shore,
'Delighted with the dashing roar;
'Or when the *North* his fleecy store
   'Drove thro' the sky,
'I saw grim Nature's visage hoar,
   'Struck thy young eye.

'Or when the deep-green-mantled Earth,
'Warm cherish'd ev'ry floweret's birth,
'And joy and music pouring forth,
   'In ev'ry grove,
'I saw thee eye the gen'ral mirth
   'With boundless love.

'When ripen'd fields, and azure skies,
'Call'd forth the *Reaper's* rustling noise,
'I saw thee leave their ev'ning joys,
   'And lonely stalk,
'To vent thy bosom's swelling rise,
   'In pensive walk.

'When *youthful Love*, warm-blushing, strong,
'Keen-shivering shot thy nerves along,
'Those accents grateful to thy tongue,
   'Th' adored *Name*,
'I taught thee how to pour in song,
   'To soothe thy flame.

'I saw thy pulse's maddening play,
'Wild-send thee Pleasure's devious way,
'Misled by Fancy's *meteor-ray*,
   'By Passion driven;
'But yet the *light* that led astray
   'Was *light* from Heaven.

14TH JANUARY

On Henry Mackenzie
from a letter to Frances Dunlop, 10th April 1790

HENRY MACKENZIE, who Burns described as his 'favourite author' and whose novel *The Man of Feeling* (1771) he claimed to 'prize most next to the Bible', died in Edinburgh on this day in 1831. Mackenzie was the founder and editor of two influential Scottish periodicals, *The Mirror* (1770) and *The Lounger* (1785–86). As such, he was often compared to the London-based editor of *The Spectator*, Joseph Addison.

Mackenzie was also the author of the most influential contemporary review of Burns's *Poems, Chiefly in the Scottish Dialect* (1786). He made much of the 'uncommon penetration and sagacity' with which 'this Heaven-taught ploughman, from his humble and unlettered station, has looked upon men and manners'. His review cemented Burns's fame and ensured his celebrity when he arrived in Edinburgh in 1786. Burns was grateful and wrote to Mackenzie in May 1787 that 'no little petulant self-conceit, no distance or absence shall ever make me forget how much I owe You'. The following is Burns's most extensive written commentary on Mackenzie and his informal 'review' of *The Man of Feeling*.

You must know, I have just met with the *Mirror* and *Lounger* for the first time, and I am quite in raptures with them.— I should be glad to have *your* opinion of some of the papers.— The one I have just read, Lounger No. 61st, has cost me more honest tears than any thing I have read of a long time.— Mackenzie has been called the Addison of the Scots, and in my opinion, Addison would not be hurt at the comparison.— If he has not Addison's exquisite humour, he as certainly outdoes him in the tender and the Pathetic. His *Man of Feeling* (but I am not counsel-learned in the laws of criticism) I estimate as the first performance in its kind I ever saw.— From what book, moral or even Pious, will the susceptible young mind receive impressions more congenial to Humanity and Kindness, Generosity and Benevolence, in short, all that ennobles the Soul to herself, or endears her to others, than from the simple, affecting tale of poor Harley? Still, with all my admiration for Mackenzie's writings I do not know if they are the fittest reading for a young Man who is about to set out, as the phrase is, to make his way into life.—

15TH JANUARY

On Fame
from a letter to Frances Dunlop, 15th January 1787

O N THIS DAY IN 1787, following publication of the Kilmarnock edition of *Poems, Chiefly in the Scottish Dialect*, Burns wrote to Frances Dunlop on the subject of his recent rise to fame. Here Burns refers to his reception among the 'enlightened' and 'polite' company of the Edinburgh literati who had (in part owing to Henry Mackenzie's review in *The Lounger*) greeted him as a celebrity. Nevertheless, Burns intimates his underlying insecurity and expresses anxiety that his popularity may be short-lived.

You are afraid I shall grow intoxicated with my prosperity as a poet. Alas! Madam, I know myself and the world too well. I do not mean any airs of affected modesty; I am willing to believe that my abilities deserved some notice; but in a most enlightened, informed age and nation, when poetry is and has been the study of men of the first natural genius, aided with all the powers of polite learning, polite books, and polite company — to be dragged forth to the full glare of learned and polite observation, with all my imperfections of awkward rusticity and crude unpolished ideas on my head — I assure you, Madam, I do not dissemble when I tell you I tremble for the consequences. The novelty of a poet in my obscure situation, without any of those advantages which are reckoned necessary for that character, at least at this time of day, has raised a partial tide of public notice, which has borne me to a height where I am absolutely feelingly certain my abilities are inadequate to support me; and too surely do I see that time when the same tide will leave me, and recede, perhaps, as far below the mark of truth. I do not say this in the ridiculous affectation of self-abasement and modesty. I have studied myself, and know what ground I occupy; and, however a friend or the world may differ from me in that particular, I stand for my own opinion, in silent resolve, with all the tenaciousness of property. I mention this to you, once for all, to disburthen my mind, and I do not wish to hear or say more about it — But "When proud fortune's ebbing tide recedes," you will bear me witness, that, when my bubble of fame was at the highest, I stood, unintoxicated, with the inebriating cup in my hand, looking forward with rueful resolve to the hastening time when the blow of Calumny should dash it to the ground, with all the eagerness of vengeful triumph.

16TH JANUARY

from **Epistle to Davie, A Brother Poet**

IT IS THOUGHT THAT 'Epistle to Davie' was written in January 1785 and the opening lines provide an atmospheric description of the harsh Scottish winter. David Sillar (1760–1830), like Burns, was the son of an Ayrshire farmer. His family farm near Tarbolton neighboured the Burnes farm at Lochlea. Sillar went into business as a grocer in the Ayrshire town of Irvine and, seemingly inspired by Burns's success, published his own volume of poetry in 1789.

In these verses, Burns addresses the social inequality that he perceives between the '*Great* folk', comfortable in their spacious dwellings, and those such as he and Davie who 'hae little gear'. He encourages his friend not to despair, but to take comfort in nature and himself, and emphasises the importance of emotional substance rather than material possession. After all, 'The *heart* ay's the part ay,/ That makes us right or wrang.'

While winds frae off Ben-Lomond blaw,
And bar the doors wi' driving snaw,
   And hing us owre the ingle,
I set me down, to pass the time,
And spin a verse or twa o' rhyme,
   In hamely, *westlin* jingle.
While frosty winds blaw in the drift,
   Ben to the chimla lug,
I grudge a wee the *Great-folk's* gift,
   That live sae bien an' snug:
      I tent less, and want less

Their roomy fire-side;
　But hanker, and canker,
　　To see their cursed pride.

It's hardly in a body's pow'r,
To keep, at times, frae being sour,
　To see how things are shar'd;
How *best o' chiels* are whyles in want,
While *Coofs* on countless thousands rant,
　And ken na how to wair't;
But DAVIE lad, ne'er fash your head,
　Tho' we hae little gear,
We're fit to win our daily bread,
　As lang's we're hale and fier:
　　Mair spier na, nor fear na,'
　　　Auld age ne'er mind a feg;
　　The last o't, the warst o't,
　　　Is only but to beg.

To lye in kilns and barns at e'en,
When banes are craz'd, and bluid is thin,
　Is, doubtless, great distress!
Yet then *content* could make us blest;
Ev'n then, sometimes we'd snatch a taste
　Of truest happiness.
The honest heart that's free frae a'
　Intended fraud or guile,
However Fortune kick the ba',
　Has ay some cause to smile:
　　And mind still, you'll find still,
　　　A comfort this nae sma';
　　Nae mair then, we'll care then,
　　　Nae *farther* can we *fa'*.

What tho', like Commoners of air,
We wander out, we know not where,

But either house or hal'?
Yet *Nature's* charms, the hills and woods,
The sweeping vales, and foaming floods,
　　Are free alike to all.
In days when Daisies deck the ground,
　　And blackbirds whistle clear,
With honest joy, our hearts will bound,
　　To see the *coming* year:
　　　　On braes when we please then,
　　　　　　We'll sit and *sowth* a tune;
　　　　Syne *rhyme* till't, well time till't,
　　　　　　And sing't when we hae done.

It's no in titles nor in rank;
It's no in wealth like *Lon'on Bank*,
　　To purchase peace and rest:
It's no in makin' muckle, *mair*:
It's no in books; it's no in Lear,
　　To make us truly blest:
If Happiness hae not her seat
　　And centre in the breast,
We may be *wise*, or *rich*, or *great*,
　　But never can be *blest*:
Nae treasures, nor pleasures
　　Could make us happy lang;
The *heart* ay's the part ay,
That makes us right or wrang.

17TH JANUARY

Up in the Morning Early

WE ARE NOW IN the very depths of winter and 'Up in the Morning Early' is a song that many of us can relate to. The long nights and extreme weather in Scotland would have presented a particular challenge to Burns and his family in their agricultural labours during this season.

Cauld blaws the wind frae east to west,
    The drift is driving sairly;
Sae loud and shill's I hear the blast,
    I'm sure it's winter fairly.

Up in the morning's no for me,
    Up in the morning early;
When a' the hills are cover'd wi' snaw,
    I'm sure it's winter fairly.

The birds sit chittering in the thorn,
    A' day they fare but sparely;
And lang's the night frae e'en to morn
    I'm sure it's winter fairly.
        Up in the morning's &c.

18TH JANUARY

On Winter
from the First Commonplace Book

Despite the challenges of winter in rural Scotland, Burns was known to favour the season above all others. In the following extract the poet explains why winter captures his imagination and extols the benefits of a winter walk. He suggests that the season appeals to him owing to the 'melancholy cast' of his mind, referring to the periods of depression to which he was prone and which were often reflected in his writing. Burns's quote is from James Thomson's *The Seasons* (1730).

As I am, what the men of the world, if they knew of such a man, would call a whimsical Mortal; I have various sources of pleasure & enjoyment which are, in a manner, peculiar to myself; or some here & there such other out-of-the-way person. Such is the peculiar pleasure I take in the season of Winter, more than the rest of the year. This, I believe, may be partly owing to my misfortunes giving my mind a melancholy cast; but there is something even in the –

> "Mighty tempest & the hoary waste
> Abrupt & deep stretch'd o'er the buried earth"

– which raises the mind to a serious sublimity, favorable to every thing great & noble.— There is scarcely any earthly object gives me more – I don't know if I should call it pleasure, but something which exalts me, something which enraptures me – than to walking in the sheltered side of a wood or high plantation, in a cloudy, winter day, and hear a stormy wind howling among the trees & raving o'er the plain – It is my best season for devotion; my mind is rapt up in a kind of enthusiasm to Him who, in the pompous language of Scripture, "Walks on the wings of the wind."

19TH JANUARY

Winter, A Dirge

BURNS WROTE IN HIS 'FIRST COMMONPLACE BOOK' that he composed these verses 'just after a tract of misfortunes'. Burns captures the violence and extremity of the Scottish winter in powerful language, referring to his predisposition for 'melancholy' (or depression) and appealing to God for assistance in resigning himself to his circumstances and state of mind.

The Wintry West extends his blast,
　　And hail and rain does blaw;
Or the stormy North sends driving forth,
　　The blinding sleet and snaw:
While, tumbling brown, the Burn comes down,
　　And roars frae bank to brae;
And bird and beast, in covert, rest,
　　And pass the heartless day.

'The sweeping blast, the sky o'ercast,'
　　The joyless *winter-day*,
Let others fear, to me more dear,
　　Than all the pride of May:

The Tempest's howl, it *soothes* my soul,
    My *griefs* it seems to join;
The leafless trees my fancy please,
    Their *fate* resembles mine!

Thou POW'R SUPREME, whose mighty Scheme,
    These *woes* of mine fulfil;
Here, firm, I rest; they *must* be best,
    Because they are *Thy* Will!
Then all I want (Oh, do thou grant
    This one request of mine!)
Since to *enjoy* Thou dost deny,
    Assist me to *resign!*

20TH JANUARY

O Lassie, Art Thou Sleeping Yet
to the tune of **Will ye lend me your loom lass**

IN THIS SONG, an insistent man appeals to his lover to 'let him in' from the cold winter night. It is based upon a traditional song which Burns collected and edited in several different versions, some more playful and more successful than others. The version below was published by George Thomson in *A Select Collection of Original Scottish Airs*. Thomson was rather prudish as an editor and Burns often teased him with bawdy verse and double entendre. In one letter to Thomson including a version of this song he wrote, 'How do you like this? And would you have the dénouement to be successful or otherwise? Should she "let him in," or not?' Thomson's response may be derived from the song itself.

O Lassie, art thou sleeping yet,
Or art thou wakin, I would wit,
For Love has bound me, hand and foot,
And I would fain be in, jo.
O let me in this ae night,
This ae, ae, ae night;
For pity's sake, this ae night,

O rise and let me in, jo.
Thou hear'st the winter wind and weet,
Nae star blinks thro' the driving sleet;
Tak pity on my weary feet,
And shield me frae the rain, jo.
O let me in this ae night, &c.

The bitter blast that round me blaws,
Unheeded howls, unheeded fa's;
The cauldness o' thy heart's the cause
Of a' my grief and pine, jo.
O let me in this ae night, &c.

Her *Answer*.

O tell na me of wind and rain,
Upbraid na me wi' cauld disdain,
Gae back the gate ye came again,
I winna let you in, jo.
I tell you how this ae night,
This ae, ae, ae night;
And ance for a' this ae night
I winna let you in, jo.

The snellest blast, at mirkest hours,
That round the pathless wanderer pours,
Is nought to what poor she endures
That's trusted faithless man, jo.
I tell you now, &c.

The sweetest flower that deck'd the mead,
Now trodden like the vilest weed,
Let simple maid the lesson read,
The wierd may be her ain, jo.
I tell you now, &c.

The bird that charm'd his summer day,
Is now the cruel fowler's prey;
Let witless, trusting woman say
How aft her fate's the same, jo.
I tell you now, &c.

21st JANUARY

from **A Winter Night**

I N THIS EXTRACT, Burns describes a winter scene reminiscent of Shakespeare's in *King Lear*, drawing also (as he does in his 'First Commonplace Book') upon the imagery of James Thomson's *The Seasons*. The poem is, however, distinctively Burnsian in its approach to nature. Burns's insistence upon recognising the plight of the animal, and the notion that human and animal suffering are one and the same, informs several of his better-known works, among them 'To a Mouse'.

When biting *Boreas*, fell and doure,
Sharp shivers thro' the leafless bow'r;
When *Phoebus* gies a short-liv'd glow'r,
   Far south the lift,
Dim-dark'ning thro' the flaky show'r,
   Or whirling drift.

Ae night the Storm the steeples rocked,
Poor Labour sweet in sleep was locked,
While burns, wi' snawy wreeths up-choked,
   Wild-eddying swirl,
Or thro' the mining outlet bocked,
   Down headlong hurl.

List'ning, the doors an' winnocks rattle,
I thought me on the ourie cattle,
Or silly sheep, wha bide this brattle
                    O' winter war,
And thro' the drift, deep-lairing, sprattle,
                    Beneath a scar.

Ilk happing bird, wee, helpless thing!
That, in the merry months o' spring,
Delighted me to hear thee sing,
                    What comes o' thee?
Whare wilt thou cow'r thy chittering wing,
                    An' close thy e'e?

Ev'n you on murd'ring errands toil'd,
Lone from your savage homes exil'd,
The blood-stain'd roost, and sheep-cote spoil'd,
                    My heart forgets,
While pityless the tempest wild
                    Sore on you beats.

Now *Phoebe*, in her midnight reign,
Dark-muffl'd, view'd the dreary plain;
Still crouding thoughts, a pensive train,
                    Rose in my soul,
When on my ear this plantive strain,
                    Slow-solemn, stole —

'Blow, blow, ye Winds, with heavier gust!
'And freeze, thou bitter-biting Frost!
'Descend, ye chilly, smothering Snows!
'Not all your rage, as now, united shows
  'More hard unkindness, unrelenting,
  'Vengeful malice, unrepenting,
'Than heaven-illumin'd Man on brother
                    'Man bestows!

22ND JANUARY

To a Mouse

L EGEND HAS IT THAT Burns composed 'To a Mouse' while standing by his plough in November 1785. Still, as the Burns Supper season is off to an enthusiastic start by this point in January, and since this is one of the most joyfully received and oft-recited of the bard's poems, it seems appropriate to include it here.

As the ploughman poet has accidentally destroyed the 'tim'rous beastie's' home and hard work, he reflects upon the vulnerability of mouse and man. That said, however difficult the creature's present, it is spared the memory of past difficulty and the dread of future hardship that preoccupies humanity.

'To a Mouse' masterfully communicates a poignant and timeless message of universal significance: 'The best-laid schemes o' *Mice* an' *Men*, / Gang aft agley'.

Wee, sleeket, cowran, tim'rous *beastie*,
O, what a panic's in thy breastie!
Thou need na start awa sae hasty,
　　　　Wi' bickering brattle!
I wad be laith to rin an' chase thee,
　　　　Wi' murd'ring *pattle*!

I'm truly sorry Man's dominion
Has broken Nature's social union,
An' justifies that ill opinion,
　　　　Which makes thee startle
At me, thy poor, earth-born companion,
　　　　An' *fellow-mortal*!

I doubt na, whyles, but thou may *thieve*;
What then? poor beastie, thou maun live!
A *daimen-icker* in a *thrave*
        'S a sma' request:
I'll get a blessin wi' the lave,
        An' never miss't!

Thy wee bit *housie*, too, in ruin!
It's silly wa's the win's are strewin!
An' naething, now, to big a new ane,
        O' foggage green!
An' bleak *December's winds* ensuin,
        Baith snell an' keen!

Thou saw the fields laid bare an' waste,
An' weary *Winter* comin fast,
An' cozie here, beneath the blast,
        Thou thought to dwell,
Till crash! the cruel *coulter* past
        Out thro' thy cell.

That wee-bit heap o' leaves an' stibble,
Has cost thee mony a weary nibble!
Now thou's turn'd out, for a' thy trouble,
        But house or hald,
To thole the winter's *sleety dribble*,
        An' *cranreuch* cauld!

But, Mousie, thou art no thy lane,
In proving *foresight* may be vain:
The best-laid schemes o' *Mice* an' *Men*,
        Gang aft agley,
An' lea'e us nought but grief an' pain,
        For promis'd joy!

Still, thou art blest, compar'd wi' *me*!
The *present* only toucheth thee:
But, Och! I backward cast my e'e,
        On prospects drear!
An' *forward*, tho' I canna *see*,
        I *guess* an' *fear*!

23RD JANUARY

Contended Wi' Little
to the tune of Lumps o' Puddins

AS THE WORLD – from Scotland to New Zealand and China to Canada – embraces the Burns Supper season, we turn our attention to works to accompany the celebrations; poems and songs that reflect Burns's talent, conviviality and *joie de vivre*.

One such song is 'Contented Wi' Little'; a drinking song, or 'Bacchanalian'. Burns wrote to George Thomson of the genre, 'Scots Bacchanalians we certainly want, though the few that we have are excellent.' In another letter to the same, Burns suggested he would like the song to accompany a miniature of his likeness in order that, 'the picture of my face and the picture of my mind may go down the stream of Time together'. The following, then, is utterly apt for a celebration of the bard's life.

Contented wi' little, and canty wi' mair,
Whene'er I forgather wi' sorrow and care,
I gie them a skelp as they're creeping alang,
Wi' a cog o' good ale, and an auld Scotish sang.

I whyles claw the elbow o' troublesome thought,
But man is a Soldier and life is a faught:
My mirth and good humour are coin in my pouch,
And my FREEDOM's my lairdship nae monarch dare touch.

A towmond o' trouble, should that be may fa',
A night o' gude fellowship sowthers it a';
When at the blythe end of our journey at last,
Wha the de'il ever thinks o' the road he has past.

Blind chance, let her snapper and stoyte on her way,
Be't to me, be't frae me, e'en let the jade gae,
Come ease, or come travail, come pleasure or pain;
My warst word is, "Welcome, and welcome again!"

24TH JANUARY

Rantin' Rovin' Robin
to the tune of Dainty Davie

T ODAY'S SONG IS AN ADAPTATION of the traditional song 'Dainty
Davie'. In this version explicit reference is made to Burns's
birthday (which falls tomorrow). The song also playfully refers to the
bard's notorious fondness for women. All of which makes it another
strong choice for performance at a Burns Supper.

There was a lad was born in Kyle,
But what na day o' what na style,
I doubt it's hardly worth the while
    To be sae nice wi' *Robin*.

Robin was a rovin' Boy,
  Rantin' rovin', rantin' rovin';
Robin was a rovin' Boy,
  Rantin' rovin' Robin.

Our monarch's hindmost year but ane
Was five and twenty days begun,
'Twas then a blast o' Janwar' Win'
  Blew hansel in on *Robin*.

The gossip keekit in his loof,
Quo' scho wha lives will see the proof,
This waly boy will be nae coof,
  I think we'll ca' him *Robin*.

He'll hae misfortunes great and sma',
But ay a heart aboon them a';
He'll be a credit 'till us a',
  We'll a' be proud o' *Robin*.

But sure as three times three mak nine,
I see by ilka score and line,
This chap will dearly like our kin',
  So leeze me on thee *Robin*.

Guid faith quo' scho, I doubt you Sir,
Ye gar the lasses * * * *
But twenty fauts ye may hae waur
  So blessins on thee, *Robin*!
    Robin was, &c.

25TH JANUARY

To a Haggis

ROBERT BURNS WAS BORN on the 25th of January 1759 in Alloway, Ayrshire. It is commonly believed that the first Burns Supper was held in Alloway in July 1801 to commemorate the fifth anniversary of the bard's death. A gathering of contemporaries and admirers paid tribute to Burns by reading from his works, raising a toast to his memory and dining on haggis, a dish traditionally regarded as peasant food. They agreed to meet again in January of the following year to celebrate the bard's birth and the tradition developed from there. Burns Night is now a truly global phenomenon: the biggest annual celebration of any author worldwide.

'To a Haggis' is the bard's ode to the dish that has since become the culinary centrepiece of any Burns Supper. Haggis is comprised of those parts of a sheep that would not fetch a good price at sale: heart, lungs and liver combined with oats and seasoning, and boiled in the sheep's stomach. In a performative piece, abundant with imagery, Burns presents the haggis as nutritious, hamely fare, unpretentious and truly worthy of celebration.

Why not try performing the poem at your own Burns Supper? By the end of this 'warm-reekin, rich' address, your company will be ravenous!

Fair fa' your honest, sonsie face,
Great Chieftain o' the Puddin-race!
Aboon them a' ye tak your place,
      Painch, tripe, or thairm:
Weel are ye wordy o'a *grace*
        As lang's my arm.

The groaning trencher there ye fill,
Your hurdies like a distant hill,
Your *pin* wad help to mend a mill
        In time o'need,
While thro' your pores the dews distil
        Like amber bead.

His knife see Rustic-labour dight,
An' cut you up wi' ready slight,
Trenching your gushing entrails bright,
        Like onie ditch;
And then, O what a glorious sight,
        Warm-reekin, rich!

Then, horn for horn they stretch an' strive:
Deil tak the hindmost, on they drive,
Till a' their weel-swall'd kytes belyve
        Are bent like drums;
Then auld Guidman, maist like to rive,
        Bethankit hums.

Is there that owre his French *ragout,*
Or *olio* that wad staw a sow,
Or *fricassee* wad mak her spew
        Wi' perfect sconner,
Looks down wi' sneering, scornfu' view
        On sic a dinner?

Poor devil! see him owre his trash,
As feckless as a' wither'd rash,
His spindle shank a guid whip-lash,
        His nieve a nit;
Thro' bluidy flood or field to dash,
        O how unfit!

But mark the Rustic, *haggis-fed*,
The trembling earth resounds his tread,
Clap in his walie nieve a blade,
          He'll mak it whissle;
An' legs, an' arms, an' heads will sned,
          Like taps o' thrissle.

Ye Pow'rs, wha mak mankind your care,
And dish them out their bill o' fare,
Auld Scotland wants nae skinking ware
          That jaups in luggies;
But, if ye wish her gratefu' pray'r,
          Gie her a *haggis*!

26TH JANUARY

The Selkirk Grace

EVEN IN THE ABSENCE of manuscript evidence, 'The Selkirk Grace' has long been attributed to Burns. Another Burns Supper favourite, it represents an important part of the almost ritualistic running order of the festivities.

Some hae meat and canna eat,
And some wad eat that want it:
But we hae meat and we can eat,
Sae let the Lord be thankit.

27TH JANUARY

from Scotch Drink

IF HAGGIS IS THE CULINARY CENTREPIECE of the Burns Supper, then whisky is its most popular accompaniment. 'Scotch Drink' is Burns's most explicit celebration of the Scottish national tipple and one of the country's most successful exports (alongside the bard himself). In the following extract, Burns wittily extols the inspirational and illuminating 'benefits' of a dram.

Let other Poets raise a fracas
'Bout vines, an' wines, an' drucken *Bacchus*,
An' crabbed names an' stories wrack us,
        An' grate our lug:
I sing the juice *Scotch bear* can mak us,
        In glass or jug.

O thou, my MUSE! guid, auld SCOTCH DRINK!
Whether thro' wimplin worms thou jink,
Or, richly brown, ream owre the brink,
        In glorious faem,
Inspire me, till I *lisp* an' *wink*,
        To sing thy name!

Let husky Wheat the haughs adorn,
And Aits set up their awnie horn,
An' Pease and Beans, at een or morn,

Perfume the plain,
Leeze me on thee, *John Barleycorn*,
Thou king o' grain!

On thee aft Scotland chows her cood,
In souple scones, the wale o' food!
Or tumbling in the boiling flood
Wi' kail an' beef;
But when thou pours thy strong *heart's blood*,
There thou shines chief.

Food fills the wame, an' keeps us livin;
Tho' life's a gift no worth receivin,
When heavy-dragg'd wi' pine an' grievin;
But oil'd by thee,
The wheels o' life gae down-hill, scrievin,
Wi' rattlin glee.

Thou clears the head o' doited Lear;
Thou chears the heart o' drooping Care;
Thou strings the nerves o' Labor-sair,
At's weary toil;
Though ev'n brightens dark Despair,
Wi' gloomy smile.

Willie Brew'd a Peck o' Maut
to the tune of Willie Brew'd a Peck o' Maut

W E DRAW TOWARDS the close of this month with another of Burns's Bacchanalian productions. Famous for its representation of conviviality and revelry in male friendship, 'Willie Brew'd a Peck o' Maut' was inspired by a meeting between Burns, William Nicol (1744–1797) and Allan Masterton (c.1750–1799). Burns recalled that, 'We had such a joyous meeting that Masterton and I agreed, each in our own way, to celebrate the business.' And so, Masterton composed the air to which Burns's song is set.

O Willie brew'd a peck o' maut,
  And Rob and Allan cam to see;
Three blyther hearts, that lee-lang night,
  Ye wadna found in Christendie.

Chorus: We are na fou, We're nae that fou,
  But just a drappie in our e'e;
The cock may craw, the day may daw,
  And aye we'll taste the barley bree.

Here are we met, three merry boys,
  Three merry boys I trow are we;
And mony a night we've merry been,
  And mony mae we hope to be!
    Chorus: We are na fou, &c.

It is the moon, I ken her horn,
　　That's blinkin' in the lift sae hie;
She shines sae bright to wyle us hame,
　　But by my sooth, she'll wait a wee!
　　　　Chorus: We are na fou, &c.

Wha first shall rise to gang awa,
　　A cuckold, coward loun is he!
Wha first beside his chair shall fa',
　　He is the King amang us three!
　　　　Chorus: We are na fou, &c.

29TH JANUARY

from Tam o' Shanter

SURELY 'TAM O' SHANTER' is Burns's most iconic and widely
commemorated poem. The wild ride of the tale's drunken
protagonist is re-enacted in lively performances at most Burns Night
celebrations. Those returning from the revelry of a Burns Supper
could do worse than take note of the bard's ominous forewarning
in the early stanzas of the poem. Tam has been enjoying good
friendship and fine ale. However, as Burns is careful to point out,
pleasure is fleeting and little does Tam know the horrors that await
him on his journey home. Look out for more from 'Tam o' Shanter'
on the 30th of October...

But to our tale: Ae market night,
Tam had got planted unco right,
Fast by an ingle, bleezing finely,

Wi reaming swats, that drank divinely;
And at his elbow, Souter Johnny,
His ancient, trusty, drouthy crony:
Tam lo'ed him like a vera brither;
They had been fou for weeks thegither.
The night drave on wi' sangs an' clatter;
And aye the ale was growing better:
The landlady and Tam grew gracious,
Wi' favours secret, sweet, and precious:
The Souter tauld his queerest stories;
The landlord's laugh was ready chorus:
The storm without might rair and rustle,
Tam did na mind the storm a whistle.

    Care, mad to see a man sae happy,
E'en drown'd himsel amang the nappy:
As bees flee hame wi' lades o' treasure,
The minutes wing'd their way wi' pleasure:
Kings may be blest, but Tam was glorious,
O'er a' the ills o' life victorious!

    But pleasures are like poppies spread,
You seize the flower, its bloom is shed;
Or like the snow falls in the river,
A moment white – then melts for ever;
Or like the Borealis race,
That flit ere you can point their place;
Or like the rainbow's lovely form
Evanishing amid the storm.—
Nae man can tether Time or Tide,
The hour approaches Tam maun ride;
That hour, o' night's black arch the key-stane,
That dreary hour he mounts his beast in;
And sic a night he taks the road in,
As ne'er poor sinner was abroad in.

30th JANUARY

from Lament for James, Earl of Glencairn

JAMES CUNNINGHAM, the 14th Earl of Glencairn, died on the 30th of January 1791. Burns was introduced to Glencairn in Edinburgh and the men quickly became close friends. The Earl was also an important patron and his influence proved invaluable in helping to secure subscriptions for the Edinburgh edition of *Poems, Chiefly in the Scottish Dialect* (1787). The poem makes clear Burns's gratitude and the keen loss that he felt following Glencairn's death.

"Awake thy last sad voice, my harp!
   The voice of woe and wild despair!
Awake, resound thy latest lay,
   Then sleep in silence evermair!
And thou, my last, best, only, friend,
   That fillest an untimely tomb,
Accept this tribute from the Bard
   Thou brought from Fortune's mirkest gloom.

"In Poverty's low barren vale,
   Thick mists obscure involv'd me round;
Though oft I turn'd the wistful eye,
   Nae ray of fame was to be found:
Thou found'st me, like the morning sun
   That melts the fogs in limpid air,
The friendless bard and rustic song,
   Became alike thy fostering care.

"O! why has Worth so short a date?
   While villains ripen grey with time!
Must thou, the noble, gen'rous, great,
   Fall in bold manhood's hardy prime!
Why did I live to see that day?
   A day to me so full of woe?
O! had I met the mortal shaft
   That laid my benefactor low!

"The bridegroom may forget the bride,
   Was made his wedded wife yestreen;
The monarch may forget the crown
   That on his head an hour has been;
The mother may forget the child
   That smiles sae sweetly on her knee;
But I'll remember thee, Glencairn,
   And a' that thou hast done for me!"

31st JANUARY

Here's a Bottle and an Honest Friend

IN A FITTING CONCLUSION to January – a month of reflection and expectation, of cold weather and warm celebration – the following verse reminds us to value friendship and to seize every opportunity for happiness and enjoyment.

> Here's a bottle and an honest friend!
>   What wad ye wish for mair, man?
> Wha kens, before his life may end,
>   What his share may be of care, man.
> Then catch the moments as they fly,
>   And use them as ye ought, man:—
> Believe me, happiness is shy,
>   And comes not ay when sought, man.

FEBRUARY

Love is the Alpha and the Omega
of human enjoyment.—

from a letter to Alexander Cunningham

1st FEBRUARY

Green Grow the Rashes
to the tune of Green Grow the Rashes

ROBERT BURNS IS indisputably Scotland's most famous poet. He is also, perhaps, the country's most famous lover. His work and correspondence feature many different love interests and – although it is impossible to know exactly how many women the poet was associated with – during his short life, he fathered at least twelve children with at least five women.

Burns's treatment of women in both life and art is complicated. He could be fickle and unfaithful; at times overtly masculinist in his approach to women and the female body. But there is evidence that he also sincerely admired and respected women, leading him to create some of the most tender, heartfelt and universally celebrated love songs ever written. Women were, after all, Burns's greatest muse – and love his dearest enjoyment. So, we begin February, a month associated with romantic love, with the bard's most famous song in praise of 'the lasses'.

> *Green grow the rashes, O;*
> *Green grow the rashes, O;*
> *The sweetest hours that e'er I spend,*
>   *Are spent amang the lasses, O.*

> There's nought but care on ev'ry han',
>   In ev'ry hour that passes, O:
> What signifies the life o' man,
>   An''twere na for the lasses, O.
>   *Green grow, &c.*

The warly race may riches chase,
    An' riches still may fly them, O;
An' tho' at last they catch them fast,
    Their hearts can ne'er enjoy them, O.
            Green grow, &c.

But gie me a cannie hour at e'en,
    My arms about my Dearie, O;
An' war'ly cares, an' warly men,
    May a' gae tapsalteerie, O!
            Green grow, &c.

For you sae douse, ye sneer at this;
    Ye're nought but senseless asses, O:
The wisest Man the warl' saw,
    He dearly lov'd the lasses, O.
            Green grow, &c.

Auld Nature swears, the lovely Dears
    Her noblest work she classes, O:
Her prentice han' she try'd on man,
    An' then she made the lasses, O.
            Green grow, &c.

2ND FEBRUARY

On Love and Poetry
from the First Commonplace Book

BURNS MADE NO SECRET of the importance that he placed upon love. It is one of the greatest preoccupations of his writing and, according to Burns himself, the first thing that inspired him to put pen to paper. Here are a young poet's early musings on the subject, entered in his 'First Commonplace Book' at the age of just twenty-four.

Notwithstanding all that has been said against Love respecting the folly and weakness it leads a young mind into, still I think it in a great measure deserves the highest encomiums that have been passed upon it. If any thing on earth deserves the name of rapture or transport it is the feelings of a youth of eighteen in the company of the mistress of his heart when she repays him with an equal return of affection.

There is certainly some connection between Love, Music and Poetry; and therefore, I have always thought it a fine touch of Nature, that passage in a modern love composition

> "As towards her cot he jogged along
> Her name was frequent in his song –"

For my own part I never had the least thought or inclination of turning Poet till I got heartily in Love, and then Rhyme and Song were, in a manner, the spontaneous language of my heart.

3rd FEBRUARY

from **The Posie**
to the tune of **There was a pretty May, and a-milkin' she went**

THOSE PLANNING FLOWERS for their valentine might consider replacing the iconic red rose with a bouquet of primroses or violets. These flowers, which bloom in the late winter and early springtime, are often associated with February. The primrose is said to represent young love, and tradition has it that gifting a lover a primrose expresses an inability to live without them.

It is appropriate that Burns begins 'The Posie' with the primrose, 'the firstling of the year'. The song was influenced by Burns's own great, inescapable love, Jean Armour Burns, who performed the tune to which the words are set.

O luve will venture in where it daur na weel be seen,
O luve will venture in where wisdom ance has been;
But I will down yon river rove, amang the woods sae green,
   And a' to pu' a posie to my ain dear May.

The primrose I will pu', the firstling o' the year;
   And I will pu' the pink, the emblem o' my Dear,
For she is the pink o' womankind, and blooms without a peer;
   And a' to be a posie to my ain dear May.

4TH FEBRUARY

On Love
from a letter to Alexander Cunningham, 24th January 1789

BURNS AGAIN PONDERS the value and meaning of love, observing that young love is often superficial, but that sincere, deep love can be mind-altering and life-changing. His humanitarian sensibility is evident as he emphasises that, unlike some things in life, love is not exclusively the privilege of the wealthy, but the lifeblood and solace of the poor. For Burns, love is life's most essential pleasure, not least because it is accessible to all.

To the hopeful youth, keen on the badger-foot of Mammon, or listed under the gaudy banners of Ambition, a love-disappointment, as such, is an easy business; nay, perhaps he hugs himself on his escape; but to your scanty tribe of mankind, whose souls bear, on the richest materials, the most elegant impress of the Great Creator, Love enters deeply into their existence, it is entwisted with the very thread of life.— I myself can affirm, both from bachelor and wedlock experience, that Love is the Alpha and the Omega of human enjoyment.— All the pleasures, all the happiness of my humble Compeers, flow immediately and directly from this delicious source.— It is that spark of celestial fire which lights up the wintry hut of Poverty and makes that cheerless mansion warm, comfortable and gay.— It is the emanation of Divinity that preserves the Sons and Daughters of rustic labour from degenerating into the brutes with which they daily hold converse.— Without it, life to the poor inmates of the Cottage would be a damning gift.—

O Poortith Cauld and Restless Love
to the tune of Cauld Kail in Aberdeen

L OVE MAY BE UNIVERSAL, but Burns was keenly aware that forces beyond reasonable control can frustrate even the most devoted lovers. 'O Poortith Cauld and Restless Love' was written in empathy with his friend and colleague in the excise, John Gillespie, and inspired by another of Burns's friends, Jean Lorimer. Jean had rejected Gillespie and eloped with another man, only to be abandoned three weeks after the marriage. The song is a clear expression of Burns's frustration that natural, sincere love can be unduly influenced by 'wealth' or 'state'.

O Poortith cauld, and restless love,
    Ye wrack my peace between ye;
Yet poortith a' I could forgive,
    An''twere na for my Jeanie.

O why should Fate sic pleasure have,
    Life's dearest bands untwining?
Or why sae sweet a flower as love,
    Depend on Fortune's shining.

This warld's wealth when I think on,
    Its pride, and a' the lave o't;
Fie, fie on silly coward man,
    That he should be the slave o't.

Her een sae bonie blue betray,
    How she repays my passion;
But prudence is her o'erword ay,
    She talks o' rank and fashion.

O wha can prudence think upon,
    And sic a lassie by him;
O wha can prudence think upon,
    And sae in love as I am?

How blest the humble cotter's fate,
    He wooes his simple dearie:
The silly bogles, Wealth and State,
    Can never make them eerie.

6TH FEBRUARY

On Fergusson's Grave
from a letter to the Honorable the Bailies of the
Canongate, Edinburgh, 6th February 1787

O N THIS DAY IN 1787, Burns wrote to the Bailies of the Canongate requesting permission to erect a gravestone over the Edinburgh poet Robert Fergusson's unmarked grave. Fergusson was another of the bard's favourite writers, and his poems – among them 'Hallow Fair', 'Leith Races' and 'The Farmers Ingle' – profoundly influenced Burns's work. Fergusson's life was cut tragically short when, afflicted with illness and following a fall, he was committed to the Darien House Asylum in Edinburgh. He died there in 1774 at the age of twenty-four. Burns was successful in his petition to commemorate Fergusson. He commissioned the architect Robert Burn to erect the gravestone and had it inscribed with the following lines:

No sculptur'd Marble here, nor pompous lay
No storied Urn nor animated Bust;
This simple Stone directs pale Scotia's way
To pour her Sorrows o'er her Poet's Dust

Burns did indeed 'direct pale Scotia's way', and in 2007 a bronze
statue of Fergusson was inaugurated at the gates of Canongate Kirk.
Since taking up Fergusson's cause, Burns himself has become the
most internationally commemorated of all poets.

Gentlemen,

I am sorry to be told that the remains of Robert Fergusson the so
justly celebrated Poet, a man whose talents for ages to come will do
honor to our Caledonian name, lie in your churchyard among the
ignoble Dead, unnoticed and unknown.— Some memorial to direct
the steps of the Lovers of Scottish Song, when they wish to shed
a tear over the "Narrow house" of the Bard who is now no more,
is surely a tribute due to Fergusson's memory: a tribute I wish to
have the honor of paying.— I petition you then, Gentlemen, for your
permission to lay a simple stone over his revered ashes, to remain an
unalienable property to his deathless fame.—

from **Epistle to Mr Tytler of Woodhouselee, Author of a Defence of Mary Queen of Scots**

WILLIAM TYTLER (1711–1793) was an acquaintance of Burns and the author of *An Historical and Critical Enquiry into the Evidence produced by the Earls of Murray and Morton, against Mary Queen of Scots* (1760). Burns shared Tytler's Jacobite sympathies, and here we see the bard in patriotic mood as he praises Tytler's defence of the 'beauteous Stuart', Mary Queen of Scots. However, skilled at treading the line, the politically aware poet is guarded as he addresses the failure of the Jacobite cause and makes sure to express a 'cordial' acceptance of the head of state, King George IV (1762–1830).

Revered defender of beauteous Stuart,
    Of Stuart, a name once respected,
A name which to love was the mark of a true heart,
    But now 'tis despis'd and neglected.

Tho' something like moisture conglobes in my eye,
    Let no one misdeem me disloyal;
A poor, friendless wand'rer may well claim a sigh,
    Still more if that wand'rer were royal.

My fathers that name have rever'd on a throne;
    My fathers have fallen to right it;
Those fathers would spurn their degenerate son
    That name should he scoffingly slight it.

Still in prayers for King George I most cordially join,
    The Queen and the rest of the gentry:
Be they wise, be they foolish, is nothing of mine,
    Their title's allow'd by the Country.

8TH FEBRUARY

from Lament of Mary Queen of Scots on the Approach of Spring

IT WAS ON THIS DAY IN 1587 that Mary Queen of Scots was beheaded for treason at Fotheringhay Castle in Northamptonshire, ending nineteen years of imprisonment in England. Her sentence was the consequence of several plots to overthrow her cousin, Queen Elizabeth I. Mary has since proven a divisive figure, vilified by some for her perceived treason and mourned by others as a martyr in service of the Catholic faith.

Burns was much taken with the story of the tragic monarch, whom he referred to as 'beautiful injured Mary Queen of Scots'. In a letter to Agnes McLehose he describes her as 'the amiable but unfortunate Mary', lamenting that 'Misfortune seems to take a peculiar pleasure in darting her arrows against "Honest Men & bony Lasses"'. Burns expresses an entirely opposing view of Elizabeth I in a letter to Dr John Moore where he proclaims, 'What a rocky-hearted perfidious Succubus was that Queen Elizabeth! Judas Iscariot was a sad dog to be sure, but still his demerits shrink to insignificance, compared with the doings of the infernal Bess Tudor.'

It is clear that the bard had no trouble forming an opinion, particularly in the face of perceived injustice.

Now blooms the lily by the bank,
  The primrose down the brae;
The hawthorn's budding in the glen,
  And milk-white is the slae:
The meanest hind in fair Scotland
  May rove their sweets amang;
But I, the Queen of a' Scotland,
  Maun lie in prison strang.

I was the Queen o' bonie France,
  Where happy I hae been;
Fu' lightly rase I in the morn,
  As blythe lay down at e'en:
And I'm the sov'reign of Scotland,
  And mony a traitor there;
Yet here I lie in foreign bands,
  And never-ending care.

But as for thee, thou false woman,
  My sister and my fae,
Grim vengeance, yet, shall whet a sword
  That thro' thy soul shall gae:
The weeping blood in woman's breast
  Was never known to thee;
Nor th' balm that draps on wounds of woe
  Frae woman's pitying e'e.

My son! my son! may kinder stars
  Upon thy fortune shine!
And may those pleasures gild thy reign,
  That ne'er wad blink on mine!
God keep thee frae thy mother's faes,
  Or turn their hearts to thee:
And where thou meet'st thy mother's friend,
  Remember him for me!

O! soon, to me, may summer-suns
    Nae mair light up the morn!
Nae mair, to me, the autumn winds
    Wave o'er the yellow corn!
And, in the narrow house o' death
    Let winter round me rave;
And the next flowers, that deck the spring,
    Bloom on my peaceful grave.

9TH FEBRUARY

from Holy Willie's Prayer

O NE OF BURNS'S MOST SCATHING religious satires, 'Holy Willie's Prayer' is also his most famous attack on religious hypocrisy. The poem was inspired by William Fisher (1737–1809), an elder of Mauchline Kirk. Burns's 'Holy Willie' considers himself to be one of the religious 'elect', preordained for heaven. In this excerpt, Burns uses biblical language to convey the obvious irony present in the idea that Holy Willie is a 'chosen sample'. Willie confesses that he has had a sexual encounter, but vows 'ne'er to lift a lawless leg / Again upon her' if God forgives him, admitting that he has broken one of the laws of religion that he claims to uphold. This is immediately followed by another confession, 'wi' Leezie's lass three times I trow', indicating not only a lack of sincerity on the part of this infamous hypocrite, but a lack of fear of God.

Burns's conflation of religious and physical language to satirise the misguided complacency of the 'elect' and to expose hypocrisy is a recurring feature of his writing. There is no escaping the biting humour of this dramatic monologue, imbued as it is with 'fleshly lust' and euphemistic 'pillars'. Its irreverent critique ensured the poem's circulation and preservation among Burns's friends, and its eventual status as one of the most celebrated and performed of the bard's works.

When frae my mither's womb I fell,
Thou might hae plunged me deep in hell,
To gnash my gums, and weep, and wail,
In burnin lakes,
Where damned devils roar and yell,
Chain'd to their stakes.

Yet I am here, a chosen sample,
To show thy grace is great and ample;
I'm here, a pillar o' Thy temple,
Strong as a rock,
A guide, a buckler, and example,
To a' Thy flock.

But yet, O Lord! confess I must,
At times I'm fash'd wi' fleshly lust;
And sometimes too, in wardly trust,
Vile self gets in;
But Thou remembers we are dust,
Defil'd wi' sin.

O Lord! yestreen, Thou kens, wi' Meg,
Thy pardon I sincerely beg,
O may't ne'er be a living plague
To my dishonour,
An' I'll ne'er lift a lawless leg
Again upon her.

Besides, I farther maun avow,
Wi' Leezie's lass, three times I trow,
But Lord, that Friday I was fou,
When I cam near her;
Or else, Thou kens, Thy servant true
Wad never steer her.

Maybe Thou lets this fleshly thorn
Buffet Thy servant e'en and morn,
Lest he owre proud and high should turn,
      That he's sae gifted:
If sae, Thy han' maun e'en be borne,
      Until Thou lift it.

10TH FEBRUARY

Epitaph on Holy Willie

IN FEBRUARY 1809 'Holy Willie' Fisher died. He succumbed to the harsh Scottish winter and froze to death having fallen into a ditch in the snow. He outlived Burns by thirteen years, but that did not prevent the poet from relishing the prospect of his adversary's death in an epitaph written in 1785: twenty-four years too early!

Burns's potent dislike for 'Holy Willie' was borne from Fisher's persecution of the poet's friend and landlord Gavin Hamilton, who found himself at the centre of a dispute concerning his supposed failure to collect 'poors rent' on behalf of the Kirk Session, and for failing to observe the Sabbath. Burns portrays the notorious hypocrite not in heaven, but in hell, where 'Justice, alas!' is being served.

Here Holy Willie's sair worn clay
    Taks up its last abode;
His saul has ta'en some other way,
    I fear, the left-hand road.

Stop! there he is, as sure's a gun,
  Poor silly body, see him;
Nae wonder he's as black's the grun,
  Observe wha's standing wi' him.

Your brunstane devilship, I see,
  Has got him there before ye;
But haud your nine-tail cat a wee,
  Till ance you've heard my story.

Your pity I will not implore,
  For pity ye have nane;
Justice, alas! has gi'en him o'er,
  And mercy's day is gane.

But hear me, Sir, deil as ye are,
  Look something to your credit;
A coof like him wad stain your name,
  If it were kent ye did it.

11TH FEBRUARY

Wilt Thou Be My Dearie
to the tune of The Sutor's Dochter

A S MANY OF US LOOK for the right words ahead of Valentine's
Day, we might turn to Burns's song 'Wilt thou be my Dearie'
for inspiration. Here an ardent lover pledges his heart and soul, if
only his lassie will 'say thou lo'es me'.

Wilt thou be my Dearie;
When sorrow wrings thy gentle heart,
O wilt thou let me chear thee:
By the treasure of my soul,
That's the love I bear thee!
I swear and vow, that only thou
Shall ever be my dearie
Only thou, I swear and vow,
Shall ever be my Dearie.

Lassie, say thou lo'es me;
Or if thou wilt na be my ain,
Say na thou'lt refuse me:
If it winna, canna be,
Thou for thine may chuse me,
Let me, Lassie, quickly die,
Trusting that thou lo'es me.
Lassie, let me quickly die,
Trusting that thou lo'es me.

12TH FEBRUARY

Anna Thy Charms

BURNS KNEW FROM PERSONAL EXPERIENCE that sometimes people set their sights on a love that is just out of reach. The song 'Anna thy Charms' was inspired by Anne Stewart, who was the love interest of Burns's friend Alexander Cunningham (1763–1812). She refused him and married elsewhere, but it is clear from Burns's correspondence that Cunningham never fully recovered from his disappointment. The sentiment is of enduring admiration, and of hope over despair.

Anna, thy charms my bosom fire,
    And waste my soul with care;
But ah! how bootless to admire,
    When fated to despair!

Yet in thy presence, lovely Fair,
    To hope may be forgiven;
For sure 'twere impious to despair
    So much in sight of Heaven.

13TH FEBRUARY

Epitaph – For the Author's Father

ON THE 13TH OF FEBRUARY 1784, Burns's father William Burnes died from physical consumption. His condition was exacerbated by years of gruelling labour, and intensified by the strain associated with legal wrangles over the family's unprosperous farm at Lochlea. He was buried in Alloway Kirkyard, which would later become the scene of Burns's iconic poem, 'Tam o' Shanter'.

Burns sincerely respected his father and was deeply affected by his death. They didn't always see eye to eye; William was obviously concerned about his son's temperament. In his autobiograhic letter to Dr John Moore, Burns recalled a disagreement that arose when he attended a country dance school in defiance of his devout father's wishes. He writes:

> In my seventeenth year, to give my manners a brush, I went to a country dancing school.— My father had an unaccountable antipathy against these meetings; and my going was, what to this hour I repent, in absolute defiance of his commands.— My father, as I said before, was the sport of strong passions: from that instance of rebellion he took a kind of dislike to me, which, I believe, was one cause of that dissipation which marked my future years.

However, in the days following William's death the poet wrote to his cousin James in the warmest of terms:

> On the 13th current I lost the best of fathers. Though to be sure we have had long warning of the impending stroke, still the feelings of Nature claim their part, and I cannot recollect the tender endearments and parental lessons of the best of friends and the ablest of instructors without feeling what, perhaps, the calmer dictates of reason would partly condemn.

Below is Burns's memorial to his father in verse; an epitaph that he made sure to include in his first published book of poetry, the Kilmarnock edition of *Poems, Chiefly in the Scottish Dialect* (1786).

O ye whose cheek the tear of pity stains,
    Draw near with pious rev'rence and attend!
Here lie the loving Husband's dear remains,
    The tender Father, and the gen'rous Friend.

The pitying Heart that felt for human Woe;
    The dauntless heart that fear'd no human Pride;
The Friend of Man, to vice alone a foe;
    'For ev'n his failings lean'd to Virtue's side.'

14TH FEBRUARY

Ae Fond Kiss
to the tune of Rory Dall's Port

THE 14TH OF FEBRUARY IS THE FEAST of St Valentine, the patron saint of love. Valentine's Day is traditionally recognised as a time for declarations of love; some expected and reciprocated, others secret and unrequited.

Given Burns's status as one of the world's greatest writers of love songs, there are a great many candidates for today's verse.

On Valentine's Day in 1788, Burns was in Edinburgh in the company of Agnes McLehose (1758–1841). In the afternoon he wrote to her planning to meet with her at eight p.m.: 'I esteem you, I love you, as a friend; I admire you, I love you, as a Woman, beyond any one in all the circle of Creation.'

Some months before this, Agnes had arranged an introduction to the bard through a mutual friend. Agnes was separated from her husband and living alone, dependent upon the generosity of her cousin. These were precarious social circumstances for a middle-class woman in the eighteenth century. Deeply concerned with propriety, to maintain her privacy and protect her reputation she suggested that she and Burns correspond using the *noms d'amour* 'Clarinda' and 'Sylvander'. They shared a lengthy, at times passionate, correspondence throughout 1787 and 1788, and enjoyed several private meetings. However, their individual circumstances ensured that nothing could come of the relationship and 'Clarinda' would become one of Burns's secret lost loves.

However, although Clarinda was lost, 'Ae Fond Kiss' is one of Burns's most famous love songs. It is the bard's heartfelt missive to Clarinda several years after their affair, written when she was due to leave Scotland for the West Indies.

Ae fond kiss, and then we sever;
Ae fareweel, and then for ever!
Deep in heart-wrung tears I'll pledge thee,
Warring sighs and groans I'll wage thee.
Who shall say that fortune grieves him,
While the star of hope she leaves him?
Me, nae chearfu' twinkle lights me;
Dark despair around benights me.

I'll ne'er blame my partial fancy,
Naething could resist my Nancy:
But to see her, was to love her;
Love but her, and love for ever.
Had we never lov'd sae kindly,
Had we never lov'd sae blindly,
Never met – or never parted,
We had ne'er been broken-hearted.

Fare thee weel, thou first and fairest!
Fare thee weel, thou best and dearest!
Thine be ilka joy and treasure,
Peace, Enjoyment, Love and Pleasure!
Ae fond kiss, and then we sever;
Ae fareweel, Alas! for ever!
Deep in heart-wrung tears I'll pledge thee,
Warring sighs and groans I'll wage thee.

15TH FEBRUARY

On That Delicious Passion
from a letter to Agnes McLehose, December 1787

BURNS WAS HIGHLY SKILLED in the art of letter-writing and in his correspondence with 'Clarinda' he makes impressive use of the sentimental 'language of feeling' fashionable at the time. Less impressive is his seeming attempt to tread the line between friendship and romantic love. Perhaps unsurprisingly, his letters and poetry for Clarinda make clear that he was unable to do so. In this letter Burns gives up the pretence and his flirtation takes full flight ...

I do love you if possible still better for having so fine a taste and turn for Poesy.— I have again gone wrong in my usual unguarded way, but you may erase the word, and put esteem, respect, or any other tame Dutch expression you please in its place.— I believe there is no holding converse or carrying on correspondence, with an amiable woman, much less a *gloriously amiable, fine woman*, without some mixture of that delicious Passion, whose most devoted Slave I have more than once had the honor of being: but why be hurt or offended on that account? Can no honest man have a prepossession for a fine woman, but he must run his head against an intrigue? Take a little of the tender witchcraft of Love, and add it to the generous, the honorable sentiments of manly Friendship; and I know but *one* more delightful morsel, which few, few in any rank ever taste.— Such a composition is like adding cream to strawberries – it not only gives the fruit a more elegant richness, but has a peculiar deliciousness of its own.—

16TH FEBRUARY

Clarinda, Mistress of My Soul

BURNS'S WORKS INSPIRED by Agnes McLehose are imbued with longing and a sense that their love is truly ill-fated. In 'Clarinda, Mistress of My Soul', parted from the 'Sun of all his joy', the poet is plunged into darkness and declares that 'No other light shall guide my steps'. Heart-breaking, yet the question mark at the end of the final stanza is perhaps telling. Burns had a roving eye and evidently even the 'glimmering Planet' Clarinda could not hold his gaze for long.

Clarinda, mistress of my soul,
   The measur'd time is run!
The wretch beneath the dreary pole,
   So marks his latest sun.

To what dark cave of frozen night
   Shall poor Sylvander hie;
Depriv'd of thee, his life and light,
   The Sun of all his joy.

We part – but by these precious drops,
   That fill thy lovely eyes!
No other light shall guide my steps,
   Till thy bright beams arise.

She, the fair Sun of all her sex,
   Has blest my glorious day:
And shall a glimmering Planet fix
   My worship to its ray?

17TH FEBRUARY

On Boundaries
from a letter to Agnes McLehose, 25th January 1788

D ID THEY, OR DIDN'T THEY? That is the unanswerable question
frequently posed by those intrigued by Burns's relationship with
Agnes McLehose. In the following extract Burns responds to a letter
from 'Clarinda' in which she declares:

> I will not deny it, Sylvander, last night was one of the most exquisite
> I ever experienced. Few such fall to the lot of mortals! Few, extremely
> few, are formed to relish such refined enjoyment. That it should be
> so vindicates the wisdom of Heaven. But, though our enjoyment did
> not lead beyond the limits of virtue, yet today's reflections have not
> been altogether unmixed with regret.

In an attempt to reassure her, Burns pledges '*Sylvander's honor*' that he
has learned from any past indiscretion. However, '*Sylvander's honor*'
might be considered a fiction, not necessarily to be relied upon.

Clarinda, my life, you have wounded my soul.— Can I think of your
being unhappy, even tho' it be not described in your pathetic elegance
of language, without being miserable? Clarinda, can I bear to be told
from you, that "you will not see me tomorrow night – that you wish
the hour of parting were come"! Do not let us impose on ourselves by
sounds: if, in the moment of fond endearment and tender dalliance,
I perhaps trespassed against the *letter* of Decorum's law; I appeal,
even to you, whether I ever sinned in the very least degree against
the *spirit* of her strictest statute.— But why, My Love, talk to me
in such strong terms; every word of which cuts me to the very soul?

You know, a hint, the slightest signification of your wish, is to me a sacred command.— Be reconciled, My Angel, to your God, your self and me; and I pledge you *Sylvander's honor*, an oath I dare say you will trust without reserve, that you shall never more have reason to complain of his conduct.— Now, my Love, do not wound our next meeting with any averted looks or restrained caresses: I have marked the line of conduct, a line I know exactly to your taste, and which I will inviolably keep; but do not *you* show the least inclination to make boundaries. Seeming distrust, where you know you may confide, is a cruel sin against sensibility.

18TH FEBRUARY

On Clarinda's Contempt
from a letter to Agnes McLehose, February 1790

BURNS, WHILE PERSISTENTLY DECLARING his love for 'Clarinda', was apparently conducting a physical relationship with her maid, Jenny Clow. Agnes McLehose did not become aware of this until some months later when, following the poet's departure from Edinburgh, Jenny gave birth to his son. This development, along with Burns's marriage to Jean Armour shortly after he left Edinburgh, understandably contributed to the collapse of their relationship. By February 1790 Burns was responding to Agnes in terms that made clear her attitude towards him had – unsurprisingly – significantly cooled.

I could not answer your last letter but one. When you in so many words tell a man that "you look on his letters with a smile of contempt", in what language, Madam, can he answer you? Though I were conscious I had acted wrong – and I am conscious that I have acted wrong – yet I would not be bullied into repentance but your last letter quite disarmed me.—

19TH FEBRUARY

Behold the Hour the Boat Arrive
to the tune of Oran Gaoil

I N HIS LAST LETTER TO Agnes McLehose in December 1791, Burns enclosed 'Ae Fond Kiss' along with 'Behold the Hour the Boat Arrive'. Both are songs of unrequited love and make explicit reference to Agnes's proposed departure for Jamaica early in 1792, where she planned to attempt a reunion with her estranged husband. It is commonly believed that Agnes arrived in the West Indies to discover that her husband had fathered children with his Jamaican mistress. As far as their troubled relationship was concerned, little had changed. This reality, combined with an aversion to the hot climate, caused Agnes to return to Scotland after a few short months. There is no evidence that she and Burns ever resumed their correspondence, although she cherished the poet's letters and retained a lifelong affection for him.

Indeed, Agnes wrote in her journal on the sixth of December 1831, forty years later: 'This day I can never forget. Parted with Burns in the year 1791, never more to meet in this world. Oh, may we meet in Heaven!'

Behold the hour, the boat arrive!
  My dearest Nancy, O fareweel!
Severed frae thee, can I survive,
  Frae thee whom I hae lov'd sae weel?

Endless and deep shall be my grief;
  Nae ray of comfort shall I see,
But this most precious, dear belief,
  That thou wilt still remember me!

Alang the solitary shore
　　Where flitting sea-fowl round me cry,
Across the rolling, dashing roar,
　　I'll westward turn my wishful eye.

"Happy thou Indian grove," I'll say,
　　"Where now my Nancy's path shall be!
While thro' your sweets she holds her way,
　　O tell me, does she muse on me?"

20TH FEBRUARY

On Politics
from a letter to Alexander Cunningham, 20th February 1793

A S IS THE CASE WITH many aspects of Burns's life and works, the poet's political position is difficult to distil; it is fraught with complexity and contradiction. Burns himself declared that, 'Politics is dangerous ground for me to tread on, and yet I cannot for the soul of me resist an impulse of anything like wit.' On this day in 1793 Burns sent his good friend Cunningham the following witty 'Catechism' on the subject.

What are you doing, what hurry have you got on your hands, my dear Cunningham, that I have not heard from you? Are you deeply engaged in the mazes of Law, the mysteries of Love, or in the profound wisdom of modern politics?— Curse on the word which ended the period!

Q. What is Politics?

A. Politics is a science wherewith, by means of nefarious cunning, and hypocritical pretence, we govern civil Polities for the emolument of ourselves and our adherents.—

Q. What is a Minister?

A. A Minister is an unprincipled fellow, who by the influence of hereditary, or acquired wealth; by superior abilities; or by a lucky conjuncture of circumstances, obtains a principal place in the administration of the affairs of government.—

Q. What is a Patriot?

A. An individual exactly of the same description as a Minister, only, out of place.—

21st FEBRUARY

from A Ballad – While Prose-work and Rhymes

BURNS'S COMPLICATED POLITICS proved the source of controversy during his lifetime. In 1792 he provoked the alarmed interest of his superiors in the excise when he – a government employee – was rumoured to have openly expressed support for the French Revolution. Whether or not this was the case, analysis of Burns's correspondence and political verse certainly points to his support for revolutionary principles, and it's safe to say that the initial success of the Revolution provided the poet with new and contemporary inspiration to convey the ideas of unity and equality which recur throughout his work.

In the bawdy political satire 'While Prose-work and Rhymes', sex and politics collide as Burns takes aim at the literary censorship sprung from the establishment's political insecurity. If he cannot write explicitly about politics, he will do so implicitly and 'chuse' to write about sex.

While Prose-work and rhymes
Are hunted for crimes,
And things are – the devil knows how;
Aware o' my rhymes,
In these kittle times,
The subject I chuse is a mowe.

Some cry, Constitution!
Some cry, Revolution!
And Politicks kick up a rowe;
But Prince and Republic,
Agree on the Subject,
No treason is in a good mowe.

22ND FEBRUARY

from Ode for General Washington's Birthday

G EORGE WASHINGTON, Commander of the American forces in
the War of Independence and the first President of the United
States, was born on the 22nd of February 1732. Today Americans
mark his birthday with a federal holiday. Burns, who greatly admired
Washington and his quest for liberty and equality, celebrated his
birthday with this rousing 'Ode'. The bard's vehement praise for the
politics of revolution, written at a period of considerable political
unrest in Europe, meant the poem could not be published during his
lifetime. It was not printed in full until 1872, the best part of a century
after its composition.

No Spartan tube, no Attic shell,
No lyre Eolian I awake;
'Tis Liberty's bold note I swell,
Thy harp, Columbia, let me take.
See gathering thousands, while I sing,
A broken chain, exulting, bring,
And dash it in a tyrant's face!
And dare him to his very beard,
And tell him he no more is feared,
No more the Despot of Columbia's race.
A tyrant's proudest insults brav'd,
They shout – a People freed! They hail an Empire saved.

Where is Man's god-like form?
Where is that brow erect and bold,
That eye that can, unmoved, behold

The wildest rage, the loudest storm,
That e'er created fury dared to raise!
Avaunt! thou caitiff, servile, base,
That tremblest at a Despot's nod,
Yet, crouching under the iron rod,
Canst laud the hand that struck th' insulting blow!
Art thou of man's imperial line?
Dost boast that countenance divine?
Each sculking feature answers, No!
But come, ye sons of Liberty,
Columbia's offspring, brave as free,
In danger's hour still flaming in the van:
Ye know, and dare maintain, the Royalty of Man.

23RD FEBRUARY

I Reign in Jeanie's Bosom

I N THIS SONG, inspired by Jean Armour, Burns defiantly elevates woman over monarchy and romantic love over political authority. He and Jeanie are answerable to one another alone.

Louis, what reck I by thee,
  Or Geordie on his ocean:
Dyvor, beggar louns to me,
  I reign in Jeanie's bosom.

Let her crown my love her law,
  And in her breast enthrone me:
Kings and nations, swith awa!
  Reif randies, I disown ye!

24TH FEBRUARY

O Leave Novels, Ye Mauchline Belles

I N 1783, BURNS'S FAMILY moved to Mossgiel Farm near Mauchline. Burns, then in his early twenties, was unsurprisingly interested in the local beauties whom he referred to as the 'Mauchline belles'. Here he portrays them as sophisticated consumers of literature, while playfully warning of the danger associated with an over-romantic sensibility. The rakish Burns, confident of his sex appeal, is the artful seducer of whom they should beware. One of the Mauchline Belles, Jean Armour, did indeed fall prey to his advances.

O leave novels, ye Mauchline belles,
    Ye're safer at your spinning-wheel;
Such witching books, are baited hooks
    For rakish rooks, like Rob Mossgiel;
Your fine Tom Jones and Grandisons,
    They make your youthful fancies reel;
They heat your brains, and fire your veins,
    And then you're prey for Rob Mossgiel.

Beware a tongue that's smoothly hung;
    A heart that warmly seems to feel;
That feeling heart but acts a part –
    'Tis rakish art in Rob Mossgiel.
The frank address, the soft caress,
    Are worse than poisoned darts of steel,
The frank address, and politesse,
    Are all finesse in Rob Mossgiel.

25TH FEBRUARY

I Love My Jean
to the tune of Miss Admiral Gordon's Strathspey

ROBERT BURNS'S WIFE, Jean Armour Burns, was born on the 25th of February 1765. 'I Love My Jean' is the most famous of Burns's songs inspired by her. The bard himself wrote in an interleaved copy of the *Scots Musical Museum* that: 'it was composed out of compliment to Mrs Burns.— N.B. it was during the honey-moon.'

The song references separations experienced by the couple prior to their marriage and expresses Burns's seemingly undeniable attraction to 'the Lassie I lo'e best'.

Of a' the airts the wind can blaw,
    I dearly like the west;
For there the bony Lassie lives,
    The Lassie I lo'e best:
There's wild-woods grow, and rivers row,
    And mony a hill between;
But day and night my fancy's flight
    Is ever wi' my Jean.

I see her in the dewy flowers,
    I see her sweet and fair;
I hear her in the tunefu' birds,
    I hear her charm the air:
There's not a bony flower that springs
    By fountain, shaw, or green;
There's not a bony bird that sings,
    But minds me o' my Jean.

26TH FEBRUARY

Inconstancy in Love

BURNS SENT 'INCONSTANCY IN LOVE' to George Thomson, who had requested some songs in the English language. The poet complained that, 'These English Songs gravel me to death.— I have not that command of the language that I have of my native tongue.— In fact, I think that my ideas are more barren in English than in Scottish.'

If Burns felt unhappy with his attempts to 'dress it in English', he was on a somewhat surer footing with the song's subject matter, which certainly chimes with the way the poet lived his life.

Let not Woman e'er complain
    Of inconstancy in love;
Let not Woman e'er complain,
    Fickle Man is apt to rove:
Look abroad through Nature's range,
Nature's mighty law is CHANGE;
Ladies would it not seem strange
    Man should then a monster prove.

Mark the winds, and mark the skies;
    Oceans ebb, and oceans flow;
Sun and moon but set to rise;
    Round and round the seasons go:
Why then ask of silly Man,
To oppose great Nature's plan?
We'll be constant while we can
    You can be no more, you know.

27TH FEBRUARY

Ca' the Yowes to the Knowes

THIS FAMOUS BALLAD, characteristically Scottish and rich in natural imagery, is an example of Burns's collection and 'improvement' of traditional Scottish songs. The poet is known to have made several emendations and to have composed and added the final two stanzas. Here two lovers come and go with one another until they pledge to be one another's 'dearie' for life.

Ca' the yowes to the knowes,
  Ca' them where the heather grows,
Ca' them where the burnie rowes,
  My bonie dearie.

As I gaed down the water-side,
  There I met my shepherd lad,
He row'd me sweetly in his plaid,
  And he ca'd me his dearie.
    Ca' the yowes &c.

Will ye gang down the water-side,
  And see the waves sae sweetly glide,
Beneath the hazels spreading wide,
  The moon it shines fu' clearly.
    Ca' the yowes &c.

I was bred up at nae sic school,
    My shepherd lad, to play the fool,
And a' the day to sit in dool,
    And naebody to see me.
        Ca' the yowes &c.

Ye sall get gowns and ribbons meet,
    Cauf-leather shoon upon your feet,
And in my arms ye'se lie and sleep,
    And ye sall be my dearie.
        Ca' the yowes &c.

If ye'll but stand to what ye've said,
    I'se gang wi' you, my shepherd lad,
And ye may rowe me in your plaid,
    And I sall be your dearie.
        Ca' the yowes &c.

While waters wimple to the sea;
    While day blinks in the lift sae hie,
Till clay-cauld death sall blin' my e'e,
    Ye sall be my dearie.
        Ca' the yowes &c.

28TH FEBRUARY

On Life
from a letter to Captain Richard Brown, February 1788

I N FEBRUARY 1788, Burns penned the following philosophy on life. While the bard certainly embraced life's pleasures, he did not do so without conscience. Pleasure, he writes, is fleeting. For Burns, stability, independence of mind and friendship are truly what matter.

Life is a fairy scene; almost all that deserves the name of enjoyment, or pleasure, is only charming delusion; and in comes ripening Age, in all the gravity of hoary wisdom, and wickedly chases away the dear, bewitching Phantoms.—

When I think of life, I resolve to keep a strict lookout in the course of Economy, for the sake of worldly convenience and independence of mind; to cultivate intimacy with a few of the companions of youth, that they may be the friends of Age; never to refuse my liquorish humour a handful of the Sweetmeats of life, where they come not too dear; and for futurity,

> "The present moment is our ain,
> The neist we never saw!"

How do you like my Philosophy?

29TH FEBRUARY

John Come Kiss Me Now

EVERY FOUR YEARS, an extra day is added to the calendar on the 29th of February. This is known as 'leap day'. The leap in time ensures that the calendar remains in time with the earth's orbit of the sun. A day that is all about redressing imbalances, tradition has it that St Patrick designated leap day as the only day on which a woman could propose to a man, following a complaint by St Bridget that they were typically unable to do so. The female protagonist in 'John Come Kiss Me Now' doesn't quite propose marriage, but neither is she a stranger to female agency when it comes to the opposite sex.

O John, come kiss me now, now, now;
   O John, my luve, come kiss me now;
O John, come kiss me by and by,
   For weel ye ken the way to woo.

O some will court and compliment,
   And ither some will kiss and daut;
But I will mak o' my gudeman,
   My ain gudeman, it is nae faute.

O some will court and compliment,
   And ither some will prie their mou,
And some will hause in ithers arms,
   And that's the way I like to do.

MARCH

The smiling spring comes in rejoicing,
And surly winter grimly flies;

from Bonie Bell

1st MARCH

I Am a Son of Mars
from Love and Liberty – A Cantata
to the tune of Soldier's Joy

THE MONTH OF MARCH (from Latin, *Martius*) was named after Mars, the Roman god of war. We begin the month, then, with Burns's most explicit reference to Mars in 'Love and Liberty – A Cantata' (also commonly known as 'The Jolly Beggars'). Burns composed the cantata, a collection of several songs punctuated with narrative verse, in 1785. However, it was never published during the poet's lifetime; it is thought that he was deterred from publishing the work by Rev. Dr Hugh Blair (1718–1800), who declared that it was 'much too licentious'.

'Love and Liberty' rejects the values of conventional society in favour of vagrancy and the satisfaction of bodily appetites with alcohol and sex, flouting the authority of kirk and state. In this song a 'staggering, an' swaggering' wounded soldier recounts his military career. His 'cuts' and 'scars' are the consequence of martial duty and illicit sex. And so, Burns conflates sex and war to represent man's struggle in an imperfect world.

I am a son of Mars, who have been in many wars,
   And show my cuts and scars wherever I come;
This here was for a wench, and that other in a trench,
   When welcoming the French at the sound of the drum.

My Prenticeship I past where my Leader breathed his last,
   When the bloody die was cast on the heights of Abram;
And I served out my trade when the gallant game was play'd,
   And the Moro low was laid at the sound of the drum.

I lastly was with Curtis among the floating batt'ries,
    And there I left for witness an arm and a limb;
Yet let my Country need me, with Elliot to head me,
    I'd clatter on my stumps at the sound of a drum.

And now tho' I must beg, with a wooden arm and leg,
    And many a tatter'd rag hanging over by bum,
I'm as happy with my wallet, my bottle and my Callet,
    As when I used in scarlet to follow a drum.

What tho' with hoary locks, I must stand the winter shocks,
    Beneath the woods and rocks oftentimes for a home,
When the t'other bag I sell and the t'other bottle tell,
    I could meet a troop of Hell at the sound of a drum.

2ND MARCH

I Once Was a Maid
from Love and Liberty – A Cantata
to the tune of Soldier Laddie

ALSO REFERRED TO AS 'Sodger Laddie', this is perhaps the most salacious of all songs included in 'Love and Liberty – A Cantata'. Here we encounter the soldier's 'doxy', whose circumstances are the product of a very different military career. Her sexuality has sustained her throughout her life, and her survival on the periphery of 'polite' society has equipped her with an alternative moral outlook, even leading her to a brief (if unsatisfying!) foray with the army chaplain.

The final stanzas convey the overarching message of 'Love and Liberty': despite misfortune, poverty and alienation from society, Burns's 'Jolly Beggars' are still able to derive pleasure from their bodies – from alcohol, conviviality and love.

I once was a maid, tho' I canna tell when,
    An' still my delight is in proper young men;
Some one of a troop of dragoons was my daddie,
    No wonder I'm fond of a sodger laddie.

The first of my loves was a swaggerin' blade,
    To rattle the thundering drum was his trade;
His leg was so tight, and his cheek was so ruddy,
    Transported I was with my sodger laddie.

But the godly old chaplain left him in the lurch,
    The sword I forsook for the sake of the church:
He ventur'd the *soul*, and I risked the *body*,
    'Twas then I proved false to my sodger laddie.

Full soon I grew sick of my sanctified sot,
    The regiment at large for a husband I got;
From the gilded spontoon to the fife I was ready,
    I asked no more but a sodger laddie.

But the peace it reduc'd me to beg in despair,
    Till I met old boy in a Cunningham fair,
His rags regimental, they flutter'd so gaudy,
    My heart it rejoic'd at a sodger laddie.

An' now I have lived – I know not how long,
    And still I can join in a cup and a song;
But whilst with both hands I can hold the glass steady,
    Here's to thee, my hero, my sodger laddie.

3RD MARCH

from A Fragment – On Glenriddell's Fox Breaking Its Chain

O N WORLD WILDLIFE DAY we might cast our minds back to Burns's compassion for the 'tim'rous beastie' in 'To a Mouse'. Burns again ponders man and creature when, incredulous that his politically progressive friend Captain Robert Riddell (1755–1794) had imprisoned a wild fox in a 'dirty kennel', he is inspired by the wily animal's escape to reflect more broadly upon the value and attainment of liberty.

Thou, Liberty, thou art my theme;
Not such as idle Poets dream,
Who trick thee up a Heathen goddess,
That a fantastic cap and rod has:
Such stale conceits are poor and silly;
I paint thee out, a Highland filly,
A sturdy, stubborn, handsome dapple,
As sleek's a mouse, as round's an apple,
That when thou pleasest can do wonders;
But when thy luckless rider blunders,
Or if thy fancy should demur there,
Wilt break thy neck ere thou go further.

These things premis'd, I sing a fox,
Was caught among his native rocks,
And to a dirty kennel chain'd,
How he his liberty regain'd.

Glenriddel, a Whig without a stain,
A Whig in principle and grain,
Couldst thou enslave a free-born creature,
A native denizen of Nature?
How couldst thou with a heart so good,
(A better ne'er was sluic'd with blood)
Nail a poor devil to a tree,
That ne'er did harm to thine or thee?

The staunchest Whig Glenriddel was,
Quite frantic in his Country's cause;
And oft was Reynard's prison passing,
And with his brother Whigs canvassing
The Rights of Men, the Powers of Women,
With all the dignity of Freemen.

[...]

Thus wily Reynard by degrees,
In kennel listening at his ease,
Suck'd in a mighty stock of knowledge,
As much as some folks at a college.
Knew Britain's rights and constitution,
Her aggrandizement, diminution,
How fortune wrought us good from evil;
Let no man then despise the devil,
As who should say, I ne'er can need him;
Since we to scoundrels owe our freedom.

4TH MARCH

On Reading
from Burns's autobiographical letter to Dr John Moore, 2nd August 1787

T HE FOURTH OF MARCH is World Book Day, and so here is Burns's joyful account of his first experiences of independent reading. The poet makes clear the passion he feels for the written word and the lifelong influence of his early reading, not least the impact that it has had upon his imagination and continued sense of patriotism.

The two first books I ever read in private, and which gave me more pleasure than any two books I ever read again, were the life of Hannibal and the history of Sir William Wallace.— Hannibal gave my young ideas such a turn that I used to strut in raptures up and down after the recruiting drum and bagpipe, and wish myself tall enough to be a soldier; while the story of Wallace poured a Scottish prejudice in my veins which will boil along there till the flood-gates of life shut in eternal rest.—

5TH MARCH

On the Monkland Friendly Society
from a letter to Sir John Sinclair

IN MARCH 1789, with the patronage and assistance of his friend Captain Robert Riddell (1755–1795), Burns founded the Monkland Friendly Society Library in the village of Dunscore, Dumfriesshire. The purpose of the library was to render books more affordable, and therefore more freely available, among the farming community in Burns's locale. Members paid a modest entry fee and monthly subscription, and the funds were used to purchase books for circulation among the subscribers.

The extract below from an account that Burns provided for John Sinclair's *Statistical Account of Scotland* (1791) is a clear articulation of his motivation in forming the society, and his commitment to the Enlightenment principle of intellectual improvement.

To store the minds of the lower classes with useful knowledge, is certainly of very great consequence, both to them as individuals, and to society at large. Giving them a turn for reading and reflection, is giving them a source of innocent and laudable amusement; and besides, raises them to a more dignified degree in the scale of rationality. Impressed with this idea, a gentleman in this parish, ROBERT RIDDELL, Esq; of Glenriddel, set on foot a species of circulating library, on a plan so simple, as to be practicable in any corner of the country; and so useful, as to deserve the notice of every country gentleman, who thinks the improvement of that part of his own species, whom chance has thrown into the humble walks of the peasant and the artisan, a matter worthy of his attention. [...]

At the breaking up of this little society, which was formed under Mr Riddell's patronage, what with benefactions of books from him, and what with their own purchases, they had collected together upwards of 150 volumes. It will easily be guessed, that a good deal of trash would be bought. Among the books, however, of this little library, were, Blair's Sermons, Robertson's History of Scotland, Hume's History of the Stewarts, the Spectator, Idler, Adventurer, Mirror, Lounger, Observer, Man of Feeling, Man of the World, Chrysal, Don Quixotte, Joseph Andrews, &c. A peasant who can read, and enjoy such books, is certainly a much superior being to his neighbour, who, perhaps, stalks beside his team, very little removed, except in shape, from the brutes he drives.

6TH MARCH

A Penitential Thought, in the Hour of Remorse – Intended for a Tragedy

SEVERAL ENTRIES IN BURNS'S 'FIRST COMMONPLACE BOOK' during March 1784 convey his dark and pensive mood as he reeled from the death of his father. 'A Penitential Thought, in the hour of Remorse', one of Burns's most solemn works, is one such entry. In another manuscript version of this poem the poet explains, 'In my early years nothing less would serve me than courting the tragic Muse.' He elaborates that he had 'sketched the outlines of a Tragedy' until 'a bursting cloud of family Misfortunes, which had for some time threatened us, prevented my farther progress'. These 'Misfortunes' were the family's financial and legal difficulties pertaining to previously unsuccessful farming ventures, something that would surely have been weighing on his mind as he contemplated the challenges faced by his father prior to his death, and his own imminent plans to lease a farm at Mossgiel with his brother, Gilbert.

All devil as I am, a damned wretch,
A hardened, stubborn, unrepenting villain:
Still my heart melts at human wretchedness;
And with sincere though unavailing sighs
I view the helpless children of distress.
With tears indignant I behold th' Oppressor,
Rejoicing in the honest man's destruction,
Whose unsubmitting heart was all his crime.

Even you, ye hapless crew, I pity you,
Ye, whom the seeming good think sin to pity;
Ye poor, despis'd, abandon'd Vagabonds,
Whom Vice, as usual, has turn'd o'er to Ruin.
If but for kind, though ill requited friends,
I had been driven forth like you forlorn,
The most detested, worthless wretch among ye!

O injur'd God! Thy goodness has endow'd me
With talents passing most of my compeers,
Which I in just proportion have abus'd;
As far surpassing other common Villains
As Thou in nat'ral parts hast given me more.

7TH MARCH

On Mossgiel Farm
from Burns's autobiographical letter to John Moore

IN MARCH 1784, Burns and his brother Gilbert leased Mossgiel Farm, between Mauchline and Tarbolton in Ayrshire, for £90 per annum. Burns composed several of his most famous works while he resided and worked at Mossgiel, and it was here that he began his career as a poet in earnest by setting in motion plans to publish *Poems, Chiefly in the Scottish Dialect* (1786). Although Burns left Mossgiel for Edinburgh and eventually Dumfriesshire, his family resided there (albeit with his financial support) until after the poet's death.

Burns's account of the difficult early days at Mossgiel is interesting also for the insight that it offers into Robert and Gilbert's very different temperaments. Gilbert was seemingly less passionate and impulsive than Robert, and took seriously his responsibilities as a carer for their mother, sisters and Burns's first-born daughter, Elizabeth. It is clear from his accounts of his famous brother, however, that he respected and depended upon Robert in his own way.

When my father died, his all went among the rapacious hell-hounds that growl in the kennel of justice; but we made a shift to scrape a little money in the family amongst us, with which, to keep us together, my brother and I took a neighbouring farm.— My brother wanted my hare-brained imagination as well as my social and amorous madness, but in good sense and every sober qualification he was far my superior.—

I entered on this farm with a full resolution, "Come, go to, I will be wise!"— I read farming books; I calculated crops; I attended markets; and, in short, in spite of "the devil, the world, and the flesh," I believe I would have been a wise man; but the first year, from unfortunately buying bad seed, the second from a late harvest, we lost half of both our crops: this overset all my wisdom, and I returned "like the dog to his vomit, and the sow that was washed to her wallowing in the mire".

8TH MARCH

The Rights of Women
spoken by Miss Fontenelle on her Benefit Night

ON INTERNATIONAL WOMEN'S DAY we turn our attention to this poem, composed for the London actress Miss Louisa Fontenelle (1773–1799).

Burns wrote to her in November 1792 offering the piece for performance at a forthcoming benefit night. In the wake of Thomas Paine's *The Rights of Man* (1791), one of the most influential and contentious books of its time owing to its defence of the French Revolution, Burns asserts that – indeed! – 'The Rights of Woman merit some attention'. The poem's concluding lines, which invoke the French revolutionary cry, '*ça ira!*', appear to have fuelled accusations that the poet led the revolutionary cry at the Dumfries Playhouse. When this was brought to the attention of his superiors in the excise, Burns was forced to address 'charges which Malice and Misrepresentation have brought against me', although he received little more than a slap on the wrist.

Burns's light-hearted poem is by no means a petition for gender equality, and it bears no resemblance to Mary Wollstonecraft's proto-feminist manifesto, *A Vindication of the Rights of Women* (1792), which appeared in the same year. Rather, Burns extols the 'majesty of women' and their ability to distract men from political matters. In proposing that women have a right to 'protection', 'decorum' (or good manners) and 'admiration', he suggests that society should protect and respect the delicacy of the female sex. Burns articulates an outlook popular in his time: that woman's crucial role within society was reflected in the positive, more passive, sympathetic effect that they supposedly had on men. There is ample evidence in the bard's correspondence, however, that he maintained a sincere respect for female intellect. Today's selection, then, serves as a glimpse into the perception of women in eighteenth-century society – and a reminder of hard-won progress!

While Europe's eye is fix'd on mighty things,
The fate of empires and the fall of kings,
While quacks of State must each produce his plan,
And even children lisp *the Rights of Man*;
Amid this mighty fuss just let me mention,
The Rights of Woman merit some attention.

First, in the sexes' intermix'd connection,
One sacred Right of Woman is *protection.*—
The tender flower that lifts its head, elate,
Helpless, must fall before the blasts of fate,
Sunk on the earth, defac'd its lovely form,
Unless your shelter ward th' impending storm.—

Our second Right — but needless here is caution,
To keep that right inviolate's the fashion,
Each man of sense has it so full before him,
He'd die before he'd wrong it – 'tis *decorum.*—
There was, indeed, in far less polish'd days,
A time, when rough rude man had naughty ways;
Would swagger, swear, get drunk, kick up a riot,
Nay even thus invade a lady's quiet.—

Now, thank our stars! those Gothic times are fled;
Now, well-bred men — and you are all well-bred —
Most justly think (and we are much the gainers)
Such conduct neither spirit, wit, nor manners.

For Right the third, our last, our best, our dearest,
That right to fluttering female hearts the nearest;
Which even the Rights of Kings, in low prostration,
Most humbly own — 'tis dear, dear *admiration!*
In that blest sphere alone we live and move;
There taste that life of life-immortal love.—
Smiles, glances, sighs, tears, fits, flirtations, airs;
'Gainst such an host what flinty savage dares —
When awful Beauty joins with all her charms,
Who is so rash as rise in rebel arms?

But truce with kings, and truce with constitutions,
With bloody armaments and revolutions;
Let Majesty your first attention summon,
Ah! ça ira! The Majesty of Woman!

9TH MARCH

On Adam Smith's *The Wealth of Nations*
from a letter to Robert Graham of Fintry, 13th May 1789

O N THIS DAY IN 1776, the Scottish economist and philosopher Adam Smith (1723–1790) published *An Enquiry into the Nature and Causes of the Wealth of Nations*. Smith's treatise, which set out the principles of free economy, was foundational for modern economics and one of the most influential works of the eighteenth century. Burns, who was profoundly influenced by the intellectual and philosophical developments of the Scottish Enlightenment, praises Smith's achievement in this extract from a letter to Robert Graham of Fintry. The other book to which he refers is William Marshal's *The Rural Economy of Yorkshire* (1788).

By-the-by, the Excise instructions you mentioned were not in the bundle.— But 'tis no matter; Marshal in his Yorkshire, and particularly that extraordinary man, Smith, in his Wealth of Nations, find my leisure employment enough.— I could not have given any mere *man* credit for half the intelligence Mr Smith discovers in his book. I would covet so much to have his ideas respecting the present state of some quarters of the world that are, or have been, the scenes of considerable revolutions since his book was written.—

10TH MARCH

There Was a Lass, and She Was Fair

WRITTEN IN 1793, this song was inspired by Jean McMurdo (1777–1839), the daughter of Burns's friend John McMurdo of Drumlanrig. To avoid offending his friend, Burns first sent it to McMurdo requesting permission to present it to his daughter, emphasising that it was not meant as a romantic overture, but as a respectful compliment: 'I assure you, I am not a little flattered with the idea, when I anticipate children pointing out in future Publications the tributes of respect I have bestowed upon their mothers.' When eventually Burns presented the song to Jean, he flattered her that, 'The personal charms, the purity of mind, the ingenious naiveté of heart and manners, in my heroine, are, I flatter myself, a pretty just likeness of Miss McMurdo in a cottager.'

This touching pastoral ballad uses natural imagery to create a scene of beauty, simplicity and innocence, even if the declaration that 'Young Robie was the brawest lad' provokes a raised eyebrow (or two).

There was a lass and she was fair,
    At kirk and market to be seen;
When a' our fairest maids were met,
    The fairest maid was bonie Jean.
And ay she wrought her mammie's wark,
    And ay she sang sae merrilie;
The blythest bird upon the bush
    Had ne'er a lighter heart than she.

But hawks will rob the tender joys
   That bless the little lintwhite's nest;
And frost will blight the fairest flowers,
   And love will break the soundest rest.
Young Robie was the brawest lad,
   The flower and pride of a' the glen;
And he had owsen, sheep, and kye,
   And wanton nagies nine or ten.

He gaed wi' Jeanie to the tryste,
   He danc'd wi' Jeanie on the down,
And, lang ere witless Jeanie wist,
   Her heart was tint, her peace was stown!
As in the bosom o' the stream,
   The moon-beam dwells at dewy e'en;
So trembling, pure, was tender love
   Within the breast of bonie Jean.

And now she works her mammie's wark,
   And ay she sighs wi' care and pain;
Yet wist na what her ail might be,
   Or what wad mak' her weel again.
But did na Jeanie's heart lowp light,
   And did na joy blink in her e'e,
As Robie tauld a tale o' love
   Ae e'ening on the lily lea?

The sun was sinking in the west,
   The birds sang sweet in ilka grove;
His cheek to her's he fondly laid,
   And whisper'd thus his tale o' love.
O Jeanie fair, I lo'e thee dear;
   O can'st thou think to fancy me!
Or wilt thou leave thy mammie's cot,
   And learn to tent the farms wi' me?

At barn or byre thou shalt na drudge,
  Or naething else to trouble thee,
But stray amang the heather bells,
  And tent the waving corn wi' me.
Now what could artless Jeanie do?
  She had na will to say him na:
At length she blush'd a sweet consent,
  And love was aye between them twa.

11TH MARCH

from The Death and Dying Words of Poor Mailie, the Author's Only Pet Yowe, an Unco Mournfu' Tale

THIS IS ONE OF BURNS's earliest works. It was inspired by an incident at the Burnes family farm at Lochlea. Gilbert Burns recounted that his brother had purchased a sheep with two lambs and tethered them in a field. One day a panicked local boy alerted him that the sheep had become tangled in her rope and was lying in a ditch. In reality, Mailie the sheep was rescued, but the events prompted Burns to imagine her 'Death and Dying Words' which, if Gilbert's account is to be believed, he had composed by the end of that same working day.

In the tradition of 'last words poetry', Mailie spends her dying moments imparting advice for Burns (her 'Master Dear') and her lambs. Among her concerns are the welfare and manners of her offspring: that at 'ridin time' her 'son and heir' remains content 'wi' yowes at hame' rather than jumping the fence; and that her daughter doesn't consort 'wi' ony blastet, moorlan toop' but with 'a sheep o' credit like thysel'! It seems Burns's sheep had good foresight: the flippancy with which Burns addresses these concerns might be considered prophetic, not least because the bard himself 'jumped the fence' on more than one occasion, and for a time was very much the 'blastet, moorlan *toop*' in the eyes of Jean Armour's parents!

O thou, whase lamentable face
Appears to mourn my woefu' case!
My *dying words* attentive hear,
An' bear them to my *Master* dear.

   Tell him, if e'er again he keep
As muckle gear as buy a *sheep*,
O, bid him never tye them mair,
Wi' wicked strings o' hemp or hair!
But ca' them out to park or hill,
An' let them wander at their will:
So, may his flock increase an' grow
To *scores* o' lambs, an' *packs* of woo'!

   Tell him, he was a Master kin',
An' ay was guid to me an' mine;
An' now my *dying* charge I gie him,
My helpless *lambs*, I trust them wi' him.

   O, bid him save their harmless lives,
Frae dogs, an' tods, an' butchers' knives!
But gie them guid *cow-milk* their fill,
Till they be fit to fend themsel;
An' tent them duly, e'en an' morn,
Wi' taets o' *hay* an' ripps o' *corn*.

   An' may they never learn the gaets,
Of ither vile, wanrestfu' *Pets*!
To slink thro' slaps, an' reave an' steal,
At stacks o' pease, or stocks o' kail.
So may they, like their great *forbears*,

For monie a year come thro' the sheers:
So *wives* will gie them bits o' bread,
An' *bairns* greet for them when they're dead.

My poor *toop-lamb*, my son an' heir,
O, bid him breed him up wi' care!
An' if he live to be a beast,
To pit some havins in his breast!
An' warn him ay at ridin time,
To stay content wi' *yowes* at hame;
An' no to rin an' wear his cloots,
Like ither menseless, graceless brutes.

An' niest, my *yowie*, silly thing,
Gude keep thee frae a *tether string*!
O, may thou ne'er forgather up,
Wi' ony blastet, moorlan *toop*;
But ay keep mind to moop an' mell,
Wi' sheep o' credit like thysel!

12TH MARCH

Poor Mailie's Elegy

Burns's homage to his (supposedly) dead sheep is made humorous by exaggeration. It provides context for its partner piece by explaining that Mailie, far from being any old common ewe, was an upstanding animal: intelligent, loyal and well behaved. Furthermore, Mailie was imported frae 'yont the TWEED' – from England – and so Burns mischievously implies that she was a superior breed to the 'moorlan toops' of whom she is so critical.

Lament in rhyme, lament in prose,
Wi' saut tears trickling down your nose
Our *Bardie's* fate is at a close,
      Past a' remead!
The last, sad cape-stane of his woes;
      Poor Mailie's dead!

It's no the loss o' warl's gear,
That could sae bitter draw the tear,
Or mak our *Bardie*, dowie, wear
      The mourning weed:
He's lost a friend an' neebor dear,
      In *Mailie* dead.

Thro' a' the town she trotted by him;
A lang half-mile she could descry him;
Wi' kindly bleat, when she did spy him,
      She ran wi' speed:
A friend mair faithfu' ne'er came nigh him,
      Than *Mailie* dead.

I wat she was a *sheep* o' sense,
An' could behave hersel' wi' mense:
I'll say't, she never brak a fence,
    Thro' thievish greed.
Our *Bardie*, lanely, keeps the spence
    Sin' *Mailie's* dead.

Or, if he wanders up the howe,
Her living image in *her yowe*,
Comes bleating to him, owre the knowe,
    For bits o' bread;
An' down the briny pearls rowe
    For *Mailie* dead.

She was nae get o' moorlan toops,
Wi' tauted ket, an' hairy hips;
For her forbears were brought in ships,
    Frae 'yont the TWEED:
A bonier *fleesh* ne'er cross'd the clips
    Than *Mailie's* dead.

Wae worth the man wha first did shape,
That vile, wanchancie thing – *a raep*!
It maks guid fellows girn an' gape,
    Wi' chokin dread;
An' *Robin's* bonnet wave wi' crape
    For *Mailie* dead.

O, a' ye *Bards* on bonie DOON!
An' wha on AIRE your chanters tune!
Come, join the melancholious croon
    O' *Robin's* reed!
His heart will never get aboon!
    His *Mailie's* dead!

.

Elegy on Peg Nicholson

CONTINUING THE ANIMAL THEME, this poem is Burns's tribute
to a horse loaned to him by his friend William Nicol (1744–1797).
In 1790 a heartsore Burns wrote, 'That damned mare of yours is dead.
I would freely have given her price to have saved her: she has vexed
me beyond description [...] While she was with me, she was under
my own eye, and I assure you, my much valued friend, everything
was done for her that could be done; and the accident has vexed me
to the heart.'

These blunt stanzas lack the humour of his poems for 'poor Mailie',
and reflect the – at times – harsh reality of farming with animals. That
said, Burns's nod to the mare's previous owner in the final stanza might
be considered a wry, if ambiguous, joke at the expense of the clergy.

Peg Nicholson was a good bay mare,
　　As ever trod on airn;
But now she's floating down the Nith,
　　And past the Mouth o' Cairn.

Peg Nicholson was a good bay mare,
　　And rode thro' thick and thin;
But now she's floating down the Nith,
　　And wanting even the skin.

Peg Nicholson was a good bay mare,
　　And ance she bore a priest;
But now she's floating down the Nith,
　　For Solway fish a feast.

Peg Nicholson was a good bay mare,
　　And the priest he rode her sair:
And much oppressed and bruised she was;
　　— As priest-rid cattle are, &c.

14TH MARCH

To Alexander Findlater

I N THIS COMIC VERSE EPISTLE to his good friend Alexander
Findlater, Burns is in bawdy mode as he fantasises about what
life would be like were he born a cockerel, free to live according to
'honest Nature's laws and ties', rather than a 'Poet poor', restrained
by law and social decorum. This poem is an example of the masculine
bravado with which Burns wrote to some of his male cronies, despite
knowing that his remarks were 'kittle'; that is, treading risky or
licentious ground.

Dear Sir,
　　　　Our Lucky humbly begs
Ye'll prie her caller, new-laid eggs:
Lord grant the Cock may keep his legs,
　　　　Aboon the Chuckies;
And wi' his kittle, forket clegs,
　　　　Claw weel their dockies!

Had Fate that curst me in her ledger,
A Poet poor, and poorer Gager,
Created me that feather'd Sodger,
　　　　A generous Cock,
How I wad craw and strut and roger
　　　　My kecklin Flock!

Buskit wi' mony a bien, braw feather,
I was defied the warst o' weather:
When corn or bear I could na gather
                    To gie my burdies;
I'd treated them wi' caller heather,
                    And weel-knooz'd hurdies.

Nae cursed CLERICAL EXCISE
On honest Nature's laws and ties;
Free as the vernal breeze that flies
                    At early day,
We'd tasted Nature's richest joys,
                    But stint or stay.—

But as this subject's something kittle,
Our wisest way's to say but little;
And while my Muse is at her mettle,
                    I am, most fervent,
Or may I die upon a whittle!
                    Your Friend and Servant —
                              Robert Burns.

15TH MARCH

O' Saw Ye My Maggie
to the tune of **Sae Ya Na My Peggy**

I N   T H E S E   V E R S E S, the communication of sexual ideas is more
erotic than bawdy. Although much less explicit and lacking the
vulgarity of yesterday's poem, the reader is left in no doubt of the
sexual dénouement of this song.

Saw ye my Maggie?
Saw ye my Maggie?
Saw ye my Maggie?
Comin o'er the lea?

What mark has your Maggie,
What mark has your Maggie,
What mark has your Maggie,
That ane may ken her be?

My Maggie has a mark,
Ye'll find it in the dark,
It's in below her sark,
A little aboon her knee.

What wealth has your Maggie,
What wealth has your Maggie,
What wealth has your Maggie,
In tocher, gear, or fee?

My Maggie has a treasure,
A hidden mine o' pleasure,
I'll howk it at my leisure,
It's alane for me.

How loe ye your Maggy,
How loe ye your Maggy,
How loe ye your Maggy,
And loe nane but she?

Een that tell our wishes,
Eager glowing kisses,
Then diviner blisses,
In holy ecstacy!

How meet ye your Maggie,
How meet ye your Maggie,
How meet ye your Maggie,
When nanes to hear or see?

Heavenly joys before me,
Rapture trembling o'er me,
Maggie I adore thee,
On my bended knee!!!

16TH MARCH

Lassie wi' the Lintwhite Locks
to the tune of Rothiemurche's Rant

THIS SONG WAS INSPIRED by Jean Lorimer (1775–1831). Jean was a famous beauty and the particular favourite of Burns's friend and colleague in the excise, John Gillespie. Jean rejected Gillespie, made an unfortunate match and was abandoned by her husband just weeks after their marriage. She returned home to her family and never married again. Burns maintained contact with Jean and his knowledge of her affairs inspired a quantity of love songs, in many of which she is given the Arcadian pseudonym, 'Chloris'. Burns maintained in a letter to George Thomson, however, that she was 'a Mistress, or Friend, or what you will, in the guileless simplicity of Platonic Love'.

This song is in the pastoral tradition and depicts a love that is both innocent and sincere. Burns's striking use of natural imagery to reflect the seasons anticipates the joyful scenes of spring and summer, although the song ends with one of those 'howling wintry blasts' that we Scots still haven't quite escaped in March!

Lassie wi' the lintwhite locks,
Bonie lassie, artless lassie!
Wilt thou wi' me tent the flocks,
Wilt thou be my dearie O?

Now Nature cleeds the flow'ry lea,
And a' is young and sweet like thee;
O wilt thou share its joys wi' me,
And say thou'lt be my dearie O?
     Lassie &c.

The primrose bank, the wimpling burn,
The cuckoo on the milkwhite thorn,
The wanton lambs at rosy morn
Shall glad thy heart, my dearie O.
    Lassie &c.

And when the welcome summer show'r
Has cheer'd ilk drooping little flow'r,
We'll to the breathing woodbine bow'r
At sultry noon, my dearie O.
    Lassie &c.

When Cynthia lights, wi' silver ray,
The weary shearer's hameward way,
Through yellow, waving fields we'll stray,
And talk of love, my dearie O.
    Lassie &c.

And when the howling, wintry blast
Disturbs my lassie's midnight rest,
Enclasped to my faithful breast,
I'll comfort thee, my dearie O.
    Lassie &c.

17TH MARCH

Their Groves o' Sweet Myrtle
to the tune of Humours of Glen

THE 17TH OF MARCH is St Patrick's Day. This feast day in commemoration of the patron saint of Ireland is enthusiastically celebrated in Ireland and by Irish diaspora all over the world. Although Burns never travelled to Ireland, there is evidence that Irish song and music was an important influence for the bard in his song-writing and collecting activities. 'Their Groves o' Sweet Myrtle' is one of several verses he wrote to Irish airs, on this occasion 'Humours of Glen' which he described as 'a great favourite of mine'.

Their groves o' sweet myrtle let foreign lands reckon,
Where bright beaming summers exalt the perfume;
Far dearer to me yon lone glen o' green breckan,
Wi' the burn stealing under the lang, yellow broom:
Far dearer to me are yon humble broom bowers,
Where the blue-bell and gowan lurk, lowly, unseen;
For there, lightly tripping amang the wild flowers,
A-listening the linnet, oft wanders my Jean.

Tho' rich is the breeze in their gay, sunny vallies,
And cauld, Caledonia's blast on the wave;
Their sweet-scented woodlands that skirt the proud palace,
What are they?— The haunt of the Tyrant and Slave!
The Slave's spicy forests, and gold-bubbling fountains,
The brave Caledonian views with disdain;
He wanders as free as the winds of his mountains,
Save Love's willing fetters, the chains o' his Jean.

18TH MARCH

Hey for a Lass wi' a Tocher
to the tune of Ballinamona Ora

THIS IS ANOTHER SONG set to an Irish air, this time 'Ballinamona Ora'. Burns wrote to Thomson in February 1796, 'I have already, you know, equipped three Irish airs with words, and the other day I strung up a kind of rhapsody to another Hibernian melody which I admire much.' On this occasion – surprisingly! – it is not 'beauty' or romance fuelling Burns's rhapsody, but the prospect of acres of lush farming land, 'weel-stockit' with 'bonie white yewes'.

A 'tocher' was a marriage settlement bestowed upon a groom by the bride's family. In this song it is the lassie's wealth that makes her desirable; her beauty is inconsequential as we are (brutally) reminded that it will 'wither' with age. The true romance here is reserved for 'the bonie green knowes' and ever-replenishing nature. That said, Burns was a much more successful lover than farmer.

Awa wi' your witchcraft o' beauty's alarms,
  The slender bit beauty you grasp in your arms;
O gie me the lass that has acres o' charms,
  O gie me the lass wi' the weel-stockit farms.

Then hey for a lass wi' a tocher,
  Then hey for a lass wi' a tocher,
Then hey for a lass wi' a tocher,
  The nice yellow guineas for me.

Your beauty's a flower, in the morning that blows,
    And withers the faster, the faster it grows;
But the rapturous charm o' the bonie green knowes,
    Ilk Spring they're new deckit wi' bonie white yewes.
        Then hey for a lass wi' a tocher, &c.

And e'en when this beauty your bosom has blest,
    The brightest o' beauty may cloy when possess'd;
But the sweet, yellow darlings wi' Geordie impress'd,
    The langer ye ha'e them, the mair they're carest.
        Then hey for a lass wi' a tocher, &c.

19TH MARCH

Address to the Woodlark
to the tune of Loch Erroch Side

WOODLARKS ARE RARE BIRDS that nest in low-lying farmland and heather bushes. Their 'sweet warbling' is most likely to be heard in February and March. In another song thought to have been inspired by Jean Lorimer (or 'Chloris'), Burns is prompted by the bird's 'soothing, fond complaining' to express the heart-breaking sorrow of unrequited love.

O stay, sweet warbling woodlark, stay,
Nor quit for me the trembling spray,
A hapless lover courts thy lay,
Thy soothing, fond complaining.
Again, again that tender part,

That I may catch thy melting art;
For surely that would touch her heart
Wha kills me wi' disdaining.

Say, was thy little mate unkind,
And heard thee as the careless wind?
Oh, nocht but love and sorrow join'd,
Sic notes of woe could wauken!
Thou tells of never ending care;
Of speechless grief, and dark despair:—
For pity's sake, sweet bird, nae mair!
Or my poor heart is broken!

20TH MARCH

Bonie Bell

THE SPRING EQUINOX occurs in the northern hemisphere around
the 20th of March. It is commonly associated with fertility, growth
and renewal. 'Bonie Bell' provides a powerfully visual celebration of
spring's arrival, while in the second stanza the promise of everlasting
love is set against the transient imagery of the changing seasons.

The smiling spring comes in rejoicing,
    And surly winter grimly flies;
Now crystal clear are the falling waters,
    And bonny blue are the sunny skies.
Fresh o'er the mountains breaks forth the morning,
    The ev'ning gilds the Ocean's swell;
All Creatures joy in the sun's returning,
    And I rejoice in my Bonie Bell.

The flowery Spring leads sunny Summer,
   The yellow Autumn presses near,
Then in his turn comes gloomy Winter,
   Till smiling Spring again appear.
Thus seasons dancing, life advancing,
   Old Time and Nature their changes tell,
But never ranging, still unchanging,
   I adore my Bonie Bell.

21st MARCH

from A Sketch – On Pastoral Poetry

O N WORLD POETRY DAY we might turn our attention to
Burns's 'Sketch' on pastoral poetry, which begins with an
emphatic salute: 'Hail Poesie!' The bard appeals for a return to
classical pastoral verse, to the 'shepherd-sangs' and bucolic scenes
of Theocrites (fl.300–260 BC), before declaring that one of his
favourite eighteenth-century writers, Allan Ramsay, is the poet
most capable of representing Nature in all her glory.

Hail, Poesie! Thou Nymph reserv'd!
In chase o' thee, what crowds hae swerv'd
Frae common sense, or sunk enerv'd
        'Mang heaps o' clavers;
And och! o'er aft thy joes hae starv'd
        'Mid a' thy favours!

Say, Lassie, why thy train amang,
While loud, the trump's heroic clang,
And Sock and buskin skelp alang
          To death or marriage;
Scarce ane has tried the shepherd-sang
          But wi' miscarriage?

In Homer's craft Jock Milton thrives;
Eschylus' pen Will Shakespeare drives;
Wee Pope, the knurlin, 'till him rives
          Horatian fame;
In thy sweet sang, Barbauld, survives
          Even Sappho's flame.

But thee, Theocritus, wha matches?
They're no' Herd's ballats, Maro's catches;
Squire Pope but busks his skinklin patches
          O' heathen tatters:
I pass by hunders, nameless wretches,
          That ape their betters.

In this braw age o' wit and lear,
Will nane the Shepherd's whistle mair
Blaw sweetly in his native air
          And rural grace;
And wi' the far-fam'd Grecian share
          A rival place?

Yes! there is ane; a Scottish callan!
There's ane; come forrit, honest Allan!
Thou need na jouk behint the hallan,
          A chiel sae clever;
The teeth o' Time may gnaw Tamtallan,
          But thou's for ever.

Thou paints auld Nature to the nines,
In thy sweet Caledonian lines;
Nae gowden stream thro' myrtles twines
        Where Philomel,
While nightly breezes sweep the vines,
        Her griefs will tell!

Thy rural loves are Nature's sel';
Nae bombast spates o' nonsense swell;
Nae snap conceits, but that sweet spell
        O' witchin' love,
That charm that can the strongest quell,
        The sternest move.

In gowany glens thy burnie strays,
Where bonie lasses bleach their claes;
Or trots by hazelly shaws and braes
        Wi' hawthorns gray,
Where blackbirds join the shepherd's lays
        At close o' day.

22ND MARCH

On Poetry
from a letter to Miss Helen Craik, 9th August 1790

I N THIS PASSAGE WE SEE how Burns, yet again, conflates his euphoric love of poetry with his passion for women. Both landed Burns in hot water during his lifetime, but this burst of enthusiasm makes clear that he believed them both to be entirely worth the trouble!

Bewitching Poesy is like bewitching Woman: she has in all ages been accused of leading Mankind from the counsels of Wisdom and the paths of Prudence; involving them in difficulties, baiting them with Poverty, branding them with Infamy, and plunging them in the Vortex of Ruin; yet, where is the Man but must own that all our happiness on earth is not worthy the Name! that even the holy hermit's solitary prospect of paradisical bliss is but the glitter of a northern sun rising over a frozen region! Compared with the many pleasures, the nameless raptures, we owe to the Queens of the Hearts of Men!!!

23rd MARCH

from The Heron Ballads: John Bushby's Lamentation

I N MARCH 1795, Burns composed a group of satirical political ballads in support of Patrick Heron's (c.1736–1803) election campaign for the Stewartry of Kirkcudbright. The poet wrote to Heron, 'I swear by the lyre of Thalia to muster on your side all the votaries of honest laughter and fair, candid ridicule.'

One of the 'Heron Ballads', 'John Bushby's Lamentation', is set on this very day. Bushby was the Sheriff Clerk of County in Dumfriesshire and a supporter of Gordon of Balmaghie, the Earl of Galloway's candidate. As is clear from the following extract, Heron's campaign was a success – and Gordon was defeated.

'Twas in the seventeen hunder year
   O' Christ and ninety-five,
That year I was the waest man
   Of any man alive.

In March, the three and twentieth morn,
   The sun raise clear and bright,
But Oh! I was a waefu' man
   Ere toofa' o' the night.

Earl Galloway lang did rule this land
   With equal right and fame;
Fast knit in chast and haly bands
   Wi Broughton's noble name.

Earl Galloway's man o' men was I,
    And chief o' Broughton's host:
So twa blind beggars, on a string,
    The faithfu' tyke will trust.

But now Earl Galloway's sceptre's broke,
    And Broughton's wi' the slain;
And I my ancient craft may try,
    Sin' honestie is gane.

24TH MARCH

from Again Rejoicing Nature Sees
to the tune of Jockey's Grey Breeks

FOR TODAY, WE HAVE ANOTHER SONG that juxtaposes the beauty and expectation of the newly sprung season with a lover's deep despair. It has been suggested that this song was inspired by Burns's relationship with Jean Armour and by their unfortunate, if impermanent, separation in spring 1786.

Again rejoicing Nature sees
    Her robe assume its vernal hues,
Her leafy locks wave in the breeze
    All freshly steep'd in morning dews.

And maun I still on Menie doat,
    And bear the scorn that's in her e'e!
For it's jet, jet black, an' it's like a hawk,
    An' it winna let a body be!

In vain to me the cowslips blaw,
  In vain to me the vi'lets spring;
In vain to me, in glen or shaw,
  The mavis and the lintwhite sing.
    And maun I still &c.

The merry Ploughboy cheers his team,
  Wi' joy the tentie Seedsman stalks,
But life to me's a weary dream,
  A dream of ane that never wauks.
    And maun I still &c.

25TH MARCH

The Slave's Lament

THE 25TH OF MARCH has been designated as the International Day of Remembrance of the Victims of Slavery and the Transatlantic Slave Trade. On this day in 1807, 'An Act for the Abolition of the Slave Trade' received Royal Assent.

Burns's attitudes towards slavery and abolition have proven a fraught area of consideration. The bard's commitment to humanitarian ideals is apparent in songs such as 'A Man's a Man', and it is true that he was involved with several prominent abolitionists during the time he spent in Edinburgh. However, this is problematised by the fact that, in 1786, threatened with a substantial fine and imprisonment following his first illicit liaison with Jean Armour, Burns made plans to emigrate to Jamaica to take up work as a clerk on a plantation. Burns did not, in the end, travel to the West Indies.

The provenance of 'The Slave's Lament' is uncertain: some argue that the poet composed the song in its entirety, others that he collected and edited the verses. It is nonetheless the most substantial piece of writing associated with Burns that relates to this horrific period in modern history.

It was in sweet Senegal that my foes did me enthral,
    For the lands of Virginia-ginia O;
Torn from that lovely shore, and must never see it more;
    And alas I am weary, weary O!
        Torn from that lovely shore, and must never see it more;
        And alas I am weary, weary O!

All on that charming coast is no bitter snow and frost,
    Like the lands of Virginia-ginia O;
There streams forever flow, and there flowers forever blow,
    And alas! I am weary, weary O!
        There streams &c.

The burden I must bear, while the cruel scourge I fear,
    In the lands of Virginia-ginia O;
And I think on friends most dear, with the bitter, bitter tear,
    And alas! I am weary, weary O!
        And I think &c.

26TH MARCH

It Is Na, Jean, Thy Bonie Face
to the tune of The Maid's Complaint

JEAN ARMOUR BURNS, the poet's wife, died on this day in 1834. She outlived her husband by thirty-eight years, and yet she never remarried. Over the course of her relationship with Burns, Jean gave birth to nine children, the youngest of whom, Maxwell Burns (1796–1799), was born on the day of his father's funeral. Jean was a devoted wife and it seems she loved Burns sincerely, not least because she was reportedly very accepting of his dalliances with other women. In one anecdote she is famously quoted as saying, 'Rab should hae had twa wives.' Jean lived long enough to witness Burns's posthumous international fame, and she generously gave time, sometimes even souvenirs, to visiting enthusiasts.

Despite his womanising, Burns ever returned to Jean and she was his only enduring love. 'It is na, Jean, thy Bonie Face' is based upon an English song. Perhaps identifying its sentiments with his own regard for his wife, the poet gave it a 'Scots dress' as a compliment to his 'bonie Jean'.

It is na, Jean, thy bonie face,
    Nor shape that I admire,
Altho' thy beauty and thy grace
    Might weel awauk desire.
Something in ilka part o' thee
    To praise, to love, I find,
But dear as is thy form to me,
    Still dearer is thy mind.

Nae mair ungen'rous wish I hae,
    Nor stronger in my breast,
Than, if I canna mak thee sae,
    At least to see thee blest.
Content am I, if Heaven shall give
    But happiness to thee:
And as wi' thee I'd wish to live,
    For thee I'd bear to die.

27TH MARCH

Postscript to The Author's Earnest Cry & Prayer

H ERE, BURNS RESPONDS to the punitive taxes levied against
Scottish distillers prior to 'the Act anent the Scottish Distilleries'
in 1786. Rich in humour and irony, he addresses the inequity with
which Scottish distillers were treated by the British state. The
postscript represents a powerfully ironic call to arms, concluding with
the famous exclamation, 'FREEDOM and WHISKY gang thegither,
Tak aff your *dram!*' The perfect toast for today – it is International
Whisky Day after all.

Let half-starv'd slaves in warmer skies,
See future wines, rich-clust'ring, rise;
Their lot auld Scotland ne'er envies,
But blythe an' frisky,
She eyes her freeborn, martial boys,
Tak aff their Whisky.

What tho' their Phebus kinder warms,
While Fragrance blooms an' Beauty charms!
When wretches range, in famish'd swarms,
The scented groves,
Or hounded forth, *dishonor* arms
In hungry droves.

Their *gun's* a burden on their shouther;
They downa bide the stink o' *powther*;
Their bauldest thought's a hank'ring swither,
       To stan' or rin,
Till skelp – a shot – they're aff, a' throw'ther,
       To save their skin.

But bring a SCOTCHMAN frae his hill,
Clap in his cheek a *Highland gill*,
Say, such is royal GEORGE's will,
       An' there's the foe,
He has nae thought but how to kill
       Twa at a blow.

Nae cauld, faint-hearted doubtings tease him;
Death comes, wi' fearless eye he sees him;
Wi' bluidy han' a welcome gies him;
       An' when he fa's,
His latest draught o' breathin lea'es him
       In faint huzzas.

Sages their solemn een may steek,
An' raise a philosophic reek,
An' physically causes seek,
       In *clime* an' *season*;
But tell me *Whisky's* name in Greek
       I'll tell the reason.

SCOTLAND, my auld, respected Mither!
Tho' whyles ye moistify your leather,
Till where ye sit, on craps o' heather;
       Ye tine your dam;
FREEDOM and WHISKY gang thegither.
       Tak aff your DRAM!

28TH MARCH

On Virtue and Vice
from the First Commonplace Book

B URNS WAS PERCEPTIVE in his scrutiny of human behaviour, and
this was one of the characteristics that made him such a talented
poet. In the following passage, written in his 'First Commonplace
Book' in March 1784, Burns sets out his position on 'goodness' and
'wickedness'; on 'virtue' and 'vice'; and on flawed humanity. This is one
of several examples from across his poetry, prose and correspondence
where Burns expresses the notion that man possesses an innate
moral sense. His reasoning here corresponds to a significant branch
of Enlightenment religious thought and resonates particularly
with the ideas articulated by the philosopher Francis Hutcheson in
*Treatise 11: An Inquiry Concerning The Original of Our Ideas of Virtue
or Moral Good* (1725), which Burns certainly read.

I have often observed in the course of my experience of human life
that every man, even the worst, have something good about them,
though very often nothing else than a happy temperament of consti-
tution inclining them to this or that Virtue. On this, likewise, depend
a great many, no man can say how many, of our vices. For this reason
no man can say in what degree any person besides himself can be,
with strict justice, called Wicked.— Let any of the strictest character
for regularity of conduct among us, examine impartially how many of
his virtues are owing to constitution and education, how many vices
he has never been guilty of, not from any care or vigilance, but from
want of opportunity or some accidental circumstance intervening,
how many of the weaknesses of mankind he had fallen into because

he was out of the line of such temptation; and what often, if not always, weighs more than all the rest; how much he is indebted to the World's good opinion, because the World does not know all. I say any man who can thus think will scan the failings, nay the faults and crimes of mankind around him, with a brother's eye.—

29TH MARCH

Address to the Unco Guid, or the Rigidly Righteous

THIS IMPORTANT POEM is a skilful expression of the ideas encountered in yesterday's selection, and essential reading for those seeking to understand Burns's stance in his notoriously scathing religious satires (among them 'Holy Willie's Prayer' and 'The Holy Fair'). Burns addresses the tension between natural human appetite and outward piety. He is, as ever, critical of the self-righteous's 'better art o' hidin' their humanity, and appeals for kindness since, as far as he is concerned, only God can truly judge his creations.

O ye wha are sae guid yoursel,
    Sae pious and sae holy,
Ye've nought to do but mark and tell
    Your Neebours' fauts and folly!
Whase life is like a weel-gaun mill,
    Supply'd wi' store o' water,
The heaped happer's ebbing still,
    An' still the clap plays clatter.

Hear me, ye venerable Core,
  As counsel for poor mortals
That frequent pass douce Wisdom's door
  For glaikit Folly's portals:
I, for their thoughtless, careless sakes,
  Would here propone defences,
Their donsie tricks, their black mistakes,
  Their failings and mischances.

Ye see your state wi' theirs compared,
  And shudder at the niffer;
But cast a moment's fair regard,
  What maks the mighty differ;
Discount what scant occasion gave,
  That purity ye pride in;
And (what's aft mair than a' the lave),
  Your better art o' hidin.

Think, when your castigated pulse
  Gies now and then a wallop,
What ragings must his veins convulse,
  That still eternal gallop:
Wi' wind and tide fair i' your tail,
  Right on ye scud your sea-way;
But in the teeth o' baith to sail,
  It maks a unco leeway.

See Social-life and Glee sit down,
  All joyous and unthinking,
Till, quite transmugrify'd, they're grown
  Debauchery and Drinking:
O would they stay to calculate
  Th' eternal consequences;
Or your more dreaded hell to state,
  Damnation of expenses!

Ye high, exalted, virtuous Dames,
    Ty'd up in godly laces,
Before ye gie poor *Frailty* names,
    Suppose a change o' cases;
A dear-lov'd lad, convenience snug,
    A treach'rous inclination —
But let me whisper i' your lug,
    Ye're aiblins nae temptation.

Then gently scan your brother Man,
    Still gentler sister Woman;
Tho' they may gang a kennin wrang,
    To step aside is human:
One point must still be greatly dark,
    The moving *Why* they do it;
And just as lamely can ye mark,
    How far perhaps they rue it.

Who made the heart, 'tis *He* alone
    Decidedly can try us;
He knows each chord its various tone,
    Each spring its various bias:
Then at the balance let's be mute,
    We never can adjust it;
What's *done* we partly may compute,
    But know not what's *resisted*.

30TH MARCH

On Blackguards
from the First Commonplace Book

BURNS ONCE AGAIN RECOGNISES inescapable human frailty when he expresses affection and empathy for those considered 'blackguards'. A 'blackguard' was a derogatory term for a man whose character was compromised by some perceived scandal or disgrace. It is for the reader to decide how 'safe' Burns's character actually was.

I have often coveted the acquaintance of that part of mankind commonly known by the ordinary phrase of BLACKGUARDS, sometimes farther than was consistent with the safety of my character; those who by thoughtless Prodigality, or headstrong Passions have been driven to ruin: though disgraced by follies, nay sometimes "Stain'd with guilt and crimson'd o'er with crimes". I have yet found among them, in not a few instances, some of the noblest Virtues, Magnanimity Generosity, disinterested friendship and even Modesty, in the highest perfection.—

31st MARCH

Yestreen I Had a Pint o' Wine
to the tune of Banks of Banna

I N 1790 ROBERT BURNS met Helen Anne Park at the Globe Tavern in Dumfries. Although married at the time, Burns hadn't quite bid 'farewell to Rakery' and his head was turned. Soon Helen was pregnant, and she gave birth to Burns's daughter Elizabeth (1791–1873), known as Betty, on the 31st of March 1791, mere days before Jean Armour gave birth to his son William Nicol. Helen died when Betty was still very young, and Jean raised her husband's daughter with the rest of the Burns family.

Burns immortalised Helen – referring to her as 'Anna' – in the song 'Yestreen I Had a Pint o' Wine' and declared it 'the best love-song I ever composed in my life; but in its original state, is not quite a lady's song'. The song conveys considerable depth of feeling alongside poignant descriptions of physical intimacy. The postscript, first published in *The Merry Muses of Caledonia* (1799), does not exist in Burns's holograph. However, it remains entirely possible that it is indeed Burns's work as it strongly represents the poet's attitudes; attitudes that are evident not only from his writing, but from the way in which he lived his life.

Yestreen I had a pint o' wine,
  A place where body saw na';
Yestreen lay on this breast of mine,
  The gowden locks of Anna.

The hungry Jew in wilderness,
  Rejoicing o'er his manna,
Was naething to my hinny bliss
  Upon the lips of Anna.

Ye monarchs, tak the east and west
  Frae Indus to Savannah;
Gie me within my straining grasp,
  The melting form of Anna.

There I'll despise Imperial charms,
  An Empress or Sultana;
While dying raptures in her arms,
  I give and take with Anna!

Awa, thou flaunting God of Day!
  Awa, thou pale Diana!
Ilk star gae hide thy twinkling ray,
  When I'm to meet my Anna.

Come in thy raven-plumage, night,
  Sun, moon and stars withdrawn a'!
And bring an angel-pen to write,
  My transports wi' my Anna!

Postscript:

The kirk and state may join and tell;
  To do sic things I manna:
The kirk an' state may gae to hell,
  An' I shall gae to Anna.

She is the sunshine o' my e'e,
  To live but her I canna;
Had I on earth but wishes three,
  The first should be my Anna.

APRIL

Drumossie moor, Drumossie day,
A waefu' day it was to me;
For there I lost my father dear,
My father dear and brethren three.

from The Lovely Lass o' Inverness

1ST APRIL

from Epistle to John Lapraik

JOHN LAPRAIK (1727–1807), like Burns, was a farmer-turned-poet who was no stranger to the financial penury of farming life. Left penniless by the failure of the Ayr Bank in 1773, he was forced to sell his property in Muirkirk and spent a time in debtors' prison. Burns sincerely admired Lapraik's work and composed the first of two verse epistles to the 'Old Scottish Bard' on this day in 1785. Several verses from this poem, in which Burns conveys his outlook on poetic inspiration, also appear as our Burnsian words for the 7th of January. In the following extract he emphasises the importance of 'social pleasure', conviviality and warmth as he extends the hand of friendship to Lapraik.

Awa ye selfish, warly race,
Wha think that havins, sense an' grace,
Ev'n love an' friendship should give place
        To *catch-the-plack*!
I dinna like to see your face,
        Nor hear your crack.

But ye whom social pleasure charms,
Whose hearts the *tide of kindness* warms,
Who hold your *being* on the terms,
        'Each aid the others,'
Come to my bowl, come to my arms,
        My friends, my brothers!

2ND APRIL

The Rantin Dog the Daddie O't
to the tune of East Hook o' Fife

B Y EARLY APRIL 1786, Burns was aware that Jean Armour, who he had been seeing for some months, was pregnant. In 'The Rantin Dog the Daddie O't' Burns ventriloquises a pregnant woman as she poses a series of fraught, very human, questions: Who will provide for her unborn child? What about emotional and practical support? And who will join her in the humiliation of public rebuke on the cutty stool? Burns, having already mounted the 'creepie chair' with Elizabeth Paton, would have anticipated a spell of public penance. Deeply in love with Jean, he took steps to avoid their public humiliation by presenting her with a type of marriage certificate. Jean's parents, however, attempted to conceal her pregnancy by, to the distress of Burns, sending her away.

O wha my babie-clouts will buy?
  O wha will tent me when I cry?
Wha will kiss me where I lie?
  The rantin dog, the daddie o't.

O wha will own he did the faut?
  O wha will buy the groanin maut?
O wha will tell me how to ca't?
  The rantin dog, the daddie o't.

When I mount the creepie-chair,
  Wha will sit beside me there?
Gie me Rob, I'll seek nae mair,
  The rantin dog, the daddie o't.

Wha will crack to me my lane?
    Wha will mak me fidgin fain?
Wha will kiss me o'er again?
    The rantin dog, the daddie o't.

3RD APRIL

On That Unlucky Paper
from a letter to Gavin Hamilton, 15th April 1786

BURNS'S CORRESPONDENCE AROUND the time of Jean Armour's pregnancy – and her consequent removal to Paisley – is beset with frustration, resentment and disappointment. And yet, his love for Jean reveals itself, even in anger. This letter from April 1786 contains Burns's famous reference to the 'unlucky paper' that would, in the eighteenth century, probably have sufficed as an irregular contract of marriage, had Jean's father not had other ideas.

I must consult with you, first opportunity, on the propriety of sending my *quondam* friend, Mr Aiken, a copy.— If he is now reconciled to my character as an honest man, I would do it with all my soul; but I would not be beholden to the noblest being ever God created, if he imagined me to be a rascal.— Apropos, old Mr Armour prevailed with him to mutilate that unlucky paper yesterday.— Would you believe it? Tho' I had not a hope, or even a wish, to make her mine after her conduct; yet when he told me the names were all cut out of the paper, my heart died within me, and he cut my very veins with the news.— Perdition seize her falsehood, and perjurious perfidy! but God bless her and forgive my poor, once dear, misguided girl.— She is ill-advised.— Do not despise me, Sir: I am indeed a fool, but a *knave* is an infinitely worse character than any body, I hope, will dare to give the unfortunate Robert Burns.

4TH APRIL

On the Houghmagandie Pack
from a letter to John Arnot, April 1786

IN EIGHTEENTH-CENTURY SCOTLAND, a man could be fined for 'seduction' and forced to pay an aliment to the 'corrupted' female. Jean Armour's father was aware of this and Burns anticipated that he would seek reparation. Heartbroken and thoroughly disillusioned, the poet put his affairs in order and set in motion his application to emigrate to Jamaica. In a letter to John Arnot in April 1786 Burns confirms that his intentions towards Jean were honourable. He expresses his frustration and sense of injustice, and refers to his 'hunted' status, though not without some typical Burnsian relish. The poet's sardonic reference to the 'holy beagles, the houghmagandie pack... snuff[ing] the scent' takes aim at those employed by the Kirk Session to spy on the community, by implying an animalistic, somewhat seedy sensuality.

I had long had a wishing eye to that inestimable blessing, a wife.— My mouth watered deliciously to see a young fellow, after a few idle, common-place stories from a gentleman in black, strip and go to bed with a young girl, and no one durst say black was his eye; while I, for just doing the same thing, only wanting that insignificant ceremony; am made a Sunday's laughing stock and abused like a pick-pocket.— I was well aware though, that if my ill-starred fortune got the least hint of my connubial wish, my schemes would go to nothing.—

[. . .]

Already the holy beagles, the houghmagandie pack, begin to snuff the scent; & I expect every moment to see them cast off, and hear them after me in full cry: but as I am an old fox, I shall give them dodging and doubling for it; and by and by, I intend to earth among the mountains of Jamaica.—

5TH APRIL

The Farewell

I N THIS POEM, BURNS CONVEYS a sense of powerlessness and alienation in the wake of his forced separation from Jean, and reluctance, too, at the prospect of his proposed emigration. As is the case in his letters on the subject, Jean's welfare is always in his mind.

There is ongoing debate among critics regarding how serious Burns was about emigrating. He delayed travel to the West Indies on several occasions and was ultimately dissuaded by the success of his Kilmarnock edition, *Poems, Chiefly in the Scottish Dialect* (1786), and the promise of a further edition to be published in Edinburgh.

Farewell, old Scotia's bleak domains,
Far dearer than the torrid plains,
    Where rich ananas blow!
Farewell, a mother's blessing dear!
A brother's sigh! a sister's tear!
    My Jean's heart-rending throe!
Farewell, my Bess! tho' thou'rt bereft
    Of my paternal care,
A faithful brother I have left,

My part in him thou'lt share!
　Adieu, too, to you too,
　　My Smith, my bosom frien';
When kindly you mind me,
　O then befriend my Jean!

What bursting anguish tears my heart;
From thee, my Jeany, must I part!
　Thou, weeping, answ'rest – 'No!'
Alas! misfortune stares my face,
And points to ruin and disgrace,
　I for thy sake must go!
Thee, Hamilton, and Aiken dear,
　A grateful, warm adieu:
I, with a much-indebted tear,
　Shall still remember you!
　　All hail then, the gale then,
　　　Wafts me from thee, dear shore!
　　It rustles, and whistles
　　　I'll never see thee more!

6TH APRIL

As I Came O'er the Cairney Mount
to the tune of The Highland Lassie

THIS DAY MARKS TARTAN DAY in Canada and the United States;
a time when the Scottish diaspora dust off their 'tartan plaidies'
in celebration of their Scottish heritage. 'As I came o'er the Cairney
Mount' is a cheerful and appropriate song for such an occasion.
Thought to be Burns's polite adaptation of a bawdy folksong, even so
the bard has neither stripped it of its tartan, nor its sexual undertones.
　On the 6th of April 1320, the Declaration of Arbroath was signed:
a most famous assertion of Scottish independence. It states, 'We

fight, not for glory nor for riches nor for honour, but only and alone for freedom, which no good man surrenders but with his life.' Burns explores the idea of liberty in 'Love and Liberty – A Cantata'; 'Ode for General Washington's Birthday' (featured later on the 4th of July); and in 'A Man's a Man' (14th of July).

As I came o'er the Cairney mount,
   And down amang the blooming heather,
Kindly stood the milking-shiel
   To shelter frae the stormy weather.
O my bonie Highland lad,
   My winsome, weelfar'd Highland laddie;
Wha wad mind the wind and rain,
   Sae weel row'd in his tartan plaidie.

Now Phebus blinkit on the bent,
   And o'er the know's the lambs were bleating:
But he wan my heart's consent,
   To be his ain at the neist meeting.
O my bonie Highland lad,
   My winsome, weelfar'd Highland laddie;
Wha wad mind the wind and rain,
   Sae weel row'd in his tartan plaidie.

7TH APRIL

The Bonie Wee Thing

THIS POEM WAS INSPIRED BY Miss Deborah Duff Davies, to whom it was sent in April 1793. She was in poor health and her fragility seems to have captured Burns's imagination. The poet described her as 'positively the least creature ever I saw, to be at the same time unexceptionably, and indeed uncommonly handsome and beautiful'. This delicate woman is not necessarily to be desired, but adored, and Burns's description of her as a 'constellation', a 'Goddess', renders her untouchable in every sense of the word. Sadly, Deborah died from consumption at a young age. In the twenty-first century, the 7th of April has been designated as World Health Day.

Bonie wee thing, canie wee thing,
   Lovely wee thing, was thou mine,
I wad wear thee in my bosom,
   Lest my jewel I should tine.

Wishfully I look and languish
   In that bonie face of thine,
And my heart it stounds wi' anguish,
   Lest my wee thing be na mine.

Wit, and Grace, and Love, and Beauty,
   In ae constellation shine;
To adore thee is my duty,
    Goddess o' this soul o' mine!
      Bonie wee &c.

8TH APRIL

I Dream'd I Lay

BURNS CLAIMED TO HAVE COMPOSED this poem when he was just seventeen years of age. The mood expressed here is as fluctuating and tempestuous as the spring weather. Burns, during periods of what he called 'melancholy', frequently juxtaposed the beauty and hope of springtime with descriptions of his dark and brooding thoughts.

I dream'd I lay where flowers were springing,
    Gaily in the sunny beam,
List'ning to the wild birds singing,
    By a falling, chrystal stream:
Straight the sky grew black and daring;
    Thro' the woods the whirlwinds rave;
Trees with aged arms were warring,
    O'er the swelling, drumlie wave.

Such was my life's deceitful morning,
    Such the pleasures I enjoy'd;
But lang or noon, loud tempests storming,
    A' my flowery bliss destroy'd.
Tho' fickle Fortune has deceiv'd me,
    She promis'd fair, and perform'd but ill;
Of mony a joy and hope bereav'd me,
    I bear a heart shall support me still.

9TH APRIL

On Making Remarks
from the Second Commonplace Book

B URNS COMMENCED WRITING his 'Second Commonplace Book'
while staying in Edinburgh in 1787. His first entry, on the 9th of
April, is an interesting example of his complicated, at times self-
contradictory, character. The poet intended his 'Commonplace Book'
as a collection of 'remarks' on 'human life' in Edinburgh. He writes
here that his vanity as an author and observer causes him to desire an
audience, and yet he also seeks someone, or something, to confide in
with 'unreserved confidence'.

I don't know how it is with the world in general, but with me, making
remarks is by no means a solitary pleasure.— I want someone to
laugh with me, someone to be grave with me; someone to please me
and help my discrimination with his or her own remark, and at times,
no doubt, to admire my acuteness and penetration.— The world are
so busied with selfish pursuits, ambition, vanity, interests or pleasure,
that very few think it worth their while to make any observation on
what passed around them, except where that observation is a sucker
or a branch of the darling plant they are rearing in their fancy.—
Nor am I sure if notwithstanding all the sentimental flights of novel
writers and the sage philosophy of Moralists, if we are capable of
so intimate and cordial a coalition of friendship as that one of us
may pour out of his bosom his every thought and floating fancy,
his very inmost soul with unreserved confidence to another, without
hazard of losing part of that respect man demands from man; of
from the unavoidable imperfections attending human nature, of one
day repenting his confidence.— For these reasons, I am determined
to make these pages my Confidante.—

10TH APRIL

Jessie – A New Scots Song
to the tune of **Bonie Dundee**

BURNS SENT 'Jessie – A New Scots Song' to Miss Jessie Staig (1775–1801), the daughter of the Provost of Dumfries, in April 1793. The poet's compliment to Jessie is bound up with a tribute to the district of Dumfriesshire which, we are told, is as rich with natural and 'feminine' beauty as Burns's native Ayrshire.

True hearted was he, the sad swain o' the Yarrow,
    And fair are the maids on the banks of the Ayr;
But by the sweet side of the Nith's winding river,
    Are lovers as faithful, and maidens as fair.
To equal young Jessie, seek Scotland all over;
    To equal young Jessie, you seek it in vain:
Grace, beauty, and elegance, fetter her lover,
    And maidenly modesty fixes the chain.

O fresh is the rose in the gay, dewy morning,
    And sweet is the lily at evening close;
But in the fair presence o' lovely young Jessie,
    Unseen is the lily, unheeded the rose.
Love sits in her smile, a wizard ensnaring;
    Enthron'd in her eyes he delivers his law:
And still to her charms she alone is a stranger!
    Her modest demeanour's the jewel of a'.

11TH APRIL

Afton Water
to the tune of Afton Water

TODAY'S OFFERING IS another song inspired by Burns's natural surroundings in Dumfriesshire. In 1789 he enclosed it in a letter to Frances Dunlop, explaining that: 'There is a small river, Afton, that falls into the Nith near New Cumnock, which has some charming, wild, romantic scenery on its banks.— I have a particular pleasure in those little pieces of poetry such as our Scots songs &c where the names and landskip-features of rivers, lakes, or woodlands that one knows are introduced.' Certainly, the celebration of Scotland's spectacular scenery, particularly the rural and the local, are a recurring feature of Burns's poetry.

Flow gently, sweet Afton, among thy green braes,
   Flow gently, I'll sing thee a song in thy praise;
My Mary's asleep by thy murmuring stream,
   Flow gently sweet Afton disturb not her dream.

Thou stock-dove, whose echo resounds thro' the glen,
   Ye wild whistling blackbirds in yon thorny den,
Thou green-crested lapwing, thy screaming forbear,
   I charge you disturb not my slumbering Fair.

How lofty, sweet Afton, thy neighbouring hills,
   Far mark'd with the courses of clear winding rills;
There daily I wander as noon rises high,
   My flocks and my Mary's sweet cot in my eye.

How pleasant thy banks and green valleys below,
 Where wild in the woodlands the primroses blow;
There oft as mild Ev'ning leaps over the lea,
 The sweet-scented birk shades my Mary and me.

Thy crystal stream, Afton, how lovely it glides,
 And winds by the cot where my Mary resides;
How wanton thy waters her snowy feet lave,
 As gathering sweet flowrets she stems thy clear wave.

Flow gently, sweet Afton, among thy green braes,
 Flow gently, sweet river, the theme of my lays;
My Mary's asleep by thy murmuring stream,
 Flow gently, sweet Afton, disturb not her dream.

12TH APRIL

A Toast. Lines on the Commemoration of Rodney's Victory

ON THIS DAY IN 1782, Admiral George Brydges Rodney (1718–1792) defeated the French Navy in the Battle of the Saintes near Dominica. It is thought that Burns composed this 'extempore' – or 'off-the-cuff' – at a celebration in the King's Arms Tavern in Dumfries in 1792. This would account for the fact that the 'Toast' is not among the most elegant of the poet's works. It is interesting, however, for its reference to what was a significant naval battle of the American War of Independence, and for the insight that it provides into Burns's complicated politics.

Instead of a song, boys, I'll give you a toast,
Here's the memory of those on the twelfth that we lost;
That we lost, did I say, nay, by heav'n that we found,
For their fame it shall last while the world goes round.
The next in succession, I'll give you the King,
Whoe'er wou'd betray him, on high may he swing;
And here's the grand fabric, our free Constitution,
As built on the base of our great Revolution;
And longer with Politics, not to be cramm'd,
Be Anarchy curs'd, and be Tyranny damn'd;
And who wou'd to Liberty e'er prove disloyal,
May his son be a hangman, and he his first trial.

There'll Never Be Peace Till Jamie Comes Hame
to the tune of There are few good fellows when Jamie's awa

THE FIRST OF SEVERAL JACOBITE SONGS selected for this month, 'There'll Never Be Peace Till Jamie Comes Hame' refers to the deposed Stuart dynasty. King James VII of Scotland and II of England (1633–1701) was deposed in the 'Glorious Revolution' of 1688 on account of his Catholicism. Following his death, his son James Frances Edward Stuart (1688–1766) laid claim to the Scottish, English and Irish thrones, and, fourteen years later, led the unsuccessful Jacobite uprising of 1715. In this song, a Jacobite laments the absence of who he perceives to be the rightful monarchs of Scotland, and the loss of his sons to the ill-fated Jacobite campaign. Despite terrible personal and political tragedy, Burns's protagonist holds true to his principles.

By yon castle wa', at the close of the day,
I heard a man sing tho' his head it was grey;
And as he was singing, the tears down came,
There'll never be peace till Jamie comes hame.
The Church is in ruins, the State is in jars,
Delusions, oppressions, and murderous wars,
We dare na weel say't, but we ken wha's to blame,
There'll never be peace till Jamie comes hame.

My seven braw sons for Jamie drew sword,
But now I greet round their green beds in the yerd;
It brak the sweet heart o' my faithful auld Dame,

There'll never be peace till Jamie comes hame.
 Now life is a burden that bows me down,
Sin I tint my bairns, and he tint his crown;
But till my last moments my words are the same,
There'll never be peace till Jamie comes hame.

14TH APRIL

On the Stuarts
from a letter for the *Edinburgh Evening Courant,*
8th November 1788

BURNS'S VIEWS ON JACOBITISM appear to have evolved over the course of his life. He was enthusiastically engaged in the collection and composition of Jacobite songs that lamented and sentimentalised the failed cause, attracted by the loyalty and doomed heroism of its followers, and seemingly roused by its associations with nationalism and patriotism.

His letters refer to Jacobite ancestry on his father's side and, while touring Stirlingshire, Clackmannanshire and Perthshire in 1787 he was 'knighted' by Mrs Catherine Bruce (1696–1791), a descendant of Robert the Bruce, with Bruce's own sword. His travelling companion, Dr James Adair (1765–1802), recalled that 'the old lady's political tenets were as Jacobitical as the poet's, a conformity which contributed not a little to the cordiality of our reception and entertainment'.

However, this is problematised by the fact that Burns also has elements of Presbyterian Whig identity – ideological positions that are at odds with Jacobitism. Burns's letter to the *Edinburgh Evening Courant* in 1788 (signed 'A BRITON') is fairly nuanced in its consideration of Jacobitism and an example of the bard's considered 'political correctness' when addressing the Uprisings of 1715 and 1745 in the public domain.

The Stuarts have been condemned and laughed at for the folly and impracticability of their attempts in 1715 and 1745. That they failed, I bless my God most fervently; but cannot join in the ridicule against them.— Who does not know that the abilities or defects of leaders and commanders are often hidden until put to the touchstone of exigence; and that there is a caprice of fortune, an omnipotence in particular accidents and conjunctures of circumstances, which exalt us as heroes, or brand us as madmen, just as they are for or against us?

[...]

To conclude, Sir; let every man who has a tear for the many miseries incident to humanity, feel for a family, illustrious as any in Europe, and unfortunate beyond historic precedent; and let every Briton, and particularly every Scotsman, who ever looked with reverential pity on the dotage of a parent, cast a veil over the fatal mistakes of the Kings of his forefathers.

A BRITON

15TH APRIL

Charlie He's My Darling

CHARLES EDWARD STUART (1720–1788), also commonly referred to as 'Bonnie Prince Charlie' or 'the Young Pretender', was the son of James Frances Edward Stuart (1688–1766). Charles was raised in Rome and travelled to Scotland in 1745 with the intention of succeeding where his father had failed, by restoring the Stuart dynasty to the British throne. He experienced some initial success, even occupying Edinburgh for a time in autumn of 1745, before the army's eventual defeat at Culloden in April 1746.

'Bonnie Prince Charlie' is often depicted in song and legend as just that: bonnie. Attractive, charming and charismatic, he seemingly knew how to play to the crowd, flamboyantly adopting Scottish Highland dress. 'Charlie He's My Darling', Burns's famous version of a traditional Jacobite song, reflects this image of the 'young Chevalier' and imagines him, energetic and full of bravado, seducing the Scottish lasses.

'Twas on a Monday morning,
    Right early in the year,
That Charlie came to our town,
    The young Chevalier.

An' Charlie he's my darling,
    My darling, my darling,
Charlie he's my darling,
    The young Chevalier.

As he was walking up the street,
    The city for to view,
O there he spied a bonie lass
    The window looking thro'.
        An' Charlie he's my darling &c.

Sae light's he jimped up the stair,
    And tirl'd at the pin;
And wha sae ready as herself,
    To let the laddie in.
        An' Charlie he's my darling &c.

He set his Jenny on his knee,
    All in his Highland dress;
For brawly weel he ken'd the way
    To please a bonie lass.
        An' Charlie he's my darling &c.

It's up yon heathery mountain,
    An' down yon scroggy glen,
We daur na gang a milking,
    For Charlie and his men.
        An' Charlie he's my darling &c.

An' Charlie, he's my darling,
    My darling, my darling,
Charlie, he's my darling,
    The young Chevalier.
        An' Charlie he's my darling &c.

16TH APRIL

The Lovely Lass o' Inverness

O N THE 16TH OF APRIL 1746, the Jacobite army was brutally defeated in the Battle of Culloden by British forces commanded by William, Duke of Cumberland (1721–1765). So ended the Jacobite uprising of 1745–46. Burns purposefully visited Culloden (and several other locations of Jacobite significance) during his tour of the Scottish Highlands in 1787, fulfilling a long-held ambition to 'make leisurely pilgrimages through Caledonia; to sit on the fields of her battles; to wander on the romantic banks of her rivers; and to muse by the stately tower or venerable ruins, once the honored abodes of her heroes'. Burns noted in his tour journal that he spent some time in 'reflection on the field of battle'.

'The Lovely Lass o' Inverness' – in which a woman grieves for the loss of generations of men and, implicitly, the failure of the Jacobite campaign – is Burns's poignant homage to those who fell at Culloden.

The lovely lass o' Inverness,
    Nae joy nor pleasure can she see;
For, e'en and morn she cries, Alas!
    And aye the saut tear blins her e'e.
Drumossie moor, Drumossie day,
    A waefu' day it was to me;
For there I lost my father dear,
    My father dear and brethren three.

Their winding sheet the bludy clay,
    Their graves are growing green to see;
And by them lies the dearest lad
    That ever blest a woman's e'e!
Now wae to thee, thou cruel lord,
    A bludy man I trow thou be;
For mony a heart thou has made sair,
    That ne'er did wrang to thine or thee!

17TH APRIL

The Highland Widow's Lament

THE HIGHLAND WIDOW'S LAMENT refers to the plight of the heartbroken Jacobite sympathisers following the failure of the 1745 uprising, and to the severe emotional and economic impact it had upon the families of those who gave their lives.

Oh, I am come to the low countrie,
    Ochon, Ochon, Ochrie!
Without a penny in my purse,
    To buy a meal to me.

It was na sae in the Highland hills,
    Ochon, Ochon, Ochrie!
Nae woman in the Country wide
    Sae happy was as me.

For then I had a score o' kye,
  Ochon, Ochon, Ochrie!
Feeding on yon hill sae high,
  And giving milk to me.

And there I had three score o' yowes,
  Ochon, Ochon, Ochrie!
Skipping on yon bonie knowes,
  And casting woo to me.

I was the happiest of a' the Clan,
  Sair, sair may I repine;
For Donald was the brawest man,
  And Donald he was mine.

Till Charlie Stewart cam at last,
  Sae far to set us free;
My Donald's arm was wanted then
  For Scotland and for me.

Their waefu' fate what need I tell,
  Right to the wrang did yield;
My Donald and his Country fell,
  Upon Culloden field.

Ochon, O, Donald, Oh!
  Ochon, Ochon, Ochrie!
Nae woman in the warld wide,
  Sae wretched now as me.

18TH APRIL

Ye Jacobites by Name
to the tune of Up Black-nebs by Name

TODAY'S VERSES WERE SET to a traditionally anti-Jacobite air, 'Up Black-nebs by Name'. Burns's song is by no means anti-Jacobite, but it is one of his more nuanced considerations of Jacobitism; truly solemn in its treatment of the political aftermath of the failed uprisings, and mindful of the dear cost of 'heroic strife'. The final stanza, defeatist and yet sympathetic in tone, is a poignant and sombre expression of the impotence of the doomed cause.

Ye Jacobites by name, give an ear, give an ear,
  Ye Jacobites by name, give an ear;
    Ye Jacobites by name,
      Your fautes I will proclaim,
       Your doctrines I maun blame,
        You shall hear.

What is Right, and what is Wrang, by the law, by the law?
  What is Right, and what is Wrang, by the law?
    What is Right, and what is Wrang?
      A short sword, and a lang,
       A weak arm, and a strang
        For to draw.

What makes heroic strife, fam'd afar, fam'd afar?
　　What makes heroic strife fam'd afar?
　　　　What makes heroic strife?
　　　　　To whet th' assassin's knife,
　　　　　Or hunt a Parent's life
　　　　　　Wi' bludie war?

Then let your schemes alone, in the state, in the state,
　　Then let your schemes alone in the state,
　　　　Then let your schemes alone,
　　　　　Adore the rising sun,
　　　　　And leave a man undone,
　　　　　　To his fate.

19TH APRIL

On Seeing a Wounded Hare Limp by Me, Which a Fellow Had Just Shot At

O N THIS DAY IN 1789, Burns was working in the fields at his Ellisland farm when he heard a gunshot. He explained in a letter to Frances Dunlop two days later that 'presently a poor little hare limped by me, apparently very much hurt.— You will easily guess, this set my humanity in tears and my indignation in arms.'

Burns's seeming disapproval of hunting for sport (which might also be deduced from 'On Glenriddell's Fox Breaking its Chain') is fully articulated in a letter to Patrick Miller in June of the same year:

I have always had an abhorrence at this way of assassinating God's creatures without first allowing them those means of defence with which he has variously endowed them; but at this season when the object of our treacherous murder is most probably a Parent, perhaps the mother, and of consequence to leave two little helpless nurslings to perish with hunger amid the pitiless wilds, such an action is not only a sin against the letter of the law, but likewise a deep crime against the *morality of the heart*.

'On Seeing a Wounded Hare Limp by Me, Which a Fellow Had Just Shot At' is Burns's sentimental and typically sympathetic tribute to the injured animal.

INHUMAN man! curse on thy barb'rous art,
  And blasted be thy murder-aiming eye;
  May never pity soothe thee with a sigh,
Nor ever pleasure glad thy cruel heart!

Go live, poor wand'rer of the wood and field,
  The bitter little that of life remains:
  No more the thickening brakes and verdant plains
To thee shall home, or food, or pastime yield.

Seek, mangled wretch, some place of wonted rest,
  No more of rest, but now thy dying bed!
  The sheltering rushes whistling o'er thy head,
The cold earth with thy bloody bosom prest.

Oft as by winding Nith I, musing, wait
  The sober eve, or hail the cheerful dawn,
  I'll miss thee sporting o'er the dewy lawn,
And curse the ruffian's aim, and mourn thy hapless fate.

20TH APRIL

To a Mountain Daisy, on Turning One Down with the Plough, in April – 1786

THE DAISY IS THE FLOWER most associated with the month of April. In a happy coincidence, on this day in 1786 Burns enclosed the newly composed 'To a Mountain Daisy' in a letter to John Kennedy. The bard wrote that he was pleased with some of the sentiments of the poem as 'they are just the native, querulous feelings of a heart which, as the elegantly melting Gray says, "Melancholy has marked for her own."' Burns's reference is to Thomas Gray's 'Elegy in a Country Churchyard' (1751).

There is, of course, an autobiographical element to this poem in which Burns compares the fragility of the 'slender' daisy (a flower commonly linked with innocence and purity) with 'the fate of artless Maid', 'By Love's simplicity betray'd', and 'the fate of simple Bard, On Life's rough ocean luckless starr'd'. It seems likely that these are references to the troubled circumstances surrounding Burns and Jean Armour's separation.

Wee, modest, crimson-tipped flow'r,
Thou's met me in an evil hour;
For I maun crush amang the stoure
      Thy slender stem:
To spare thee now is past my pow'r,
      Thou bonie gem.

Alas! it's no thy neebor sweet,
The bonie *Lark*, companion meet!
Bending thee 'mang the dewy weet!
          Wi' spreckl'd breast,
When upward-springing, blythe, to greet
          The purpling East.

Cauld blew the bitter-biting *North*
Upon thy early, humble birth;
Yet cheerfully thou glinted forth
          Amid the storm,
Scarce rear'd above the *Parent-earth*
          Thy tender form.

The flaunting *flow'rs* our Gardens yield,
High-shelt'ring woods and wa's maun shield,
But thou, beneath the random bield
          O' clod or stane,
Adorns the histie *stibble field*,
          Unseen, alane.

There, in thy scanty mantle clad,
Thy snawie bosom sun-ward spread,
Thou lifts thy unassuming head
          In humble guise;
But now the *share* uptears thy bed,
          And low thou lies!

Such is the fate of artless Maid,
Sweet *flow'ret* of the rural shade!
By Love's simplicity betray'd,
          And guileless trust,
Till she, like thee, all soil'd, is laid
          Low i' the dust.

Such is the fate of simple Bard,
On Life's rough ocean luckless starr'd!
Unskilful he to note the card
   Of *prudent Lore*,
Till billows rage, and gales blow hard,
    And whelm him o'er!

Such fate to *suffering worth* is giv'n,
Who long with wants and woes has striv'n,
By human pride or cunning driv'n
   To Mis'ry's brink,
Till wrench'd of ev'ry stay but HEAV'N
    He, ruin'd, sink!

Ev'n thou who mourn'st the *Daisy's* fate,
That fate is thine – no distant date;
Stern Ruin's plough-share drives elate,
   Full on thy bloom,
Till crush'd beneath the *furrow's* weight,
    Shall be thy doom!

21st APRIL

Dedication to the Noblemen and Gentlemen of the Caledonian Hunt from the Edinburgh Edition of *Poems, Chiefly in the Scottish Dialect* (1787)

BURNS'S SECOND EDITION of *Poems, Chiefly in the Scottish Dialect* (commonly referred to as the Edinburgh edition) was published by William Creech (1745–1815) in April 1787 to the significant demand of over 1,300 subscribers. It was printed by William Smellie (1740–1795), the first editor of the *Encyclopedia Britannica*, with whom Burns became fast friends. Burns dedicated the Edinburgh edition to 'The Noblemen and Gentlemen of the Caledonian Hunt', a society club that organised field sports and social events. Several members of the club had befriended and patronised Burns during his time in the capital.

Written in markedly confident prose, this 'Preface' very much plays to the poet's reputation as the 'Heaven-taught ploughman' (established in the wake of his first published collection, the Kilmarnock edition of 1786) by emphasising the divine inspiration of his muse Coila, described here as 'the Poetic Genius of my Country'. By the time the Edinburgh edition was published Burns was very much affirmed in his status as 'A Scottish Bard'.

A Scottish Bard, proud of the name, and whose highest ambition is to sing in his Country's service, where shall he so properly look for patronage as to the illustrious Names of his native Land; those who bear the honours and inherit the virtues of their Ancestors?— The

Poetic Genius of my Country found me as the prophetic bard Elijah did Elisha – at the plough; and threw her inspiring mantle over me. She bade me sing the loves, the joys, the rural scenes and rural pleasures of my natal Soil, in my native tongue: I tuned my wild, artless notes, as she inspired.— She whispered me to come to this ancient metropolis of Caledonia, and lay my Songs under your honoured protection: I now obey her dictates.

Though much indebted to your goodness, I do not approach you, my Lords and Gentlemen, in the usual stile of dedication, to thank you for past favours; that path is so hackneyed by prostituted Learning, that honest Rusticity is ashamed of it.— Nor do I present this Address with the venal soul of a servile Author, looking for a continuation of those favours: I was bred to the Plough, and am independent. I come to claim the common Scottish name with you, my illustrious Countrymen; and to tell the world that I glory in the title.— I come to congratulate my Country, that the blood of her ancient heroes still runs uncontaminated; and that from your courage, knowledge, and public spirit, she may expect protection, wealth, and liberty.— In the last place, I come to proffer my warmest wishes to the Great Fountain of Honour, the Monarch of the Universe, for your welfare and happiness.

When you go forth to waken the Echoes, in the ancient and favourite amusement of your Forefathers, may Pleasure ever be of your party; and may Social-joy await your return! When harassed in courts or camps with the justlings of bad men and bad measures, may the honest consciousness of injured Worth attend your return to your native Seats; and may Domestic Happiness, with a smiling welcome, meet you at your gates! May Corruption shrink at your kindling indignant glance; and may tyranny in the Ruler and licentiousness in the People equally find you an inexorable foe!

22ND APRIL

Sonnet on the Death of Robert Riddell Esq. of Glenriddell, April 1794

B URNS'S FRIENDSHIP WITH Captain Robert Riddell (1755–1794) was one of his most important and influential relationships. Riddell's home at Friars Carse in Dumfriesshire was near to Burns's farm at Ellisland. He shared the poet's interest in Scottish song, his progressive views on contemporary politics, and he collaborated with Burns to establish the Monkland Friendly Society Library at Dunscore. Burns compiled the volumes of poetry and prose now referred to as 'The Glenriddell Manuscripts' for presentation to Riddell and his wife Elizabeth, 'as a sincere though small tribute of gratitude for the many, many happy hours the Author has spent under their roof'.

The men appear to have been boon companions – their conviviality and companionship informed 'The Whistle' – however their relationship cooled following a drunken incident at Riddell's home in December of 1793 whereby Burns, having offended Riddell's wife, was asked to leave. Burns sincerely regretted this offence, but sadly the men were not reconciled prior to Riddell's death in April 1794. The bard was deeply affected by Riddell's death and composed this sonnet as 'a small heart-felt tribute to the memory of the *man I loved*'. It was printed in the *Dumfries Journal* on this day in 1794.

No more, ye warblers of the wood, no more,
Nor pour your descant grating on my soul:
Thou young-eyed spring, gay in thy verdant stole,
More welcome were to me grim winter's wildest roar.

How can ye charm, ye flow'rs, with all your dyes?
Ye blow upon the sod that wraps my friend:
How can I to the tuneful strain attend?
That strain flows round th'untimely tomb where Riddel lies.

Yes, pour, ye warblers, pour the notes of woe,
And soothe *the Virtues* weeping on this bier:
The *Man of Worth*, and has not left his peer,
Is in his "narrow house" for ever darkly low.

Thee, Spring, again with joy shall others greet,
Me, mem'ry of my loss will only meet.

23RD APRIL

On Expressing Gratitude
from a letter to James Sibbald, January 1787

TODAY IS ST GEORGE'S DAY, the feast day of the patron saint
of England. It is also the day on which William Shakespeare,
the celebrated English bard, died in 1616. Burns greatly admired
Shakespeare; and he frequently quoted from Shakespeare's plays in
his letters, among them *As You Like It, Hamlet, Henry VIII,* and *Julius
Caesar.*

We commemorate Shakespeare today with an extract from Burns's
letter of introduction to the bookseller James Sibbald (1747–1803).
Here Burns – recently arrived in the Scottish capital and possibly
somewhat overwhelmed by his reception – paraphrases Act I Scene
3 of Shakespeare's *Othello* in modest reference to his own perceived
position on the periphery of polite society.

So little am I acquainted with the Modes and Manners of the more public and polished walks of life, that I often feel myself much embarrassed how to express the feelings of my heart, particularly Gratitude.—

> "— Rude am I in speech,
> And little blest with the set, polish'd phrase;
> For since these arms of mine had seven year's pith,
> Till now, some nine moons wasted, they have us'd
> Their dearest effort in the rural field;
> And therefore, little can I grace my cause
> In speaking for myself —"

The warmth with which you have befriended an obscure man and young Author in your three last Magazines — I can only say, Sir, I feel the weight of the obligation and wish I could express my sense of it.—

24TH APRIL

Adown Winding Nith I Did Wander
to the tune of Geordie's Byre

ADOWN WINDING NITH I DID WANDER was inspired by Phillis McMurdo (1779–1835), John McMurdo's daughter. The McMurdo women obviously left their mark on Burns: Phillis was the sister of Jean, the subject of 'There Was A Lass And She Was Fair' (see 10th March). This song is set on an idyllic spring day and refers also to an 'artless', 'simple', 'wild' daisy: the flower for the month of April.

Adown winding Nith I did wander,
   To mark the sweet flowers as they spring;
Adown winding Nith I did wander,
   Of Phillis to muse and to sing.
Awa wi' your belles and your beauties,
   They never wi' her can compare:
Wha-ever has met wi' my Phillis,
   Has met wi' the queen o' the Fair.

The daisy amus'd my fond fancy,
   So artless, so simple, so wild;
Thou emblem, said I, of my Phillis,
   For she is simplicity's child.
The rose-bud's the blush of my charmer,
   Her sweet balmy lip when 'tis prest:
How fair and how pure is the lily,
   But fairer and purer her breast.

Yon knot of gay flow'rs in the arbour,
   They ne'er wi' my Phillis can vie:
Her breath is the breath of the woodbine,
   Its dew-drop of diamond, her eye.
Her voice is the song of the morning,
   That wakes thro' the green-spreading grove;
When Phebus peeps over the mountains,
   On music, and pleasure, and love.

But beauty, how frail and how fleeting,
   The bloom of a fine summer's day!
While worth, in the mind of my Phillis
   Will flourish without a decay.
Awa wi' your Belles and your Beauties,
   They never wi' her can compare:
Whaever has met wi' my Phillis,
   Has met wi' the queen o' the fair.

Young Peggy
to the tune of Loch Erroch Side

INSPIRED BY MARGARET (PEGGY) KENNEDY (1766–1795), the niece of Burns's friend Gavin Hamilton, 'Young Peggy' depicts a springtime scene of pastoral beauty, entirely appropriate for this time of year.

Young Peggy blooms our boniest lass,
    Her blush is like the morning,
The rosy dawn, the springing grass,
    With early gems adorning:
Her eyes outshine the radiant beams
    That gild the passing shower,
And glitter o'er the crystal streams,
    And cheer each fresh'ning flower.

Her lips more than the cherries bright,
    A richer die has grac'd them,
They charm th' admiring gazer's sight,
    And sweetly tempt to taste them:
Her smile is as the ev'ning mild,
    When feath'red pairs are courting,
And little lambkins wanton wild,
    In playful bands disporting.

Were Fortune lovely Peggy's foe,
    Such sweetness would relent her,
As blooming spring unbends the brow
    Of surly, savage winter.
Detraction's eye no aim can gain,

Her winning pow'rs to lessen;
And fretful envy grins in vain,
The poison'd tooth to fasten.

Ye Pow'rs of Honor, Love and Truth,
From ev'ry ill defend her;
Inspire the highly-favour'd Youth
The Destinies intend her;
Still fan the sweet, connubial flame
Responsive in each bosom;
And bless the dear parental name
With many a filial blossom.

26TH APRIL

from Again Rejoicing Nature Sees
to the tune of Jockey's Grey Breeks

IN THIS SONG, Burns contrasts the glorious natural imagery of the
season with profound human sorrow. The final stanza expresses a
longing for winter, that nature might align with the 'chearless soul'. It
is possible, if uncertain, that today's words are another composition
referring to the unfortunate circumstances in which Burns and Jean
Armour found themselves during the spring of 1786.

The wanton coot the water skims,
Amang the reeds the ducklings cry,
The stately swan majestic swims,

And ev'ry thing is blest but I.
    And maun I still &c.

The Shepherd steeks his faulding slap,
    And owre the moorlands whistles shill,
Wi' wild, unequal, wand'ring step,
    I meet him on the dewy hill.
        And maun I still &c.

And when the lark, 'tween light and dark,
    Blythe waukens by the daisy's side,
And mounts and sings on flittering wings,
    A woe-worn ghaist I hameward glide.
        And maun I still &c.

Come Winter, with thine angry howl,
    And raging bend the naked tree;
Thy gloom will soothe my chearless soul,
    When Nature all is sad like me!
        And maun I still &c.

27TH APRIL

O Whistle, and I'll Come to Ye

HERE WE HAVE BURNS'S VERSION of a traditional song. It is not difficult to understand why 'O Whistle, and I'll Come to Ye' would have appealed to him; its reference to illicit love and disapproving parents certainly resonates with the bard's early dealings with Jean Armour and her family.

O Whistle, and I'll come to ye, my lad,
O whistle, and I'll come to ye, my lad;
Tho' father, and mother, and a' should gae mad,
Thy Jeanie will venture wi' ye, my lad.

But warily tent when ye come to court me,
And come nae unless the back-yett be a-jee;
Syne up the back-stile and let naebody see,
   And come as ye were na comin' to me,
   And come as ye were na comin' to me.—

At kirk, or at market, whene'er ye meet me,
Gang by me as tho' that ye car'd nae a flie;
But steal me a blink o' your bonie black e'e,
   Yet look as ye were na lookin' at me,
   Yet look as ye were na lookin' at me.—

Aye vow and protest that ye care na for me,
And whyles ye may lightly my beauty a wee;
But court nae anither, tho' jokin' ye be,
   For fear that she wyle your fancy frae me,
   For fear that she wyle your fancy frae me.

On Marrying Jean
from a letter to James Smith, April 1788

FOLLOWING THE SUCCESS of the Kilmarnock and Edinburgh editions of Burns's poetry, perhaps worn down by the couple's defiance and Jean's recurring pregnancies, the Armours eventually conceded defeat and accepted Burns as their son-in-law (although, from existing correspondence, the relationship was – perhaps unsurprisingly – always somewhat strained).

In this letter to James Smith, Burns refers to the couple's 'official' marriage in April 1788. Two years after the drama of Jean's first pregnancy, and two sets of twins later, the bard makes clear his happiness and playfully boasts about their expert ability to conceive.

There is no understanding a man properly, without knowing something of his previous ideas (that is to say if the Man has any ideas; for I know many who in the Animal-muster pass for Men that are the scanty masters of only one idea on any given subject, and by far the greatest part of your acquaintances and mine can barely boast of Ideas, 1.25, 1.5, 1.75, or some such fractional matter) so to let you a little into the secrets of my Pericranium, there is, you must know, a certain clean-limb'd, handsome bewitching young hussy of your acquaintance to whom I have lately and privately given a matrimonial title to my Corpus.—

> "Bode a robe, and wear it;
> "Bode a pock, and bear it,"

says the wise old Scots Adage! I hate to presage ill-luck; and as my girl in some late random trials has been *doubly* kinder to me than even the best of women usually are to their Partners of our Sex, in similar circumstances; I reckon on twelve times a brace of children against I celebrate my twelfth wedding-day: these twenty four will give me twenty four Gossipings, twenty four christenings (I mean, one equal to two) and I hope by the blessing of the God of my fathers to make them twenty four dutiful children to their Parents, twenty four useful Members of society, and twenty four approven servants of their God; not to mention, twenty four times a hundred and eighty two Mason-meetings on the business that I hope to have with their Mother into the bargain.—

29TH APRIL

It Was A' For Our Rightfu' King
to the tune of Mally Stewart

THIS IS BURNS'S FAMOUS VERSION of a traditional song, 'Mally Stewart' (c.1746). In this song, a young woman laments the failure of the Jacobite uprising and the departure of her fugitive lover for Ireland. Following defeat at Culloden, government forces were brutal in their treatment of rebels and sympathisers, arresting Jacobite soldiers for treason, burning meeting houses and confiscating livestock. Many fled, including Bonnie Prince Charlie who escaped to the Highlands. He eventually reached Europe via the Western Isles, and lived, an exile, in Rome until his death over forty years later.

It was a' for our rightfu' king
  We left fair Scotland's strand;
It was a' for our rightfu' king
  We e'er saw Irish land, my dear,
    We e'er saw Irish land.

Now a' is done that men can do,
  And a' is done in vain:
My Love and Native Land fareweel,
  For I maun cross the main, my dear,
    For I maun cross the main.

He turn'd him right and round about,
  Upon the Irish shore,
And gae his bridle reins a shake,
  With adieu for evermore, my dear,
    With adieu for evermore.

The soger frae the wars returns,
  The sailor frae the main,
But I hae parted frae my Love,
  Never to meet again, my dear,
    Never to meet again.

When day is gane, and night is come,
  And a' folk bound to sleep;
I think on him that's far awa,
  The lee-lang night and weep, my dear,
    The lee-lang night and weep.

30TH APRIL

The Small Birds Rejoice
to the tune of Captain O'Kean

OUR FINAL BURNSIAN OFFERING for April conflates two of this month's recurring themes: springtime and Jacobitism. Burns sent the first stanza of this song to Robert Cleghorn (d.1798), farmer at Saughton Mills, in March 1788. Cleghorn responded, 'I would have it in the Jacobite style. Suppose it should be sung after the fatal field of Culloden by the unfortunate Charles.' Burns duly obliged, and the song ends with the fugitive 'Bonnie Prince Charlie' mourning the 'ruin' of his followers and his powerlessness in the wake of defeat.

The small birds rejoice in the green leaves returning,
The murmuring streamlet winds clear thro' the vale,
The primroses blow in the dews of the morning,
And wild-scattered cowslips bedeck the green dale:
But what can give pleasure, or what can seem fair,
When the lingering moments are number'd wi' care?
No birds sweetly singing, nor flowers gayly springing,
Can soothe the sad bosom of joyless despair.

The deed that I dared, could it merit their malice?
A king and a father to place on his throne?
His right are these hills, and his right are these vallies,
Where wild beasts find shelter, but I can find none:
But 'tis not my sufferings thus wretched, forlorn,
My brave gallant friends, 'tis your ruin I mourn;
Your faith proved so loyal, in hot bloody trial,
Alas! can I make it no better return!

MAY

Now rosy May comes in wi' flowers,
To deck her gay, green-spreading bowers;

from Dainty Davie

1st MAY

Such a Parcel of Rogues in a Nation

THE POLITICAL UNION of Scotland and England became effective on this day in 1707, and the Kingdom of Great Britain was created. In 'Such a Parcel of Rogues in a Nation' Burns invokes several traditional sources condemning the dealings of corrupt Scottish nobility with peers south of the border. The 'rogues' here are the Scottish Commissioners responsible for negotiating the preceding 1706 Treaty of Union. A devolved Scottish Parliament was re-established some 292 years after the 1707 Union.

Another of Burns's songs, 'A Man's a Man', was performed to rousing applause at the formal opening ceremony for the Scottish Parliament on the first of July 1999. Designed by Enric Miralles (1955–2000), the spectacular parliamentary building of steel, oak and granite sits between the foot of Edinburgh's Royal Mile and the crags of Arthur's Seat. Donald Dewar (1937–2000), Scotland's first First Minister, said of the bard in his opening address, 'Burns believed that sense and worth ultimately prevail. He believed that was the core of politics; that without it, ours would be an impoverished profession.'

Fareweel to a' our Scottish fame,
    Fareweel our ancient glory;
Fareweel even to the Scottish name,
    Sae fam'd in martial story.
Now Sark rins o'er the Solway sands,
    And Tweed rins to the ocean,
To mark where England's province stands,
Such a parcel of rogues in a nation.

What force or guile could not subdue,
    Thro' many warlike ages,
Is wrought now by a coward few
    For hireling traitor's wages.
The English steel we could disdain;
    Secure in valour's station;
But English gold has been our bane,
Such a parcel of rogues in a nation.

O would, or I had seen the day
    That treason thus could sell us,
My auld gray head had lien in clay,
    Wi' Bruce and loyal Wallace!
But pith and power, till my last hour,
    I'll mak' this declaration;
We're bought and sold for English gold,
Such a parcel of rogues in a nation.

2ND MAY

Dainty Davie

MAY IS THE LAST MONTH of spring when nature, now fully emerged from winter, transitions to its full glory. The spectacle was not lost on Burns, who makes many references to the month of May in poetry and song. In 'Dainty Davie' the bard's female protagonist looks forward to all that nature has to offer, and, of course, to sharing it with her lover.

206

Now rosy May comes in wi' flowers,
To deck her gay green-spreading bowers;
And now come in my happy hours,
    To wander wi' my Davie.

Meet me on the warlock knowe,
    Dainty Davie, dainty Davie;
There I'll spend the day wi' you,
    My ain dear, dainty Davie.

The chrystal waters round us fa',
The merry birds are lovers a',
The scented breezes round us blaw,
A-wandering wi' my Davie.
    Meet me on the warlock knowe, &c.

When purple morning starts the hare,
To steal upon her early fare,
Then thro' the dews I will repair,
To meet my faithful Davie.
    Meet me on the warlock knowe, &c.

When day, expiring in the west,
The curtain draws of Nature's rest,
I flee to 's arms I lo'e the best,
And that's my ain dear Davie.
    Meet me on the warlock knowe, &c.

3RD MAY

To Miss Cruickshank, a Very Young Lady

BURNS COMPOSED THIS as a compliment to Miss Jean Cruickshank (1775–1835). The poet lodged with Jean's family during his second winter in Edinburgh (1787–1788). Jean, twelve years old at the time, was a gifted harpsichordist and singer. She reportedly played for Burns, assisting the poet as he set words to existing airs. Here Burns makes much of the common association of May with youth and beauty in wishing Jean a long life, safe from harm or corruption.

Beauteous rose-bud, young and gay,
Blooming on thy early May,
Never may'st thou, lovely Flower,
Chilly shrink in sleety shower!
Never Boreas' hoary path,
Never Eurus' pois'nous breath,
Never baleful stellar lights,
Taint thee with untimely blights!
Never, never reptile thief
Riot on thy virgin leaf!
Nor even Sol too fiercely view
Thy bosom blushing still with dew!

Mayst thou long, sweet crimson gem,
Richly deck thy native stem;
Till some evening, sober, calm,
Dropping dews, and breathing balm,
While all around the woodland rings,

And ev'ry bird thy requiem sings;
Thou, amid the dirgeful sound,
Shed thy dying honours round,
And resign to Parent Earth
The loveliest form she e'er gave birth.

4TH MAY

On Poetic Ability
from a letter to Frances Dunlop, 4th May 1788

IT'S REASSURING TO KNOW THAT, for all his success, Burns was still prone to the occasional crisis of confidence. On this day in 1788, the bard wrote to Frances Dunlop in praise of John Dryden's translation of *The Works of Virgil* (1697). Burns's humorous comparison of his own writing abilities is modest, but it also serves as a reminder that the 'heaven-taught ploughman' was far from an unread farmer.

Dryden's Virgil has delighted me.— I don't know whether the critics will agree with me, but the Georgics are to me by far the best of Virgil.— It is indeed a species of writing entirely new to me, and has filled my head with a thousand fancies of emulation: but alas! When I read the Georgics, and then survey my own powers, 'tis like the idea of a Shetland Pony drawn up by the side of a thorough bred Hunter, to start for the Plate.—

5TH MAY

On Leaving Edinburgh
from a letter to Mr Fyfe, 5th May 1787

BURNS DEPARTED EDINBURGH on this day in 1787, having spent six months in the capital. The poet had enjoyed good company, fine dining and the attention of several women. He had completed an extended edition of *Poems, Chiefly in the Scottish Dialect*, published a fortnight earlier, and it was time to set off on his next adventure: a tour of the Scottish Borders and the north of England. Here Burns takes a cheerful farewell of the city referred to as 'Auld Reekie' ('Old Smoky'), although it would not be long before he returned.

My dear Sir,
    My loins are girded, my sandals on my feet, and my staff is in my hand; and in half an hour I shall set off from this venerable, respectable, hospitable, social, convivial, Queen of cities, AULD REEKIE.— [...] Farewell!

> Now, God in heaven bless REEKIE's town,
>   With plenty joy and peace!
> And may her wealth and fair renown,
>   To latest times increase!!!— Amen

> Robert Burns

6TH MAY

To Miss Ainslie in Church

O N THIS DAY IN 1787 – which fell on a Sunday – Burns enjoyed the first stop on his tour of the Scottish Borders and the north of England. His travel companion, Robert Ainslie (1766–1838), introduced the bard to his family at Berrywell, Dunse. Burns comments affectionately on Ainslie's parents in his tour journal, but he was, of course, particularly taken with Ainslie's sister, Rachel (b.1768):

> Miss Ainslie an angel — her person a little of the embonpoint, but handsome her face, particularly her eyes full of sweetness and good humour — She unites three qualities rarely to be found together; keen, solid penetration; sly, witty observation and remark; and the gentlest, most unaffected female Modesty.

Burns noted later in the day that he attended church with the family. It is clear from this epigram that, rather than give his full attention to the church service, he continued to indulge his admiration for the 'fair maid'. The implication is that Miss Ainslie's beauty, rather than her piety or devotion, sets her apart from the rest of the congregation.

Fair maid, you need not take the hint,
Nor idle texts pursue;
'Twas guilty sinners that he meant,
Not angels such as you.

from The Cotter's Saturday Night

O N THIS DAY IN 1787, Burns crossed the River Tweed via the Coldstream Bridge, and in doing so he set foot on English soil for the first time. Robert Ainslie recalled several years later that, having crossed the border, Burns was so overcome with emotion that he kneeled on the ground with his arms in the air and recited aloud the concluding stanzas of 'The Cotter's Saturday Night'. In the poem, Burns expresses an impassioned love for his country and prays that Scotland's 'hardy sons of rustic toil' prioritise simple values over '*Luxury's* contagion'. For Burns, love and friendship, rather than wealth, are what is truly important.

o SCOTIA! my dear, my native soil!
　　For whom my warmest wish to heaven is sent!
Long may thy hardy sons of *rustic toil*,
　　Be blest with health, and peace, and sweet content!
And O may Heaven their simple lives prevent
　　From *Luxury's* contagion, weak and vile!
Then howe'er *crowns* and *coronets* be rent,
　　A *virtuous Populace* may rise the while;
And stand a wall of fire around their much-lov'd ISLE.

o THOU! who pour'd the *patriotic tide*,
　　That stream'd thro' great, unhappy WALLACE' heart;
Who dar'd to, nobly, stem tyrannic pride,
　　Or *nobly die*, the second glorious part:
(The Patriot's God, peculiarly thou art,

His *friend, inspirer, guardian,* and *reward!*)
O never, never SCOTIA's realm desert;
But still the *Patriot,* and the *Patriot-Bard,*
In bright succession raise, her *Ornament* and *Guard!*

8TH MAY

The Braw Wooer
to the tune of The Lothian Lassie

BURNS OFTEN REPRESENTED female personae in the words of his
songs and he could ventriloquise the female voice with striking
effect. Burns's attempts to inhabit the female psyche reveal much
about his own understanding of women, and about women's position
in eighteenth-century Scottish society (from a man's point of view,
at least).

In 'The Braw Wooer' an intelligent and wry-humoured young
woman plays hard to get when, rather than swooning at her suitor's
sentimental declaration of love, she has some fun at his expense.

Last May a braw wooer cam' down the lang glen,
    And sair wi' his love he did deave me;
I said there was naething I hated like men,
    The deuce gae wi him to believe me, believe me,
    The deuce gae wi him to believe me.

He spak o' the darts in my bonie black een,
    And vow'd for my love he was dying;
I said he might die when he liked for Jean;
    The Lord forgi'e me for lying, for lying;
    The Lord forgi'e me for lying!

A weel stocked mailen, himsel' for the laird,
    And marriage aff hand, were his proffers:
I never loot on that I kend it, or car'd;
    But thought I might hae waur offers, waur offers;
    But thought I might hae waur offers.

But what wad ye think? in a fortnight or less
    The de'il tak his taste to gae near her!
He up the lang loan to my black cousin Bess
    Guess ye how the jad! I could bear her, could bear her;
    Guess ye how the jad! I could bear her.

But a' the niest week as I petted wi' care,
    I gaed to the tryst o' Dalgarnock;
But wha but my fine fickle wooer was there,
    I glowr'd as I'd seen a warlock, a warlock,
    I glowr'd as I'd seen a warlock.

But owre my left shouther I ga'e him a blink,
    Leest neebours might say I was saucy:
My wooer he caper'd as he'd been in drink,
    And vow'd I was his dear lassie, dear lassie,
    And vow'd I was his dear lassie.

I spier'd for my cousin fu' couthy and sweet,
    Gin she had recover'd her hearing;
And how her new shoon fit her auld shachl't feet;
    But heavens! how he fell a-swearing, a-swearing,
    But heavens! how he fell a-swearing.

He begged, for gude-sake! I wad be his wife,
    Or else I wad kill him wi' sorrow:
So e'en to preserve the poor body in life,
    I think I maun wed him to-morrow, to-morrow;
    I think I maun wed him to-morrow.

9TH MAY

On Miss Lindsay
from Burns's Borders Tour Journal

BURNS'S 'BORDERS TOUR JOURNAL' contains a great deal of commentary on the manners and appearance of individuals he encountered on his travels, with his keenest observations focused upon the ladies. His entry for this day in 1787 is a striking example of Burns at his most complimentary, and also his most scathing. Making use of powerful and explicit language, the poet describes a walk with a group of ladies in Jedburgh, one of whom is singled out for his highest praise, and two of whom are subject to his fiercest flyting.

Miss Lindsay is a good-humor'd amiable girl; rather short et embonpoint, but handsome and extremely graceful — beautiful hazle eyes full of spirit and sparkling with delicious moisture — an engaging face and manner, *un tout ensemble* that speaks her of the first order of female minds — Her sister is a bonie, strappan, rosy, sonsie lass — Shake myself loose, after several unsuccessful efforts, of Mrs Fair & Miss Lookup and somehow or other get hold of Miss Lindsay's arm — My heart thawed into melting pleasure after being so long frozen up in the Greenland bay of Indifference amid the noise and nonsense of Edinburgh. Miss seems very well pleased with my Bardship's distinguishing her, and after some slight qualms which I could easily mark, she sets the titter round at defiance and kindly allows me to keep my hold; and when parted by the ceremony of my introduction to Mr Somerville, she met me half to resume my situation — Nota Bene — The Poet within a point and a half of being damnably in love — I am afraid my bosom still nearly as much tinder as ever —

The old, cross-grained, whiggish, ugly, slanderous hag, Miss Lookup with all the poisonous spleen of a disappointed, ancient maid, stops me very unseasonably to ease her hell-rankling, bursting breast by falling abusively foul on the Miss Lindsays, particularly on my Dulcinea; I hardly refrain from cursing her to her face — May she, for her pains, be curst with eternal desire and damn'd with endless disappointment! Hear me, O Heavens and give ear, O Earth! May the burden of antiquated Virginity crush her down to the lowest region of the bottomless Pit for daring to mouth her calumnious slander on one of the finest pieces of the workmanship of Almighty Excellence.

10TH MAY

Highland Lassie, O

BURNS'S REAL-LIFE 'HIGHLAND LASSIE' was Mary Campbell (c.1763/66–86). Although very little hard detail is known about her or her relationship with Burns, it is believed that Burns and Mary's affair took place in the spring of 1786, following his separation from the then pregnant Jean Armour. In the song 'Highland Lassie, O', Burns refers to his intended emigration to the West Indies, lamenting that he must leave his 'Highland Lassie' behind, and implying a love that is both faithful and enduring. In reality, however, their relationship was tragically short-lived.

Nae gentle dames, tho' ne'er sae fair
Shall ever be my muse's care;
Their titles a' are empty show,
Gie me my Highland Lassie, O.

Within the glen sae bushy, O,
Aboon the plain sae rashy, O,
I set me down wi' right gude will,
To sing my Highland Lassie, O.

O were yon hills and vallies mine,
Yon palace and yon gardens fine!
The world then the love should know
I bear my Highland Lassie, O.
    Within the glen &c.

But fickle fortune frowns on me,
And I maun cross the raging sea;
But while my crimson currents flow,
I love my Highland Lassie, O.
    Within the glen &c.

Altho' thro' foreign climes I range,
I know her heart will never change,
For her bosom burns with honor's glow,
My faithful Highland Lassie, O.
    Within the glen &c.

For her I'll dare the billow's roar;
For her I'll trace a distant shore;
That Indian wealth may lustre throw
Around my Highland Lassie, O.
    Within the glen &c.

She has my heart, she has my hand,
By secret truth and honor's band!
'Till the mortal stroke shall lay me low,
I'm thine, my Highland Lassie, O.

Farewel, the glen sae bushy, O!
Farewel, the plain sae rashy, O!
To other lands I now must go
To sing my Highland Lassie, O!

11TH MAY

The Highland Lassie Note

IT IS THOUGHT THAT BURNS invited Mary Campbell to travel
to the West Indies with him, and that they parted in May 1786 to
make individual arrangements for their proposed emigration. Shortly
after their farewell, Mary contracted a fever. She died within a matter
of days, and before Burns had learned of her illness. His 'Highland
Lassie Note', written to accompany the song of the same name in an
interleaved copy of the *Scots Musical Museum*, is the most substantial
piece of evidence for this episode in the poet's life. Here he refers to
their 'proposed change of life', and to Mary's untimely death.

This was a composition of mine in very early life, before I was
known at all in the world. My Highland lassie was a warm-hearted,
charming young creature as ever blessed a man with generous love.
After a pretty long tract of the most ardent reciprocal attachment,
we met by appointment on the second Sunday of May, in a seques-
tered spot by the Banks of Ayr, where we spent the day in taking
a farewell, before she should embark for the West-Highlands, to
arrange matters among her friends for our projected change of life.
At the close of Autumn following she crossed the sea to meet me at
Greenock, where she had scarce landed when she was seized with a
malignant fever which hurried my dear girl to the grave in a few days,
before I could even hear of her illness.

12TH MAY

Will Ye Go to the Indies, My Mary
to the tune of Ewe Bughts Marion

I N 'WILL YE GO TO THE INDIES, MY MARY' the male protagonist refers to having 'plighted our troth'. It is thought that Burns presented Mary Campbell with a two-volume Bible as a token of his attachment; one inscribed, 'And ye shall not swear by my name falsely—I am the Lord' (Leviticus xvi. 12), and the other, 'Thou shalt not forswear thyself, but shalt perform unto the Lord thine oath' (Matthew v. 33).

The volumes are believed to have been passed down through Mary's family, travelling to Canada and back before they were reverentially placed in the Alloway Burns Monument on the 25th of January 1841 with a lock of Mary's hair. In the end, Burns did not travel to 'the Indies', but instead remained in Scotland to further his career as a poet.

Will ye go to the Indies, my Mary,
    And leave old Scotia's shore?
Will ye go to the Indies, my Mary,
    Across th' Atlantic roar.

O sweet grows the lime and the orange,
    And the apple on the pine,
But a' the charms o' the Indies
    Can never equal thine.

I hae sworn by the Heavens to my Mary,
   I hae sworn by the Heavens to be true;
And sae may the Heavens forget me,
   When I forget my vow!

O plight me your faith, my Mary,
   And plight me your lily-white hand;
O plight me your faith, my Mary,
   Before I leave Scotia's strand.

We hae plighted our troth, my Mary,
   In mutual affection to join:
And curst be the cause that shall part us!
   The hour and the moment o' time!

13TH MAY

To Mary in Heaven
to the tune of Captain Cook's Death

THREE YEARS AFTER Mary Campbell's death, Burns composed 'To Mary in Heaven'. The song laments Mary's passing in dramatic, exclamatory verse and makes clear Burns's enduring affection. This song in particular did much to ensure that the memory of Mary remained in the popular consciousness. Several statues by the nineteenth-century sculptor John Steel (1804–1891) – inaugurated in Dundee, Dunedin, London and New York – depict Burns gazing heavenward, quill in hand, as he composes these very words.

Thou ling'ring star, with less'ning ray
   That lov'st to greet the early morn,
Again thou usher'st in the day
   My Mary from my Soul was torn.
O Mary! Dear, departed Shade!
   Where is thy place of blissful rest?
Seest thou thy Lover lowly laid?
   Hear'st thou the groans that rend his breast?

That sacred hour can I forget,
   Can I forget the hallow'd grove,
Where, by the winding Ayr, we met,
   To live one day of Parting Love!
Eternity cannot efface
   Those records dear of transports past;
Thy image at our last embrace,
   Ah, little thought we 'twas our last!

Ayr gurgling kiss'd his pebbled shore,
   O'erhung with wild-woods, thickening green;
The fragrant birch, and hawthorn hoar,
   Twin'd, amorous round the raptur'd scene:
The flowers sprang wanton to be prest,
   The birds sang love on every spray;
Till too, too soon the glowing west
   Proclaim'd the speed of winged day.

Still o'er these scenes my mem'ry wakes,
   And fondly broods with miser-care;
Time but th' impression stronger makes,
   As streams their channels deeper wear,
My Mary, dear departed Shade!
   Where is thy place of blissful rest?
Seest thou thy Lover lowly laid?
   Hear'st thou the groans that rend his breast!

14TH MAY

Highland Mary
to the tune of Katherine Ogie

BURNS AND MARY CAMPBELL parted forever on this day in 1786. In 'Highland Mary' the poet describes their last meeting and refers to Mary's death in powerfully emotive language. The song was written several years after the affair, but the final stanza suggests that the ill-fated Mary still occupied a place in the poet's heart. Burns's poetry inspired by this brief yet tragic affair captured the imagination of his audience to the extent that, over the course of the nineteenth century, 'Highland Mary' became the most widely commemorated of all the bard's love interests.

Ye banks, and braes, and streams around
    The castle of Montgomery,
Green be your woods, and fair your flowers,
    Your waters never drumlie!
There Simmer first unfauld her robes,
    And there the langest tarry;
For there I took the last farewell
    Of my sweet Highland Mary.

How sweetly bloom'd the gay, green birk,
    How rich the hawthorn's blossom,
As underneath their fragrant shade,
    I clasp'd her to my bosom!
The golden hours on angel wings,
    Flew o'er me and my dearie;
For dear to me, as light and life,
    Was my sweet Highland Mary.

Wi' mony a vow, and lock'd embrace,
  Our parting was fu' tender;
And, pledging aft to meet again,
  We tore ourselves asunder.
But oh! fell death's untimely frost,
  That nipt my flower sae early!
Now green's the sod, and cauld's the clay
  That wraps my Highland Mary!

O pale, pale now, those rosy lips,
  I aft hae kiss'd sae fondly!
And clos'd for aye, the sparkling glance
  That dwalt on me sae kindly!
And mouldering now in silent dust,
  That heart that lo'ed me dearly!
But still within my bosom's core
  Shall live my Highland Mary.

15TH MAY

from Epistle to a Young Friend

O N THIS DAY IN 1786, Burns completed 'Epistle to a Young Friend' for Andrew Hunter Aiken. Andrew was the son of Burns's close friend and confidant, the lawyer Robert Aiken (1739–1807). The poet advises his young friend in matters of the heart, finances and the importance of religion. In a case of 'do as I say, not as I do', his warning Andrew to 'never tempt th' *illicit rove*' might be considered a *bit* rich given that Burns was romancing Highland Mary at the time, while also being the father of Jean Armour's as yet unborn twins. Burns alludes to this in the final couplet where he wishes that Andrew may 'better reck the *rede* [heed the advice] / Than ever did th' *Adviser!*'

The *sacred lowe* o' weel plac'd love,
    Luxuriantly indulge it;
But never tempt th' *illicit rove*,
    Tho' naething should divulge it:
I waive the quantum o' the sin,
    The hazard of concealing;
But Och! it hardens *a' within*,
    And petrifies the feeling!

To catch Dame Fortune's golden smile,
    Assiduous wait upon her;
And gather gear by ev'ry wile
    That's justified by Honour;
Not for to *hide* it in a *hedge*,
    Nor for a *train-attendant*;
But for the glorious privilege
    Of being *independent*.

The *fear o' Hell's* a hangman's whip,
    To haud the wretch in order;
But where ye feel your *Honor* grip,
    Let that aye be your border:
Its slightest touches, instant pause –
    Debar a' side-pretences;
And resolutely keep its laws,
    Uncaring consequences.

The great Creator to revere,
    Must sure become the *Creature*;
But still the preaching cant forbear,
    And ev'n the rigid feature:

Yet ne'er with Wits profane to range,
  Be complaisance extended;
An *atheist-laugh's* a poor exchange
  For *Deity offended*!

When ranting round in Pleasure's ring,
  Religion may be blinded;
Or if she gie a *random-sting*,
  It may be little minded;
But when on life we're tempest-driven
  A Conscience but a canker –
A correspondence fix'd wi' Heav'n,
  Is sure a noble *anchor*!

Adieu, dear, amiable Youth!
  Your *heart* can ne'er be wanting!
May Prudence, Fortitude, and Truth,
  Erect your brow, undaunting!
In *ploughman phrase*, 'God send you speed,'
  Still daily to grow wiser;
And may ye better reck the *rede*,
  Than ever did th' *Adviser*!

16TH MAY

The Charming Month of May

TODAY'S CHOICE IS BURNS'S English language version of a
traditional Scots song that was first printed in Allan Ramsay's
Tea Table Miscellany (1723). Here the poet creates yet another vivid
image of this naturally spectacular month.

It was the charming month of May,
When all the flowers were fresh and gay,
One morning, by the break of day,
   The youthful charming Chloe;
From peaceful slumber she arose,
Girt on her mantle and her hose,
And o'er the flowery mead she goes,
   The youthful, charming Chloe.
     Lovely was she by the dawn,
       Youthful Chloe, charming Chloe,
     Tripping o'er the pearly lawn,
      The youthful, charming Chloe.

The feather'd people, you might see,
Perch'd all around on every tree,
In notes of sweetest melody
   They hail the charming Chloe;
Till, painting gay the eastern skies,
The glorious sun began to rise;
Out-rival'd by the radiant eyes
   Of youthful, charming Chloe.
     Lovely was she by the dawn, &c.

17TH MAY

The First Psalm

BURNS WAS, IN MANY WAYS, a sincerely religious man. He possessed a confident knowledge of the Bible, which he frequently quoted in his correspondence, moving fluently between serious scripture and pithy proverb. Burns's independent approach to matters religious and his personal control of ideas is apparent in his version of Psalms 1. His words are infused with the glorious natural imagery that recurs in many of this month's selections.

The man, in life where-ever plac'd,
    Hath happiness in store,
Who walks not in the wicked's way,
    Nor learns their guilty lore!

Nor from the seat of scornful Pride
    Casts forth his eyes abroad,
But with humility and awe
    Still walks before his God.

That man shall flourish like the trees
    Which by the streamlets grow;
The fruitful top is spread on high,
    And firm the root below.

But he whose blossom buds in guilt
    Shall to the ground be cast,
And like the rootless stubble tost,
    Before the sweeping blast.

For why? That God the good adore
    Hath giv'n them peace and rest,
But hath decreed that wicked men
    Shall ne'er be truly blest.

18TH MAY

from To W. Simpson, Ochiltree

WILLIAM SIMPSON (1758–1815) was a schoolmaster at Ochiltree, East Ayrshire. Impressed by Burns's religious satire, 'The Holy Tulzie', he sent the poet a verse epistle to which Burns replied in May 1785. In the following stanzas the bard provides an insight into his understanding of poetic sensibility. For Burns, a poet cannot be truly inspired until he gives himself over to 'pensive pondering', the full force of emotion, and the beauty of nature.

The *Muse*, nae *Poet* ever fand her,
Till by himsel he learn'd to wander,
Adown some trottin burn's meander,
        An' no think lang;
O sweet, to stray, an' pensive ponder
        A heart-felt sang!

The warly race may drudge an' drive,
Hog-shouther, jundie, stretch, an' strive,
Let me fair NATURE's face descrive,
        And I, wi' pleasure,
Shall let the busy, grumbling hive
        Bum owre their treasure.

19TH MAY

You're Welcome, Willie Stewart

THE SUBJECT OF THIS CHEERFUL DRINKING SONG is William Stuart (c.1749–1812), the son of a publican in Closeburn and factor to the Closeburn estate. From Burns's correspondence, William was one of the cronies who shared the bard's enjoyment of conviviality and bawdy song. A welcome from the bard was a warm welcome indeed!

You're welcome, Willie Stewart,
   You're welcome, Willie Stewart,
There's ne'er a flower that blooms in May
   That's half sae welcome's thou art.

Come, bumpers high, express your joy,
   The bowl we maun renew it;
The tappit-hen, gae bring her ben,
   To welcome Willie Stewart,
      You're welcome, Willie Stewart, &c.

May foes be strang, and friends be slack,
   Ilk action may he rue it,
May woman on him turn her back,
   That wrangs thee, Willie Stewart.
      You're welcome, Willie Stewart, &c.

20TH MAY

My Girl She's Airy
to the tune of **Black Joke**

TODAY WE CAN ENJOY one of Burns's earliest productions of bawdy song. The opening lines are indeed 'as sweet as the blossoms in May'. However, the description becomes increasingly erotic and considerably more suggestive until, in the final lines, it loses any sense of tact. Burns's very deliberate 'spelling' of words explicitly associated with sex might be considered a wry comment on attempted subtlety. The inevitable triumph of sexual desire over attempted modesty is a recurring theme in Burns's bawdry.

My Girl she's airy, she's buxom and gay,
Her breath is as sweet as the blossoms in May;
   A touch of her lips it ravishes quite;
She's always good natur'd, good humor'd, and free;
She dances, she glances, she smiles with a glee;
   Her eyes are the lightenings of joy and delight;
Her slender neck, her handsome waist,
Her hair well buckl'd, her stays well lac'd,
Her taper white leg with an et, and a, c,
   For her a, b, e, d, and her c, u, n, t,
   And Oh, for the joys of a long winter night!!!

21st MAY

The Fornicator
to the tune of Clout the Cauldron

IN EIGHTEENTH-CENTURY SCOTLAND, fornicators and adulterers were policed by the local Kirk Session. They were often sentenced to a spell upon the 'cutty stool', a wooden structure that stood in front of the pulpit. Offenders were dressed in sackcloth and made to stand at the entrance of the church as parishioners arrived for Sunday worship. They were then led to the cutty stool before the sermon, where they would stand, bare-legged and hatless, to be publicly rebuked by the minister.

'The Fornicator' was inspired by Burns's first experience of kirk discipline in 1784 or 1785, the consequence of his fathering a child with a young woman named Elizabeth Paton. It is one of a number of bawdy songs by Burns included in *The Merry Muses of Caledonia* (1799). The song draws attention to Burns's unwillingness to take seriously the punishment imposed by the Kirk for 'fornication'. The poet and his lover stand side by side on the cutty stool. However, rather than attentively receiving his rebuke he is distracted by the 'bare-legs' of his 'handsome Betsey', and the couple reoffend on the way home! Burns's declaration that he is a 'Fornicator' is intended as a defiant affirmation of his sexuality, rather than a label of debauchery and impiety – a reclamation of a word if ever there was one.

Ye jovial boys who love the joys.
   The blissful joys of Lovers,
Yet dare avow, wi dauntless brow,
   When the bony lass discovers,

I pray draw near, and lend an ear,
  And welcome in a Frater,
For I've lately been on quarantine,
  A proven Fornicator.

Before the Congregation wide,
  I pass'd the muster fairly,
My handsome Betsey by my side,
  We gat our ditty rarely;
But my downcast eye by chance did spy
  What made my lips to water,
Those limbs so clean where I between,
  Commenc'd a Fornicator.

With rueful face and signs of grace
  I pay'd the buttock-hire,
The night was dark and thro' the park
  I could not but convoy her;
A parting kiss, what could I less,
  My vows began to scatter,
My Betsey fell-lal de dal lal lal,
  I am a Fornicator.

But for her sake this vow I make,
  And solemnly I swear it,
That while I own a single crown,
  She's welcome for to share it;
And my roguish boy his Mother's joy,
  And the darling of his Pater,
For him I boast my pains and cost,
  Although a Fornicator.

Ye wenching blades whose hireling jades
  Have tipt you off blue-joram,
I tell ye plain, I do disdain
  To rank you in the Quorum;

But a bony lass upon the grass
   To teach her esse Mater,
And no reward but fond regard,
   O that's a Fornicator.

Your warlike Kings and Heroes bold,
   Great Captains and Commanders;
Your mighty Cesars fam'd of old,
   And Conquering Alexanders;
In fields they fought and laurels bought,
   And bulwarks strong did batter,
But still they grac'd our noble list
   And ranked Fornicator!!!

22ND MAY

A Poet's Welcome to his Love-Begotten Daughter; the First Instance That Entitled Him to the Venerable Appellation of Father

BURNS'S AFFAIR WITH ELIZABETH PATON, who worked at his family's farm, resulted in his first-born child. Their daughter Elizabeth was born on the 22nd of May and her birth inspired Burns to write 'A Poet's Welcome to his Love-Begotten Daughter'. Burns circulated the poem among several correspondents, in one manuscript version giving it the bold title, 'A Poet's Welcome to his Bastart Wean'.

In the poem, Burns adopts positively defiant language to welcome his daughter with sincere paternal love, disregarding the Kirk's zealous disapproval of his fathering an illegitimate child. Although he admits that his child could have arrived under more advantageous circumstances, he emphasises that, 'by his faith', her existence is of greater importance than the puritanical notions of the Kirk Session, or the judgement of his community.

Thou's welcome, Wean! Mischanter fa' me,
If thoughts o' thee, or yet thy Mamie,
Shall ever daunton me or awe me,
    My bonie lady;
Or if I blush when thou shalt ca' me
     Tyta, or Daddie.

Tho' now they name me, Fornicator,
And tease my name in kintra clatter,
The mair they talk, I'm kend the better;
     E'en let them clash!
An auld wife's tongue's a feckless matter
    To gie ane fash.

Welcome! my bonie, sweet, wee Dochter!
Tho' ye come here a wee unsought for;
And tho' your comin' I hae fought for,
     Baith Kirk & Queir;
Yet by my faith, ye-re no unwrought for,
    That I shall swear!

Wee image o' my bonie Betty,
As fatherly I kiss and daut thee,
As dear and near my heart I set thee,
     Wi' as gude will,
As a' the Priests had seen me get thee
    That's out o' h—

Sweet fruit o' monie a merry dint,
My funny toil is no a' tint;
Tho' ye come to the warld asklent,
     Which fools may scoff at,

In my last plack your part's be in't
              The better half o't.

Tho' I should be the waur bestead,
Thou's be as braw & bienly clad,
And thy young years as nicely bred
              Wi' education,
As ony brat o' Wedlock's bed,
              In a' thy station.

Lord grant that thou may ay inherit
Thy Mither's looks an' gracefu' merit;
An' thy poor, worthless Daddie's spirit,
              Without his failins!
'Twad please me mair to see thee heir it
              Than stocked mailins!

For if thou be, what I wad hae thee,
And tak the counsel I shall gie thee,
I'll never rue my trouble wi' thee,
              The cost nor shame o't,
But be a loving Father to thee,
              And brag the name o't.

23RD MAY

from The Inventory

BURNS DESCRIBES HIS BABY DAUGHTER, 'dear-bought Bess', with affectionate good humour in 'The Inventory'. The 'tax' he mentions was the Kirk's compulsory fine for the act of fornication, sarcastically – and pithily – referred to in 'The Fornicator' as 'buttock-hire'.

I ha'e nae wife; and that my bliss is,
An' ye have laid nae tax on misses;
An' then if kirk folks dinna clutch me,
I ken the devils dare na touch me.
Wi' weans I'm mair than weel contented,
Heav'n sent me ane mae than I wanted.
My sonsie smirking dear-bought Bess,
She stares the daddy in her face,
Enough of ought ye like but grace;
But her, my bonny sweet wee lady,
I've paid enough for her already,
An' gin ye tax her or her mither,
B' the L—d! ye'se get them a' thegither.

24TH MAY

Braw Lads o Galla Water

ON HIS TOUR OF THE SCOTTISH BORDERS in May 1787, Burns would have enjoyed the fine scenery of the three rivers mentioned in 'Braw Lads o Galla Water': Yarrow Water and Ettrick Water near Selkirk and, of course, Gala Water by Galashiels. In this song, a shepherdess declares that the natural beauty of these landmarks pales in comparison to the local 'lads'. In keeping with Burns's philosophy, she eschews wealth and aspires to a simple life, content with true love.

Braw, braw lads on Yarrow braes,
    Ye wander thro' the blooming heather;
But Yarrow braes, nor Ettrick shaws
    Can match the lads o' Galla Water.

But there is ane, a secret ane,
    Aboon them a' I lo'e him better:
And I'll be his, and he'll be mine,
    The bonie lad o' Galla Water.

Altho' his daddie was nae laird,
    And tho' I hae nae meikle tocher,
Yet rich in kindest, truest love,
    We'll tent our flocks by Galla Water.

It ne'er was wealth, it ne'er was wealth,
    That coft contentment, peace, or pleasure;
The bands and bliss o' mutual love,
    O that's the chiefest warld's treasure!

25TH MAY

Logan Braes
to the tune of **Logan Water**

THE 'MERRY MONTH OF MAY' offers little consolation to the troubled wife in 'Logan Braes' whose husband has been called away to the army, leaving her to pass 'widow'd nights and joyless days', and to raise her 'sweet nurslings' alone.

O Logan! sweetly didst thou glide,
That day I was my Willie's bride;
And years sin syne hae o'er us run,
Like Logan to the simmer sun.
But now thy flow'ry banks appear
Like drumlie winter, dark and drear,
While my dear lad maun face his faes,
Far, far frae me and Logan braes.

Again the merry month o' May
Has made our hills and valleys gay;
The birds rejoice in leafy bowers,
The bees hum round the breathing flow'rs:
Blythe morning lifts his rosy eye,
And ev'ning's tears are tears o' joy:
My soul, delightless, a' surveys,
While Willie's far frae Logan braes.

Within yon milk-white hawthorn bush,
Amang her nestlings sits the thrush;
Her faithfu' mate will share her toil,
Or wi' his song her cares beguile:-
But I, wi' my sweet nurslings here,

238

Nae mate to help, nae mate to cheer,
Pass widow'd nights, and joyless days,
While Willie's far frae Logan braes.

O wae upon you, men o' state,
That brethren rouse in deadly hate!
As ye make mony a fond heart mourn,
Sae may it on your heads return!
How can your flinty hearts enjoy
The widow's tears, the orphan's cry!
But soon may peace bring happy days,
And Willie hame to Logan braes!

26TH MAY

On Marriage
from a letter to Robert Ainslie

ON THIS DAY IN 1788, Burns wrote to Robert Ainslie with happy news of his marriage to Jean Armour. The bard suggests that marriage has brought him a sense of 'stability' and it seems that he had resolved, at least, to be faithful. In a letter written to James Johnson the previous day Burns declared, 'I am so enamoured with a certain girl's twin-bearing merit that I have given her a *legal* title to the best blood in my body; and so farewell Rakery!'

I have the pleasure to tell you that I have been extremely fortunate in all of my bargainings hitherto; Mrs Burns not only excepted, which title I now avow to the World.— I am truly pleased with this last affair: it has indeed added to my anxieties for Futurity, but it has given a stability to my mind and resolutions unknown before, and the poor girl has the most sacred enthusiasm of attachment to me, and has not a wish but to gratify my every idea of her deportment.—

27TH MAY

from Epistle to Davie, A Brother Poet

I N 'EPISTLE TO DAVIE' Burns juxtaposes the harsh reality of
agricultural labour, and social disparity in eighteenth-century
Scotland, with a description of 'joys that riches ne'er could buy'; the
comforting influence of his love for 'darling Jean'. Written early in
their relationship, it is apparent from these lines that Burns felt a
sincere affinity with the woman who would be his wife, and who he
valued not only as a lover, but as a friend.

But tent me, Davie, *Ace o' Hearts*!
(To say aught less wad wrang the *cartes*,
 And flatt'ry I detest)
This life has joys for you and I;
And joys that riches ne'er could buy;
 And joys the very best.
There's a' the *Pleasures o' the Heart*,
 The *Lover* an' the *Frien'*;
Ye hae your Meg, your dearest part,
 And I my darling Jean!
 It warms me, it charms me,
 To mention but her *name*:
 It heats me, it beets me,
 And sets me a' on flame!

O, all ye *Pow'rs* who rule above!
O Thou, whose very self art *love*!
 Thou know'st my words sincere!
The *life blood* streaming thro' my heart,
Or my more dear *Immortal part*,

Is not more fondly dear!
When heart-corroding care and grief
   Deprive my soul of rest,
Her dear idea brings relief,
   And solace to my breast.
     Thou Being, Allseeing,
       O hear my fervent pray'r!
     Still take her, and make her
       Thy most peculiar care!

All hail! ye tender feelings dear!
The smile of love, the friendly tear,
   The sympathetic glow!
Long since, this world's thorny ways
Had number'd out my weary days,
   Had it not been for you!
Fate still has blest me with a friend,
   In ev'ry care and ill;
And oft a more *endearing* band,
   A tye more tender still.
     It lightens, it brightens,
       The tenebrific scene,
     To meet with, and greet with,
       My Davie, or my Jean!

28TH MAY

On Blythe Hae I Been on Yon Hill
from a letter to Miss Lesley Baillie of Mayville, enclosing a
song I had composed on her, May 1793

TOWARDS THE END OF MAY 1793, Burns wrote to Lesley Baillie
(1768–1843), the daughter of an acquaintance, enclosing the song
'Blythe Hae I Been on Yon Hill'. He met Lesley only once when she
visited him in Dumfries with her father. And yet she obviously made
a lasting impression: this letter is very forthright in its flattery, and as
remarkable for its wit as its bravado.

Madam,

I have just put the last hand to the enclosed song; and I think that
I may say of it, as Nature can of you — "There is a work of mine,
finished in my very finest style!"—

Among your sighing swains, if there should be one whose ardent
sentiment and ingenuous modesty fetter his powers of speech in your
presence; with that look and attitude so native to your manner, and of
all others the most bewitching — Beauty listening to Compassion —
put my Ballad in the poor fellow's hand, just to give a little breathing
to the fervour of his soul.—

I have some pretence, Madam, to make you up the theme of
my song, as you and I are two downright singularities in human
nature. You will probably start at this assertion; but I believe it will
be allowed that a woman exquisitely charming, without the least
seeming consciousness of it, and a poet who never paid a compliment
but where it was justly due, are two of the greatest rarities on earth.—

29TH MAY

Blythe Hae I Been on Yon Hill
to the tune of Liggeram Cosh

AND HERE IS THE SONG enclosed with yesterday's letter. Burns would later refer to 'Blythe Hae I Been on Yon Hill' as 'one of the finest songs I ever made in my life; and, besides, is composed on a young lady, positively the most beautiful, lovely woman in the world'.

Blythe ha'e I been on yon hill,
　As the lambs before me;
Careless ilka thought and free,
　As the breeze flew o'er me:
Now nae langer sport and play,
　Mirth or sang can please me;
Lesley is sae fair and coy,
　Care and anguish seize me.

Heavy, heavy is the task,
　Hopeless love declaring;
Trembling, I dow nocht but glowr,
　Sighing, dumb, despairing!
If she winna ease the throes,
　In my bosom swelling;
Underneath the grass-green sod
　Soon maun be my dwelling.

30TH MAY

Address to the Toothache

BURNS WROTE TO HIS BOOKSELLER Peter Hill (1754–1837) on this day in 1795 that 'at present the delightful sensations of an omnipotent toothache so engross all my inner man as to put it out of my power even to write nonsense'. He bemoaned that 'fifty troops of infernal Spirits are riding post from ear-to-ear along my jaw-bones'. Just as relatable now as it was then, 'Address to the Toothache' is Burns's witty and remarkably accurate description of that most 'gnawing' and 'grim' of afflictions. That said, treatment for toothache in the eighteenth century was primitive at best and brutal at worst. The most a patient like Burns could hope for was a swift extraction that didn't fracture the jaw. Thank goodness for modern dentistry!

My curse upon your venom'd stang,
That shoots my tortur'd gums alang,
An' thro' my lug gies mony a twang,
⠀⠀⠀⠀⠀Wi' gnawing vengeance,
Tearing my nerves wi' bitter pang,
⠀⠀⠀⠀⠀Like racking engines!

When fevers burn, or ague freezes,
Rheumatics gnaw, or colics squeezes;
Our neighbour's sympathy may ease us,
⠀⠀⠀⠀⠀Wi' pitying moan;
But thee – thou hell o' a' diseases,
⠀⠀⠀⠀⠀Aye mocks our groan.

Adown my beard the slavers trickle;
I throw the wee stools o'er the meikle,
As round the fire the giglets keekle,
          To see me loup;
While, raving mad, I wish a heckle
          Were in their doup.

O' a' the num'erous human dools,
Ill har'sts, daft bargains, cutty stools,
Or worthy frien's raked i' the mools,
          Sad sight to see!
The tricks o' knaves or fash o'fools,
          Thou bear'st the gree!

Where'er that place be priests ca' hell,
Whence a' the tones o' mis'ry yell,
And ranked plagues their numbers tell,
          In dreadfu' raw,
Thou, Tooth-ache, surely bear'st the bell,
          Amang them a'!

O thou grim, mischief-making chiel,
That gars the notes o' discord squeal,
'Till daft mankind aft dance a reel
          In gore a shoe-thick;
Gie a' the faes o' Scotland's weel
          A townmond's Tooth-Ache!

31st MAY

O Were My Love Yon Lilac Fair

TODAY MARKS THE END of the month and, likewise, the end of spring. And so, we conclude May with 'O Were My Love Yon Lilac Fair': a song rich with seasonal imagery and full of references to nature, beauty and change, as feature in so many of Burns's works inspired by this bountiful time of year.

O were my Love yon Lilac fair,
   Wi' purple blossoms to the Spring;
And I a bird to shelter there,
   When wearied on my little wing.
How I wad mourn, when it was torn,
   By Autumn wild, and Winter rude!
But I would sing on wanton wing,
   When merry May its bloom renew'd.

O were my love yon vi'let sweet,
   That peeps frae 'neath the hawthorn spray;
And I mysel' the zephyr's breath,
   Amang its bonnie leaves to play.
I'd fan it wi' a constant gale,
   Beneath the noontide's scorching ray;
And sprinkle it wi' freshest dews
   At morning dawn and parting day.

O gin my love were yon red rose,
   That grows upon the castle wa'!
And I mysel' a drap of dew,
   Into her bonnie breast to fa'!
Oh, there, beyond expression blest,
   I'd feast on beauty a' the night;
Seal'd on her silk-saft falds to rest,
   Till fley'd awa' by Phebus' light.

JUNE

O my Luve's like a red, red rose,
That's newly sprung in June;
O my Luve's like the melodie,
That's sweetly play'd in tune.

from O My Luve's Like a Red, Red Rose

1st JUNE

O My Luve's Like a Red, Red Rose
to the tune of Low Down in the Broom

As one of burns's most famous love songs (alongside 'Ae Fond Kiss', which appears on Valentine's Day), 'O My Luve's Like a Red, Red Rose' adopts that ubiquitous symbol of love, the red rose, which also happens to be the flower for the month of June. A flower's bloom may indeed be fleeting, but the song's powerful natural imagery emphasises an everlasting love, capable of surviving both distance and time.

O my Luve's like a red, red rose,
    That's newly sprung in June;
O my Luve's like the melodie,
    That's sweetly play'd in tune.

As fair art thou, my bonie lass,
    So deep in luve am I;
And I will luve thee still, my dear,
    Till a' the seas gang dry.

Till a' the seas gang dry, my Dear,
    And the rocks melt wi' the sun:
O I will luve thee still my dear,
    While the sands o' life shall run.

And fare-thee-weel, my only Luve!
    And fare-thee-weel, a while!
And I will come again, my Luve,
    Tho' it were ten thousand mile!

2ND JUNE

Written in Friar's Carse Hermitage

BURNS ENTERED THE FIRST DRAFT of 'Written in Friar's Carse Hermitage' in his 'Second Commonplace Book' in June 1788. Several different versions exist; the version chosen here is from the 1793 Edinburgh edition of Burns's poems. It was written as a compliment to Robert Riddell of Glenriddell who had crafted for himself the (anonymous) literary persona of 'the bedesman on nydside'. In medieval times a beadsman would offer prayers in exchange for alms. Riddell went so far as to construct a hermitage (or a hermit's dwelling) on his land and Burns, upon visiting the imagined dwelling of Riddell's wise and humble alter ego, assumed his persona in this reflection on life and morality. The sentiments of the poem are very much in keeping with Burns's New Year compositions and thus we might reflect upon them in terms of a mid-year reaffirmation to live in the moment, and to live well.

Thou whom chance may hither lead,
Be thou clad in russet weed,
Be thou deckt in silken stole,
Grave these counsels on thy soul.

Life is but a day at most,
Sprung from night, in darkness lost;
Hope not sunshine ev'ry hour,
Fear not clouds will always lour.

As Youth and Love with sprightly dance,
Beneath thy morning star advance,
Pleasure with her siren air
May delude the thoughtless pair;

Let Prudence bless enjoyment's cup,
Then raptur'd sip, and sip it up.

As thy day grows warm and high,
Life's meridian flaming nigh,
Dost thou spurn the humble vale?
Life's proud summits would'st thou scale?
Check thy climbing step, elate,
Evils lurk in felon wait:
Dangers, eagle-pinioned, bold,
Soar around each cliffy hold,
While cheerful peace, with linnet song,
Chants the lowly dells among.

As the shades of ev'ning close,
Beck'ning thee to long repose;
As life itself becomes disease,
Seek the chimney-nook of ease.
There ruminate, with sober thought,
On all thou'st seen, and heard, and wrought;
And teach the sportive younkers round,
Saws of experience, sage and sound.
Say, man's true genuine estimate,
The grand criterion of his fate,
Is not, art thou high or low?
Did thy fortune ebb or flow?
Did many talents gild thy span?
Or frugal Nature grudge thee one?
Tell them, and press it on their mind,
As thou thyself must shortly find,
The smile or frown of aweful Heav'n,
To Virtue or to Vice is giv'n.
Say, to be just, and kind, and wise,
There solid self-enjoyment lies;
That foolish, selfish, faithless ways
Lead to the wretched, vile, and base.

Thus, resign'd and quiet, creep
To the bed of lasting sleep;
Sleep, whence thou shalt ne'er awake,
Night, where dawn shall never break,
Till future Life, future no more,
To light and joy the good restore,
To light and joy unknown before.

Stranger, go! Hea'vn be thy guide!
Quod the Beadsman of Nith-side.

3RD JUNE

from Address of Beelzebub

THE MONTH OF JUNE can be warm, but not, surely, as warm as hell. Both set the scene for this ironic political satire in which Satan salutes John, Earl of Breadalbane (1762–1834), for his efforts in 1786 to thwart further emigration of the 'rebel generation' of Highlanders and prevent the loss of labouring workers from Britain. In particular, in this opening section, it is worth noting Burns's mock incredulity that the 'Highland hounds' should ever have subsistence or, indeed, their 'Liberty' – in Scotland, or in any other land.

To the Right Honorable the Earl of Breadalbane, President of the Right Honorable and Honorable the Highland Society, which met on the 23d of May last, at the Shakespeare, Covent Garden, to concert ways and means to frustrate the designs of five hundred Highlanders who, as the Society were informed by Mr. M'Kenzie of Applecross, were so audacious as to attempt an escape from their lawful lords and masters whose property they were, by emigrating from the lands of Mr. M'Donald of Glengary to the wilds of Canada, in search of that fantastic thing — Liberty.

Long Life, my lord, an' health be yours,
Unskaith'd by hunger'd Highland boors;
Lord grant me nae duddie, desperate beggar,
Wi' dirk, claymore, and rusty trigger,
May twin auld Scotland o' a life
She likes – as lambkins like a knife.

Faith you and Applecross were right
To keep the Highland hounds in sight:
I doubt na! they wad bid nae better,
Than let them ance out owre the water,
Then up amang thae lakes and seas,
They'll mak what rules and laws they please:
Some daring Hancock, or a Franklin,
May set their Highland bluid a-ranklin;
Some Washington again may head them,
Or some Montgomery, fearless, lead them;
Till (God knows what may be effected
When by such heads and hearts directed),
Poor dunghill sons of dirt an' mire
May to Patrician rights aspire!
Nae sage North now, nor sager Sackville,
To watch and premier o'er the pack vile,
An' whare will ye get Howes and Clintons
To bring them to a right repentance
To cowe the rebel generation,
An' save the honour o' the nation?

They, an' be damn'd! what right hae they
To meat, or sleep, or light o' day?
Far less — to riches, pow'r, or freedom,
But what your lordship likes to gie them?

4TH JUNE

from Libel Summons

ALSO COMMONLY REFERRED TO as 'The Court of Equity'
or 'The Fornicator's Court', 'Libel Summons' satirises the
eighteenth-century Presbyterian Kirk's seeming voyeurism – not to
mention their perceived relish – in bringing the sexual activity of
parishioners to public attention. In this bawdy poem, presented as
a legal writ – *'Pro bono amor'* – Burns's imagined 'court of equity'
upholds the rules of sexuality. According to Burns, a man should
act when 'lasses haflins offer favour', but a fornicator must not
'refuse assistance' to 'them whom he has given existence'. Sex is not
a transgression, but failure to show respect for the act itself and for
one's partner is to 'Disdain the Fornicator's honour'. These extracts
detail the humiliating treatment of the abominable 'Clocky Brown'.
Note how Burns heightens the comedy, skilfully using language to
craft euphemisms inspired by Brown's profession as a clockmaker.

In truth and honour's name.— Amen.
Know all men by these presents plain,
The fourth of June, at Mauchline given,
The year 'tween eighty-five and seven;
We Fornicators by profession,
As by extraction from each session,
In way and manner here narrated,
Pro bono amor congregated,
Are by our brethren constituted,
A court of equity deputed:
With special authoriz'd direction,
To take beneath our strict inspection,
The stays unlacing *quondam maiden,*

With growing life, and anguish laden,
Who by the rascal is denied,
That led her thoughtless steps aside;
The wretch who can refuse assistance,
To them whom he has given existence,
He who when at a lass's by-job,
Defrauds her wi' a frig or dry-bob,
The coof who stands on *clish ma claver*,
When lasses haflins offer favour;
All who in ony way and manner,
Disdain the Fornicators honour,
We take cognizance there anent,
The proper judges competent.

First, poet BURNS he takes the chair,
Allow'd by all his title's fair,
And pass'd nem con without dissention,
He has a duplicate pretension.

[...]

Then, first, our fiscal by petition
Informs us, there is strong suspicion
That Coachman Dow, and Clocky Brown,
Baith residenters in this town;
In other words, you *Jock* and *Sandy*,
Hae been at warks of *Houghmagandy*,
And now when facts are come to light,
The matter ye deny outright.

First, Clocky *Brown*, there's witness borne,
And affidavit made and sworn,
Ae evening of a Mauchline fair,
That Jeanie's masts they were seen bare,
For ye had furl'd up her sails,
And was at play at heads and tails;

That ye hae made a *hurly burly*,
About Jean Mitchell's *tirly whorly*;
That ye here pendulum tried to alter,
And grizzled at her regulator;
And further still, ye cruel vandal,
A tale might even in hell be scandal;
That ye hae made repeated trials,
Wi' dregs and drugs, in doctor's vials,
Just as ye thought, wi' full infusion,
Your ain begotten wean to poison;
An' yet ye are sae scant o' grace,
As dared to lift your brazen face,
And offered to gie your aith,
Ye never lifted Jeanie's claith.

[…]

For you, John Brown, we gie ye notice,
So deep, so great, so black, your faut is,
Without ye by a quick repentance,
Acknowledge your's and Jean's acquaintance,
Remember this shall be your sentence:-

Our Beagles to the cross shall tak' ye,
And there shall mither naked mak' ye;
A rape they round the rump shall tak',
An' tye your hands behind your back,
Wi' joost an ell o' string allow'd,
To jink and hid ye frae the crowd;
Then shall ye stand a lawfu' seizure,
Induring Jeanine Mitchell's pleasure,
So be her pleasure don't surpass,
Five turnings o' a hauf hour glass;
Nor shall it in her pleasure be,
To turn you loose in less than three.

5TH JUNE

On a Bank of Flowers

HERE BURNS OFFERS his own adaptation of a traditional Scottish song. On a fine summer day, an admirer gazes upon the sleeping object of his affection and, overcome with desire, he steals a kiss. Scenes of male voyeurism and female vulnerability are a common motif in Scottish ballads although, traditionally, not all lovers are as naïve, 'faltering' or 'ardent' as 'Willie'.

On a bank of flowers, in a summer day,
    For summer lightly drest,
The youthful, blooming Nelly lay,
    With love and sleep oprest;
When Willie, wand'ring thro' the wood,
    Who for her favour oft had su'd;
He gaz'd, he wish'd, he fear'd, he blush'd,
    And trembled where he stood.

Her closed eyes like weapons sheath'd,
    Were seal'd in soft repose;
Her lips, still as she fragrant breath'd,
    It richer dy'd the rose;
The springing lilies, sweetly prest,
    Wild, wanton kissed her rival breast;
He gaz'd, he wish'd, he fear'd, he blush'd,
    His bosom ill at rest.

Her robes, light-waving in the breeze,
  Her tender limbs embrace;
Her lovely form, her native ease,
  All harmony and grace:
Tumultuous tides his pulses roll,
  A faltering, ardent kiss he stole;
He gaz'd, he wish'd, he fear'd, he blush'd,
  And sigh'd his very soul.

As flies the partridge from the brake,
  On fear-inspired wings,
So Nelly, starting, half-awake,
  Away affrighted springs:
But Willie follow'd — as he should,
  He overtook her in the wood;
He vow'd, he pray'd, he found the maid
  Forgiving all and good.

6TH JUNE

Ay Waukin O

IN CONTRAST WITH YESTERDAY'S SONG, the subject of today's summer reverie, 'Ay Waukin O', is female desire. Here Burns's protagonist is a woman who, distracted by thoughts of her 'true lover', cannot sleep for longing.

Simmer's a pleasant time,
　　Flowers of ev'ry colour;
The water rins o'er the heugh,
　　And I long for my true lover!

Ay waukin, O,
　　Waukin still and weary:
Sleep I can get nane,
　　For thinking on my Dearie.

When I sleep I dream,
　　When I wauk I'm irie;
Sleep can I get nane
　　For thinking on my Dearie.
　　　　Ay waukin &c.

Lanely night comes on,
　　A' the lave are sleepin:
I think on my bony lad,
　　And I bleer my een wi' greetin.
　　　　Ay waukin &c.

7TH JUNE

Thou Fair Eliza

BURNS'S REFERENCE TO the 'simmer moon' and to 'fairies' in this atmospheric song conjures images of a midsummer night. In folklore, midsummer is a magical time when the boundary between the human world and the world of the fae is at its most penetrable, enabling fairies to 'sport' with human emotions. Here it seems that 'fair Eliza' is sporting with the feelings of her 'despairing Lover'.

Turn again, thou fair Eliza,
    Ae kind blink before we part,
Rue on thy despairing Lover,
    Canst thou break his faithfu' heart?
Turn again, thou fair Eliza,
    If to love thy heart denies,
For pity hide the cruel sentence
    Under friendship's kind disguise!

Thee, dear maid, hae I offended,
    My offence is loving thee;
Canst thou wreck his peace for ever,
    Wha for thine would gladly die!
While the life beats in my bosom,
    Thou shalt mix in ilka throe:
Turn again, thou lovely maiden,
    Ae sweet smile on me bestow.

Not the bee upon the blossom,
    In the pride o' sinny noon;
Not the little sporting fairy,

All beneath the simmer moon;
Not the Poet in the moment
　　Fancy lightens in his e'e,
Kens the pleasure, feels the rapture,
　　That thy presence gies to me.

8TH JUNE

from The Twa Dogs, A Tale

T HAT BURNS TOOK PRIDE IN 'The Twa Dogs, A Tale' is clear
from the fact that he chose it as the opening poem for his first
published collection of poetry: the Kilmarnock edition of *Poems,
Chiefly in the Scottish Dialect* (1786). This social satire is presented
as a conversation between a 'ploughman's collie', Luath, and a more
refined, exotic breed of dog, Caesar. Luath was named in memory
of Burns's favourite collie who, in turn, was named after the Celtic
warrior Cú Chulainn's dog (a reference to James MacPherson's
translation of Ossian's *Fingal*). The opening dialogue presents a
direct comparison of the landed gentry with the peasant class. Burns
satirises the insatiable consumption of the 'Lairds', juxtaposing their
excess with the humble contentment of the 'Cotter'.

'Twas in that place o' Scotland's isle,
That bears the name o' auld King Coil,
Upon a bonie day in June,
When wearin' thro' the afternoon,
Twa Dogs, that were na thrang at hame,
Forgather'd ance upon a time.

The first I'll name, they ca'd him *Caesar*,
Was keepet for His Honor's pleasure;
His hair, his size, his mouth, his lugs,
Shew'd he was nane o' Scotland's dogs;
But whalpet some place far abroad,
Whare sailors gang to fish for cod.

His locked, letter'd, braw brass collar
Shew'd him the *gentleman* an' *scholar*;
But though he was o' high degree,
The fient a pride, nae pride had he,
But wad hae spent an hour caressan,
Ev'n wi' al Tinkler-gipsey's *messan*:
At Kirk or Market, Mill or Smiddie,
Nae tawted *tyke*, tho' e'er sae duddie,
But he wad stan't, as glad to see him,
An' stroan't on stanes an' hillocks wi' him.

The tither was a *ploughman's collie*,
A rhyming, ranting, raving billie,
Wha for his friend an' comrade had him,
And in his freaks had *Luath* ca'd him,
After some dog in *Highland sang*,
Was made lang syne, lord knows how lang.

He was a gash an' faithfu' *tyke*,
As ever lap a sheugh or dyke.
His honest, sonsie, baws'nt face,
Aye gat him friends in ilka place;
His breast was white, his towzie back
Weel clad wi' coat o' glossy black;
His gawsie tail, wi' upward curl,
Hung owre his hurdie's wi' a swirl.

Nae doubt but they were fain o' ither,
And unco pack an' thick thegither;

Wi' social nose whiles snuff'd an' snowket;
Whiles mice an' moodewurks they howket;
Whiles scour'd awa in lang excursion,
An' worry'd ither in diversion;
Till tir'd at last wi' mony a farce,
They set them down upon their arse,
An' there began a lang digression
About the *lords o' the creation.*

Caesar.

I've aften wonder'd, honest *Luath,*
What sort o' life poor dogs like you have;
An' when the *gentry's* life I saw,
What way *poor bodies* liv'd ava.

Our *Laird* gets in his racked rents,
His coals, his kane, an' a' his stents:
He rises when he likes himsel;
His flunkies answer at the bell;
He ca's his coach; he ca's his horse;
He draws a bonie, silken purse
As lang's my tail, where thro' the steeks,
The yellow letter'd *Geordie* keeks.

Frae morn to een, it's nought but toiling
At baking, roasting, frying, boiling;
An' tho' the gentry first are steghan,
Yet ev'n the *ha' folk* fill their peghan
Wi' sauce, ragouts, an' sic like trashtrie,
That's little short o' downright wastrie.
Our *Whipper-in,* wee, blasted wonner,
Poor, worthless elf, it eats a dinner,
Better than ony *Tenant-man*
His Honor has in a' the lan':
An' what poor *Cot-folk* pit their painch in,

I own it's past my comprehension.

Luath.

Trowth, Caesar, whiles they're fash't enough:
A *Cotter* howkan in a sheugh,
Wi' dirty stanes biggan a dyke,
Bairan a quarry, an' sic like;
Himsel, a wife, he thus sustains,
A smytrie o' wee, duddie weans,
An' nought but his han'-daurk, to keep
Them right an' tight in thack an' raep.

An' when they meet wi' sair disasters,
Like loss o' health or want o' masters,
Ye maist wad think, a wee touch langer,
An' they maun starve o' cauld an' hunger:
But how it comes, I never kent yet,
They're maistly wonderfu' contented;
An' buirdly chiels, an' clever hizzies,
Are bred in sic a way as this is.

9TH JUNE

On the Prospect of Ellisland
from a letter to Margaret Chalmers, 14th March 1788

BURNS SPENT MOST OF 1787 AND 1788 in Edinburgh making the most of his success as a celebrated poet. The city also served as a base for his tours of Scotland and the north of England. However, he was aware that this way of life, although enjoyable, was untenable. And so the poet focused his attention on provisions for the future. He set in motion an application to become an officer of the excise, and also decided to return to farming and settle down to a family with Jean Armour. Burns's resolve is clear from this letter, as is his trepidation at the prospect of resuming manual, agricultural labour.

Yesternight I completed a bargain with Mr. Miller of Dalswinton for the farm of Ellisland on the banks of the Nith, between five and six miles above Dumfries. I begin at Whitsunday to build a house, drive lime, &c. and heaven be my help! For it will take a strong effort to bring my mind into the routine of business. I have discharged all the army of my former pursuits, fancies and pleasures; a motley host! And have literally and strictly retained only the ideas of a few friends, which I have incorporated into a life-guard. I trust in Dr. Johnson's observation, 'Where much is attempted, something is done.' Firmness both in sufferance and exertion, is a character I would wish to be thought to possess; and have always despised the whining yelp of complaint, and the cowardly, feeble resolve.

10TH JUNE

Awa Whigs Awa

J AMES FRANCIS EDWARD STUART, 'the Old Pretender', was born on this day in 1688. His birth exacerbated political unrest at the prospect of ongoing rule by a Catholic monarchy and set in motion the 'Glorious Revolution'. His father, King James VII of Scotland and II of England (1633–1701), was deposed and replaced by his half-sister Mary II (1662–1694) alongside her husband, William of Orange (1650–1702). Thereafter, the white rose became a Jacobite symbol of the exiled Stuart dynasty.

'Awa Whigs Awa' makes explicit reference to 'our ancient crown', 'fa'n in the dust', and to the symbolic rose and thistle (the thistle is the national flower of Scotland). That an unseasonable June frost 'withers' these 'posies' is a metaphor for the disturbance of the natural order; an allusion to the ancient belief that monarchs are ordained by God, not appointed by man.

Awa whigs awa,
Awa whigs awa,
Ye're but a pack o' traitor louns,
    Ye'll do nae gude at a'.

Our thrissles flourish'd fresh and fair,
    And bonie bloom'd our roses;
But whigs cam like a frost in June,
    And wither'd a' our posies.
        Awa whigs &c.

Our ancient crown's fa'n in the dust;
    Deil blin' them wi' the stoure o't,
And write their names in his black beuk
    Wha gae the whigs the power o't!
        Awa whigs &c.

Our sad decay in church and state
    Surpasses my descriving:
The whigs cam o'er us for a curse,
    And we have done wi' thriving.
        Awa whigs &c.

Grim Vengeance lang has taen a nap,
    But we may see him wauken:
Gude help the day when royal heads
    Are hunted like a maukin.
        Awa whigs &c.

11TH JUNE

Epistle to Hugh Parker, June 1788

BURNS TOOK OVER Ellisland Farm on the eleventh of June 1788. It was no small undertaking. In a letter of negotiation to his landlord several months earlier Burns wrote:

> the farm is so worn out, and every bit of it good for any thing is this year under tillage; at least the fields are so intersected with pieces under crop that four horses which I will need this summer for driving lime and materials for building, with a cow for a married servant perhaps the first year, and one for myself as I must be on the spot, will eat up the whole pasture.

The land would prove difficult to cultivate and Burns would have to build a house for himself and Jean Armour to inhabit. Daunted by the enormity of the task, separated from his new wife and isolated with his thoughts, Burns conveys his declining mood in 'Epistle to Hugh Parker'. The poet's dismal and lonely new dwelling leads him to elevate the familiar in an overblown passage about his horse Jenny Geddes: 'my Pegasean Pride!' Finally, he expresses his longing to escape the 'peat reek i' my head', by rejoining his friends and family in Tarbolton.

In this strange land, this uncouth clime,
A land unknown to prose or rhyme;
Where words ne'er crost the muse's heckles,
Nor limpet in poetic shackles;
A land that prose did never view it,
Except when drunk he stacher't thro' it;
Here, ambush'd by the chimla cheek,
Hid in an atmosphere of reek,

I hear a wheel thrum i' the neuk,
I hear it – for in vain I leuk.
The red peat gleams, a fiery kernel,
Enhusked by a fog infernal:
Here, for my wonted rhyming raptures,
I sit and count my sins by chapters;
For life and spunk like ither Christians,
I'm dwindled down to mere existence,
Wi' nae converse but Gallowa' bodies,
Wi' nae kend face but Jenny Geddes.
Jenny, my Pegasean pride!
Dowie she saunters down Nithside,
And aye a westlin leuk she throws,
While tears hap o'er her auld brown nose!
Was it for this, wi' canny care,
Thou bure the Bard through many a shire?
At howes or hillocks never stumbled,
And late or early never grumbled?
O, had I power like inclination,
I'd heeze thee up a constellation,
To canter with the Sagitarre,
Or loup the ecliptic like a bar;
Or turn the pole like any arrow;
Or, when auld Phebus bids good-morrow,
Down the zodiac urge the race,
And cast dirt on his godship's face;
For I could lay my bread and kail
He'd ne'er cast saut upo' thy tail.
Wi' a' this care and a' this grief,
And sma', sma' prospect of relief,
And nought but peat reek i' my head,
How can I write what ye can read?
Tarbolton, twenty-fourth o' June,
Ye'll find me in a better tune;
But till we meet and weet our whistle,
Tak this excuse for nae epistle.

12TH JUNE

On Ellisland
from a letter to Frances Dunlop, 13th June 1788

IT IS APPARENT FROM the following extract that Burns, recently set to work at Ellisland, was nervous about the farm's prospects. The poet attempts to rationalise his dreary outlook, suggesting that the trials of his formative years have led to his depression. It seems likely that his own father's unfortunate farming ventures were playing on his mind.

This is the second day, my honored Friend, that I have been on my farm.— A solitary inmate of an old, smoky 'SPENCE'; far from every Object I love, or by whom I am belov'd, nor any acquaintance older than yesterday except Jenny Geddes the old mare I ride on; while uncouth Cares and novel Plans hourly insult my awkward Ignorance & bashful inexperience.— There is a foggy Atmosphere native to my soul in the hour of care, consequently the dreary Objects seem larger than the life.— Extreme Sensibility, irritated and prejudiced on the gloomy side by a series of Misfortunes and Disappointments at that period of my existence when the soul is laying in her cargoe of ideas for the voyage of Life is, I believe, the principal cause of this unhappy frame of mind.—

13TH JUNE

In the Character of a Ruined Farmer
to the tune of Go from my window, love, do!

T ODAY'S SONG IS ONE OF BURNS'S EARLIEST WORKS, thought
to have been inspired by the misfortunes of his father. In 1777
William Burnes leased Lochlea, a farm of a hundred and thirty acres
near Tarbolton, from the Ayr merchant David McLure. McLure
was supportive of the family in the early days of their tenancy.
However, over time, Burnes's efforts to cultivate the boggy land
proved futile and he soon fell into arrears. His relationship with
McLure deteriorated to the extent that, in May 1783, the landlord
had a warrant of sequestration issued against Burnes. Burns's
father successfully challenged the warrant at the Court of Session
in Edinburgh, winning his case on 27th January 1784. However, the
considerable legal fees meant that the family were nearly bankrupted
in the process. Burnes, whose health had deteriorated significantly
over the course of these events, died on the 13th of February 1784,
just a few weeks after his vindication in court. It is little wonder
that Robert Burns, who had experienced the tragic consequences of
his hard-working father's misfortune, was plagued by anxiety and
self-doubt as he commenced his own farming endeavour at Ellisland.

The sun he is sunk in the west;
All creatures retired to rest,
While here I sit, all sore beset,
    With sorrow, grief, and woe:
And it's O, fickle Fortune, O!

The prosperous man is asleep,
Nor hears how the whirlwinds sweep;
But Misery and I must watch
   The surly tempest blow:
And it's O, fickle Fortune, O!

There lies the dear Partner of my breast;
Her cares for a moment at rest:
Must I see thee, my youthful pride,
   Thus brought so very low!
And it's O, fickle Fortune, O!

There lie my sweet babies in her arms;
No anxious fear their little hearts alarms;
But for their sake my heart does ache,
   With many a bitter throe:
And it's O, fickle Fortune, O!

I once was by Fortune carest:
I once could relieve the distrest:
Now life's poor support, hardly earn'd
   My fate will scarce bestow:
And it's O, fickle Fortune, O!

No comfort, no comfort I have!
How welcome to me were the grave!
But then my wife and children dear
   O, whither would they go!
And it's O, fickle Fortune, O!

O whither, O whither shall I turn!
All friendless, forsaken, forlorn!
For in this world, Rest or Peace,
   I never more shall know!
And it's O, fickle Fortune, O!

14TH JUNE

On Responsibility
from a letter to Robert Ainslie, 8th June 1788

IN THIS EXTRACT FROM A LETTER to his bachelor friend Robert Ainslie, Burns demonstrates a keen awareness of his responsibilities as a husband and father. He advises that 'rakehelly dogs' – or, rather, promiscuous young men as he himself once was – should not boast of their recklessness and freedom from commitment. Hindsight, after all, is a wonderful thing. Certainly, it's apparent from Burns's writing around the time of his marriage and move to Ellisland that this episode represented a period of significant growth as regards the poet's mindset.

Life, my dear Sir, is a serious matter. You know by experience that a man's individual self is a good deal, but believe me, a wife and family of children, whenever you have the honour to be a husband and a father, will show you that your present and most anxious hours of solitude are spent on trifles. The welfare of those who are very dear to us, whose only support, hope, and stay we are — this, to a generous mind, is another sort of more important object of care than any concerns whatever which centre merely in the individual. On the other hand, let no young, rakehelly dog among you, make a song of his pretended liberty and freedom from care.

15TH JUNE

Country Lassie

W HEN BURNS FIRST MOVED to Ellisland in June 1788 his own 'Country Lassie', Jean, was not with him. The farm was not yet properly cultivated and the farmhouse was unhabitable, particularly for Jean and their young son, Robert. It would be a year before the family could properly set up home. That said, whatever their hardships, Burns's correspondence makes clear that the poet was assured of Jean's devotion to him; a devotion that had survived even the most determined meddling from her own family.

In 'Country Lassie' a young woman shuns the advice of an old 'dame' and expresses her intention to marry for love rather than material possession. The pastoral imagery of the opening stanza paints an idyllic picture, inspired by this time of year.

In simmer when the hay was mawn,
    And corn wav'd green in ilka field,
While claver blooms white o'er the lea,
    And roses blaw in ilka beild;
Blythe Bessie in the milking shiel,
    Says, I'll be wed come o't what will;
Out spak a dame in wrinkled eild,
    O' gude advisement comes nae ill.

Its ye hae wooers mony ane,
    And lassie ye're but young ye ken;
Then wait a wee, and canie wale,
    A routhie butt, a routhie ben:

There's Johnie o' the Buskie glen,
  Fu' is his barn, fu' is his byre;
Take this frae me, my bonie hen,
  It's plenty beets the luver's fire.

For Johnie o' the Buskie glen,
  I dinna care a single flie;
He loes sae weel his craps and kye,
  He has nae love to spare for me:
But blythe's the blink o' Robie's e'e,
  And weel I wat he loes me dear;
Ae blink o' him I wad na gie
  For Buskie glen and a' his gear.

O thoughtless lassie, life's a faught,
  The canniest gate, the strife is sair;
But aye fu'-han't is fechtin' best,
  A hungry care's an unco care:
But some will spend, and some will spare,
  An' wilfu' folk maun hae their will;
Syne as ye brew, my maiden fair,
  Keep mind that ye maun drink the yill.

O gear will buy me rigs o' land,
  And gear will buy me sheep and kye;
But the tender heart o' leesome loove,
  The gowd and siller canna buy:
We may be poor, Robie and I,
  Light is the burden Loove lays on;
Content and Loove brings peace and joy,
  What mair hae Queens upon a throne.

16TH JUNE

On Marriage and Friendship
from a letter to 'E', c.1781

O UR NAME FOR THE MONTH OF JUNE is thought to be derived from 'Juno', the Roman goddess of marriage and childbirth. It is perhaps unsurprising, given Burns's history with women, that Jean Armour was not the only woman to whom he proposed marriage. A series of letters believed to have been written to the elusive 'E' (thought now to be Eliza Gebbie, a farmer's daughter from Galston) around 1781, refer both to the bard's proposal and to her refusal. These are often read in the context of Burns's autobiographical letter to John Moore where he explains that: 'a belle-fille whom I adored, and who had pledged her soul to meet me in the field of matrimony, jilted me with peculiar circumstances of mortification'. It is thought that Burns was refused again by Margaret (Peggy) Chalmers in 1787. A laird's daughter, Margaret was just out of the ploughman poet's reach (see 5th November).

In this extract from a letter to 'E', the young Burns takes a very pragmatic view of marriage, emphasising the importance of friendship and understanding, rather than passion, or 'flames and raptures'.

People may talk of flames and raptures as long as they please; and a warm fancy, with a flow of youthful spirits, may make them feel something like what they describe; but sure I am, the nobler faculties of the mind with kindred feelings of the heart, can only be the foundation of friendship, and it has always been my opinion, that the married life was only friendship in a more exalted degree.

17TH JUNE

Sandy and Jockie

TODAY'S LINES OFFER a light-hearted articulation of a message already encountered in works such as 'The Twa Dogs' and 'Country Lassie': that true happiness cannot be bought. Burns's views are very clear: people should marry for love, not money.

Twa bony lads were Sandy and Jockie;
　　Jockie was lo'ed but Sandy unlucky;
Jockie was laird baith of hills and of vallies,
　　But Sandy was nought but the king o' gude fellows.

Jockie lo'ed Madgie, for Madgie had money,
　　And Sandy lo'ed Mary, for Mary was bony:
Ane wedded for Love, ane wedded for treasure,
　　So Jockie had siller, and Sandy had pleasure.

18TH JUNE

My Wife's a Winsome Wee Thing

THE REFRAIN IN 'My Wife's a Winsome Wee Thing' might objectify the woman in this partnership (Burns was writing in the eighteenth century, after all), but the second and final stanzas describe an ardent love and a couple truly united as they navigate life, with all of its complications and responsibilities.

My wife's a winsome wee thing,
She is a handsome wee thing,
She is a lo'esome wee thing,
    This sweet wee wife o' mine.

I never saw a fairer,
I never lo'ed a dearer,
And neist my heart I'll wear her,
    For fear my jewel tine.

She is a winsome wee thing,
She is a handsome wee thing,
She is a lo'esome wee thing,
    This dear wee wife o' mine.

The warld's wrack we share o't,
The warstle and the care o't;
Wi' her I'll blythely bear it,
    And think my lot divine.

19TH JUNE

On Marriage

BURNS RECOGNISED THAT marriage was not always straightforward, and he attributed this to human nature. Burns's view was that men were prone to 'Inconstancy in Love' (see 26th February), and although he expressed his desire to be married on more than one occasion, marriage simply wasn't compatible with his nature as a self-confessed 'fickle man'. These lines 'On Marriage' capture his frustration.

That hackney'd judge of human life,
    The Preacher and the King,
Observes:– 'The man that gets a wife
    He gets a noble thing.'

But how capricious are mankind,
    Now loathing, now desirous!
We married men, how oft we find
    The best of things will tire us!

20TH JUNE

John Anderson My Jo

HERE WE HAVE BURNS'S polite version of the traditional bawdy
song of the same name. The bard's version has become one of the
most famous Scottish songs ever written. Here a woman reminisces
about her lover in his youth, the couple's shared life as they 'clamb the
hill thegither', and their mutual physical decline. Finally, the ageing
lovers of Burns's song resolve to 'sleep the gither at the foot' in this
understated, yet extremely romantic song about human relationships.

John Anderson my jo, John,
   When we were first acquent;
Your locks were like the raven,
   Your bonie brow was brent;
But now your brow is beld, John,
   Your locks are like the snaw;
But blessings on your frosty pow,
   John Anderson my Jo.

John Anderson my jo, John,
   We clamb the hill thegither;
And mony a canty day, John,
   We've had wi' ane anither:
Now we maun totter down, John,
   And hand in hand we'll go;
And sleep the gither at the foot,
   John Anderson my Jo.

21st JUNE

On Marriage
from a letter to Alexander Cunningham, 10th September 1792

HERE IS BURNS'S tongue-in-cheek account of married life, written some years after his and Jean's marriage. Burns's advice to his newly-wed crony regarding 'Good-wife-ship' is in part sound, as he places emphasis on the importance of personality: 'Good Nature', 'Good Sense' and 'Wit'. His typically forthright masculinity is apparent, however, from the relish with which he refers to women's physical charms and to 'fine waists', which are 'spoilt' (it is implied) by child-bearing.

Apropos, how do you like, I mean *really* like, the Married Life?— Ah, my Friend! Matrimony is quite a different thing from what your love-sick youths and sighing girls take it to be!— But Marriage, we are told, is appointed by God and I shall never quarrel with any of His Institutions.— I am a Husband of older standing than you, and shall give you *my* ideas of the Conjugal State.— (*En passant*, you know I am no Latin, is not "Conjugal" derived from "Jugum" a yoke?) Well then, the scale of Good-wife-ship I divide into ten parts.— Good Nature, four; Good Sense, two; Wit, one; Personal Charms, viz. a sweet face, eloquent eyes, fine limbs, graceful carriage, (I would add a fine waist too, but that is so soon spoilt you know) all these, one. As for the other qualities belonging to, or attending on, a Wife, such as, fortune, connections, education, (I mean, education extraordinary) family-blood, &c. divide the two remaining degrees among them as you please; only, remember that all these minor properties must be expressed by *fractions*; for there is not any one of them, in the aforesaid scale, entitled to the dignity of an *integer*.—

22ND JUNE

In Anticipation of Another Child
from a letter to Frances Dunlop, 22nd June 1789

FATHER'S DAY IS CELEBRATED ANNUALLY on the third Sunday of June. Robert Burns first became a father to Elizabeth, or 'dear-bought Bess', in 1785 and we know that he fathered at least twelve children with at least five women in the eleven years between then and his death in 1796.

On the third of September 1786, although she wasn't married to Burns at the time, Jean Armour gave birth to their twins, Robert and Jean (named after their parents). Jean died in infancy on the 20th of October 1787. In May 1787, less than one year after the birth of Jean's twins, Burns accepted paternal responsibility for a child born to an Edinburgh servant, May (or Meg) Cameron. It would appear that the bard embarked on several affairs over the course of 1787–1788 when he was residing in Edinburgh, as he is also known to have fathered a child with Agnes McLehose's maid Jennie Clow, who gave birth to a boy late in 1788. Burns had, all the time, maintained contact with Jean Armour who in 1788 delivered a second set of twins, both of whom sadly died shortly thereafter.

Following the couple's marriage, Jean gave birth to five further children: Francis Wallace Burns (1789–1803), William Nicol Burns (1791–1872), Elizabeth Riddell Burns (1792–1795), James Glencairn Burns (1794–1865) and Maxwell Burns (1796–1799). Furthermore, William Nicol's birth coincided with that of Burns's daughter Elizabeth (1791–1873), known as Betty, who was the result of his extramarital affair with Helen Anne Park.

He was undeniably promiscuous, but Burns appears to have sincerely loved his family. He took great pride in his children and was beset by grief following the loss of those who died in infancy. In the following letter to Frances Dunlop, Burns looks forward to the arrival of Francis Wallace Burns and writes of his aspirations for his son, who was to be named in honour of his correspondent and the Scottish hero she claimed was her ancestor: Sir William Wallace.

Your little dear namesake has not yet made his appearance, but he is every day expected.— I promise myself great assistance in training up his young mind to dignity of sentiment and greatness of soul, from the honoured name by which he is called.— I know many would despise and more would laugh at such a way of thinking, but with all reverence to the cold theorems of Reason, a few honest Prejudices and benevolent Prepossessions, are of the utmost consequence, and give the finishing polish to the illustrious characters of Patriot, Benefactor, Father and Friend; and all the tender relations included in the endearing word, Family.— What a poor, blighted, rickety breed are the Virtues and charities when they take their birth from geometrical hypothesis and mathematical demonstration? And what a vigorous Offspring are they when they owe their origin to, and are nursed with the vital blood of a heart glowing with the noble enthusiasm of Generosity, Benevolence and Greatness of Soul?— The first may do very well for those philosophers who look on the world of man as one vast ocean, and each individual as a little vortex in it whose sole business and merit is to absorb as much as it can in its own centre; but the last is absolutely and essentially necessary when you would make a Leonidas, a Hannibal, an Alfred or a WALLACE.—

23RD JUNE

On William Wallace
from a letter to Frances Dunlop, 15th November 1786

IN HIS FIRST LETTER to Frances Dunlop, Burns provides an account of his youthful hero-worship of her 'Illustrious Ancestor', Sir William Wallace (c.1270–1305). Wallace was a leader in the Scottish War of Independence against Edward I of England, and famously led the Scots to victory in the 1297 Battle of Stirling Bridge. Following defeat in 1298, Wallace was eventually captured and taken to London where he was hung, drawn and quartered for treason. Burns's quotes here are from James Thomson's *Autumn* (1730) and William Hamilton of Gilbertfield's *The Life and Heroick Actions of the Renoun'd Sir William Wallace* (1722). Of particular note is Burns's wish to 'make a song' on Wallace, 'equal to his merits'.

Had you been thoroughly acquainted with me, Madam, you could not have touched my darling heart-chord more sweetly than by noticing my attempts to celebrate your illustrious Ancestor, the SAVIOUR OF HIS COUNTRY—

> "Great Patriot hero! Ill-requited Chief!"

The first books I met with in my early years were the lives of Hannibal, and Sire William Wallace.— For several of my earlier years I had few other Authors: and many a solitary hour have I stole out, after the laborious vocations of the day, to shed a tear over their glorious, but unfortunate Story.— In those boyish days, I remember in particular being much struck with that part of Wallace's history where these lines occur –

"Syne to the Leglen wood when it was late
To make a silent and safe retreat."—

I chose a fine summer Sunday, the only day of the week in my power, and walked half a dozen miles to pay my respects to the "Leglen Wood," with as much devout enthusiasm as ever Pilgrim did to Loretto; and as I explored every den and dell where I could suppose my heroic Countryman to have sheltered, I recollect (for even then I was a Rhymer) that my heart glowed with a wish to be able to make a Song on him equal to his merits.—

24TH JUNE

Scots Wha Hae

BURNS IMMORTALISED William Wallace and Robert the Bruce (1274–1329) in the opening lines of one of the most rousing and patriotic Scottish songs ever written: 'Scots Wha Hae' (or 'Robert Bruce's March to Bannockburn').

On this day in 1314, Bruce led the Scottish army to victory against Edward II of England in the battle of Bannockburn, fought near Stirling. It was a pivotal moment in the Scottish War of Independence. In a letter to George Thomson, Burns writes that he was inspired to compose the song in 'a pitch of enthusiasm on the theme of Liberty and Independence' declaring, 'May God ever defend the cause of Truth and Liberty, as he did that day!— Amen!'

Scots, wha hae wi' Wallace bled,
Scots, wham Bruce has aften led,
Welcome to your gory bed,
   Or to Victorie.

Now's the day, and now's the hour;
See the front o' battle lour;
See approach proud Edward's power
   Chains and Slaverie.

Wha will be a traitor knave?
Wha can fill a coward's grave?
Wha sae base as be a Slave?
   Let him turn and flie.—

Wha for Scotland's King and Law,
Freedom's sword will strongly draw,
Freeman stand, or Freeman fa',
   Let him follow me.

By Oppression's woes and pains,
By your Sons in servile chains,
We will drain our dearest veins,
   But they shall be free!

Lay the proud Usurpers low!
Tyrants fall in every foe!
Liberty's in every blow!—
   Let us Do — or Die!!!

25TH JUNE

On Bannockburn
from a letter to the Earl of Buchan, 12th January 1794

I N A LETTER TO THE EARL OF BUCHAN, Burns expresses his
fascination with the history of the Battle of Bannockburn and
provides some insight into the reasons for which it fuelled his sense
of patriotism.

Independent of my enthusiasm as a Scotchman, I have rarely met
with any thing in History which interests my feelings as a Man
equally with the story of Bannockburn.— On the one hand, a cruel
but able Usurper, leading on the finest army in Europe, to extinguish
the last spark of Freedom among a greatly-daring and greatly injured
People; on the other hand, the desperate relics of a gallant Nation,
devoting themselves to rescue their bleeding Country, or perish with
her.—

Liberty! Thou art a prize truly and indeed invaluable!— For never
canst thou be too dearly bought!

26TH JUNE

On Burns's Final Illness
from a letter to James Clarke, 26th June 1796

B URNS WAS PLAGUED by ill heath during his short life and there are references throughout his poems and letters to periods of 'melancholy', physical injuries and rheumatic complaints. The first signs of the illness which would eventually prove fatal began in the winter of 1795 when the poet was confined to bed for several weeks. In the months that followed, his health steadily declined, and by the 26th of June 1796 Burns had fully realised that he was not going to recover. To make matters worse, Burns's illness and the reduction in his wages from the excise meant that he was in serious financial difficulty and facing the threat of debtors' jail. This letter conveys the full morbid force of Burns's awareness of his own mortality, along with his dire financial circumstances.

My dear Clarke,

Still, still the victim of affliction, were you to see the emaciated figure who now holds the pen to you, you would not know your old friend.— Whether I shall ever get about again, is only known to Him, the Great Unknown, whose creature I am.— Alas, Clarke, I begin to fear the worst!— As to my individual Self, I am tranquil;— I would despise myself if I were not; but Burns's poor widow! And half a dozen of his dear little ones, helpless orphans, there I am weak as a woman's tear.— Enough of this! 'tis half my disease!—

I duly received your last, inclosing the note.— It came extremely in time, and I was much obliged to your punctuality.— Again I must request you to do me the same kindness.— Be so very good as *by return of post* to inclose me another note.— I trust you can do it without much inconvenience, and it will seriously oblige me.— If I must go, I leave a few friends behind me whom I shall regret while consciousness remains — I know I shall live in their remembrance.—

Adieu dear Clarke! That I shall ever see you again, is, I am afraid, highly improbable.—

R Burns

27TH JUNE

To Miss Jessy Lewars

JESSY LEWARS (1778–1855) helped to care for Burns during his final illness. She was, according to Burns, a good singer, and so Jean had her husband write to James Johnson requesting a copy of *The Scots Musical Museum* as a gift for their kind friend. Burns did so, emphasising that he was 'anxious to have it soon', possibly so that he could inscribe it with the following touching lines. Burns dated the verse on the 26th of June 1796, less than a month prior to his death.

Thine be the volumes, Jessy fair,
And with them take the Poet's prayer;—
That Fate may in her fairest page,
With every kindliest, best presage
Of future bliss, enrol thy name:
With native worth, and spotless fame,
And wakeful caution to beware
Of ill, but chief, man's felon snare;
All blameless joys on earth we find,
And all the treasures of the mind —
These be thy guardian and reward!
So prays thy faithful friend, The Bard.

R Burns

28TH JUNE

Epigram

A T THE END OF JUNE 1787, Burns made a short tour taking in Glasgow, Dumbarton, Loch Lomond, Arrochar, Inverary and Greenock. It is possible that Burns visited Inverary with the intention of calling on the Duke of Argyll – one of the subscribers to the Edinburgh edition of Burns's *Poems, Chiefly in the Scottish Dialect* (1787) – at Inverary Castle. Anecdote has it that, when staying at the inn there, Burns and his companion found themselves overlooked in favour of several of the Duke's guests. Burns is thought to have vented his frustration in the following lines.

Whoe'er he be that sojourns here,
    I pity much his case,
Unless he come to wait upon
    The Lord their God, his Grace.

There's naething here but Highland pride,
    And Highland scab and hunger;
If Providence has sent me here,
    'Twas surely in an anger.

29TH JUNE

from Second Epistle to Davie

BURNS'S SECOND VERSE EPISTLE to his poet friend David Sillar was composed around this time in 1786. In the following stanzas Burns once again proclaims his love of poetry. He emphasises that 'rhyme' is his enduring pleasure, and he encourages his friend to make 'the muse' his solace in a world that plays 'monie a shavie', or many a trick.

> Leeze me on rhyme! it's aye a treasure,
> My chief, amaist my only pleasure;
> At hame, a-fiel', at wark, or leisure,
> The Muse, poor hizzie!
> Tho' rough an' raploch be her measure,
> She's seldom lazy.
>
> Haud to the Muse, my daintie Davie:
> The warl' may play you mony a shavie;
> But for the Muse, she'll never leave ye,
> Tho' e'er sae puir,
> Na, even tho' limpin wi' the spavie
> Frae door tae door.

30TH JUNE

On Burns's West Highland Tour
from a letter to James Smith, 30th June 1787

T HIS MONTH DRAWS TO A CLOSE with the young, carefree poet's account of a drunken horse race at Loch Lomond-side on this day in 1787; a highlight of his tour of the west Highlands. Ironically, given one of this month's recurring themes – marriage – Burns insists in this letter that his poetic temperament means that he 'must never marry'. Contradictions such as this are abundant in the biography and literary works of Robert Burns; contradictions which have served only to fuel our ongoing fascination with this most intriguing and talented of bards.

My two friends and I rode soberly down the Loch side, till by came a Highlandman at the gallop, on a tolerably good horse, but which had never known the ornaments of iron or leather. We scorned to be out-galloped by a Highlandman, so off we started, whip and spur. My companions, though seemingly gaily mounted, fell sadly astern; but my old mare, Jenny Geddes, one of the Rosinante family, she strained past the Highlandman in spite of all his efforts, with the hair-halter: just as I was passing him, Donald wheeled his horse, as if to cross before me to mar my progress, when down came his horse, and threw his rider's breekless a—e in a clipt hedge; and down came Jenny Geddes over all, and my bardship between her and the Highlandman's horse. Jenny Geddes trod over me with such cautious reverence, that matters were not so bad as might well have been expected; so I came off with a few cuts and bruises, and a thorough resolution to be a pattern of sobriety for the future.

I have yet fixed nothing with respect to the serious business of life. I am, just as usual, a rhyming, mason-making, raking, aimless, idle fellow. However, I shall somewhere have a farm soon. I was going to say a wife; but that must never be my blessed lot. I am but a younger son of the house of Parnassus, and, like other sons of great families, I may intrigue, if I choose to run all risks, but must not marry.

JULY

Now Robin lies in his last lair,
He'll gabble rhyme, nor sing nae mair;
Cauld poverty, wi' hungry stare,
Nae mair shall fear him;
Nor anxious fear, nor cankert care,
E'er mair come near him.

from Elegy on the Death of Robert Ruisseaux

The Farewell. To the Brethren of St James's Lodge, Tarbolton

BURNS'S ACTIVITIES AS A FREEMASON have been well documented in his writing and by his biographers. Initiated to St David's Lodge, No. 174, Tarbolton in July 1781, he then became a Master of St James's Lodge, Tarbolton in July 1784, and was made a member of Canongate Kilwinning Lodge, No. 2, during his time in Edinburgh in 1786. The Freemasons offered an important network for Burns, particularly as an emerging poet, and did much to promote his work during and beyond his lifetime. Much more than this, however, Freemasonry in the eighteenth century represented an enlightened cultural space which appealed to the sociable bard's enjoyment of male conviviality, as well as his proclivity for intellectual improvement. 'The Farewell', one of several poems inspired by Burns's Masonic brethren, appeared in the Kilmarnock Edition of *Poems, Chiefly in the Scottish Dialect* (1786). Composed when Burns was still contemplating emigration to the West Indies, the poem is testament to the fact that Burns valued his connection to Freemasonry: its rationale, its symbolism and its community.

Adieu! a heart-warm, fond adieu!
   Dear brothers of the *mystic tye*!
Ye favoured, *enlighten'd* Few,
   Companions of my social joy!
Tho' I to foreign lands must hie,
   Pursuing Fortune's slidd'ry ba',
With melting heart, and brimful eye,
   I'll mind you still, tho' far awa'.

Oft have I met your social Band,
    And spent the chearful, festive night;
Oft, honor'd with supreme command,
    Presided o'er the *Sons of light*:
And by that *Hieroglyphic* bright,
    Which none but *Craftsmen* ever saw!
Strong Mem'ry on my heart shall write
    Those happy scenes when far awa'!

May Freedom, Harmony and Love
    Unite you in the *grand Design*,
Beneath th' Omniscient Eye above,
    The glorious ARCHITECT Divine!
That you may keep th' *unerring line*,
    Still rising by the *plummet's law*,
Till *Order* bright, completely shine,
    Shall be my Pray'r when far awa'.

And *YOU*, farewell! whose merits claim,
    Justly that *highest badge* to wear!
Heav'n bless you honor'd, noble Name,
    To MASONRY and SCOTIA dear!
A last request, permit me here,
    When yearly ye assemble a',
One *round*, I ask it with a *tear*,
    To him, *the Bard, that's far awa'*.

2ND JULY

To Dr John Mackenzie

IN THIS LIGHT-HEARTED VERSE, Burns – in his capacity as Depute Master of St James's Lodge, Tarbolton – invites his friend and fellow Mason Dr John Mackenzie (d.1837) to a Masonic procession marking the Nativity of St John the Baptist. Mackenzie was a local medic and is known to have attended Burns's family. Obviously keen for his company, the bard jokes that should 'Death' come calling for any of the doctor's patients in the run-up to the event on Friday, he should 'fecht' (or fight) him on Saturday!

Friday first's the day appointed
By the Right Worshipful Anointed,
   To hold our grand Procession,
To get a blade o' Johnie's Morals,
And taste a swatch o' Manson's barrels,
   I' the way of our Profession:
Our Master and the Brotherhood
   Wad a' be glad to see you;
For me, I would be mair than proud
   To share the Mercies wi' you.
      If Death then wi' skaith then
        Some mortal heart is hechtin,
     Inform him, an' storm him,
        That Saturday ye'll fecht him.

3RD JULY

from Libel Summons

IN ANOTHER EXTRACT FROM 'LIBEL SUMMONS' (see 4th June), Burns's imagined 'Court of Equity' treats coachman 'Sandy Dow' with relative leniency 'for that *ancient secret* sake', or rather, owing to his status as a Freemason. Dow, who is humorously encouraged to 'confess and join our core' – to take responsibility for his actions and proudly declare that he is a fornicator – is spared the excruciating public humiliation handed down to 'Clocky Brown'.

Exculpate proof ye needna bring,
For we've due notice o' the thing,
But as reluctantly we punish,
And rather mildly would admonish,
We for that *ancient secret* sake,
You have the honour to partake,
An' for that noble badge you wear,—
You, Sandy Dow, our brother dear,
We give you as a man an' mason,
This serious, sober, friendly lesson,
Your crime a manly deed we verit,
As man alone can only do it;
But in denial persevering,
Is to a scoundrel's name adhering;
Far best confess, and join our core,
As be reproach'd for ever more;

The best o' men hae been surpris'd,
The dousest women been advis'd,
The cleverest lads hae had a trick o't,
The bonniest lasses ta'en a lick o't;
Kings hae been proud our name to own,
The brightest jewel in their crown;
The rhyming sons o' bleak Parnassus,
Were ay red wood about the lasses,
And saul and body, all would venture,
Rejoicing in our list to enter;
E'en (wha wad trow't,) the cleric order,
Aft slyly break the hallow'd border,
An' show in proper time an' place,
They are as ascant o' boasted grace,
As ony o' the human race.
Then, brother Dow, be not asham'd,
In sic a quorum to be nam'd,
But lift a dauntless brow upon it,
An' say I am the man has done it,—
I, Sandy Dow, got Meg wi' bairn,
An' fit to do as much again.

4TH JULY

A Fragment – *or* Ballad on the American War
to the tune of Killiecrankie

TODAY IS INDEPENDENCE DAY in the United States of America. On the fourth of July 1776 the Declaration of Independence was passed by the Continental Congress, asserting the independence of thirteen American states from Great Britain. Burns took considerable interest in the American Revolution (1775–1783) – of which the Declaration was a pivotal development. 'A Fragment', also commonly referred to as 'Ballad on the American War', is Burns's comic poetic account of the key political moments of the American War of Independence, and of the ensuing parliamentary turmoil in Britain.

When *Guilford* good our Pilot stood,
   An' did our hellim thraw, man,
Ae night, at tea, began a plea,
   Within *America*, man:
Then up they gat the maskin-pat,
   And in the sea did jaw, man;
An' did nae less, in full Congress,
   Than quite refuse our law, man.

Then thro' the lakes *Montgomery* takes,
   I wat he was na slaw, man;
Down *Lowrie's burn* he took a turn,
   And *Carleton* did ca', man;
But yet, whatreck, he, at *Quebec*,

Montgomery-like did fa', man,
Wi' sword in hand, before his band,
 Amang his en'mies a', man.

Poor *Tammy Gage* within a cage
 Was kept at *Boston-ha'*, man;
Till *Willie Howe* took o'er the knowe
 For *Philadelphia*, man;
Wi' sword an' gun he thought a sin
 Guid Christian bluid to draw, man;
But at *New-York*, wi' knife an' fork,
 Sir Loin he hacked sma', man.

Burgoyne gaed up, like spur an' whip,
 Till *Fraser* brave did fa', man;
Then lost his way, ae misty day,
 In *Saratoga* shaw, man.
Cornwallis fought as lang's he dought,
 An' did the Buckskins claw, man;
But *Clinton's* glaive frae rust to save
 He hung it to the wa', man.

Then *Montague*, an' *Guilford* too,
 Began to fear, a fa', man;
And *Sackville* doure, wha stood the stoure,
 The German Chief to thraw, man:
For Paddy *Burke*, like ony Turk,
 Nae mercy had at a', man;
An' *Charlie Fox* threw by the box,
 An' lows'd his tinkler jaw, man.

Then *Rockingham* took up the game;
 Till Death did on him ca', man;
When *Shelburne* meek held up his cheek,
 Conform to Gospel law, man:
Saint Stephen's boys, wi' jarring noise,

They did his measures thraw, man,
For *North* an' *Fox* united stocks,
  An' bore him to the wa', man.

Then Clubs an' Hearts were *Charlie's* cartes,
  He swept the stakes awa', man,
Till the Diamond's Ace, of *Indian* race,
  Led him a sair *faux pas*, man:
The Saxon lads, wi' loud placads,
  On *Chatham's Boy* did ca', man;
An' Scotland drew her pipe an' blew,
  'Up, Willie, waur them a', man!'

Behind the throne then *Granville's* gone,
  A secret word or twa, man;
While slee *Dundas* arous'd the class
  Be-north the Roman wa', man:
An' *Chatham's* wraith, in heav'nly graith,
  (Inspired Bardies saw, man)
Wi' kindling eyes, cry'd, '*Willie*, rise!
  'Would I hae fear'd them a', man!'

But, word an' blow, *North, Fox*, and *Co.*
  Gowff'd *Willie* like a ba', man,
Till *Suthron* raise, an' coost their claise
  Behind him in a raw, man:
An' *Caledon* threw by the drone,
  An' did her whittle draw, man;
An' swoor fu' rude, thro' dirt an' blood,
  To mak it guid in law, man.

5TH JULY

On America
from a letter for the *Edinburgh Evening Courant,* 8th November 1788

I N HIS LETTER TO THE *Edinburgh Evening Courant,* Burns is as 'politically correct' in his comments on the American Revolution as he is in his remarks on Jacobitism (see 14th April). The poet does not stop short, however, of pointing out the irony he perceives in the similarities between Congress's rejection of British rule and the deposition of the Stuart dynasty in the Glorious Revolution (which commenced on the fifth of November 1688). Although the bard 'will not' and 'cannot, enter into the merits of the cause', his general support for revolutionary principles is implied in the final lines of this excerpt, as it is in several different places across his poetry, song and correspondence.

Man, Mr. Printer, is a strange, weak, inconsistent being — Who could believe, Sir, that in our Augustan age of liberality and refinement, while we seem so justly sensible and jealous of our rights and liberties, and animated with such indignation against the very memory of those who would have subverted them, who would suppose that a certain people, under our national protection, should complain, not against a Monarch and a few favourite advisers, but against our whole legislative body, of the very same imposition and oppression, the Romish religion not excepted, and almost in the very same terms as our forefathers did against the family of Stuart! I will not, I cannot, enter into the merits of the cause; but I dare say the American Congress, in 1776, will be allowed to have been as able and as enlightened, and, a whole empire will say, as honest, as the English Convention in 1688; and that the fourth of July will be as sacred to their posterity as the fifth of November is to us.

6TH JULY

On the Excise
from a letter to James, Earl of Glencairn, 1st February 1788

BY JULY 1788, Burns was fully trained and commissioned as an officer for the Scottish Board of Excise, and he received instructions regarding his appointment to the Dumfries division in July 1789. A career in the excise was one that Burns had been contemplating for several years. He pondered making an application as early as 1786, when he was also considering emigration to the West Indies. By early 1788 the bard was more or less fixed in his goal, even if he was still grappling with the prospect of taking on another farm (Ellisland). He made overtures to several trusted patrons – among them Robert Graham of Fintry (1749–1815) and James, Earl of Glencairn – in the hope that he might secure a commission.

In this letter to Glencairn, Burns's resolve is undeniable as he sets out his reasons for pursuing this dramatic change of career, from a 'will o' the wisp' ploughman poet to an excise officer and government employee.

My Lord,

I know your Lordship will disapprove of my ideas in the request I am going to make to you, but I have weighed seriously my situation, my hopes and turn of mind, and am fully fixed to my scheme if I can possibly effectuate it. I wish to get into the Excise; I am told that your Lordship's interest will easily procure me the grant from the Commissioners; and your Lordship's Patronage and Goodness, which have already rescued me from obscurity, wretchedness and exile, embolden me to ask that interest.— You have put it in my power to save the little home that sheltered an aged mother, two brothers, and three sisters. from destruction.— My brother's lease is but a wretched one, though I think he will probably weather out the remaining seven years of it.— After what I have given and will give him as a small farming capital to keep the family together, I guess my remaining all will be about two hundred pounds. Instead of beggaring myself with a small dear farm, I will lodge my little stock, a sacred deposit, in a banking-house.— Extraordinary distress, or helpless old age have often harrowed my soul with fears; and I have one or two claims on me in the name of father: I will stoop to any thing that honesty warrants to have it in my power to leave them some better remembrance of me than the odium of illegitimacy.—

These, my Lord, are my views: I have resolved on the maturest deliberation; and now I am fixed, I shall leave no stone unturned to carry my resolve into execution.— Your Lordship's Patronage is by far the strength of my hopes; nor have I yet applied to anybody else. Indeed I know not how to apply to anybody else.— I am ill qualified to dog the heels of Greatness with the impertinence of Solicitation, and tremble nearly as much at the idea of the cold promise as the cold denial; but to your Lordship I have not only the honor, the happiness, but the pleasure of being,

My Lord,
your lordship's much obliged and deeply indebted
humble servant,
Robert Burns

7TH JULY

On the Excise
from a letter to Margaret Chalmers, 17th February 1788

WRITING TO MARGARET CHALMERS several weeks after setting in motion his plans to become an excise officer, Burns reiterates that circumstances, not least his family's financial difficulties, have forced him to 'alter all my plans of future life'. Furthermore, the bard expresses his need of *'un but'* – a goal – following eighteen months of exuberance as the toast of Edinburgh and the celebrated new Scottish poet.

I have altered all my plans of future life. A farm that I could live in, I could not find; and indeed, after the necessary support my brother and the rest of the family required, I could not venture on farming in that style suitable to my feelings. You will condemn me for the next step I have taken. I have entered into the excise. I stay in the west about three weeks, and then return to Edinburgh for six weeks instructions. Afterwards, for I get employ instantly, I go *où il plait a Dieu — et mon Roi.* I have chosen this, my dear friend, after mature deliberation. The question is not at what door of fortune's palace shall we enter in; but what doors does she open to us? I was not likely to get any thing to do. I wanted *un but*, which is a dangerous, an unhappy situation. I got this without any hanging on or mortifying solicitation; it is immediate bread, and though poor in comparison of the last eighteen months of my existence, 'tis luxury in comparison of all my preceding life: besides, the commissioners are some of them my acquaintances, and all of them my firm friends.

8TH JULY

On the Excise
from a letter to Robert Graham Esq. of Fintry,
10th September 1788

IF BURNS FELT HE HAD AVOIDED 'hanging on or mortifying solicitation' in securing his excise commission, then that all changed when, increasingly aware that Ellisland Farm was an unprofitable venture, he became impatient to be assigned an excise division. Burns solicited the help of Excise Commissioner Robert Graham of Fintry, and went so far as to suggest the removal of the existing Dumfriesshire exciseman on account of the fact he was wealthy enough to forego the position. This forwardness is enough to make Burns himself 'shudder at my own hardiesse', but, then as now, desperate times call for desperate measures.

Your Honourable Board, sometime ago, gave me my Excise Commission; which I regard as my sheet anchor in life.— My farm, now that I have tried it a little, though I think it will in time be a saving bargain, yet does by no means promise to be such a penny-worth as I was taught to expect.— It is in the last stage of worn-out poverty, and will take some time before it pays the rent [. . .] But I am embarked now in the farm; I have commenced married man; and I am determined to stand by my lease till resistless Necessity compel me to quit my ground.—

There is one way by which I might be enabled to extricate myself from this embarrassment, a scheme which I hope and am certain is in your power to effectuate.— I live here, Sir, in the very centre of a country Excise-Division; the present Officer lately lived on a farm which he rented in my nearest neighbourhood; and as the gentleman, owing to some legacies, is quite opulent, a removal could do him no manner of injury; and on a month's warning, to give me a little time to look again over my Instructions, I would not be afraid to enter on business. [...]

When I think how and on what I have written to you, Sir, I shudder at my own hardiesse.— Forgive me, Sir! I have told you my situation.— If asking anything less could possibly have done, I would not have asked so much.

9TH JULY

To Mr Graham of Fintry, On Being Appointed to My Excise Division

BURNS'S APPEAL TO GRAHAM for the Dumfries excise division was successful, and the bard commenced in post in 1789. From his correspondence it can be deduced that Burns did very well as an exciseman. The £50 salary helped to alleviate his financial concerns (for a time, anyway) and, with that, the anxiety that he had expressed regarding the maintenance of his wife, children and extended family. Burns's relief and his overwhelming gratitude is apparent from the following gushing lines sent to Graham as a token of thanks.

I call no goddess to inspire my strains,
A fabled Muse may suit a Bard that feigns:
'Friend of my life!' my ardent spirit burns,
And all the tribute of my heart returns,
For boons accorded, goodness ever new,
The Gift still dearer, as the Giver You.

Thou Orb of Day! Thou Other Paler Light!
And all ye many-sparkling Stars of Night!
If aught that Giver from my mind efface;

If I that Giver's bounty e'er disgrace;
Then roll, to me, along your wandering spheres,
Only to number out a Villain's Years!

I lay my hand upon my swelling breast,
And grateful would – but cannot speak the rest.

10TH JULY

On the Excise
from a letter to Robert Graham Esq. of Fintry, 9th December 1789

W HILE BURNS WAS GLAD of the salary, work as an excise officer
was by no means easy employment. Burns was regularly
required to travel for miles on horseback, during which time his
exposure to the changeable, often bitter, Scottish weather likely
exacerbated his recurring rheumatic complaint and took its toll
on the bard's seemingly precarious health. Despite this, Burns was
needful of the steady income and pleased when, at times, his new
occupation – although often busy and distracting – aligned with his
poetic endeavours.

I have found the Excise business goes on a great deal smoother with
me than I apprehended; owing a good deal to the generous friendship
of Mr Mitchel my Collector, and the kind assistance and instruction
of Mr Findlater my Supervisor.— I dare to be honest, and I fear
no Labor.— Nor do I find my hurried life greatly inimical to my
correspondence with the Muses.— Their visits to me indeed, and I
believe to most their acquaintances, like the visits of good angels are
short, and far between; but still I meet them now and then as I jog
through the wild hills of Nithsdale.—

11TH JULY

The Deil's Awa wi' th' Exciseman

EXCISE OFFICERS WERE CROWN EMPLOYEES who collected taxes for the government and intercepted illegal goods. It is not difficult to imagine why they were unpopular among eighteenth-century communities! Burns seemingly accepted this in good humour – it seems likely that on a personal, rather than a professional, level he even empathised with such feelings. In 'The Deil's Awa Wi' Th' Exciseman' he imagines a community revelling in the absence of the loathed exciseman, who has been danced off to hell by Satan. They defiantly 'mak maut', 'brew drink' and 'rejoice' in his absence, in direct contravention of those government regulations that Burns was employed to uphold.

The deil cam fiddlin' thro' the town,
　　And danc'd awa wi' th' Exciseman;
And ilka wife cries, auld Mahoun,
　　I wish you luck o' the prize, man.

The deil's awa the deil's awa,
　　The deil's awa wi' th' Exciseman,
He's danc'd awa he's danc'd awa
　　He's danc'd awa wi' th' Exciseman.

We'll mak our maut and we'll brew our drink,
　　We'll laugh, sing, and rejoice, man;
And mony braw thanks to the meikle black deil,
　　That danc'd awa wi' th' Exciseman.
　　　　The deil's awa &c

314

There's threesome reels, there's foursome reels,
   There's hornpipes and strathspeys, man,
But the ae best dance e're cam to the Land
   Was, the deil's awa wi' th' Exciseman.
      The deil's awa &c

12TH JULY

Here's a Health to Ane I Loe Dear
to the tune of Here's a Health to Them That's Awa'

BURNS SENT THIS SONG to Alexander Cunningham on the twelfth of July 1796, just nine days before he died. He described it as 'the last I made or probably will make for some time'. It was indeed to be one of his last works. Burns did in fact send another song, 'Fairest Maid on Devon Banks', to George Thomson on the same day, but it was 'Here's a Health to Ane I Loe Dear' that Burns set to his 'favourite' air. The song is inspired by Jessy Lewars, who helped nurse Burns through his final illness. It seems apt that, even on his deathbed, Burns was coveting – and celebrating – the great pleasure of his life: women. And yet, there is no escaping the poet's sincere and melancholic sense of hopelessness.

Here's a health to ane I lo'e dear,
   Here's a health to ane I lo'e dear;
Thou art sweet as the smile when fond lovers meet,
   And soft as their parting tear – Jessy.
Altho' thou maun never be mine,
   Altho' even hope is denied;
'Tis sweeter for thee despairing,
   Than aught in the warld beside – Jessy.

Here's a health to ane I lo'e dear,
　　Here's a health to ane I lo'e dear;
Thou art sweet as the smile when fond lovers meet,
　　And soft as their parting tear – Jessy.
I mourn through the gay, gaudy day,
　　As, hopeless I muse on thy charms,
But welcome the dream o' sweet slumber,
　　For then I am lock'd in thy arms – Jessy.

13TH JULY

On the French Revolution
from a letter to Robert Graham Esq. of Fintry, 5th January 1793

CRITICS HAVE FOUND IT DIFFICULT to reconcile Burns's role as a government excise officer with his seemingly Republican political outlook. It appears that the poet himself struggled to tread that precarious line, and his superiors in the excise service were forced to pay attention to his politics when the poet was accused of leading the French Revolutionary cry – '*Ça ira!*' – at the Dumfries playhouse in 1792 (see 8th of March for an explanation of this). In this letter to his commissioner Burns makes his defence and praises the constitution, but he cannot commend its execution and instead highlights the corruption that he perceives in British politics.

I never uttered any invectives against the king.— His private worth, it is altogether impossible that such a man as I can appreciate; and in his Public capacity, I always revered, and always will, with the soundest loyalty, revere the monarch of Great Britain as, to speak in Masonic, the sacred KEYSTONE of Our ROYAL ARCH CONSTITUTION.—

As to REFORM PRINCIPLES, I look upon the British Constitution, as settled at the Revolution, to be the most glorious Constitution on earth, or that perhaps the wit of man can frame; at the same time, I think, and you know what high and distinguished characters have for some time thought so, that we have a good deal deviated from the original principles of that Constitution; particularly, that an alarming system of corruption has pervaded the connection between the Executive Power and the House of Commons.— This is the truth, the whole truth, of my Reform opinions; opinions which, before I was aware of the complexion of these innovating times, I too unguardedly (now I see it) sported with: but henceforth I seal up my lips.—

14TH JULY

A Man's a Man for A' That
to the tune of **For A' That**

THE 14TH OF JULY IS BASTILLE DAY: a national holiday in France. It commemorates the storming of the Bastille in Paris on this day in 1789, when a mob overwhelmed the infamous state prison, releasing its prisoners and gaining access to armaments in a defining moment of the French Revolution. We mark Bastille Day – known as La Fête Nationale in France – with one of Burns's most famous and rousing songs.

'A Man's a Man' is often considered an expression of the bard's support for Republicanism. His emphasis on notions of equality and brotherhood chime with the motto of the French Revolution: '*Liberté, égalité, fraternité*'. In this Burns is also responding to Thomas Paine's (1737–1809) controversial pro-revolutionary publication, *The Rights of Man* (1791). The song, which represents one of Burns's most optimistic and universal statements on class, concludes with the bard's 'prayer' that 'man to man, the world o'er / Shall brothers be for a' that'.

Is there for honest poverty
   That hings his head, an' a' that;
The coward slave, we pass him by,
   We dare be poor for a' that!
     For a' that, and a' that.
       Our toils obscure and a' that,
     The rank is but the guinea's stamp,
      The man's the gowd for a' that.

What though on hamely fare we dine,
   Wear hoddin grey, and a that;
Gie fools their silks, and knaves their wine;
   A man's a man for a' that!
     For a' that, and a' that,
       Their tinsel show, and a' that,
     The honest man, tho' e'er sae poor,
      Is king o' men, for a' that.

Ye see yon birkie, ca'd a lord,
   Wha struts and stares, and a' that;
Tho' hundreds worship at his word,
   He's but a coof for a' that:
     For a' that, and a' that,
       His ribband, star, and a' that,
     The man o' independent mind,
      He looks and laughs at a' that.

A prince can mak a belted knight,
   A marquis, duke, and a' that,
But an honest man's aboon his might,
   Gude faith, he maunna fa' that!
     For a' that, and a' that,

Their dignities, and a' that,
 The pith o' sense, and pride o' worth,
  Are higher rank than a' that.

Then let us pray that come it may,
 As come it will, for a' that,
That sense and worth, o'er a' the earth,
 Shall bear the gree, and a' that!
  For a' that, and a' that,
   It's coming yet, for a' that,
  That man to man, the warld o'er,
   Shall brothers be, for a' that.

15TH JULY

Why Should Na Poor Folk Mowe
to the tune of The Campbells Are Coming

ALTHOUGH BURNS DECLARED his intention to 'seal up' his lips regarding political matters for the purposes of portraying his 'official' self, he certainly retained freedom of political expression in his bawdy satires, probably because these were never intended for public consumption. Sexually explicit writing in Burns's day was often less concerned with sexual arousal than with religious and political arousal. 'Why should na poor folk mowe' (commonly published using the more polite title 'When Princes and Prelates') is a defiant song that advocates the triumph of sex over social class. Here the so-called 'poor folk' command a powerful political weapon – their expert ability to reproduce – and the driving force of their sexuality is symbolised by the success of the French Revolution. The European ruling class, on the other hand, are portrayed as sexually and politically impotent. The common man, Burns suggests, is comparatively content when considered alongside the fraught monarchs of Europe and their unsuccessful battles with Republican France.

When Princes and Prelates and het-headed zealots
 All Europe hae set in a lowe,
The poor man lies down, nor envies a crown,
 And comforts himsel with a mowe.

And why shouldna poor folk mowe, mowe, mowe,
 And why shouldna poor folk mowe:
The great folk hae siller, and houses and lands,
 Poor bodies hae naething but mowe.

When Brunswick's great Prince cam a cruising to France,
 Republican billies to cowe,
Bauld Brunswick's great Prince wad hae shawn better sense,
 At hame with his Princess to mowe.
  And why shouldna &c.

Out over the Rhine proud Prussia wad shine,
 To *spend* his best blood he did vow;
But Frederic had better ne'er forded the water,
 But spent as he docht in a mowe.
  And why shouldna &c.

By sea and by shore! the Emperor swore,
 In Paris he'd kick up a row;
But Paris sae ready just leugh at the laddie
 And bad him gae tak him a mowe.
  And why shouldna &c.

Auld Kate laid her claws on poor Stanislaus,
 And Poland has bent like a bow:
May the deil in her a—e ram a huge pr-ck o' brass!
 And damn her in h-ll with a mowe!
  And why shouldna &c.

320

But truce with commotions and new-fangled notions,
    A bumper I trust you'll allow:
Here's George our gude king and Charlotte his queen,
    And lang may they tak a gude mowe!
        And why shouldna &c.

16TH JULY

The Dumfries Volunteers
to the tune of Push About the Jorum

I N 1793, POST-REVOLUTIONARY FRANCE declared war with Great
Britain. Amid the threat of an invasion by France, local volunteers
were organised into civilian companies. In 1795 Burns took an oath
of allegiance to serve as one of the Royal Dumfries Volunteers and
promptly penned this stirring song inspired by the company and his
comrades. Unlike yesterday's song, it was very much intended for
public consumption.

First published in the local newspaper, the *Dumfries Weekly Journal*,
in April 1795 it was received with patriotic enthusiasm. The song and
its context do introduce further complexity regarding Burns's politics,
and we might consider that he himself struggled to align his desire
to defend his country and locale from invasion with his seemingly
Republican political predilections. Burns's rallying cry to defend the
country against 'a foreign foe' is likely sincere, but the concluding
lines of his song direct us back to his overriding preoccupation with
'the People', rather than his more contrived expressions of loyalty to
the ruling monarch.

Does haughty Gaul invasion threat?
    Then let the louns beware, Sir;
There's wooden walls upon our seas,
    And Volunteers on shore, Sir:

The Nith shall run to Corsincon,
   And Criffel sink in Solway,
Ere we permit a foreign foe
   On British ground to rally!
     We'll ne'er permit &c.

O let us not, like snarling curs,
   In wrangling be divided,
Till, slap! come in an unco loun,
   And wi' a rung decide it:
Be Britain still to Britain true,
   Amang oursels united:
For never but by British hands
   Maun British wrangs be righted!
     For never but &c.

The kettle o' the Kirk and State,
   Perhaps a clout may fail in't;
But deil a foreign tinkler loun
   Shall ever ca' a nail in't:
Our father's blude the kettle bought,
   And wha wad dare to spoil it,
By Heavens, the sacrilegious dog
   Shall fuel be to boil it!
     By Heavens &c.

The wretch that would a Tyrant own,
   And the wretch, his true sworn brother,
Who would set the Mob above the throne,
   May they be damn'd together.
Who will not sing God save the king,
   Shall hang as high's the steeple;
But while we sing, God save the King,
   We'll ne'er forget the People!
     But while we sing &c.

17TH JULY

On the French Revolution
from a letter to Frances Dunlop, 12th January 1795

I N HIS CORRESPONDENCE WITH FRANCES DUNLOP, Burns was
considerably more forthright in his expressions of sympathy for
the French Revolution, but his confidence was clearly misplaced.
Eventually, Burns's failure to condemn the execution of the French
monarchs, Louis XVI and Marie Antoinette, prompted his friend and
patron to cease correspondence altogether (although anecdote has it
that the last thing Burns read on his deathbed in 1796 was Frances's
letter of reconciliation). Here is the offending letter. The following
comments regard the correspondents' mutual acquaintance and the
man for whom Burns composed his extensive autobiographical letter,
Dr John Moore. Burns's quote is from a song by William Roscoe
beginning, 'O'er the vine-covered hills and gay regions of France'.

Entre nous, you know my Politics; & I cannot approve of the
honest Doctor's whining over the deserved fate of a certain pair
of Personages.— What is there in the delivering over a perjured
Blockhead & and unprincipled Prostitute into the hands of the
hangman, that it should arrest for a moment, attention, in an eventful
hour when, as my friend Roscoe in Liverpool gloriously expresses it —

> "When the welfare of millions is hung in the scale
> And the balance yet trembles with fate!"

But our friend is already debted to People in power, and still looks
forward for his family, so I can apologise for him; for at bottom I am

sure he is a staunch friend to liberty.— Thank God, these London trials have given us a little more breath, and I imagine that the time is not far distant when a man may freely blame Billy Pit, without being called an enemy to his Country.—

18TH JULY

Burns's Last Written Words
from a letter to James Armour, 18th July 1796

OVER THE COURSE OF JULY 1796, Burns's health was in rapid decline. He wrote to George Thomson on the 4th of July, 'I received your songs, but my health being so precarious nay dangerously situated, that as a last effort I am here at sea-bathing quarters.— Besides my inveterate rheumatism, my appetite is quite gone; & I am so emaciated as to be scarce able to support myself on my own legs.'

Sea-bathing – walking into the freezing cold Solway Firth each day – was unlikely to do anything other than exacerbate his 'inveterate rheumatism', yet such was the inadequacy of eighteenth-century medicine. Burns soon became aware that the sea-bathing was ineffective. He wrote to his father-in-law James Armour on the 10th of July, 'I have now been a week at salt water, and though I think I have got some good by it, yet I have some secret fears that this business will be dangerous if not fatal.'

To his brother Gilbert, he wrote in desperate concern for the welfare of his family – 'God help my wife & children if I am taken from their head! – They will be poor indeed' – making clear once again his dire financial circumstances (see 26th June). Burns last put pen to paper on this day in 1796, to compose the following frantic letter to his father-in-law. In it, the ailing bard requests assistance for Jean, who was due to give birth to his last-born child.

My dear Sir,

Do, for heaven's sake, send Mrs Armour here immediately. My wife is hourly expecting to be put to bed. Good God! What a situation for her to be in, poor girl, without a friend! I returned from sea-bathing quarters today, and my medical friends would almost persuade me that I am better, but I think and feel that my strength is so gone that the disorder will prove fatal to me.

Your son-in-law,
R.B.

19TH JULY

Sensibility How Charming

IN JULY 1791, BURNS ENCLOSED this song in a letter to Agnes McLehose. Their relationship had long since cooled, and their letters were few and far between. Burns offers some insight into this in the accompanying letter in which he wrote, 'How can you expect a Correspondent should write you, when you declare that you mean to preserve his letters with a view, sooner or later, to expose them on the pillory of derision and the rack of criticism? This is gagging me completely as to speaking the sentiments of my bosom.'

Burns was nonetheless inspired by Agnes's letters to compose the following verses, which imply more than a lingering fondness.

Sensibility how charming,
    Dearest Nancy, thou canst tell;
But distress with horrors arming,
    Thou hast also known too well.
Fairest flower, behold the lily,
    Blooming in the sunny ray:

Let the blast sweep o'er the valley,
   See it prostrate on the clay.

Hear the woodlark charm the forest,
   Telling o'er his little joys:
Hapless bird! a prey the surest
   To each pirate of the skies.
Dearly bought the hidden treasure,
   Finer Feelings can bestow:
Chords that vibrate sweetest pleasure,
   Thrill the deepest notes of woe.

20TH JULY

Remorse

ONE OF THE BARD'S EARLIEST POEMS, today's choice was entered in Burns's 'First Commonplace Book' in 1783. It was inspired by Adam Smith's *Theory of Moral Sentiments* (1759). In his preface to the poem, Burns writes that: 'I entirely agree with that judicious Philosopher Mr Smith in his excellent *Theory of Moral Sentiments*, that Remorse is the most painful sentiment that can embitter the human bosom.' One would hope that these were not his sentiments as, on the 20th of July 1796, the poet lay on his deathbed, although his correspondence from that time certainly implies a mind wrought with anguish.

Of all the numerous ills that hurt our peace;
That press the soul, or wring the mind with anguish;
Beyond comparison the worst are those
That to our Folly, or our Guilt we owe.
In ev'ry other circumstance, the mind
Has this to say, It was no deed of mine:
But, when to all the evil of misfortune
This sting is added, blame thy foolish self;
Or worser far, the pangs of keen remorse:
The tort'ring, gnawing consciousness of guilt
Of guilt, perhaps, where we've involved others;
The young, the innocent, who fondly lov'd us:
Nay more, that very love their cause of ruin
O! burning Hell! in all thy store of torments
There's not a keener Lash —
Lives there a man so firm who, while his heart
Feels all the bitter horrors of his crime,
Can reason down its agonizing throbs,
And, after proper purpose of amendment,
Can firmly force his jarring thoughts to peace?
O happy, happy, enviable man!
O glorious magnanimity of soul!

21st JULY

A Prayer in the Prospect of Death

R OBERT BURNS DIED AT HIS HOUSE in Dumfries, surrounded by friends and family, on the 21st of July 1796. He was thirty-seven years old. The cause of his death has been the subject of considerable speculation among biographers and critics. Beginning in the nineteenth century, several elaborate theories have been proffered, some going so far as to imply that Burns's death was the consequence of a conspiracy to silence the, at times, politically outspoken poet. Such fanciful theories are entirely without evidence. Ultimately, scholars and medics who have examined the poet's own account of his illness, together with testimonies from his contemporaries, agree that the most likely cause of death was bacterial endocarditis: a complication arising from Burns's recurring rheumatic illness.

We mark this sombre anniversary with a poem written by Burns in his early twenties and entered in his 'First Commonplace Book' with the more revealing title, 'A Prayer, when fainting fits, & other alarming symptoms of a Pleurisy or some other dangerous disorder, which indeed still threaten me, first put Nature on the alarm'. It seems that the threat of ill health never left the bard. It is a poignant poem that sees him take full account of his character, his humanity and his 'Passions' while expressing his sincere belief in an 'Unknown', but all-knowing and forgiving deity.

O Thou unknown, Almighty Cause
　　Of all my hope and fear!
In whose dread presence, ere an hour,
　　Perhaps I must appear!

If I have wander'd in those paths
　　Of life I ought to shun;
As *Something*, loudly, in my breast,
　　Remonstrates I have done;

Thou know'st that Thou hast formed me,
　　With Passions wild and strong;
And list'ning to their witching voice
　　Has often led me wrong.

Where human *weakness* has come short,
　　Or *frailty* stept aside,
Do Thou, ALL-GOOD, for such Thou art,
In shades of darkness hide.

Where with *intention* I have err'd,
　　No other plea I have,
But, *Thou art good*; and Goodness still
　　Delighteth to forgive.

22ND JULY

Stanzas on the Same Occasion

IN A POEM WRITTEN BY BURNS to accompany yesterday's entry, the poet contemplates the fickleness of humanity, acknowledging that returned health might lead to further temptation, and appealing for help to control his 'headlong furious passions'.

Why am I loth to leave this earthly scene?
   Have I so found it full of pleasing charms?
Some drops of joy with draughts of ill between;
   Some gleams of sunshine mid renewing storms:
Is it departing pangs my soul alarms?
   Or Death's unlovely, dreary, dark abode?
For guilt, for guilt, my terrors are in arms;
   I tremble to approach an angry GOD,
And justly smart beneath his sin-avenging rod.

Fain would I say, 'Forgive my foul offence!'
   Fain promise never more to disobey;
But, should my Author health again dispense,
   Again I might desert fair Virtue's way;
Again in Folly's path might go astray;
   Again exalt the brute and sink the man;
Then how should I for Heavenly Mercy pray
   Who act so counter Heavenly Mercy's plan?
Who sin so oft have mourn'd, yet to temptation ran?

O Thou, Great Governor of all below!
   If I may dare a lifted eye to Thee,
Thy nod can make the tempest cease to blow,

Or still the tumult of the raging sea:
With that controlling pow'r assist ev'n me,
　　Those headlong furious passions to confine;
For all unfit I feel my powers be,
　　To rule their torrent in th' allowed line;
O, aid me with Thy help, *Omnipotence Divine*!

23RD JULY

from Burns's Deed of Assignment, July 1786

I N JULY 1786, BURNS, separated from Jean Armour, seeking to evade the fine sought by her father for her seduction, and contemplating emigration to the West Indies, legally signed his worldly belongings, the care of his daughter and the copyright for his forthcoming edition of *Poems, Chiefly in the Scottish Dialect* over to his brother Gilbert. The deed proved superfluous, but it serves as an interesting glimpse into Burns's circumstances and state of mind at a particularly fraught time in his life. Whether the poet truly intended to walk away from everything outlined in this extract, we will never know.

Know all men by these presents that I Robert Burns in Mossgiel: whereas I intend to leave Scotland and go abroad, and having acknowledged myself the father of a child named Elizabeth, begot upon Elizabeth Paton in Largieside: and whereas Gilbert Burns in Mossgiel, my brother, has become bound, and hereby binds and obliges himself to aliment, clothe and educate my said natural child in a suitable manner as if she was his own, in case her Mother choose to part with her, and that until she arrives at the age of fifteen years. Therefore, and to enable the said Gilbert Burns to make good his engagement, Wit ye me to have assigned, disponed, conveyed and made over to, and in favours of, the said Gilbert Burns his Heirs,

Executors and Assignees, who are always to be bound in like manner with himself, all and Sundry Goods, Gear, Corns, Cattle, Horses, Nolt, Sheep, Household furniture, and all other moveable effects of whatever kind that I shall leave behind me on my departure from the kingdom, after allowing for my part of the conjunct debts due by the said Gilbert Burns and me as joint Tacksmen of the farm of Mossgiel.— And particularly, without prejudice of the aforesaid generality, the profits that may arise from the Publication of my Poems presently in the press.— And also, I hereby dispose and convey to him in trust for behoof of my said natural daughter, the Copyright of said Poems in so far as I can dispose of the same by law, after she arrives at the above age of fifteen years complete.—

24TH JULY

The Song of Death
to the tune of Orananoig

S ENT TO FRANCES DUNLOP in 1791, 'The Song of Death' conflates two of July's recurring themes: death and liberty. Burns, in a patriotic mood, celebrates the bravery of warriors past and praises their heroic demise. His accompanying letter states that the song, 'to a lady the descendant of Wallace and many heroes of his truly illustrious Line, and herself the mother of several soldiers, needs neither preface nor apology'.

Farewell, thou fair day; thou green earth; and ye skies,
    Now gay with the broad setting sun!
Farewell, loves and friendships, ye dear tender ties!
    Our race of existence is run.

Thou grim king of terrors, Thou life's gloomy foe,
  Go frighten the coward and slave!
Go teach them to tremble, fell tyrant! but know,
  No terrors hast thou to the Brave.

Thou strik'st the dull peasant, he sinks in the dark,
  Nor saves e'en the wreck of a name:
Thou strik'st the young hero, a glorious mark!
  He falls in the blaze of his fame.
In the field of proud honor, our swords in our hands,
  Our King and our Country to save,
While victory shines on life's last ebbing sands,
  O, who would not die with the Brave!

25TH JULY

A Bard's Epitaph

BURNS'S FUNERAL TOOK PLACE at midday on the 25th of July 1796 in St Michael's Kirkyard, Dumfries. His status as a member of the Royal Dumfries Volunteers entitled him to a military funeral, one which his regiment attended in full regalia, firing several shots over the bard's humble grave. Thousands of mourners lined the streets of Dumfries in an unprecedented show of respect for the poet. As tragic circumstance would have it, Burns's wife Jean was unable to attend his funeral. On the same day that her husband was laid to rest, she gave birth to his youngest child, Maxwell Burns (1796–1799). It seems apt to commemorate the anniversary of Burns's funeral with an epitaph he wrote with himself in mind, and that he chose as the closing poem for his seminal first collection of poetry.

Is there a whim-inspir'd fool,
Owre fast for thought, owre hot for rule,
Owre blate to seek, owre proud to snool,
            Let him draw near;
And owre this grassy heap sing dool,
            And drap a tear.

Is there a Bard of rustic song,
Who, noteless, steals the crowds among,
That weekly this area throng,
            O, pass not by!
But with a frater-feeling strong,
            Here, heave a sigh.

Is there a man whose judgment clear,
Can others teach the course to steer,
Yet runs, himself, life's mad career,
            Wild as the wave,
Here pause — and thro' the starting tear,
            Survey this grave.

The poor Inhabitant below
Was quick to learn and wise to know,
And keenly felt the friendly glow,
            And *softer flame*;
But thoughtless follies laid him low,
            And stain'd his name!

Reader attend — whether thy soul
Soars fancy's flights beyond the pole,
Or darkling grubs this earthly hole,
            In low pursuit,
Know, prudent, cautious, *self-controul*
            Is Wisdom's root.

26TH JULY

Elegy on the Death of Robert Ruisseaux

Ruisseaux is the french word for 'streams', which many refer to as 'burns'. The title for this mock elegy is, of course, a play on words and refers to the bard himself. In the opening lines Burns imagines that he 'lies in his last lair', but the poet could never have envisaged that the grave in which he was buried in July 1796 would not prove to be his final resting place. The first grave in St Michael's Kirkyard was extremely modest, marked only by a solitary and plain gravestone.

In the years following his death, enthusiasts – who felt that the original grave was an insufficient tribute to Burns's genius – petitioned for a more suitable resting place for the Scottish national bard. Subscriptions were gathered from admirers worldwide to commission a mausoleum by the architect Thomas Frederick Hunt (c.1790–1831). And so, on the 19th of September 1815, Robert Burns's body was exhumed from his humble grave and reinterred in an impressive dome-shaped building over twenty-five feet in height. Inside is an elaborate design of Burns with his muse Coila in a scene from the bard's poem 'The Vision' (see 8th January), sculpted by the artist Peter Turnerelli (1774–1839).

Now Robin lies in his last lair,
He'll gabble rhyme, nor sing nae mair;
Cauld poverty, wi' hungry stare,
         Nae mair shall fear him;
Nor anxious fear, nor cankert care,
         E'er mair come near him.

To tell the truth, they seldom fash't him,
Except the moment that they crush't him;
For sune as chance or fate had husht 'em
        Tho' e'er sae short,
Then wi' a rhyme or sang he lasht 'em,
        And thought it sport.—

Tho' he was bred to kintra wark,
And counted was baith wight and stark,
Yet that was never Robin's mark
        To mak a man;
But tell him, he was learn'd and clark,
        Ye roos'd him then!

27TH JULY

Killiecrankie

ON THIS DAY IN 1689, a Jacobite army commanded by John Graham of Claverhouse (1648–1689) – the Viscount of Dundee – defeated William of Orange's forces under the leadership of General Hugh Mackay (c.1640–1692) in the Battle of Killiecrankie. Burns commemorates this brutal and bloody battle in a song of the same name. Certainly, there were considerable losses on both sides, among them the Viscount of Dundee himself who 'gat a clankie' – or took a knock – and died in the hours following his victory.

Whare hae ye been sae braw, lad!
  Whare hae ye been sae brankie O?
Whare hae ye been sae braw, lad?
  Cam ye by Killiecrankie O?

An ye had been whare I hae been,
  Ye wad na been sae cantie O;
An ye had seen what I hae seen,
  I' th' braes o' Killiecrankie O.

I faught at land, I faught at sea,
  At hame I faught my Auntie, O;
But I met the Devil and Dundee
    On th' Braes o' Killiecrankie, O.
      An ye had been &c.

The bauld Pitcur fell in a furr,
  An' Clavers gat a clankie, O;
Or I had fed an Athole Gled
    On th' braes o' Killiecrankie, O.
      An ye had been &c.

28TH JULY

To Alexander Cunningham

THIS VERSE EPISTLE FORMS the first part of a letter to Burns's good friend Alexander Cunningham on the 27th of July 1788 (yesterday's anniversary means that it has been delayed for one day). Here the poet refers again to Cunningham's unrequited love for Anne Stewart, which also inspired the selection for the 12th of February. The bard emphasises the intensity of Cunningham's 'volcanic', 'immortal' love, implying that he is indeed hopelessly 'bewitched'.

My godlike Friend — nay do not stare,
　　You think the phrase is odd like;
But 'God is love', the Saints declare,
　　Then surely thou art Godlike.

And is thy Ardour still the same?
　　And kindled still at Anna?
Others may boast a partial flame,
　　But thou art a Volcano.

Even Wedlock asks not Love beyond
　　Death's tie-dissolving Portal;
But thou, omnipotently fond,
　　May'st promise Love Immortal.

Prudence, the Bottle and the Stew
　　Are fam'd for Lovers' curing:
Thy Passion nothing can subdue,
　　Nor Wisdom, Wine nor Whoring.

Thy Wounds such healing powers defy;
    Such Symptoms dire attend them,
That last great Antihectic try,
    Marriage, perhaps, may mend them.

Sweet Anna has an air, a grace,
    Divine magnetic touching!
She takes, she charms — but who can trace
    The process of Bewitching?

29TH JULY

The Mauchline Wedding

BURNS REMINISCED IN A LETTER to Frances Dunlop that the following 'burlesque' on a wedding brawl was composed 'in the heat of my resentment' when he was snubbed by the groom's sister. According to the opening line, it is set in July 1785.

When Eighty-five was seven month auld,
    And wearing thro the aught,
When rotting rains and Boreas bauld
    Gied farmer-folks a faught;
Ae morning quondam Mason Will,
    Now Merchant Master Miller,
Gaed down to meet wi' Nansie Bell
    And her Jamaica siller,
            To wed, that day.

The rising sun o'er Blacksideen
    Was just appearing fairly,
When Nell and Bess get up to dress
    Seven lang half-hours o'er early!
Now presses clink and drawers jink,
    For linnens and for laces;
But modest Muses only *think*
    What ladies' under dress is,
            On sic a day.

But we'll suppose the stays are lac'd,
    And bony bosoms steekit;
Tho, thro the lawn — but guess the rest —
    An Angel scarce durst keekit:
Then stockins fine, o' silken twine,
    Wi cannie care are drawn up;
And gartened tight, whare mortal wight.—

                * * *

But now the gown wi rustling sound,
    Its silken pomp displays;
Sure there's no sin in being vain
    O siccan bony claes!
Sae jimp the waist, the tail sae vast —
    Trouth, they were bony Birdies!
O Mither Eve, ye wad been grave
    To see their ample hurdies
            Sae large that day!!!

Then Sandy wi's red jacket braw
    Comes, whip-jee-whoa! about,
And in he gets the bony twa —
    Lord send them safely out!
And auld John Trot wi' sober phiz
    As braid and braw's a Bailie,

> His shouthers and his Sunday's giz
>   Wi powther and wi ulzie
>   Weel smear'd that day.

30TH JULY

On Emigration
from a letter to John Richmond, 30th July 1786

O N THIS DAY IN 1786, Burns wrote to his friend and confidante, John Richmond (1765–1846), that his departure for Jamaica was imminent. From this letter he appears fixed upon this course of action. However, as we know, he did not board the 'Nancy' and instead travelled from Ayrshire to Edinburgh where he lodged with Richmond in Baxter's Close for several months. Whether Burns landed in Jamaica or Edinburgh, it seems that remaining in Ayrshire was not an option!

My hour is now come.— You and I will never meet in Britain more.— I have orders within three weeks at farthest to repair aboard the Nancy, Capn. Smith, from Clyde to Jamaica, and to call at Antigua.— This, except to our friend Smith, whom God long preserve, is a secret about Mauchline. Would you believe it? Armour has got a warrant to throw me in jail till I find security for an enormous sum.— This they keep an entire secret, but I got it by a channel they little dream of; and I am wandering from one friend's house to another, and like a true son of the Gospel "have no where to lay my head."

31st JULY

from the Preface to Burns's Kilmarnock Edition of *Poems, Chiefly in the Scottish Dialect* (1786)

ROBERT BURNS PUBLISHED his first volume of poetry, *Poems, Chiefly in the Scottish Dialect*, on this day in 1786. The edition was printed by John Wilson in Kilmarnock and 612 copies were issued at a price of three shillings each. An immediate and unprecedented success, it included several of what have since become Burns's most famous works. Burns's 'Preface' to the Kilmarnock edition, where he provides some insight into his motivations for composing and publishing his poetry, casts light on Henry MacKenzie's famous description of him as 'the heaven-taught ploughman'. Burns refers his readership to his rural roots and describes himself modestly as an 'obscure, nameless Bard', fearful of a poor reception. He is, nonetheless, 'possest of some poetic abilities'. The talented, well-read poet, who was skilled in the art of crafting personae, seemingly enjoyed playing – with comparable skill and ingenuity – the part of the 'rustic bard'.

The following trifles are not the production of the Poet, who, with all the advantages of learned art, and perhaps amid the elegancies and idlenesses of upper life, looks down for a rural theme, with an eye to Theocrites or Virgil. To the Author of this, these and other celebrated names their countrymen are, in their original languages, 'A fountain shut up, and a book sealed.' Unacquainted with the necessary requisites for commencing Poet by rule, he sings the sentiments and manners, he felt and saw in himself and his rustic compeers around him, in his and their native language. Though a Rhymer from his earliest years, at least from the earliest impulses of the softer passions, it was not till very lately, that the applause, perhaps the partiality, of

Friendship, wakened his vanity so far as to make him think any thing of his was worth showing; and none of the following works were ever composed with a view to the press. To amuse himself with the little creations of his own fancy, amid the toil and fatigues of a laborious life; to transcribe the various feelings, the loves, the griefs, the hopes, the fears, in his own breast; to find some kind of counterpoise to the struggles of a world, always an alien scene, a task uncouth to the poetical mind; these were his motives for courting the Muses, and in these he found Poetry to be its own reward.

Now that he appears in the public character of an Author, he does it with fear and trembling. So dear is fame to the rhyming tribe, that even he, an obscure, nameless Bard, shrinks aghast, at the thought of being branded as 'An impertinent blockhead, obtruding his nonsense on the world; and because he can make a shift to jingle a few doggerel, Scotch rhymes together, looks upon himself as a Poet of no small consequence forsooth.'

It is an observation of that celebrated Poet,* whose divine Elegies do honor to our language, our nation, and our species, that 'Humility has depressed many a genius to a hermit, but never raised one to fame.' If any Critic catches at the word genius, the Author tells him, once for all, that he certainly looks upon himself as possest of some poetic abilities, otherwise his publishing in the manner he has done, would be a manœuvre below the worst character, which, he hopes, his worst enemy will ever give him: but to the genius of a Ramsay, or the glorious dawnings of the poor, unfortunate Ferguson, he, with equal unaffected sincerity, declares, that, even in his highest pulse of vanity, he has not the most distant pretensions. These two justly admired Scotch Poets he has often had in his eye in the following pieces; but rather with a view to kindle at their flame, than for servile imitation.

To his Subscribers, the Author returns his most sincere thanks. Not the mercenary bow over a counter, but the heart-throbbing gratitude of the Bard, conscious how much he is indebted to Benevolence and Friendship, for gratifying him, if he deserves it, in that dearest wish of every poetic bosom – to be distinguished. He begs his readers, particularly the Learned and the Polite, who may honor him with a perusal, that they will make every allowance for Education and Circumstances of Life: but, if after a fair, candid, and impartial criticism, he shall stand convicted of Dulness and Nonsense, let him be done by, as he would in that case do by others – let him be condemned, without mercy, to contempt and oblivion.

*Shenstone

AUGUST

*"Lord grant that we may lead a gude life! for
a gude life maks a gude end; at least it helps weel!"*

from a letter to Agnes McLehose

1st AUGUST

It Was Upon a Lammas Night
to the tune of Corn Rigs Are Bonie

THE FIRST DAY OF AUGUST is known in some Christian communities as 'Lammas' (or 'Loaf Mass'), when loaves baked using freshly harvested grain were taken to Christian churches to give thanks for the new crop. The tradition can be traced back to the classical festival of 'First Fruits'.

We begin August, then, with a song set upon a 'Lammas night' when 'corn rigs are bonie'. Corn rigs were an agricultural drainage system whereby fields were ploughed into three-foot-high ridges and, according to several traditional Scottish songs, these ridges concealed many a lovers' tryst! In his notes to the 'Interleaved' *Scots Musical Museum*, Burns recorded an old, more explicit chorus for a song set to the same air:

> O corn-rigs & rye-rigs,
> O corn-rigs is bonie;
> Whare e'er ye meet a bonie lass,
> Preen up her apron, Johnie.—

Although Burns's version is considerably more romantic, erotic even, we might consider that the 'dénouement' – to use the bard's own word – is the same. Nevertheless, this is another example of his ability to make the bawdy very beautiful indeed.

It was upon a Lammas night,
   When corn rigs are bonie,
Beneath the moon's unclouded light,
   I held awa to Annie:
The time flew by, wi' tentless heed,
   Till 'tween the late and early;
Wi' sma' persuasion she agreed,
   To see me thro' the barley.

The sky was blue, the wind was still,
   The moon was shining clearly;
I set her down, wi' right good will,
   Amang the rigs o' barley:
I ken't her heart was a' my ain;
   I lov'd her most sincerely;
I kiss'd her owre and owre again,
   Amang the rigs o' barley.

I lock'd her in my fond embrace;
   Her heart was beating rarely:
My blessings on that happy place,
   Amang the rigs o' barley!
But by the moon and stars so bright,
   That shone that night so clearly!
She ay shall bless that happy night
   Amang the rigs o' barley.

I hae been blythe wi' Comrades dear;
   I hae been merry drinking;
I hae been joyfu' gath'rin gear;
   I hae been happy thinking:
But a' the pleasures e'er I saw,
   Tho' three times doubl'd fairly,
That happy night was worth them a',
   Amang the rigs o' barley.

chorus.

Corn rigs, an' barley rigs,
   An' corn rigs are bonie:
I'll ne'er forget that happy night,
   Amang the rigs wi' Annie.

2ND AUGUST

On the Religious Satires
from Burns's autobiographical letter to Dr John Moore, 2nd August 1787

PERHAPS ROBERT BURNS'S most famous letter – and certainly his longest – is his 'history of MYSELF' for Dr John Moore, which is dated on this day in 1787. The importance of this narrative of Burns's life is such that several extracts appear over the course of this book. Today we read his account of the emergence of some of his most famous works, the religious satires, paving the way for a more substantial consideration of Burns and religion over the course of the month of August.

The first of my poetic offspring that saw the light was a burlesque lamentation on a quarrel between two reverend Calvinists, both of them dramatis personae in my Holy Fair.— I had an idea myself that the piece had some merit; but to prevent the worst, I gave a copy of it to a friend who was very fond of these things, and told him I could not guess who was the Author of it, but that I thought it pretty clever.— With a certain side of both clergy and laity it met with a roar of applause.— Holy Willie's Prayer next made its appearance, and alarmed the kirk-Session so much that they held three several meetings to look over their holy artillery, if any of it was pointed against profane Rhymers. Unluckily for me, my idle wanderings led me, on another side, point blank within the reach of their heaviest metal.—

3RD AUGUST

from The Holy Tulzie

FOLLOWING ON FROM YESTERDAY'S ENTRY, here is an extract from 'the first of Burns's poetic offspring that saw the light' – 'The Holy Tulzie' or, as it appeared in a 1786 pamphlet, 'An Unco Mournfu' Tale'. Burns explained in a manuscript copy of the poem that, 'The occasion was a bitter and shameless quarrel between two reverend gentlemen – Mr Moodie of Riccarton and Mr Russell of Kilmarnock.' Moodie and Russell were 'Auld Licht' Presbyterian ministers.

Burns lived in a century of ongoing religious unrest in the Scottish Kirk, which had split into two factions: the 'Auld Licht' and the 'New Licht'. The Auld Licht was staunchly Calvinist in its outlook, held to the doctrine of predestination (which contended that God had irrevocably mapped the lives of the blessed and the damned), and believed that the church should come before the state. The New Licht, to which Burns more broadly leaned, emphasised such principles as private judgement and freedom of conscience, but also believed in Patronage; that ministers should be assigned by lay patrons without the need for consent from parish elders or the congregation. The New Licht held that education and intellect played an important part in the selection of more moderate ministers, as opposed to the public preaching contests frequently entered into by over-zealous Auld Licht evangelicals – contests that Burns satirises in poems such as 'The Holy Fair' (see 6th August).

In these stanzas, Burns ridicules the ministers' ungodly public 'tulzie', or brawl, over parish boundaries. Their 'pious godly flocks' are sardonically referred to as the 'brutes' who elected them without, it is implied, due diligence regarding their abilities or temperament. The clergymen themselves are the subject of derision by the New Lichts, who perceive in both ministers the characteristics that they detest in one another: 'villainy' and 'hypocrisy'.

O a' ye pious, godly flocks,
Weel fed on pastures orthodox,
Wha now will keep you frae the fox,
      Or worrying tykes?
Or wha will tent the waifs an' crocks,
      About the dykes?

The twa best herds in a' the west,
That e'er ga'e gospel horns a blast
These five an' twenty simmers past
      O dool to tell!
Hae had a bitter black outcast
      Atween themsel'.

O, Moodie man, an' wordy Russell,
How could ye breed sae vile a bustle;
Ye'll see how New-Light herds will whistle,
      An' think it fine!
The Lord's cause ne'er gat sic a twistle,
      Sin' I hae min'.

O, sirs! whae'er wad expeckit
Your duty ye wad sae negleckit?
Ye wha were ne'er by lairds respeckit,
      To wear the plaid;
But by the brutes themselves eleckit,
      To be their guide.

What flock wi' Moodie's flock could rank,
Sae hale and hearty every shank?
Nae poison'd soor Arminian stank
          He let them taste;
But Calvin's fountain-head they drank,
          O, sic a feast!

The thummart, willcat, brock, an' tod,
Weel kend his voice thro' a' the wood,
He smell'd their ilka hole an' road,
          Baith out an in;
An' weel he lik'd to shed their bluid,
          An' sell their skin.

What herd like Russell tell'd his tale;
His voice was heard thro' muir and dale,
He ken'd the Lord's sheep, ilka tail,
          Owre a' the height;
An' saw gin they were sick or hale,
          At the first sight.

He fine a mangy sheep could scrub,
Or nobly fling the Gospel club,
And New-Light herds could nicely drub
          Or pay their skin;
Could shake them o'er the burning dub,
          Or heave them in.

Sic twa — O! do I live to see't?
Sic famous twa should disagree't,
And names, like "villain," "hypocrite,"
          Ilk ither gi'en,
While New-Light herds, wi' laughin spite,
          Say neither's liein!

4TH AUGUST

On Procrastination
from a letter to Helen Maria Williams, 1789

GIVEN THE EXTENT OF HIS writings, his busy family life, his 'colourful' social activities and the reality of his very demanding occupation, we could be forgiven for thinking that Burns never stopped. However, just like the rest of us, there were days when the bard's motivation took a dip. How many of us can relate to his thoughts here, particularly in the heat of summer?

Of the many problems in the nature of that wonderful creature, Man, this is one of the most extraordinary, that he shall go on from day to day, from week to week, from month, or perhaps from year to year, suffering a hundred times more in an hour from the impotent consciousness of neglecting what he ought to do, than the very doing of it would cost him.

5TH AUGUST

On Poetry and Marriage
from a letter to David Sillar, 5th August 1789

F OR BURNS, POETRY AND LOVE went hand in hand – most of the
time, anyway ... Here he warns his 'brother poet' that poetry and
marriage don't necessarily make a fruitful combination.

I hear you have commenced Married Man; so much the better,
though perhaps your Muse may not fare the better for it.— I know
not whether the NINE GIPSEYS are jealous of my Lucky, but they
are a good deal shyer since I could boast the important relation of
Husband.—

6TH AUGUST

from The Holy Fair

THIS FAMOUS RELIGIOUS SATIRE is a brawling, satirical account of the Mauchline annual communion. Communions were held in the summer and, as an eagerly anticipated opportunity for different communities to enjoy the hospitality and company of neighbouring parishes, they formed an important and enjoyable part of ecclesiastical life in the eighteenth century.

Although essentially a sacramental occasion, Burns's 'The Holy Fair' concentrates on the social and convivial aspects of these gatherings, which were held in notorious regard by those who complained that they became, in practice, more of a festival than a religious occasion. Burns skilfully adopts the Christis Kirk stanza form, a genre commonly associated with carnivalesque celebration, to emphasise the contrast between the behaviour of the devout religious, intent on worship, and those more light-hearted attendees who see the occasion as an opportunity to attract members of the opposite sex. True to form, Burns takes aim at the 'elect swatch' for their pride and self-importance, with his most scathing attacks reserved for 'sober ministers and orthodoxy laity', among them Alexander Moodie of Riccarton (1728–99), who Burns refers to as 'Sawnie'.

In this extract Burns focuses on the mixed motivations of the congregation, and on the delivery of Sawnie's dogmatic sermon. Ironically, Sawnie is portrayed as a man possessed with demonic qualities, more 'frightful' than Satan himself. His fanaticism is extended to the pious members of the congregation when the grotesque, bestial delivery of his sermon (as opposed to its content) is said to 'fire the heart devout / Like cantharidian plaisters'; like an aphrodisiac!

Here stands a shed to fend the show'rs,
    An' screen our countra Gentry;
There, *Racer Jess*, an' twathree whores,
    Are blinkan at the entry.
Here sits a raw o' tittlin jads,
    Wi' heaving breast an' bare neck;
An' there, a batch o' *Wabster lads*,
    Blackguarding frae Kilmarnock,
                        For *fun* this day.

Here, some are thinkan on their sins,
    An' some upo' their claes;
Ane curses feet that fyl'd his shins,
    Anither sighs an' prays:
On this hand sits an *Elect* swatch,
    Wi' screwed-up, grace-proud faces;
On that, a set o' chaps, at watch,
    Thrang winkan on the lasses
                        To *chairs* that day.

O happy is that man, an' blest!
    Nae wonder that it pride him!
Whase ain dear lass, that he likes best,
    Comes clinkin down beside him!
Wi' arm repos'd on the *chair-back*,
    He sweetly does compose him;
Which, by degrees, slips round her *neck*,
    An's loof upon her *bosom*,
                        Unkend that day.

Now a' the congregation o'er
    Is silent expectation;
For Moodie speels the holy door,
    Wi' tidings o' salvation.
Should *Hornie*, as in ancient days,
    'Mang sons o' God present him,

The vera sight o' Moodie's face,
   To 's ain *het hame* had sent him
               Wi' fright that day.

Hear how he clears the points o' Faith
   Wi' rattlin an' thumpin!
Now meekly calm, now wild in wrath,
   He's stampin, an' he's jumpan!
His lengthen'd chin, his turn'd up snout,
   His eldritch squeel an' gestures,
O how they fire the heart devout,
   Like *cantharidian* plaisters
               On sic a day!

7TH AUGUST

from Holy Willie's Prayer

IN THE OPENING STANZAS of this poem Burns draws attention
to 'Holy Willie's' firm belief that he is 'a burning and a shining
light'; one of the 'elect', preordained for heaven. As we see in the
entry for the ninth of February, the lecherous Willie, far from being
a 'shining light', is susceptible to drunkenness and – to use the kirk's
term – fornication. Burns uses this religious satire, then, to point out
the misguided complacency that might be derived from the Calvinist
doctrine of predestination by those who consider themselves to be
'elect'. For the bard, it is individuals such as 'Holy Willie' who traduce
religion from the inside.

O Thou, who in the heavens does dwell,
Who, as it pleases best thysel',
Sends ane to heaven an' ten to hell,
                    A' for Thy glory,
And no for ony gude or ill
                    They've done afore Thee!

I bless and praise Thy matchless might,
When thousands Thou hast left in night,
That I am here afore Thy sight,
                    For gifts an' grace,
A burning and a shining light
                    To a' this place.

What was I, or my generation,
That I should get sic exaltation?
I wha deserve most just damnation
                    For broken laws,
Sax thousand years ere my creation,
                    Thro' Adam's cause!

8TH AUGUST

On Being Busy
from a letter to Alexander Cunningham, 8th August 1790

THE AUGUST OF 1790 was clearly a busy time of year for Burns the ploughman-poet-exciseman, so much so that he was not always entirely up to date with his correspondence. But who wouldn't forgive his 'negligence' following several such 'pat similes' for his chaotic life?

Forgive me, my once dear and ever dear Friend, my seeming negligence.— You cannot sit down and fancy the busy life I lead.— I laid down my Goose-feather to beat my brains for a pat Simile, and had some thoughts of a country Grannum at a family-christening; a bride on the market-day before her marriage; an Orthodox Clergyman at a Paisley Sacrament; an Edinburgh Bawd on a Sunday evening; a tavern-keeper at an Election dinner &c. &c. &c. but the resemblance that hits my fancy best is that poor, blackguard miscreant, Satan, who, as Holy Writ tells us, roams about like a roaring lion, seeking, *searching*, whom he may devour.— However, tossed about as I am, if I chuse (and who would not chuse) to bind down with the crampets of Attention the brazen foundation of Integrity, I may rear up the Superstructure of Independence, and from its daring turrets bid defiance to the storms of Fate.

9TH AUGUST

On Poets
from a letter to Miss Helen Craik, 9th August 1790

O N THIS DAY IN 1790, it seems that the bard was suffering
with a bout of 'melancholy' – and so he turned his attention
to the disposition of the 'Rhyming tribe'. This extract from his
correspondence is particularly interesting for the insight it offers
regarding Burns's perspective on the complexities, tensions and
contradictions that he considered to be inherent in the character of a
poet. These features of his personality clearly had a significant impact
upon his life and literature.

It is often a reverie of mine, when I am disposed to be melancholy,
the characters and fates of the Rhyming tribe.— There is not among
all the Martyrologies that ever were penned, so rueful a narrative as
Johnson's Lives of the Poets.— In the comparative view of Wretches,
the criterion is not what they are doomed to suffer, but how they
are formed to bear.— Take a being of our kind; give him a stronger
imagination and more delicate sensibility, which will ever between
them engender a more ungovernable set of Passions than the usual
lot of man; implant in him an irresistible impulse to some idle vagary,
such as arranging wild flowers in fantastical nosegays, tracing the
grasshopper to his haunt by his chirping song, watching the frisks of
the little minnows in the sunny pool, or hunting after the intrigues of
wanton butterflies — in short, send him adrift after some wayward
pursuit which shall eternally mislead him from the paths of Lucre; yet
curse him with a keener relish than any man living for the pleasures
that only Lucre can bestow; lastly, fill up the measure of his woes by
bestowing on him a spurning sense of his own dignity; and you have
created a wight nearly as miserable as a Poet.—

10TH AUGUST

On Religion and Moral Sense
from a letter to James Burness, 3rd August 1784

I N TODAY'S EXTRACT, Burns establishes that the ideas and beliefs of individuals should not necessarily be accepted by the multitude as the 'immediate influences of the deity'. In fact, he suggests that the only immediate influences of the deity that man can be sure of are the 'sacred Monitors' supplied to his person by God in order to discourage the fanaticism disseminated by disturbed, misinformed or delusional individuals. The 'sacred Monitors' to which Burns refers are 'sound reason' and 'common sense'.

This My Dear Sir, is one of the many instances of folly in leaving the guidance of sound reason, and common sense in matters of Religion.— Whenever we neglect or despise these sacred Monitors, the whimsical notions of a perturbated brain are taken for the immediate influences of the Deity, and the wildest fanaticism, and the most inconsistent absurdities will meet with abettors and converts.— Nay I have often thought, that the more out-of-the-way and ridiculous their fancies are, if once they are sanctified under the sacred name of RELIGION, the unhappy, mistaken votaries are the more firmly glued to them.

11TH AUGUST

from The Kirk of Scotland's Garland – A New Song

BURNS REFERS ONCE AGAIN to the importance of 'sense' rather than strict Calvinist orthodoxy in this flyting poem – 'flyting' being a ritual exchange of insults, often in verse form – which mentions one or two names with which the reader will now be familiar.

Burns once again takes aim at 'Holy Will', this time adding theft to his list of ungodly transgressions. 'Daddy Auld' is the Rev. William Auld who publicly rebuked Burns in 1786 for his affair with Jean Armour, subsequently issuing the dejected poet with a certificate of bachelorhood. Burns also refers to himself and his 'priest-skelping' turns – his anti-clerical satires – emphasising that there is no insult he could level at the clergymen that would be 'waur', or worse, than they already are.

Orthodox, Orthodox, who believe in John Knox,
    Let me sound an alarm to your conscience;
A heretic blast has been blown i' the West
    That what is not sense must be Nonsense, Orthodox,
    That what is not sense must be Nonsense.

[...]

Daddy Auld, Daddy Auld, there's a tod in the fauld,
    A tod meikle waur than the clerk:
Tho' ye do little skaith, ye'll be in at the death,
    For if ye canna bite ye can bark,
    Daddy Auld! If ye canna bite ye can bark.

Holy Will, Holy Will, there was wit i' your skull,
    When ye pilfer'd the alms o' the poor;
The timmer is scant when ye're ta'en for a saint,
    Wha should swing in a rape for an hour,
    Holy Will! Wha should swing in a rape for an hour.

Poet Burns, Poet Burns, wi' your priest-skelping turns,
    Why desert ye your auld native shire?
Tho' your Muse is a gipsey, yet were she even tipsey,
    She could ca' us nae waur than we are, Poet Burns,
    She could ca' us nae waur than we are.

12TH AUGUST

On Religion
from a letter to Agnes McLehose, 8th January 1788

R OBERT BURNS'S DESCRIPTION of his creed is meticulously considered in this letter which contains the most extensive and, perhaps, the most articulate expression of Burns's religious beliefs. The bard demonstrates his profound theological awareness, but concludes by lightening the tone with a pithy, yet meaningful and entirely appropriate, proverb: 'Lord grant that we may lead a gude life! for a gude life maks a gude end; at least it helps weel!'

He, who is our Author and Preserver, and will one day be our Judge, must be, (not for his sake in the way of duty, but from the native impulse of our hearts,) the object of our reverential awe and grateful adoration: He is almighty and all-bounteous, we are weak and dependent; hence, prayer and every other sort of devotion.— "He is not willing that any should perish, but that all should come to everlasting life;" consequently it must be in every one's power to embrace His offer of "everlasting life;" otherwise He could not, in justice, condemn those who did not. A mind pervaded, actuated and governed by purity, truth and charity, though it does not merit heaven, yet is an absolutely necessary pre-requisite, without which heaven can neither be obtained nor enjoyed; and, by Divine promise, such a mind shall never fail of attaining "everlasting life:" hence, the impure, the deceiving, and the uncharitable, extrude themselves from eternal bliss, by their unfitness for enjoying it. The Supreme Being has put the immediate administration of all this, for wise and good ends known to himself, into the hands of Jesus Christ, a great Personage, whose relation to Him we cannot comprehend, but whose relation to us is a Guide and Saviour; and who, except for our own obstinacy and misconduct, will bring us all, through various ways and by various means, to bliss at last. These are my tenets, my lovely friend; and which, I think, cannot be well disputed. My creed is pretty nearly expressed in the last clause of Jamie Dean's grace, an honest weaver in Ayrshire: "Lord grant that we may lead a gude life! for a gude life maks a gude end; at least it helps weel!"

13TH AUGUST

from The Cotter's Saturday Night

FOLLOWING ITS PUBLICATION in the Kilmarnock edition of 1786, and all throughout the nineteenth century, 'The Cotter's Saturday Night' was one of Burns's most well-received works. This was in part owing to those passages of the lengthy poem – four of which are extracted here – that depict a humble and pious scene of family worship. The poem was also appreciated for its perceived biographical elements, and for the compliment that it seemingly pays Burns's father William, 'The saint, the father, and the husband'. This work certainly offers an alternative perspective on eighteenth-century religious life when considered alongside Burns's religious satires, although it is the case that the poem as a whole is considerably more complex in its consideration of eighteenth-century rural life than nineteenth-century critics and biographers gave Burns credit for.

The chearfu' supper done, wi' serious face,
    They, round the ingle, form a circle wide;
The Sire turns o'er, with patriarchal grace,
    The big *ha'-Bible*, ance his *Father's* pride:
His bonnet rev'rently is laid aside,
    His *lyart haffets* wearing thin and bare;
Those strains that once did sweet in Zion glide,
    He wales a portion with judicious care;
'And let us worship God!' he says with solemn air.

They chant their artless notes in simple guise,
    They tune their *hearts*, by far the noblest aim:
Perhaps *Dundee's* wild warbling measures rise,
    Or plaintive *Martyrs*, worthy of the name;

Or noble *Elgin* beets the heaven-ward flame;
    The sweetest far of SCOTIA's holy lays:
Compar'd with these, *Italian trills* are tame;
    The tickl'd ears no heart-felt raptures raise;
Nae unison hae they, with our CREATOR's praise.

[…]

Then, kneeling down to HEAVEN'S ETERNAL KING,
    The *Saint*, the *Father*, and the *Husband* prays:
Hope 'springs exulting on triumphant wing,'
    That *thus* they all shall meet in future days:
There, ever bask in *uncreated rays*,
    No more to sigh, or shed the bitter tear,
Together hymning their CREATOR's praise,
    In *such society*, yet still more dear;
While circling Time moves round in an eternal sphere.

Compar'd with *this*, how poor Religion's pride,
    In all the pomp of *method*, and of *art*,
When men display to congregations wide,
    Devotion's ev'ry grace, except the *heart*!
The POWER, incens'd, the Pageant will desert,
    The pompous strain, the sacerdotal stole;
But haply, in some *Cottage* far apart,
    May hear, well pleas'd, the language of the Soul;
And in His *Book of Life* the Inmates poor enroll.

14TH AUGUST

On a Scotch Bard Gone to the West Indies

O N THIS DAY IN 1786, Burns wrote to James Smith in Mauchline that his plans to emigrate to Jamaica had been frustrated. This was on account of the fact that, 'to send me from Savannah la Mar to Port Antonio will cost my Master, Charles Douglas, upwards of fifty pounds; besides running the risk of throwing myself into a pleuritic fever in consequence of hard travelling in the sun'. Burns states his intention to delay travel until the first of September when another more direct vessel was due to depart from Greenock. He still, however, seems to be resolved on leaving the country. This poem, published in the Kilmarnock edition a fortnight before Burns wrote the letter, is his imagined 'send-off' for the journey that he would never make.

A' ye wha live by sowps o' drink,
A' ye wha live by crambo-clink,
A' ye wha live and never think,
            Come, mourn wi' me!
Our *billie's* gien us a' a jink,
            An' owre the Sea.

Lament him a' ye rantan core,
Wha dearly like a random-splore;
Nae mair he'll join the *merry roar*,
            In social key;
For now he's taen anither shore,
            An' owre the Sea!

The bonie lasses weel may wiss him,
And in their dear *petitions* place him:
The widows, wives, an' a' may bless him,
        Wi' tearfu' e'e;
For weel I wat they'll sairly miss him
        That's owre the Sea!

O Fortune, they hae room to grumble!
Hadst thou taen aff some drowsy bummle,
Wha can do nought but fyke an' fumble,
        'Twad been nae plea;
But he was gleg as ony wumble,
        That's owre the Sea!

Auld, cantie Kyle may weepers wear,
An' stain them wi' the saut, saut tear:
'Twill mak her poor, auld heart, I fear,
        In flinders flee:
He was her *Laureat* monie a year,
        That's owre the Sea!

He saw Misfortune's cauld *Nor-west*
Lang-mustering up a bitter blast;
A Jillet brak his heart at last,
        Ill may she be!
So, took a birth afore the mast,
        An' owre the Sea.

To tremble under Fortune's cummock,
On a scarce a bellyfu' o' *drummock*,
Wi' his proud, independant stomach,
        Could ill agree;
So, row't his hurdies in a *hammock*,
        An' owre the Sea.

He ne'er was gien to great misguidin,
Yet coin his pouches wad na bide in;
Wi' him it ne'er was *under hidin*;
   He dealt it free:
The *Muse* was a' that he took pride in,
    That's owre the Sea.

Jamaica bodies, use him weel,
An' hap him in cozie biel:
Ye'll find him ay a dainty chiel,
   An' fou o' glee:
He wad na wrang'd the vera *Deil*,
    That's owre the Sea.

Farewell, my *rhyme-composing billie*!
Your native soil was right ill-willie;
But may ye flourish like a lily,
   Now bonilie!
I'll toast ye in my hindmost *gillie*,
    Tho' owre the Sea!

15TH AUGUST

Song – Composed in August
to the tune of I had a horse, I had nae mair

NOW THAT WE ARE MIDWAY through the month there are subtle signs of autumn on the horizon. Not only that, but as we have passed the 'Glorious Twelfth' of August, the shooting season – which typically lasts until October – is now underway. Burns captures this time of year perfectly in this beautiful song, which powerfully juxtaposes stunning natural imagery and tender love, with the 'slaught'ring guns' of 'tyrannic man'.

Now westlin winds, and slaught'ring guns
    Bring Autumn's pleasant weather;
And the moorcock springs, on whirring wings,
    Amang the blooming heather:
Now waving grain, wide o'er the plain,
    Delights the weary Farmer;
And the moon shines bright, when I rove at night,
    To muse upon my Charmer.

The Partridge loves the fruitful fells;
    The Plover loves the mountains;
The Woodcock haunts the lonely dells;
    The soaring Hern the fountains:
Thro' lofty groves the Cushat roves,
    The path of man to shun it;
The hazel bush o'erhangs the Thrush,
    The spreading thorn the Linnet.

Thus ev'ry kind their pleasure find,
  The savage and the tender;
Some social join, and leagues combine;
  Some solitary wander:
Avaunt, away! the cruel sway,
  Tyrannic man's dominion;
The Sportsman's joy, the murd'ring cry,
  The flutt'ring, gory pinion!

But, Peggy dear, the ev'ning's clear,
  Thick flies the skimming Swallow;
The sky is blue, the fields in view,
  All fading – green and yellow:
Come let us stray our gladsome way,
  And view the charms of Nature;
The rustling corn, the fruited thorn,
  And ev'ry happy creature.

We'll gently walk, and sweetly talk,
  Till the silent moon shine clearly;
I'll grasp thy waist, and fondly prest,
  Swear how I love thee dearly:
Not vernal show'rs to budding flow'rs,
  Not Autumn to the Farmer,
So dear can be, as thou to me,
  My fair, my lovely Charmer!

16TH AUGUST

On Moral Sense
from a letter to Alexander Cunningham, 25th February 1794

BURNS'S 'REASON' CAUSED HIM to question religious orthodoxy, though not God. Here he develops the idea that reason and sense have a part to play in the understanding and practice of religion, and also the notion that these are a gift from God, part of an innate 'sense of the mind' that he believes to be 'an original and component part of the human soul' instilled in the conscience of man.

Burns's creed might be considered progressive in that it is very much in keeping with the Enlightenment philosophy of Francis Hutcheson in *Treatise II: An Inquiry Concerning the Original of Our Ideas of Virtue or Moral Good* (1725); the idea that mankind are born with an innate moral sense and a natural inclination to do what is right.

Still there are two great pillars that bear us up, amid the wreck of misfortune and misery. The ONE is composed of the different modifications of a certain noble, stubborn something in man, known by the names of courage, fortitude, magnanimity. The OTHER is made up of those feelings and sentiments, which, however the sceptic may deny them, or the enthusiastic disfigure them, are yet, I am convinced, original and component parts of the human soul; those senses of the mind, if I may be allowed the expression, which connect us with and link us to, those awful obscure realities – an all-powerful and equally beneficent God; and a world to come, beyond death and the grave. The first gives the nerve of combat, while a ray of hope beams on the field:– the last pours the balm of comfort into the wounds which time can never cure.

17TH AUGUST

The Solemn League and Covenant

O N THIS DAY IN 1643, the Scottish Kirk accepted the terms of 'The Solemn League and Covenant, for Reformation and Defence of Religion, the honour and happiness of the King, and the peace and safety of the three kingdoms of England, Scotland and Ireland'. It pledged to 'sincerely, really and constantly, through the grace of God, endeavour in our several places and callings, the preservation of the reformed religion in the Church of Scotland, in doctrine, worship, discipline and government, against our common enemies'. Ultimately, it sought the religious and political union of the three kingdoms under Presbyterianism, and it represented an incendiary moment in the English Civil War. Here are Burns's lines about the Covenant.

The Solemn League and Covenant
    Now brings a smile, now brings a tear.
But sacred Freedom, too, was theirs;
    If thou 'rt a slave, indulge thy sneer.

18TH AUGUST

Had I a Cave on Some Wild Distant Shore
to the tune of Robin Adair

I T WAS MID-AUGUST 1793 when Burns wrote to George Thomson
– the editor of *A Select Collection of Original Scottish Airs* – 'That
crinkum crankum tune, Robin Adair, has run so in my head, and
I succeeded so ill in my last attempt, that I have ventured in this
morning's walk, one essay more.' Another song inspired by Alexander
Cunningham's unrequited love for Anne Stewart, it is extremely
dramatic in its portrayal of heartbreak – this time, with more than a
hint of bitterness. It must have been a brooding walk indeed!

Had I a cave on some wild, distant shore,
Where the winds howl to the waves' dashing roar:
   There would I weep my woes,
   There seek my lost repose,
   'Till Grief my eyes should close,
   Ne'er to wake more.

Falsest of woman-kind, canst thou declare,
All thy fond plighted vows, fleeting as air!
   To thy new lover hie,
   Laugh o'er thy perjury—
   Then in thy bosom try,
   What peace is there!

19TH AUGUST

Allan Water

THIS SONG WAS COMPOSED in August as Burns 'sat and raved under the shade of an old thorn' and he then sent it to Thomson on this day in 1793. With striking images of 'waving corn' and the 'shortening day', it paints the perfect picture of late summertime. The bard, for one, was pleased with his efforts: 'Bravo! Say I: it is a good song.'

By Allan-side I chanc'd to rove,
　　While Phoebus sank beyond Benledi;
The winds were whispering thro' the grove,
　　The yellow corn was waving ready:
I listen'd to a lover's sang,
　　And thought on youthful pleasures many;
And ay the wild wood echoes rang,
　　O dearly do I lo'e thee, Annie.

O happy be the woodbine bower,
　　Nae nightly bogle make it eerie;
Nor ever sorrow stain the hour,
　　The place and time I met my dearie!
Her head upon my throbbing breast,
　　She, sinking, said, 'I'm thine for ever!'
While many a kiss the seal imprest,
　　The sacred vow, we ne'er should sever.

The haunt o' spring's the primrose-brae,
  The Simmer joys the flocks to follow;
How cheery, thro' her shortening day,
  Is autumn in her weeds o' yellow:
But can they melt the glowing heart,
  Or chain the soul in speechless pleasure;
Or thro' each nerve the rapture dart,
  Like meeting Her, our bosom's treasure.

20TH AUGUST

from Epistle to John Goldie in Kilmarnock, Author of *The Gospel Recovered*

JOHN GOLDIE (1717–1811) was a Kilmarnock wine merchant and the author of several tracts on science and religion, among them *Essays on Various Important Subjects, Moral and Divine: Being an Attempt to Distinguish True from False Religion* (1779) and *The Gospel Recovered from its Captive State* (1785). Burns subscribed to Goldie's progressive outlook regarding the importance of reason and common sense in matters religious, and he shared Goldie's opposition to Auld Licht Presbyterianism. As such, the opening stanzas of this verse epistle gloat that Goldie's works have left the comically personified 'Bigotry', 'Superstition', 'Enthusiasm' (or fanaticism), and 'Orthodoxy' fighting for life.

O: Gowdie, terror o' the whigs,
Dread o' blackcoats and reverend wigs!
Sour Bigotry on his last legs
          Girns and looks back,

Wishing the ten Egyptian plagues
       May sieze you quick.—

Poor gapin, glowrin Superstition!
Waes me, she's in a sad condition:
Fye! bring Black Jock her state-physician,
       To see her water:
Alas! there's ground great suspicion,
       She'll ne'er get better.—

Enthusiasm's past redemption,
Gane in a gallopin consumption:
Not a' her quacks wi' a' their gumption
       Can ever mend her;
Her feeble pulse gies strong presumption,
       She'll soon surrender.—

Auld Orthodoxy lang did grapple
For every hole to get a stapple,
But now, she fetches at the thrapple
       And fights for breath;
Haste, gie her name up in the Chapel
       Near unto death.—

21st AUGUST

from Tam Samson's Elegy

TAM SAMSON (1722–1795) was a friend of Burns and a keen grouse shooter. In a note accompanying this poem Burns writes, 'When this worthy old Sportsman went out last muir-fowl season, he supposed it was to be, in Ossian's phrase, "the last of his fields", and expressed an ardent wish to die and be buried in the muirs. On this hint the Author composed his Elegy and Epitaph.'

And so, although 'Tam' was very much alive, Burns granted his friend's wish – imaginatively, at least – even printing the poem in his Edinburgh edition of 1787.

When August winds the heather wave,
And Sportsmen wander by yon grave,
Three vollies let his mem'ry crave,
      O' pouther an' lead,
Till Echo answer frae her cave,
      Tam Samson's dead!

Heav'n rest his saul whare'er he be!
Is th' wish o' mony mae than me:
He had twa fauts, or maybe three,
      Yet what remead?
Ae social, honest man want we:
      Tam Samson's dead!

The Epitaph

Tam Samson's weel-worn clay here lies,
   Ye canting Zealots, spare him!
If Honest Worth in Heaven rise,
   Ye'll mend or ye win near him.

Per Contra

Go, Fame, an' canter like a filly
Thro' a' the streets an' neuks o' *Killie*;
Tell ev'ry social honest billie
   To cease his grievin,
For yet, unskaithed by Death's gleg gullie,
   Tam Samson's livin'!

22ND AUGUST

O Saw Ye Bonie Lesley
to the tune of The Collier's Dochter

BURNS SENT A VERSION of this song to Frances Dunlop on this day in 1792. He writes of Lesley Bailie (1768–1843), who inspired the ballad, 'Apropos (though how it is apropos I have not leisure to explain) do you know that I am almost in love with an acquaintance of yours. "Almost!" said I – I am in love, souse! Over head and ears, deep as the most unfathomable abyss of the boundless ocean.'

O saw ye bonie Lesley,
　　As she gaed o'er the Border?
She's gane, like Alexander,
　　To spread her conquests farther.
To see her is to love her,
　　And love but her for ever;
For Nature made her what she is,
　　And ne'er made sic anither!

Thou art a queen, fair Lesley,
　　Thy subjects we before thee:
Thou art divine, fair Lesley,
　　The hearts of men adore thee.
The Deil he could na skaithe thee,
　　Or aught that wad belang thee!
He'd look into thy bonie face,
　　And say, 'I canna wrang thee.'

The powers aboon will tent thee,
　　Misfortune sha'na steer thee;
Thou'rt like themsels sae lovely,
　　That ill they'll ne'er let near thee.
Return again, fair Lesley,
　　Return to Caledonie!
That we may brag we hae a lass,
　　There's nane again sae bonie.

23RD AUGUST

from To W. Simpson, Ochiltree

ON THIS DAY IN 1305, Sir William Wallace – one of Scotland's most famed leaders and greatest heroes – was executed in London for treason. Wallace denied this accusation until his dying moments on account of the fact he had never sworn allegiance to his enemy, King Edward I, in the first place. In a brutal execution, he was hung, drawn and quartered; his head displayed on London Bridge and his limbs sent to Newcastle, Berwick, Perth and Stirling to deter further insurrection. The fight for Scottish sovereignty continued, however, and Robert the Bruce led Scotland to independence in 1306 – the year following Wallace's death. In the following lines from a verse epistle to a fellow poet William Simpson, Burns – inspired by his Scottish muse Coila – commemorates the legendary Scot and his legacy.

We'll sing auld COILA's plains an' fells,
Her moors red-brown wi' heather bells,
Her banks an' braes, her dens an' dells,
   Where glorious WALLACE
Aft bure the gree, as story tells,
   Frae Suthron billies.

At WALLACE' name, what Scottish blood,
But boils up in a spring-tide flood!
Oft have our fearless fathers strode
   By WALLACE' side,
Still pressing onward, red-wat-shod,
   Or glorious dy'd!

24TH AUGUST

On Lord Balmerino's Durk
from a letter to David Blair, 25th August 1795

B URNS'S SENTIMENTAL CONNECTION to Scottish history is nicely illustrated by his possession of a most remarkable Jacobite relic; a dirk belonging to Arthur Elphinstone, the 6th Lord of Balmerino (1688–1746), one of the leaders of the 1745 Jacobite uprising.

A 'durk', or a dagger, was one of the weapons typically carried by Highland soldiers. In a letter written on the 25th of August 1795, Burns explains the history and provenance of the prized object, which after the poet's death was held for many years at Dean Castle in Kilmarnock and might now be viewed as part of the Burns collections held in East Ayrshire.

The following, my dear Sir, is the history of Lord Balmerino's durk which you now have.— In the year 1745, a Bailie in Glasgow (I once knew his name, but have forgotten it) who was a secret abettor of the Jacobite interest, sent some hundred pairs of shoes to the Prince's army through the medium of Lord Balmerino; and that with many compliments to my Lord's personal character.— His Lordship, who was truly a brave, generous, worthy character, wrote back a grateful letter of thanks to the Bailie, and accompanied the letter with a present of his own durk.— This durk and letter came into the possession of a son of the Bailie, a dissipated worthless fellow, who sold the durk to a particular friend of mine for an anchor of Ferintosh whisky.— My friend, who is a gentleman of the most undoubted probity, has often perused the letter; and well had it been for the interests of the durk had my friend's chastity been equal to his integrity! For one evening the devil and the flesh tempted him, in the moment of intoxication, to a house of a certain description, where he was

384

despoiled of his durk, and that durk despoiled of its knife and fork, and silver mounting which had been indeed very rich; His Lordship's arms, cypher, crest, &c. being elegantly engraved on several places of it.— My friend, after a diligent search, at last recovered his durk in this mutilated situation; from him it came to me.—

     This history, I pledge myself to you, is authentic.—

Yours ever

Robert Burns

25TH AUGUST

On the Prospect of Touring Scotland
from a letter to David Erskine, Lord Buchan, 7th February 1787

O N THIS DAY IN 1787, Burns set off on an eagerly anticipated tour of the Scottish Highlands, accompanied by his friend, the Edinburgh schoolmaster William Nicol (1744–1797). At Nicol's suggestion, the companions travelled by chaise (a type of horse-drawn carriage). This was a luxury, but Burns explained in a letter to Robert Ainslie that 'Nicol thinks it more comfortable than horse-back, to which I say, Amen: so Jenny Geddes goes home to Ayrshire, to use a phrase of my Mother's, "wi' her finger in her mouth".'

    This did free up the bard's own hand for writing in what is now known as his 'Highland Tour Journal', a wonderful, messy document in bumpy shorthand, presumably written en route. Burns, then, was able to fulfil the wish expressed in this letter, written some months earlier. And so, over the course of the next few weeks we will join Burns on those parts of his tour that inspired him to 'fire his muse' at 'Scottish story and Scottish scenes'.

Your Lordship touches the darling chord of my heart when you advise me to fire my muse at Scottish story and Scottish scenes — I wish for nothing more than to make a leisurely Pilgrimage through my native country; to sit and muse on those once hard-contended fields, where Caledonia, rejoicing, saw her bloody lion borne through broken ranks to victory and fame; and thus catching the inspiration, to pour the death-less Names in song.— But, my Lord, in the midst of these delighting, enthusiastic Reveries, a long-visaged, dry, moral looking Phantom strides across my imagination, and with the frigid air of a declaiming Preacher sets off with a text of Scripture — "I, Wisdom, dwell with Prudence".

26TH AUGUST

On Visiting Stirlingshire
from a letter to Robert Muir, 26th August 1787

BURNS SPENT THIS DAY IN 1787 making a pilgrimage through those parts of Stirlingshire made famous in the Scottish Wars of Independence, pondering the events in Scottish history that he immortalised with patriotic effect in 'Scots Wha Hae' (see 24th June). The bard was clearly taken with the romance of the locations. Yet, ever the farmer, he also maintained a keen eye on Highland agricultural practice. The romanticisation of Scottish scenery in song, and the practical scrutiny of the land in his journal, were recurring features of Burns's Highland tour.

This morning I kneel'd at the tomb of Sir John the Graham, the gallant friend of the immortal Wallace; and two hours ago, I said a fervent prayer for old Caledonia over the hole in a blue whin-stone where Robert the Bruce fixed his royal standard on the banks of Bannockburn; and just now from Stirling Castle I have seen by the setting sun the glorious prospect of the windings of Forth through the rich carse of Stirling, and skirt the equally rich carse of Falkirk.— The crops are very strong, but so very late that there is no harvest, except a ridge of two perhaps in ten miles, all the way I have travelled from Edinburgh.—

27TH AUGUST

Lines Written by SOMEBODY on the Window of an Inn at Stirling on Seeing the Royal Palace in Ruins

ON THIS DAY IN 1787, Burns stayed at James Wingate's Inn – now the Golden Lion – on Quality Street in Stirling. He famously engraved the following lines on the hotel window using a diamond stylus. Unsurprisingly this verse proved a source of controversy for its emphatically anti-Hanoverian sentiment.

> Here Stewarts once in triumph reign'd;
> And laws for Scotland's weal ordain'd;
> But now unroof'd their Palace stands,
> Their sceptre's fall'n to other hands;
> Fallen indeed, and to the earth,
> Whence grovelling reptiles take their birth.—
> The injur'd STEWART line are gone,
> A Race outlandish fill their throne;
> An idiot race, to honor lost;
> Who know them best despise them most.—

28TH AUGUST

Come, Let Me Take Thee to My Breast
to the tune of Cauld Kail in Aberdeen

O N THIS DAY IN 1793 Burns was once again colluding with his Scottish muse Coila to create a beautiful song. Burns playfully suggests to George Thomson that, in the absence of any new poets, Coila has followed him from Ayrshire to Dumfriesshire:

> That tune, Cauld Kail in Aberdeen, is such a favourite of yours that I once more roved out yesterevening for a gloaming-shot at the Muses; when the Muse that presides o'er the shores of Nith, or rather my old inspiring dearest Nymph, Coila, whispered me the following.— I have two reasons for thinking that it was my early, sweet simple Inspirer that was by my elbow, "smooth gliding without step" and pouring the song on my glowing fancy; In the first place, since I left Coila's native haunts, not a fragment of a Poet has arisen to cheer her solitary musings by catching inspiration from her; so I more than suspect that she has followed me hither, or at least makes me occasional visits. Secondly, the last stanza of this song I send you is the very words that Coila taught me many years ago, and which I set to an old Scots reel in Johnson's *Museum*.

Note here that the first stanza is in English, and the last in Scots.

Come, let me take thee to my breast,
  And pledge we ne'er shall sunder;
And I shall spurn, as vilest dust,
  The warld's wealth and grandeur:

And do I hear my Jeanie own,
    That equal transports move her?
I ask for dearest life alone
    That I may live to love her.

When in my arms, wi' a thy charms,
    I clasp my countless treasure;
I seek nae mair o' Heaven to share,
    Than sic a moment's pleasure:
And by thy een, sae bonie blue,
    I swear I'm thine for ever!
And on thy lips I seal my vow,
    And break it shall I never.

29TH AUGUST

Written with a Pencil Over the Chimney-Piece, in the Parlour of the Inn at Kenmore, Taymouth

IT WOULD APPEAR THAT BURNS dispensed with the need for paper on his Highland tour … This overblown, romantic description of the scenery around Kenmore – visited on this day in 1787 – takes in Taymouth Castle, which is the seat of the Campbells of Breadalbane.

Admiring Nature in her wildest grace,
These northern scenes with weary feet I trace;
O'er many a winding dale and painful steep,
Th' abodes of coveyed grouse and timid sheep,
My savage journey, curious, I pursue,
Till fam'd Breadalbaine opens to my view.—
The meeting cliffs each deep-sunk glen divides,
The woods, wild-scattered, clothe their ample sides;

Th' outstretching lake, imbosomed 'mong the hills,
The eye with wonder and amazement fills;
The Tay meandering sweet in infant pride,
The palace rising on his verdant side;
The lawns wood-fringed in Nature's native taste;
The hillocks dropt in Nature's careless haste,
The arches striding o'er the new-born stream;
The village glittering in the noontide beam.

Poetic ardours in my bosom swell,
Lone wandring by the hermit's mossy cell:
The sweeping theatre of hanging woods;
The incessant roar of headlong tumbling floods.—

Here Poesy might wake her heaven taught lyre,
And look through Nature with creative fire;
Here, to the wrongs of Fate half reconcil'd,
Misfortune's lightened steps might wander wild;
And Disappointment, in these lonely bounds,
Find balm to soothe her bitter rankling wounds:
Here heart-struck Grief might heavenward stretch her scan,
And injured Worth forget and pardon Man.

30TH AUGUST

The Birks of Aberfeldy
to the tune of Birks of Abergeldie

BURNS CLAIMED TO HAVE COMPOSED this song 'on the spot' as he stood 'under the falls of Aberfeldy, at, or near, Moness' on this day in 1787. For Burns, it would seem, the romance of the watery scene invites female company.

Bonie lassie, will ye go,
 Will ye go, will ye go;
Bonie lassie, will ye go
 To the birks of Aberfeldy?

Now Simmer blinks on flowery braes,
 And o'er the chrystal streamlets plays;
Come let us spend the lightsome days
 In the birks of Aberfeldy.
  Bonie lassie &c.

The little birdies blythely sing
 While o'er their heads the hazels hing;
Or lightly flit on wanton wing,
 In the birks of Aberfeldy.
  Bonie lassie &c.

The braes ascend like lofty wa's,
 The foamy stream deep-roaring fa's,
O'erhung wi' fragrant-spreading shaws,
 The birks of Aberfeldy.
  Bonie lassie &c.

The hoary cliffs are crown'd wi' flowers,
 White o'er the linns the burnie pours,
And rising, weets wi' misty showers
 The birks of Aberfeldy.
  Bonie lassie &c.

Let Fortune's gifts at random flee,
 They ne'er shall draw a wish frae me;
Supremely blest wi' love and thee,
 In the birks of Aberfeldy.
  Bonie lassie &c.

31st AUGUST

from The Humble Petition of Bruar Water to the Noble Duke of Athole

O N FRIDAY THE 31ST OF AUGUST 1787, Burns visited Blair Atholl, taking in Blair Castle – the seat of John Murray, the 4th Duke of Atholl (1755–1830). The poet's fame was opening some very special doors: he was honoured with an invitation to dine with the Duke and Duchess, and to stay at the castle as their guest. It was here that he was introduced to Robert Graham of Fintry who would later become his Commissioner in the Board of Excise.

Burns was inspired by his visit to compose 'The Humble Petition of Bruar Water to the noble Duke of Athole'. In a note to the text in his Edinburgh edition he explained, 'Bruar Falls in Athole are exceedingly picturesque and beautiful; but their effect is much impaired by the want of trees and shrubs.' In the poem, Burns imagines the river's petition for 'towering trees' and 'bonie spreading bushes'.

My lord, I know your noble ear
    Woe ne'er assails in vain;
Embolden'd thus, I beg you'll hear
    Your humble slave complain,
How saucy Phoebus' scorching beams,
    In flaming summer-pride,
Dry-withering, waste my foamy streams,
    And drink my crystal tide.

The lightly-jumping, glowrin trouts,
    That thro' my waters play,
If, in their random, wanton spouts,
    They near the margin stray;

If, hapless chance! they linger lang,
    I'm scorching up so shallow,
They're left, the whitening stanes amang,
    In gasping death to wallow.

Last day I grat wi' spite and teen,
    As poet Burns came by,
That, to a Bard, I should be seen
    Wi' half my channel dry:
A panegyric rhyme, I ween,
    Ev'n as I was he shor'd me;
But, had I in my glory been,
    He, kneeling, wad ador'd me.

Here, foaming down the skelvy rocks,
    In twisting strength I rin;
There, high my boiling torrent smokes,
    Wild-roaring o'er a linn:
Enjoying each large spring and well,
    As Nature gave them me,
I am, altho' I say't mysel,
    Worth gaun a mile to see.

Would then my noble master please
    To grant my highest wishes,
He'll shade my banks wi' towering trees,
    And bonie spreading bushes.
Delighted doubly then, my lord,
    You'll wander on my banks,
And listen mony a grateful bird
    Return you tuneful thanks.

SEPTEMBER

The sober Autumn enter'd mild,
*   When he grew wan and pale;*
His bending joints and drooping head
*   Show'd he began to fail.*

from John Barleycorn – A Ballad

1st SEPTEMBER

Address to the Shade of Thomson

TODAY MARKS THE FIRST DAY of autumn, a season that, despite the leaves falling, was fruitful in creative terms for Burns. The bard wrote to George Thomson in 1793, 'Autumn is my propitious season.— I make more verses in it than in all the year else.'

Our poem for today is Burns's sincere tribute to another poet profoundly inspired by the seasons, James Thomson (1700–1748). Thomson's series of four poems *The Seasons* (1726–1730) was one of the most popular poetic works of the eighteenth century and Burns quotes from Thomson on several occasions throughout his correspondence.

In 1791, David Erskine, Earl of Buchan (1742–1829) invited Burns to the inauguration of a commemorative bust at Thomson's birthplace in Ednam in the Scottish Borders. It was planned to coincide with the anniversary of Thomson's birth early in September. Burns responded that he would be unable to attend the event, explaining, 'a week or two in the very middle of my harvest is what I dare not venture on'. He did, however, enclose the following verses which pay tribute to Thomson, 'sweet Poet of the Year', by taking the subject of his most celebrated work.

While virgin Spring, by Eden's flood,
    Unfolds her tender mantle green,
Or pranks the sod in frolic mood,
    Or tunes Eolian strains between.

While Summer with a matron grace
   Retreats to Dryburgh's cooling shade,
Yet oft, delighted, stops to trace
   The progress of the spiky blade.

While Autumn, benefactor kind,
   By Tweed erects his aged head,
And sees, with self-approving mind,
   Each creature on his bounty fed.

While maniac Winter rages o'er
   The hills whence classic Yarrow flows,
Rousing the turbid torrent's roar,
   Or sweeping, wild, a waste of snows.

So long, sweet Poet of the Year,
   Shall bloom that wreath thou well hast won;
While Scotia, with exulting tear,
   Proclaims that *Thomson* was her son.

2ND SEPTEMBER

On Women
from a letter to John Richmond, 1st September 1786

EARLY IN SEPTEMBER 1786, Burns's planned emigration had been delayed yet again. Although a new departure date loomed, so too did impending fatherhood. From this letter to John Richmond, it appears that Burns's anger towards Jean Armour had subsided. He expresses concern regarding the forthcoming birth of their twins, but he is not yet sufficiently recovered from their estrangement to contemplate reconciliation. Remarkably, Burns takes up the cause of Jenny Surgeoner, with whom Richmond had an affair and then seemingly disowned following the discovery of her pregnancy. Burns obviously perceived significant differences in the circumstances surrounding his and Richmond's relationships, although one does wonder whether he wasn't indeed taking a 'liberty' in chastising his friend, given his own lingering plans to leave the country.

I am still here in statu quo, tho I well expected to have been on my way over the Atlantic by this time.— The Nancy, in which I was to have gone, did not give me warning enough.— Two days notice was too little for me to wind up my affairs and go for Greenock. I now am to be a passenger aboard the Bell, Captain Cathcart, who sails at the end of this month. I am under little apprehension now about Armour. The warrant is still in existence, but some of the first Gentlemen in the county have offered to befriend me; and besides, Jean will not take any step against me without letting me know, as nothing but the most violent menaces could have forced her to sign the Petition.— I have called on her once and again of late; as she, at this moment, is threatened with the pangs of approaching travail; and I assure you, my dear Friend, I cannot help being anxious, very anxious for her situation.— She would gladly now embrace that offer she once rejected, but it shall never more be in her power.—

I saw Jenny Surgeoner of late, and she complains bitterly against you. You are acting very wrong. My friend; her happiness or misery is bound up in your affection or unkindness. Poor girl! she told me with tears in her eyes that she had been at great pains since she went to Paisley, learning to write better; just on purpose to be able to correspond with you; and had promised herself great pleasure in your letters.— Richmond, I know you to be a man of honour, but this conduct of yours to a poor girl who distractedly loves you, and whom you have ruined — forgive me, my friend, when I say it is highly inconsistent with the manly Integrity that I know your bosom glows with.—Your little sweet innocent too — but I beg your pardon; 'tis taking an improper liberty.—

3RD SEPTEMBER

Nature's Law

BURNS FIRST BECAME A FATHER on this day in 1786. In a short letter to his good friend Richmond, Burns, obviously elated, exclaims, 'Wish me luck, dear Richmond! Armour has just now brought me a fine boy and girl at one throw. God bless them, poor little dears!' To another friend, Gavin Hamilton, Burns sent today's poem, which makes explicit reference to 'The third of Libra's equal sway, / That gave another Burns'. Libra – symbolised by balanced scales – is one of the astrological signs associated with the month of September. Here Burns, invigorated and full of masculine bravado following the birth of his 'double portion' (named Robert and Jean after their parents), positively and wittily espouses what he refers to as 'Nature's Law': humanity's inescapable desire to procreate.

Let other heroes boast their scars,
  The marks of sturt and strife;
And other poets sing of wars,
  The plagues of human life;
Shame fa' the fun; wi' sword and gun
  To slap mankind like lumber!
I sing his name, and nobler fame,
  Wha multiplies our number.

Great Nature spoke, with air benign,
  'Go on, ye human race;
This lower world I you resign;
  Be fruitful and increase.
The liquid fire of strong desire
  I've pour'd it in each bosom;
Here, on this hand, does Mankind stand,
  And there, is Beauty's blossom.'

The Hero of these artless strains,
  A lowly bard was he,
Who sung his rhymes in Coila's plains,
  With meikle mirth an' glee;
Kind Nature's care had given his share
  Large, of the flaming current;
And, all devout, he never sought
  To stem the sacred torrent.

He felt the powerful, high behest
  Thrill, vital, thro' and thro';
And sought a correspondent breast,
  To give obedience due:
Propitious Powers screen'd the young flow'rs,
  From mildews of abortion;
And lo! the Bard – a great reward –
  Has got a double portion!

Auld cantie Coil may count the day,
    As annual it returns,
The third of Libra's equal sway,
    That gave another Burns,
With future rhymes, an' other times,
    To emulate his sire,
To sing auld Coil in nobler style,
    With more poetic fire.

Ye Powers of peace, and peaceful song,
    Look down with gracious eyes;
And bless auld Coila, large and long,
    With multiplying joys;
Lang may she stand to prop the land,
    The flow'r of ancient nations;
And Burnses spring, her fame to sing,
    To endless generations!

4TH SEPTEMBER

On the Harvest
from a letter to Frances Dunlop, 5th September 1788

EARLY IN THE SEPTEMBER OF 1788, Burns was battling both melancholy and the weather as he attempted to manage the harvest of his Ellisland crop amid thunderstorms and fog. True to form, he turned to his muse – to the composition of poetry – for comfort and distraction.

Here am I again, dear Madam, dating my letter from this haunt of the CUMMINS, this elbow of existence;— and here am I in the middle of my harvest, without good weather when I may have Reapers, and without Reapers when I may have good weather.— The tremendous thunder-storm of yesternight and the lurid fogs of this morning have driven me, for refuge from the Hypochondria which I fear worse than the devil, to my Muse[.]

5TH SEPTEMBER

Lines on the Fall of Fyers, Near Loch Ness

O N THIS DAY IN 1787, Burns, midway through his tour of the Scottish Highlands, visited the Falls of Foyers. This dramatic waterfall, located in a steep, wooded gorge just beyond the south-east bank of Loch Ness, was already a significant tourist attraction in the eighteenth century. Burns notes in the Glenriddell manuscript, 'I composed these lines standing on the brink of the hideous caldron below the water-fall.' The bard's imagery here certainly captures the full force of this magnificent scene.

Among the heathy hills and ragged woods
The roaring Fyers pours his mossy floods;
Till full he dashes on the rocky mounds,
Where, thro' a shapeless breach, his stream resounds.
As high in air the bursting torrents flow,
As deep recoiling surges foam below,
Prone down the rock the whitening sheet descends,
And viewless Echo's ear, astonished, rends.
Dim-seen, through rising mists and ceaseless showers,
The hoary cavern, wide-surrounding, lowers:
Still thro' the gap the struggling river toils,
And still, below, the horrid cauldron boils.

6TH SEPTEMBER

On the Excise
from a letter to John Mitchell Esq, c. September 1790

M OST OF US HAVE EXPERIENCED the occasional bad day at
work, and Burns was no exception. For the bard, this day in 1790
really was 'one of those days'. Here he writes to his colleague John
Mitchell, Collector of Excise in Dumfries, of a long and frustrating
journey, an exhausted and incredulous horse, and 'offenders' – or tax
evaders – who only add insult to a very unpleasant injury!

I have galloped over my ten parishes these four days, until this moment
that I am just alighted, or rather, that my poor jackass skeleton of a
horse has let me down; for the miserable devil has been on his knees
half a score of times within the last twenty miles, telling me in his
own way— "Behold, am not I thy faithful jade of a horse, on which
thou hast ridden these many years!!!" In short, Sir, I have broke my
horse's wind, and almost broke my own neck, besides some injuries
in a part that shall be nameless, owing to a hard-hearted stone of a
saddle; and I find that every Offender has so many Great Men to
espouse his cause, that I shall not be surprised if I am committed
to the strong Hold of the Law tomorrow for insolence to the dear
friends of the Gentlemen of the Country.—

7TH SEPTEMBER

Castle Gordon
to the tune of Morag

A S PART OF HIS HIGHLAND TOUR, Burns visited Castle Gordon near Fochabers on this day in 1787. Burns describes his hosts, Alexander Gordon, 4th Duke of Gordon (1743–1827) and his wife, Jane, Duchess of Gordon (1748/9–1812), in his tour journal: 'The Duke makes me happier than ever great man did – noble princely yet mild condescending and affable gay and kind – The Duchess charming witty kind and sensible. God bless them.'

Burns clearly kept very distinguished company on parts of his tour; he was invited to stay and to dine with the Duke and Duchess. However, his travelling companion William Nicol, seemingly envious and furious at being left behind at the inn, readied the chaise and issued Burns with an ultimatum, forcing the bard to cut short his time at Gordon Castle. In a letter to the Castle librarian, James Hoy, Burns's witty criticism of Nicol plays upon his occupation as a schoolmaster:

> I shall certainly, among my legacies, leave my latest curse to that unlucky predicament which hurried me, tore me away from Castle Gordon.— May that obstinate Son of Latin Prose be curst to Scotch-mile periods, and damn'd to seven-league paragraphs; while Declension and Conjugation, Gender, Number and Time, under the raged banners of Dissonance and Disarrangement eternally rank against him in hostile array!!!!!!

Today's song was enclosed with this letter, composed as a compliment – and perhaps an apology – to his hosts.

Streams that glide in orient plains,
Never bound by Winter's chains;
Glowing here on golden sands,
There immixed with foulest stains
From Tyranny's empurpled hands:
These, their richly gleaming waves,
I leave the tyrants and their slaves;
Give me the stream that sweetly laves
       The banks by Castle Gordon.

Torrid forests, ever gay,
Shading from the burning ray
Hapless wretches sold to toil;
Or the ruthless Native's way,
Bent on slaughter, blood, and spoil:
Woods that ever verdant wave,
I leave the tyrant and the slave,
Give me the groves that lofty brave
       The storms, by Castle Gordon.

Wildly here without control,
Nature reigns and rules the whole;
In that sober, pensive mood,
Dearest to the feeling soul,
She plants the forest, pours the flood:
Life's poor day I'll musing rave,
And find at night a sheltering cave,
Where waters flow and wild woods wave,
       By bonny Castle Gordon.

8TH SEPTEMBER

Comin Thro' the Rye

HARVEST TIME IS ONGOING at this point in September and, during his farming years, Burns would have been hard at work gathering. This well-known song is set in fields of tall waving rye, perfect for concealing a lovers' embrace, and refers to the seemingly boundless curiosity – or common gossip! – aroused by romantic liaisons. This 'polite' version is based upon a bawdy song in *The Merry Muses of Caledonia* (1799), which follows much the same pattern, but in which the 'bodies' do more than 'kiss'. Even so, the sexual undercurrent is not entirely eradicated from this version. After all, how are we to suppose Jenny 'draigl't' a' her petticoatie'?

Comin thro' the rye, poor body,
   Comin thro' the rye,
She draigl't a' her petticoatie
   Comin thro' the rye.

Oh Jenny's a' weet, poor body,
   Jenny's seldom dry,
She draigl't a' her petticoatie
   Comin thro' the rye.

Gin a body meet a body
   Comin thro' the rye,
Gin a body kiss a body
   Need a body cry.
     Oh Jenny's, &c.

Gin a body meet a body
  Comin thro' the glen;
Gin a body kiss a body
  Need the warld ken!
    Oh Jenny's, &c.

9TH SEPTEMBER

Wha'll M-w Me Now
to the tune of Comin' Thro' the Rye

THIS BAWDY SONG IS SET TO the tune 'Comin' thro' the Rye', which was the title for yesterday's selection. It offers a more serious perspective on human relationships, however, as Burns ventriloquises the female voice to highlight the personal and social consequences of illicit sex in the eighteenth century, and to advocate responsibility and mutual respect between sexual partners. This song shows that, even in his bawdy verse, Burns was capable of taking account of female sexuality, and that he did in fact possess a conscience when it came to sex.

O Wha'll m-w me now, my jo,
  An' wha'll m-w me now:
A sodger wi' his bandileers
  Has bang'd my belly fu'.

O' I hae tint my rosy cheek,
  Likewise my waste sae sma';
O wae gae by the sodger lown,
  The sodger did it a'.
    An' wha'll, &c.

Now I maun thole the scornfu' sneer
    O' mony a' saucy quine;
When, curse upon her godly face!
    Her c--t's as merry's mine.
        An' wha'll, &c.

Our dame hauds up her wanton tail,
    As due as she gaes lie;
An' yet misca's a young thing,
    The trade if she but try.
        An' wha'll, &c.

Our dame can lae her ain gudeman,
    An' m-w for glutton greed;
An' yet misca' a poor thing
    That's m--n' for its bread.
        An' wha'll, &c.

Alake! sae sweet a tree as love,
    Sic bitter fruit should bear!
Alake, that e'er a merry a--e,
    Should draw a sa'tty tear.
        An' wha'll, &c.

But deevil damn the lousy loun,
    Denies the bairn he got!
Or lea's the merry a--e he loe'd
    To wear a ragged coat!
        An' wha'll, &c.

10TH SEPTEMBER

Robin Shure in Hairst

TODAY'S BURNSIAN WORDS are based on a traditional song that the bard adapted for his friend Robert Ainslie. The song refers to Ainslie's family home at Dunse and also to his profession: the goose feather and 'whittle' (pen knife) were tools commonly associated with clerks and lawyers. Here a young woman – a kirk elder's daughter – is partnered up with 'Robin' for the harvest, only to be seduced by him and then disappointed that he has but three quills, rather than an ample store of winter 'vittle', or grain.

Robin shure in hairst,
  I shure wi' him.
Fient a heuk had I,
  Yet I stack by him.

I gaed up to Dunse,
  To warp a wab o' plaiden;
At his daddie's yet,
  Wha met me but Robin.
      Robin shure in hairst, &c

Was na Robin bauld,
  Tho' I was a cotter,
Play'd me sic a trick
  And me the Eller's dochter?
      Robin shure in hairst, &c

Robin promis'd me
  A' my winter vittle;
Fient haet he had but three
  Goose feathers and whittle.
    Robin shure in hairst, &c

11TH SEPTEMBER

John Barleycorn – A Ballad

T HIS STRIKING ALLEGORY conflates the crop year with a powerful
  religious metaphor in its representation of the natural lifecycle
of 'John Barleycorn' – the personification of malting barley. The song
describes Barleycorn's death, resurrection, execution and eventual
transubstantiation from grain to whisky – or 'his very heart's blood'.

There was three kings into the east,
  Three kings both great and high,
And they hae sworn a solemn oath
  John Barleycorn should die.

They took a plough and plough'd him down,
  Put clods upon his head,
And they hae sworn a solemn oath
  John Barleycorn was dead.

But the chearful Spring came kindly on,
  And show'rs began to fall;
John Barleycorn got up again,
  And sore surpris'd them all.

The sultry suns of Summer came,
  And he grew thick and strong,
His head weel arm'd wi' pointed spears,
  That no one should him wrong.

The sober Autumn enter'd mild,
  When he grew wan and pale;
His bending joints and drooping head
  Show'd he began to fail.

His colour sicken'd more and more,
  He faded into age;
And then his enemies began
  To show their deadly rage.

They've taen a weapon, long and sharp,
  And cut him by the knee;
Then ty'd him fast upon a cart,
  Like a rogue for forgerie.

They laid him down upon his back,
  And cudgell'd him full sore;
They hung him up before the storm,
  And turn'd him o'er and o'er.

They filled up a darksome pit
  With water to the brim;
They heaved in John Barleycorn,
  There let him sink or swim.

They laid him out upon the floor,
  To work him farther woe;
And still, as signs of life appear'd,
  They toss'd him to and fro.

They wasted, o'er a scorching flame,
    The marrow of his bones;
But a Miller us'd him worst of all,
    For he crush'd him between two stones.

And they hae taen his very heart's blood,
    And drank it round and round;
And still the more and more they drank,
    Their joy did more abound.

John Barleycorn was a hero bold,
    Of noble enterprise;
For if you do but taste his blood,
    'Twill make your courage rise.

'Twill make a man forget his woe;
    'Twill heighten all his joy:
'Twill make the widow's heart to sing,
    Tho' the tear were in her eye.

Then let us toast John Barleycorn,
    Each man a glass in hand;
And may his great posterity
    Ne'er fail in old Scotland!

12TH SEPTEMBER

The Lea-rig

T HE LOVERS IN THIS ATMOSPHERIC PASTORAL SONG arrange
to meet in the low light of 'gloamin', or dusk, when shepherds
gather in sheep for milking – milk which would then be made into
cheese. This time the lovers' rendezvous takes place, not in the corn
fields, but on the 'lea-rig' (or pasture).

When o'er the hill the eastern star,
   Tells bughtin-time is near, my jo,
And owsen frae the furrow'd field
   Return sae dowf and weary O;
Down by the burn, where scented birks
   Wi' dew are hanging clear, my jo,
I'll meet thee on the lea-rig,
   My ain kind dearie O.

At midnight hour, in mirkest glen,
   I'd rove and ne'er be irie O,
If thro' that glen I gaed to thee,
   My ain kind dearie O.
Altho' the night were ne'er sae wet,
   And I were ne'er sae weary O,
I'll meet thee on the lea-rig,
   My ain kind dearie O.

The hunter lo'es the morning sun;
   To rouse the mountain deer, my jo;
At noon the fisher seeks the glen,
   Adown the burn to steer, my jo:
Gie me the hour o' gloamin grey,
   It maks my heart sae cheary O
To meet thee on the lea-rig,
   My ain kind dearie O.

13TH SEPTEMBER

Third Epistle to Lapraik

BURNS'S THIRD VERSE EPISTLE to John Lapraik was dated on this day in 1785. This extract offers a striking description of harvest time, during which both farmer-poets would have been particularly busy – or 'skelpin at it'. Burns explains that 'bitter daudin' showers' have wet his crop and frustrated his efforts, so he has replaced his scythe with his pen while he waits for the sun to reappear. In a witty and typically defiant reference to his religious satires, Burns rejects the censure of 'kirk-folks', redirecting his and Lapraik's attention to women and whisky, for '*They* are the muses'. He looks forward to a dram with his friend, with the proviso, of course, that their harvested crops are properly 'theckit'.

Guid speed and furder to you, Johny,
Guid health, hale han's, an' weather bony;
Now, when ye're nickan down fu' cany
       The staff o' bread,
May ye ne'er want a stoup o' brany
       To clear your head.

May Boreas never thresh your rigs,
Nor kick your rickles aff their legs,
Sendin' the stuff o'er muirs an' haggs
                    Like drivin wrack;
But may the tapmast grain that wags
                    Come to the sack.

I'm bizzie too, an' skelpin at it,
But bitter, daudin showers hae wat it;
Sae my auld stumpie pen I gat it
                    Wi' muckle wark,
An' took my jocteleg an whatt it,
                    Like ony clark.

It's now twa month that I'm your debtor,
For your braw, nameless, dateless letter,
Abusin' me for harsh ill-nature
                    On holy men,
While deil a hair yoursel ye're better,
                    But mair profane.

But let the kirk-folk ring their bells,
Let's sing about our noble sels;
We'll cry nae jads frae heathen hills
                    To help, or roose us,
But browster wives an' whiskie stills,
                    They are the muses.

Your friendship, Sir, I winna quat it,
An' if ye mak' objections at it,
Then han' in neive some day we'll knot it,
                    An' witness take,
An' when wi' usquabae we've wat it
                    It winna break.

417

But if the beast an' branks be spar'd
Till kye be gaun without the herd,
And a' the vittel in the yard,
                    An' theckit right,
I mean your ingle-side to guard
                    Ae winter night.

Then muse-inspirin' aqua-vitae
Shall make us baith sae blythe an' witty,
Till ye forget ye're auld an' gatty,
                    An' be as canty
As ye were nine year less than thretty,
                    Sweet ane an' twenty!

But stooks are cowpet wi' the blast,
An' now the sinn keeks in the west,
Then I maun rin amang the rest
                    An' quat my chanter;
Sae I subscribe mysel in haste,
                    Yours, Rab the Ranter.

14TH SEPTEMBER

A Sonnet Upon Sonnets

E VER CONSCIOUS OF HIS CRAFT and keen to experiment with different poetic forms, Burns here tries his hand at a sonnet by playing upon the verse form's traditional composition of fourteen lines.

Fourteen, a sonneteer thy praises sings;
What magic myst'ries in that number lie!
Your hen hath fourteen eggs beneath her wings
That fourteen chickens to the roost may fly.
Fourteen full pounds the jockey's stone must be;
His age fourteen – a horse's prime is past.
Fourteen long hours too oft the Bard must fast;
Fourteen bright bumpers – bliss he ne'er must see!
Before fourteen, a dozen yields the strife;
Before fourteen – e'en thirteen's strength is vain.
Fourteen good years – a woman gives us life;
Fourteen good men – we lose that life again.
What lucubrations can be more upon it?
Fourteen good measur'd verses make a sonnet.

15TH SEPTEMBER

Yon Wild Mossy Mountains

BURNS NOTED IN AN 'INTERLEAVED' COPY of the *Scots Musical Museum* that this song 'alludes to a part of my private history, which it is of no consequence to the world to know'. And, indeed, Burns seems to have maintained his silence regarding the identity of this mysterious woman, here praised for her modesty and loved for her kindness. Burns's rich language does justice to the wild and spectacular Scottish scenery.

Yon wild, mossy mountains sae lofty and wide,
That nurse in their bosom the youth o' the Clyde;
Where the grouse lead their coveys thro' the heather to feed,
And the shepherd tents his flock as he pipes on his reed.

Not Gowrie's rich valley, nor Forth's sunny shores,
To me hae the charms o' yon wild, mossy moors;
For there, by a lanely, sequestered stream,
Resides a sweet Lassie, my thought and my dream.

Amang thae wild mountains shall still be my path,
Ilk stream foaming down its ain green, narrow strath,
For there, wi' my Lassie, the day-lang I rove,
While o'er us unheeded, flee the swift hours o' Love.

She is not the fairest, altho' she is fair;
O' nice education but sma' is her skair;
Her parentage humble as humble can be;
But I loe the dear Lassie because she loes me.

To Beauty what man but maun yield him a prize,
In her armour of glances, and blushes, and sighs;
And when Wit and Refinement hae polish'd her darts,
They dazzle our een, as they flie to our hearts.

But Kindness, sweet Kindness, in the fond-sparkling e'e,
Has lustre outshining the diamond to me;
And the heart beating love as I'm clasp'd in her arms,
O, these are my Lassie's all-conquering charms.

16TH SEPTEMBER

On Contributions for *A Select Collection of Original Scottish Airs* *from* a letter to George Thomson, 16th September 1792

I N SEPTEMBER OF 1792, Burns was approached by George Thomson
(1757–1851) with a request to 'improve' the poetry of some traditional
Scottish songs. Thomson's intention was to pair them with settings
of Scottish airs by European composers including Pleyel, Haydn,
Beethoven, Weber and Kozeluch. In this extract Burns expresses his
enthusiasm for the project, and so began his work as a song collector
and songwriter for *A Select Collection of Original Scottish Airs* (1793–
1841). Alongside his work for James Johnson's *Scots Musical Museum*
(1787–1818), this would prove one of the bard's most important and
prolific creative collaborations.

As the request you make to me will positively add to my enjoyments
in complying with it, I shall enter into your undertaking with all the
small portion of abilities I have, strained to their utmost exertion by
the impulse of Enthusiasm.— Only, don't hurry me: "Deil tak the
hindmost" is by no means the crie de guerre of my Muse.— […]

As for any remuneration, you mat think my Songs either *above* or *below* price; for they shall absolutely be one or the other.— In the honest enthusiasm with which I embark in your undertaking, to talk of money, wages, fee, hire, &c. would be downright Sodomy of Soul!— A proof each of the Songs that I compose or amend I shall receive as a favour.— In the rustic phrase of the Season: "Gude speed the wark!"

17TH SEPTEMBER

On the Highland Tour
from a letter to Gilbert Burns, 17th September 1787

O N THIS DAY IN 1787, Burns wrote to his brother Gilbert with news that he had completed his tour of the Scottish Highlands. Although Burns's tour journal is fascinating and provides essential context for the poems and songs related to his travels, it reads simply as a series of notes. Today's selection is, therefore, the most fluent and concise prose account of the bard's travels. It is particularly interesting for the insight that it offers regarding him as a tourist. As well as visiting beauty spots and sites of historical significance, the bard clearly indulged in some 'literary tourism', purposefully stopping at locations connected with his own reading.

He could never have imagined that, in the nineteenth century, the Burns tourist trail – referred to on souvenirs and various parapher-nalia as 'The Land of Burns' – would become a significant attraction in Scotland and one of Great Britain's most popular 'pilgrimages' for literary tourists. Why not take your own literary tour and visit the 'Land of Burns'? Or perhaps you could use this account of Burns's own tour to follow in the bard's footsteps, while viewing Scotland through the lens of his poetry.

I arrived here safe yesterday evening, after a tour of twenty-two days, and travelling near six hundred miles; windings included.— My farthest stretch was about ten miles beyond Inverness.— I went through the heart of the Highlands, by Crieff, Taymouth the famous seat of the Lord Breadalbine, down the Tay, among cascades and Druidical circles of stones, to Dunkeld, a seat of the Duke of Athole, thence cross Tay, and up one of his tributary streams to Blair of Athole, another of the Duke's seats, where I had the honor of spending nearly two days with his Grace and Family, thence many miles through a wild country, among cliffs gray with eternal snows and gloomy, savage glens, till I crossed Spey and went down the stream through Strathspey, so famous in Scottish music, Badenoch, &c. till I reached Grant Castle, where I spent half a day with Sir James Grant and family; then cross the country for Fort George, cald by the way at Cawdor, the ancient seat of M'beth you know in Shakespeare, there I saw the identical bed in which Tradition says king Duncan was murdered, lastly from Fort George to Inverness.—

I returned by the coast; Nairn, Forrse and so on to Aberdeen, thence to Stonehive where James Burness from Montrose met me by appointment.— […] The rest of my stages are not worth rehearsing — warm as I was from Ossian's country where I had seen his very grave, what cared I for fisher-towns and fertile Carses?— I slept at the famous Brodie of Brodie's one night and dined at Gordon Castle next day with the Duke, Duchess and Family.—

from To the Rev. John McMath, Enclosing a Copy of Holy Willie's Prayer, which he had requested

W HEN BURNS COMPOSED this verse epistle on the 17th of September 1785, John McMath (1755–1825) was a Presbyterian minister and an assistant at Tarbolton Kirk. The moderate McMath had supported Burns's friend Gavin Hamilton in his dispute with 'Holy Willie' Fisher (see 10th February). That McMath was liberal in his outlook is clear from this extract in which Burns, once again prevented by bad weather from the harvest, feels comfortable expressing some of his more direct criticisms of the 'grace-proud' (or self-righteous), while praising religion itself and declaring that he would rather be an 'atheist clean' than a hypocrite.

While at the stook the shearers cow'r
To shun the bitter blaudin' show'r,
Or in gulravage rinnin scow'r
      To pass the time,
To you I dedicate the hour
      In idle rhyme.

My musie, tir'd wi' mony a sonnet
On gown, an' ban', an' douse black bonnet,
Is grown right eerie now she's done it,
      Lest they should blame her,
An' rouse their holy thunder on it
      And anathem her.

I own 'twas rash, an' rather hardy,
That I, a simple, countra bardie,
Should meddle wi' a pack sae sturdy,
      Wha, if they ken me,
Can easy, wi' a single wordie,
      Lowse hell upon me.

But I gae mad at their grimaces,
Their sighan, cantan, grace-proud faces,
Their three-mile prayers, an' hauf-mile graces,
      Their raxan conscience,
Whase greed, revenge, an' pride disgraces
      Waur nor their nonsense.

There's Gaw'n, misca'd waur than a beast,
Wha has mair honour in his breast
Than mony scores as guid's the priest
      Wha sae abus'd him.
And may a bard no crack his jest
      What way they've use't him.

See him, the poor man's friend in need,
The gentleman in word an' deed,
An' shall his fame an' honour bleed
      By worthless skellums,
An' not a muse erect her head
      To cowe the blellums?

O Pope, had I thy satire's darts
To gie the rascals their deserts,
I'd rip their rotten, hollow hearts,
      An' tell aloud
Their jugglin hocus-pocus arts
      To cheat the crowd.

God knows, I'm no the thing I should be,
Nor am I even the thing I cou'd be,
But twenty times, I rather would be
    An atheist clean,
Than under gospel colours hid be
    Just for a screen.

An honest man may like a glass,
An honest man may like a lass,
But mean revenge, an' malice fause
    He'll still disdain,
An' then cry zeal for gospel laws,
    Like some we ken.

They take religion in their mouth;
They talk o' mercy, grace an' truth,
For what? to gie their malice skouth
    On some puir wight,
An' hunt him down, o'er right an' ruth,
    To ruin streight.

All hail, religion! maid divine!
Pardon a muse sae mean as mine,
Who in her rough imperfect line
    Thus daurs to name thee;
To stigmatise false friends of thine
    Can ne'er defame thee.

19TH SEPTEMBER

Fair Jenny
to the tune of **The Grey Cock**

BURNS COMPOSED THIS SONG on an autumn walk in September 1793. He wrote to George Thomson, 'The evening before last, I wandered out and began a tender song in what I think is its native style.' It was inspired by Janet Miller (c.1770–1825) of Dalswinton, to whom the bard also sent his song having 'taken the Liberty' of making her the 'Heroine'. He writes, 'I have formed in my fancy a little love-story for you; and a lamentable ditty I have put in your Lover's mouth.' Certainly, it is another tale of unrequited love, and it hints at the transitional time of year that is early autumn; when summer isn't quite gone, but 'grim, surly winter is near'.

Where are the joys I have met in the morning,
    That danc'd to the lark's early song?
Where is the peace that awaited my wand'ring,
    At evening the wild-woods among?

No more a winding the course of yon river,
    And marking sweet flowerets so fair;
No more I trace the light footsteps of pleasure,
    But sorrow and sad-sighing care.

Is it that summer's forsaken our valleys,
    And grim, surly winter is near?
No, no! the bees humming round the gay roses,
    Proclaim it the pride of the year.

Fain would I hide what I fear to discover,
    Yet long, long too well have I known;
All that has caused this wreck in my bosom,
    Is Jenny, fair Jenny alone.

Time cannot aid me, my griefs are immortal,
    Nor hope dare a comfort bestow:
Come, then, enamour'd and fond of my anguish,
    Enjoyment I'll seek in my woe.

20TH SEPTEMBER

On Conscience
from a letter to William Corbet, September 1792

IN THIS VERY RELATABLE EXTRACT, Burns expresses the guilt that creeps in when life runs away with him and his endeavours are unequal to his sense of duty. At this point in his life Burns was managing a promoted position to the Dumfries Port Division of the excise and an ever-expanding young family, in addition to his activities as a collector and songwriter for two major compendiums of Scottish song.

When a man is strongly impressed with a sense of something he ought to do; at the same time, that want of leisure, or want of opportunity, or want of assistance, or want of information, or want of paper, pen and ink, or any other of the many wants which Flesh is heir to — when Sense of duty pulls one way, and Necessity (or, Alas! too often Indolence under Necessity's garb) pulls another; you are too well acquainted with poor Human Nature, to be told what a devil of a life that arch-vixen, Conscience leads us.—

21st SEPTEMBER

from Johnie Cope

SIR JOHN COPE (1668–1760), Commander-in-Chief of George II's army in Scotland, met Charles Edward Stuart's Jacobite forces in battle at Prestonpans on this day in 1745. Legend has it that the Jacobites' brutal defeat of Cope's less experienced army took less than one hour. Prior to this, Cope had his troops race to Dunbar by sea to intercept the Jacobites as they, on foot, advanced on Edinburgh. However, he was too late. This song adopts a wry humour in its references to Cope's poor timing, his defeat at Prestonpans and his swift retreat.

Sir John Cope trode the north right far,
Yet ne'er a rebel he cam naur,
Until he landed at Dunbar
Right early in a morning.

Hey Johnie Cope are ye wauking yet,
Or are ye sleeping I would wit;
O haste ye get up for the drums do beat,
O fye Cope rise in the morning.

He wrote a challenge from Dunbar,
Come fight me Charlie an ye daur;
If it be not by the chance of war
I'll give you a merry morning.
    Hey Johnie Cope, &c.

When Charlie look'd the letter upon
He drew his sword the scabbard from
"So Heaven restore to me my own,
"I'll meet you, Cope, in the morning."
   Hey Johnie Cope, &c.

Cope swore with many a bloody word
That he would fight them gun and sword,
But he fled frae his nest like an ill scar'd bird,
And Johnie he took wing in the morning.
   Hey Johnie Cope, &c.

It was upon an afternoon,
Sir Johnie march'd to Preston town
He says, my lads come lean you down,
And we'll fight the boys in the morning.
   Hey Johnie Cope, &c.

But when he saw the Highland lads
Wi' tartan trews and white cockauds,
Wi' swords and guns and rungs and gauds,
O Johnie he took wing in the morning.
   Hey Johnie Cope, &c.

On the morrow when he did rise,
He look'd between him and the skies;
He saw them wi' their naked thighs,
Which fear'd him in the morning.
   Hey Johnie Cope, &c.

On then he flew into Dunbar,
Crying for a man of war;
He thought to have pass'd for a rustic tar,
And gotten awa in the morning.
   Hey Johnie Cope, &c.

22ND SEPTEMBER

from The Brigs of Ayr (i)

THE OPENING VERSES of 'The Brigs of Ayr' paint a vivid picture of this time of year in Burns's rural Ayrshire. The bard, on another imagined autumn ramble, describes perfectly the end of harvest time, farms readied for winter, the gunshots of 'tyrant' hunters and the 'brimstone reek' of gunpowder in the air.

'Twas when the stacks get on their winter hap,
And thack and rape secure the toil-won crap;
Potato-bings are snugged up frae skaith
O' coming Winter's biting, frosty breath;
The bees, rejoicing o'er their summer toils,
Unnumber'd buds an' flow'rs' delicious spoils,
Seal'd up with frugal care in massive waxen piles,
Are doom'd by Man, that tyrant o'er the weak,
The death o' devils, smoor'd wi' brimstone reek:
The thundering guns are heard on ev'ry side,
The wounded coveys, reeling, scatter wide;
The feather'd field-mates, bound by Nature's tie,
Sires, mothers, children, in one carnage lie:
(What warm, poetic heart but inly bleeds,
And execrates man's savage, ruthless deeds!)
Nae mair the flow'r in field or meadow springs,
Nae mair the grove with airy concert rings,
Except perhaps the Robin's whistling glee,
Proud o' the height o' some bit half-lang tree:
The hoary morns precede the sunny days,
Mild, calm, serene, wide spreads the noontide blaze,
While thick the gosamour waves wanton in the rays.

23RD SEPTEMBER

from The Brigs of Ayr (ii)

T HE LATTER PART OF THIS LENGTHY POEM takes the form
of an imagined flyting – or contest of insults – between the old
Brig (or bridge) of Ayr, 'the very wrinkles Gothic in his face', and
the new Brig, 'buskit in a braw new coat'. We might think of this
as a reflection on the tensions between old ways and new, between
tradition and modernisation.

Auld Brig

"I doubt na, frien', ye'll think ye're nae sheepshank,
Ance ye were streekit owre frae bank to bank!
But gin ye be a brig as auld as me
Tho' faith, that date, I doubt, ye'll never see
There'll be, if that day come, I'll wad a boddle,
Some fewer whigmaleeries in your noddle."

New Brig

"Auld Vandal! ye but show your little mense,
Just much about it wi' your scanty sense:
Will your poor, narrow foot-path of a street,
Where twa wheel-barrows tremble when they meet,
Your ruin'd, formless bulk o' stane and lime,
Compare wi' bonie brigs o' modern time?
There's men of taste wou'd tak the Ducat stream,
Tho' they should cast the very sark and swim,
E'er they would grate their feelings wi' the view
O' sic an ugly, Gothic hulk as you."

Auld Brig

"Conceited gowk! puff'd up wi' windy pride!
This mony a year I've stood the flood an' tide;
And tho' wi' crazy eild I'm sair forfairn,
I'll be a brig when ye're a shapeless cairn!
As yet ye little ken about the matter,
But twa-three winters will inform ye better.
When heavy, dark, continued, a'-day rains,
Wi' deepening deluges o'erflow the plains;
When from the hills where springs the brawling Coil,
Or stately Lugar's mossy fountains boil;
Or where the Greenock winds his moorland course.
Or haunted Garpal draws his feeble source,
Aroused by blustering winds an' spotting thowes,
In mony a torrent down the snaw-broo rowes;
While crashing ice, borne on the rolling spate,
Sweeps dams, an' mills, an' brigs, a' to the gate;
And from Glenbuck, down to the Ratton-key,
Auld Ayr is just one lengthen'd, tumbling sea
Then down ye'll hurl, (deil nor ye never rise!)
And dash the gumlie jaups up to the pouring skies!
A lesson sadly teaching, to your cost,
That Architecture's noble art is lost!"

New Brig

"Fine architecture, trowth, I needs must say't o't,
The Lord be thankit that we've tint the gate o't!
Gaunt, ghastly, ghaist-alluring edifices,
Hanging with threat'ning jut, like precipices;
O'er-arching, mouldy, gloom-inspiring coves,
Supporting roofs, fantastic, stony groves;
Windows and doors in nameless sculptures drest
With order, symmetry, or taste unblest;

Forms like some bedlam Statuary's dream,
The craz'd creations of misguided whim;
Forms might be worshipp'd on the bended knee,
And still the second dread command be free;
Their likeness is not found on earth, in air, or sea!
Mansions that would disgrace the building taste
Of any mason reptile, bird or beast:
Fit only for a doited monkish race,
Or frosty maids forsworn the dear embrace,
Or cuifs of later times, wha held the notion,
That sullen gloom was sterling, true devotion:
Fancies that our guid Brugh denies protection,
And soon may they expire, unblest wi' resurrection!"

24TH SEPTEMBER

On Children
from a letter to Frances Dunlop, 24th September 1792

B URNS COULD BE every inch the doting father. On this day in 1792, with another baby on the way, the bard found himself 'prattling' on about his children as parents do. We might wonder why he felt unequal to the task of raising girls. Was he parroting the status quo regarding eighteenth-century attitudes towards gender? Or was he perhaps concerned for his daughters, having amassed rather too much knowledge – and experience – of men's attitudes towards women?

Well, your kind wishes will be gratified, as to seeing me when I make my Ayrshire visit.— I cannot leave Mrs. B— until her nine-month race is run, which may perhaps be in three or four weeks.— She too seems determined to make me the Patriarchal leader of a

434

band.— However, if Heaven will be so obliging as let me have them in the proportion of three boys to one girl, I shall be so much the more pleased.— I hope, if I am spared with them, to shew a set of boys that will do honor to my cares and name; but I am not equal to the task of rearing girls.— Besides, I am too poor; a girl should always have a fortune.— Apropos, your little godson is thriving charmingly, but is a very devil.— He, though two years younger, has completely mastered his brother.— Robert is indeed the mildest, gentlest creature I ever saw.— He has a most surprising memory, and is quite the pride of his schoolmaster.—

You know how readily we can get into prattle upon a subject dear to our heart: you can excuse it.— God bless you and yours!

Robert Burns

25TH SEPTEMBER

On the Bard
from the First Commonplace Book

WRITING IN HIS 'FIRST COMMONPLACE BOOK' in September 1785, Burns contemplates the legacy of 'the Bard' and all those who have gone before him. He emphasises the notion that love and poetry are intrinsically linked, and affirms the importance of 'native genius'. We might, however, detect more than a hint of insecurity that the work of a 'poor rustic Bard unknown' might be 'buried 'mongst the wreck of things which were'. Of course, we know now that Burns need not have worried.

There is a noble sublimity, a heart-melting tenderness in some of these ancient fragments, which show them to be the work of a masterly hand; and it has often given me many a heartache to reflect that such glorious old Bards — Bards who, very probably, owed all their talents

435

to native genius yet have described the exploits of Heroes, the pangs of Disappointment, and the meltings of Love with such fine strokes of Nature, and, mortifying to a Bard's vanity, their very names are "buried 'mongst the wreck of things which were" —

O ye illustrious Names unknown! who could feel so strongly and describe so well! the last, the meanest of the Muses train — one who, though far inferior to your flights yet eyes your path, and with trembling wing would sometimes soar after you — a poor rustic Bard unknown, pays this sympathetic pang to your memory! Some of you tell us, with all the charms of Verse, that you have been unfortunate in the world — unfortunate in love; he too, has felt all the unfitness of a Poetic heart for the struggle of a busy, bad world; he has felt the loss of his little fortune, the loss of friends, and worse than all, the loss of the woman he adored! Like you, all his consolation was his Muse: She taught him in rustic measures to complain — Happy could he have done it with your strength of imagination, and flow of verse! May the turf rest lightly on your bones! And may you now enjoy that solace and rest which this world rarely gives to the heart tuned to all the feelings of Poesy and Love!—

26TH SEPTEMBER

On the Human Heart
from a letter to John Kennedy, 26th September 1786

B Y THIS TIME IN 1786, Burns was speculating about his planned
emigration to the West Indies. He wrote that, 'My departure is
uncertain, but I do not think it will be till after harvest.' He was
obviously having second (or even third) thoughts. The prospect of his
leaving the country had rumbled on for some time, but the following
rapturous lines to Kennedy suggest that the arrival of the bard's
newborn twins was bringing about a profound change in his outlook.

My Dr Sir

I this moment receive yours — receive it with the honest hospitable
warmth of a friend's welcome.— Whatever comes from you wakens
always up the better blood about my heart; which your kind, little
recollections of my Parental FRIEND carries as far as it will go.— 'Tis
there, Sir, Man is blest! 'Tis there, my Friend, man feels a conscious-
ness of something within him, above the trodden clod! The grateful
reverence to the hoary, earthly Authors of his being — The burning
glow when he clasps the Woman of his Soul to his bosom — the
tender yearnings of heart for the little Angels to whom he has given
existence — These, Nature has pour'd in milky streams about the
human heart; and the Man who never rouses them into action by
the inspiring influences of their proper objects, loses by far the most
pleasurable part of his existence.

A Mother's Lament for the Death of her Son

O N THIS DAY IN 1788, Burns wrote to Frances Dunlop, 'I was on horseback this morning, for between my Wife and my farm is just 46 miles, by three o'clock.— As I jogged on in the dark, I was taken with a Poetic-fit, as follows.'

The poem Burns enclosed was described as 'Mrs Fergusson of Craigdarroch's lamentation for the death of her son, an uncommonly promising Youth of 18 or 19 years of age'. It seems likely that these poignant and affecting lines were informed by the bard's own experiences of loss. By the time of composition, three of Burns's children had sadly died in infancy.

Fate gave the word, the arrow sped,
    And pierc'd my Darling's heart;
And with him all the joys are fled
    Life can to me impart.
By cruel hands the sapling drops,
    In dust dishonor'd laid;
So fell the pride of all my hopes,
    My age's future shade.

The mother linnet in the brake
    Bewails her ravish'd young;
So I, for my lost Darling's sake,
    Lament the live-day long.
Death, oft I've feared thy fatal blow,
    Now, fond, I bare my breast;
O, do thou kindly lay me low
    With him I love at rest!

28TH SEPTEMBER

Hunting Song
to the tune of I Rede You Beware at the Hunting

WE ARE STILL IN PEAK HUNTING SEASON in September. In this song, grouse hunting is adopted as a sexual metaphor. The ambiguity of Burns's words was not lost on Agnes McLehose – or 'Clarinda'– who pleaded with him in January of 1788, 'Do not publish the "Moor Hen". Do not, for your sake and for mine.'

Burns did care about Agnes and seemingly understood the importance she placed upon her reputation. Separated from her husband – an uncommon circumstance in the eighteenth century – her position in society was somewhat delicate. The last thing she needed was for a scandal to arise from her relationship with the charismatic, rakish poet. And, indeed, the song did not appear in print until 1808, some twelve years after the bard's death.

The heather was blooming, the meadows were mawn,
Our lads gaed a-hunting, ae day at the dawn,
O'er moors and o'er mosses and mony a glen,
At length they discovered a bonie moor-hen.

I rede you beware at the hunting, young men;
I rede you beware at the hunting, young men;
Tak some on the wing, and some as they spring,
But cannily steal on a bonie moor-hen.

Sweet brushing the dew from the brown heather bells,
Her colors betray'd her on yon mossy fells;
Her plumage outlustred the pride o' the spring,
And O! as she wantoned gay on the wing.
  I rede, &c.

Auld Phoebus himsel, as he peep'd o'er the hill;
In spite at her plumage he tryed his skill;
He levell'd his rays where she bask'd on the brae —
His rays were outshone, and but mark'd where she lay.
  I rede, &c.

They hunted the valley, they hunted the hill;
The best of our lads wi' the best o' their skill;
But still as the fairest she sat in their sight,
Then, whirr! she was over, a mile at a flight.—
  I rede, &c.

29TH SEPTEMBER

My Nanie's Awa
to the tune of There'll Never Be Peace

IN TODAY'S SONG, also inspired by Burns's ill-fated affair with
Agnes McLehose, the poet invites autumn to 'soothe' his heartache
with 'tidings of nature's decay', and looks forward to 'dark, dreary
winter', that nature might once again align with his feelings.

Now in her green mantle blythe Nature arrays,
And listens the lambkins that bleat o'er the braes,
While birds warble welcomes in ilka green shaw;
But to me it's delightless,— my Nanie's awa.

The snaw-drap and primrose our woodlands adorn,
And violets bathe in the weet of the morn;
They pain my sad bosom, sae sweetly they blaw,
They mind me o' Nanie — and Nanie's awa.

Thou lavrock that starts frae the dews of the lawn
The shepherd to warn of the grey-breaking dawn,
And thou mellow mavis that hails the night fa',
Give over for pity — my Nanie's awa.

Come Autumn, sae pensive, in yellow and grey,
And soothe me wi' tydings o' Nature's decay;
The dark, dreary Winter, and wild-driving snaw,
Alane can delight me — now Nanie's awa.

30TH SEPTEMBER

Tibbie, I Hae Seen the Day
to the tune of Invercald's Reel – Strathspey

B URNS ENTERED TODAY'S SONG in his 'First Commonplace
Book' in September 1784. It is thought to have been one of his
earliest works, composed following his seeming rejection by a girl
on account of his 'laik o' gear'. A defiant Burns exposes 'Tibbie's'
snobbery, responding with the typically Burnsian sentiment that
'sense', 'lear' (learning), and kindness are all more important than
pride or material possession.

Tibbie, I hae seen the day,
   Ye would na been sae shy;
For laik o' gear ye lightly me,
   But trowth, I care na by.

Yestreen I met you on the moor,
   Ye spak na, but gaed by like stoure;
Ye geck at me because I'm poor,
   But fient a hair care I.
     Tibbie, I hae, &c.

When coming hame on Sunday last,
   Upon the road as I cam past,
Ye snufft and ga'e your head a cast –
   But trowth I care't na by.

I doubt na, lass, but ye may think,
 Because ye hae the name o' clink,
That ye can please me at a wink,
 Whene'er ye like to try.
  Tibbie, I hae, &c.

But sorrow tak' him that's sae mean,
 Altho' his pouch o' coin were clean,
Wha follows ony saucy quean
 That looks sae proud and high.
  Tibbie, I hae, &c.

Altho' a lad were e'er sae smart,
 If that he want the yellow dirt,
Ye'll cast your head anither airt,
 And answer him fu' dry.
  Tibbie, I hae, &c.

But, if he hae the name o' gear,
 Ye'll fasten to him like a brier,
Tho' hardly he, for sense or lear
 Be better than the kye.
  Tibbie, I hae, &c.

But, Tibbie, lass, tak my advice,
 Your daddie's gear maks you sae nice;
The deil a ane wad speir your price,
 Were ye as poor as I.
  Tibbie, I hae, &c.

There lives a lass beside yon park,
 I'd rather hae her in her sark,
Than you wi' a' your thousand mark;
 That gars you look sae high.
  Tibbie, I hae, &c.

OCTOBER

Let Warlocks grim, an' wither'd Hags,
Tell how wi' you on ragweed nags,
They skim the muirs an' dizzy crags,
                    Wi' wicked speed;
And in kirk-yards renew their leagues,
                    Owre howket dead.

from Address to the Deil

1st OCTOBER

How Lang and Dreary Is the Night
to the tune of A Galick Air

As we enter october, the long nights are drawing in and the clocks will soon turn back. We are also in the run-up to Halloween, and so this time of year is often associated with the strange, the supernatural and with remembrance of the dead. Today's atmospheric song tells of a woman's 'dreary', 'restless' nights, 'eerie' dreams and 'joyless' days in the absence of her lover. It certainly conveys the 'heaviness', or the shift in atmosphere, that causes many of us to seek refuge indoors late in the autumn.

How lang and dreary is the night,
 When I am frae my Dearie!
I restless lie frae e'en to morn,
 Tho' I were ne'er so weary.

For Oh, her lanely nights are lang;
 And Oh, her dreams are eerie;
And Oh, her widow'd heart is sair,
 That's absent frae her Dearie!

When I think on the lightsome days
 I spent wi' thee, my dearie,
And now what seas between us roar,
 How can I be but eerie?
  For Oh, &c.

How slow ye move, ye heavy hours!
   The joyless day how dreary:
It was na sae ye glinted by,
    When I was wi' my Dearie.—
      For Oh, &c.

2ND OCTOBER

On Quitting Ellisland
from a letter to Robert Cleghorn, October 1791

BY OCTOBER 1791, following three years of hard labour to cultivate the land at his Ellisland farm, Burns was convinced that his efforts were in vain. In this extract from a letter to Robert Cleghorn (d.1798) – a farmer at Saughton Mills near Edinburgh and a good friend of the poet – Burns seems relieved to be rid of the last of several troublesome farming ventures he'd had the misfortune to experience. The bard obviously craved financial stability and was fixed upon a career in the excise, even if, in his closing remarks, he refers to his chosen occupation with wry, self-deprecating humour.

I am giving up my farm: it is a bad bargain; and as my Landlord is offering the lands to sale, I took the hint, and have got some little consideration for my lease.— The Excise, after all has been said against it, is the business for me.— I find no difficulty in being an honest man in it; the work of itself is easy; and it is a devilish different affair, managing money matters where I care not a damn if the money is paid or not; from the long faces made to a haughty Laird or still more haughty Factor, when rents are demanded, and money, Alas! not to be had!— Besides, I am now ranked on the Supervisor list, which will in a little time, place me in a respectable situation, even as an Excise-man.—

3RD OCTOBER

The Lover's Morning Salute to His Mistress

TODAY'S SONG WAS ENCLOSED with several sent to George Thomson, editor of a *Select Collection of Original Scottish Airs*, in October 1794. In another reverie inspired by Jean Lorimer (see 16th March), Burns makes use of light and dark imagery to emphasise the lover's feelings of 'gloom' when parted from his 'Chloris', described as 'Beauty's light'. We might pay particular attention to Burns's reference to 'twining hazel bowers'. In folklore, the hazel is a magical tree which has the ability to ward off evil spirits. Furthermore, one might use the branches of a hazel tree as a wand, or for water-divining, or for 'witching a well'.

Sleep'st thou, or wauk'st thou, fairest creature;
 Rosy morn now lifts his eye,
Numbering ilka bud which Nature
 Waters wi' the tears o' joy.
Now, to the streaming fountain,
Or up the heathy mountain,
The hart, hind, and roe, freely, wanton stray;
 In twining hazel bowers,
 His lay the linnet pours;
 The laverock, to the sky
 Ascends, wi' sangs o' joy:
While the sun and thou arise to bless the day.

Phebus, gilding the brow of morning,
    Banishes ilk darksome shade,
Nature gladdening and adorning;
    Such to me, my lovely maid.
When frae my Chloris parted,
Sad, cheerless, broken-hearted,
Then night's gloomy shades o'ercast my sky:
    But when she charms my sight,
    In pride of Beauty's light;
    When through my very heart,
    Her beaming glories dart;
'Tis then – 'tis then I wake to life and joy!

4TH OCTOBER

On Chloris
from a letter to George Thomson, 19th October 1794

BURNS WROTE MORE SONGS inspired by Jean Lorimer, or 'Chloris', than any other woman, although he insisted to George Thomson that their relationship was based upon 'Platonic Love'. In this letter the bard recognises that she is a marked favourite of his, but he also explains an important aspect of his creative process – or his 'glorious recipe' for the creation of love songs. Burns mischievously suggests that the success of his songs is in direct correlation with the 'charms' of the woman who inspired them. Given the extent to which the bard 'fired' himself up with 'enthusiasm', making potent use of his imagination and poetic licence, it is perhaps little wonder that Burns often changed the names of his female muses in verse. It seems likely that adopting their real names could have invited gossip or, at worst, incited a full-blown scandal.

I assure you that to my lovely Friend you are indebted for many of your best songs of mine.— Do you think that the sober, gin-horse routine of existence could inspire a man with life, and love, and joy — could fire him with enthusiasm, or melt him with pathos, equal to the genius of your Book?— No! No!!!— Whenever I want to be more than ordinary *in song*, to be in some way equal to your diviner airs; do you imagine I fast and pray for the celestial emanation?— Tout au contraire! I have a glorious recipe, the very one that for his own use was invented by the Divinity of Healing and Poesy when erst he piped to the flocks of Admetus.— I put myself in a regimen of admiring a fine woman, and in proportion to the adorability of her charms, in proportion you are delighted with my verses.—

The lightening of her eye is the godhead of Parnassus, and the witchery of her smile the divinity of Helicon!—

5TH OCTOBER

She Says She Lo'es Me Best of A'

IN ANOTHER SONG FOR 'CHLORIS', Burns describes her beauty in exquisite detail and makes much of those 'bewitching' facial features that would 'make a wretch forget his woe', or 'make a saint forget the sky'. This is not quite the naïve 'artless lassie' of 'Lassie Wi' the Lintwhite Locks' (see 16th March), for this 'wyling' woman is more of a temptress, and 'Her's are the willing chains o' love'.

Sae flaxen were her ringlets,
   Her eyebrows of a darker hue,
Bewitchingly o'er arching
   Twa laughing e'en o' bonie blue;

Her smiling, sae wyling,
    Wad make a wretch forget his woe;
What pleasure, what treasure,
    Unto these rosy lips to grow:
Such was my Chloris' bonie face,
    When first that bonie face I saw;
And aye my Chloris' dearest charm,
    She says, she lo'es me best of a'.

Like harmony her motion;
    Her pretty ancle is a spy,
Betraying fair proportion,
    Wad make a saint forget the sky.
Sae warming, sae charming,
    Her fautless form and gracefu' air;
Ilk feature – auld Nature
    Declar'd that she could do nae mair:
Her's are the willing chains o' love,
    By conquering Beauty's sovereign law;
And still my Chloris' dearest charm,
    She says, she lo'es me best of a'.

Let others love the city,
    And gaudy shew, at sunny noon;
Gie me the lonely valley,
    The dewy eve, and rising moon
Fair beaming, and streaming
    Her silver light the boughs amang;
While falling, recalling,
    The amorous thrush concludes his sang;
There, dearest Chloris, wilt thou rove
    By wimpling burn and leafy shaw,
And hear my vows o' truth and love,
    And say, thou lo'es me best of a'.

6TH OCTOBER

On Religion
from a letter to Frances Dunlop, 6th October 1790

ON THIS DAY IN 1790, Burns wrote to Frances Dunlop that he had recently recovered from 'a malignant squinancy and slow fever which had tormented me for three weeks and had actually brought me to the brink of the grave'. The bard, clearly relieved to have recovered his health – 'the greatest enjoyment on earth, and wanting which, all other enjoyments are of poor avail' – expresses an upbeat, yet philosophical mood as he contemplates 'the genuine spirit' of religion.

We can no more live without Religion, that we can live without air; but give me the Religion of Sentiment and Reason.— You know John Hildebroad's famous epitaph—

> "Here lies poor old John Hildebroad;
> "Have mercy on his soul, Lord God,
> "As he would do, were he Lord God,
> "And thou wert poor John Hildebroad."—

This speaks more to my heart, and has more of the genuine spirit of Religion in it, than is to be found in whole waggon-loads of Divinity.—

7th OCTOBER

Beware o' Bonie Ann

IT IS THOUGHT THAT THIS SONG was composed as a compliment to Ann Masterton. Ann was the daughter of Allan Masterton (d.1799), an accomplished composer and close friend of Burns. In October 1789, the bard described Allan Masterton as 'one of the worthiest men in the world and a man of real genius'. Masterton composed airs for several of Burns's songs, including 'Beware o' Bonie Ann'. We might wonder what Masterton thought when he first read this detailed description of a dangerously beautiful woman, capable of 'trepanning', or beguiling, a gallant's heart, and enslaving him with her feminine charms. Beware, indeed!

Ye gallants bright I rede you right,
    Beware o' bonie Ann;
Her comely face sae fu' o' grace,
    Your heart she will trepan.
Her een sae bright, like stars by night,
    Her skin sae like the swan;
Sae jimply lac'd her genty waist,
    That sweetly ye might span.

Youth, grace and love attendant move,
    And pleasure leads the van:
In a' their charms and conquering arms,
    They wait on bonie Ann.
The captive bands may chain the hands,
    But loove enslaves the man:
Ye gallants braw, I rede you a',
    Beware o' bonie Ann.

8TH OCTOBER

On the *Scots Musical Museum*
from a letter to Rev. John Skinner, 25th October 1787

IT WAS IN OCTOBER 1787 that Burns commenced his most extensive activities as a collector and songwriter towards the production of James Johnson's *Scots Musical Museum* (1788–1803). Johnson (1753–1811) was an Edinburgh engraver and music-seller who had set out to print all of Scotland's traditional songs, as Burns explained to James Hoy, 'not from mercenary views, but from an honest Scotch enthusiasm'.

Burns's role, as he understood it, was to 'assist in collecting the old poetry, or sometimes for a fine air to make a stanza where it has no words'. Burns did collect vast quantities of traditional verse, but he also composed a significant number of original contributions, more than any other contributor. This extract is a clear expression of the enthusiasm with which Burns conducted these activities and sought to recruit other writers. It also provides a fascinating insight into the poet's preoccupation with the attribution of songs – even if he is less concerned with issues of copyright.

There is a work going on in Edinburgh just now which claims your best assistance. An Engraver in this town has set about collecting and publishing all the Scotch songs, with the Music, that can be found. Songs in the English language, if by Scotchmen, are admitted; but the music must all be Scotch. Drs Beattie and Blacklock are lending a hand, and the first musician in town presides over that department. I have been absolutely crazed about it, collecting old stanzas, and every information remaining respecting their origin, authors, &c.

This last is but a very fragment business; but at the end of his second number,— the first is already published,— a small account will be given of the Authors, particularly to preserve those of latter times. Your three songs, *"Tullochgorum"*, *"John of Badenyon"* and *"Ewie wi' the Crookit Horn,"* go in this second number. I was determined, before I got your letter, to write you, begging that you would let me know where the editions of these pieces may be found, as you would wish them to continue in future times; and if you would be so kind to this undertaking, as send any songs, of your own or others, that you would think proper to publish. Your name will be inserted among the other authors, *"Nill ye, will ye."* One half of Scotland already give your songs to other authors.

9TH OCTOBER

On the Death of Mrs Susan Henri
from a letter to Frances Dunlop, October 1792

IN OCTOBER 1792, Burns wrote to Frances Dunlop regarding the death of her daughter, Susan Henri. Susan's husband James had passed away in 1789, just one year after their marriage, and shortly before she gave birth to their only child. In 1792 she travelled to Muges in France with her young son to claim his father's estate, where she tragically died. Burns's affinity with Frances led him to sympathise with her in the strongest terms. Here he acknowledges the bereft mother's profound grief and misfortune, while dispensing with any pretence that she could be comforted.

What shall I say to comfort you, my much-valued, much-afflicted friend! I can but grieve with you; consolation I have none to offer,

except that which religion holds out to the children of affliction —
Children of affliction!— How just the expression! and, like every other
family, they have matters among them which they hear, see and feel
in a serious, all-important manner, of which the world has not, nor
cares to have, any idea. The world looks indifferently on, makes the
passing remark, and proceeds to the next novel occurrence.

Alas, Madam! who would wish for many years? What is it but
to drag existence until our joys gradually expire, and leave us in a
night of misery; like the gloom which blots out the stars one by one,
from the face of night, and leaves us, without a ray of comfort, in the
howling waste!

10TH OCTOBER

On Anguish and Low Spirits
from a letter to Frances Dunlop, 21st January 1788

THIS DATE NOW MARKS WORLD MENTAL HEALTH DAY, and it is
thus one on which we might contemplate Burns's own recurring
struggles with what he referred to as 'melancholy', or what would, in
the twenty-first century, most likely be referred to as depression.

In this extract Burns refers to the debilitating effects of 'anguish
and low spirits', to the times he wished he could 'resign life', and to
the feelings of shame he felt at a time when mental ill health was
even less well understood than it is in the present day. Thankfully
Burns seems instinctively to have known that to suffer in silence was
unhealthy. He did seek support by confiding in a select number of
friends, and most often in Frances Dunlop who, from her letters,
appears to have struggled with depression herself.

After six weeks confinement, I am beginning to walk across the room. They have been six horrible weeks, anguish and low spirits made me unfit to read, write, or think.

I have a hundred times wished that one could resign life as an officer resigns a commission: for I would not *take in* any poor ignorant wretch by *selling out*. Lately I was a sixpenny private, and, God knows, a miserable soldier enough: now I march to the campaign, a starving cadet; a little more conspicuously wretched.

I am ashamed of all this; for though I do want bravery for the warfare of life, I could wish, like some other soldiers, to have as much fortitude or cunning as to dissemble or conceal my cowardice.

11TH OCTOBER

Epigram – Under the Portrait of Miss Burns

MARGARET BURNS (c.1769–1792) was an Edinburgh bawd who catered for wealthy clients. In 1789 she was at the centre of a sensational legal dispute when her neighbours in Rose Street objected to the comings and goings at her house. She was banished from the city only to have the case overturned at an appeal, where she was represented by Burns's acquaintance Henry Erskine (1746–1817).

The poet enquired about 'the fate of my poor Namesake' in a letter to his bookseller Peter Hill in February 1790 and asked, 'Which of their grave Lordships can lay his hand on his heart and say that he has not taken the advantage of such frailty; nay, if we may judge by near six thousand years experience, can the World do without such frailty?'

Burns blames man's 'selfish appetites' for Margaret's ruin, derides 'those flinty-bosomed, puritanical Prosecutors of Female Frailty and Persecutors of Female Charms' and invites woman to 'curse them!' by tempting them with their sexuality and then denying them. He could be critical of the sex trade, or sex as a transaction rather than a direct expression of humanity. In another letter he warned his brother

William against 'that universal vice, bad women'. However, as we will come to see, the ever-complicated poet appears to be interested, from a creative perspective, in what he perceives as the subversive qualities of 'bewitching' female sexuality.

Cease, ye prudes, your envious railings,
    Lovely Burns has charms: confess!
True it is that she's had one failing:
    Had a woman ever less?

12TH OCTOBER

The Hue and Cry of John Lewars

IN AN INTRODUCTION TO TODAY'S POEM, Burns described its namesake as: 'A poor man ruined and undone by Robbery and Murder. Being an awful WARNING to the young men of this age, how they look well to themselves in this dangerous, terrible WORLD.'

It is likely that this is Burns's tongue-in-cheek salute to John Lewars, his friend and colleague in the excise. On reading the poem it becomes clear that Lewars has been 'robbed' of his heart, his peace 'murdered' by the bewitching lover, 'Woods'. Burns riffs on the fact that, despite the abolition of statutes criminalising witchcraft in 1736, a superstitious fear of witches remained in Scotland in the eighteenth century. Such fear can be traced back to the *Malleus Malleficarum* – or 'The Witch Hammer' – a monumental religious tract against witchcraft commissioned by Pope Innocent VIII (c.1486). It describes women as 'sinful', 'bitter', 'wheedling', a 'secret enemy' and 'a snare' of devils. Their powers to tempt men render them powerful agents of evil and disorder. Furthermore, it sexualises woman and 'witch' by claiming that woman is driven to witchcraft – to 'consort with devils' – by her insatiable bodily appetite. Burns does not, of course, subscribe to these ideas, but makes playful use of them to undermine superstition and any lingering fear of the feminine, particularly when Woods herself is 'captured' in a forthright reassertion of masculinity.

A THIEF, AND A MURDERER! Stop her who can!
　　Look well to your lives and your goods!
Good people, ye know not the hazard you run,
　　'Tis the far-famed and much-noted Woods.—

While I looked at her eye, for the devil is in it,
　　In a trice she whipt off my poor heart:
Her brow, cheek and lip — in another sad minute,
　　My peace felt her murderous dart.—

Her, features, I'll tell you them over — but hold!
　　She deals with your wizards and books;
And to peep in her face, if but once you're so bold,
　　There's witchery kills in her looks.—

But softly — I have it — her haunts are well known,
　　At midnight so slily I'll watch her;
And sleeping, undrest, in the dark, all alone —
　　Good lord! the dear THIEF HOW I'LL CATCH HER!

13TH OCTOBER

On Two Bewitching Young Ladies
from a letter to Mr William Dunbar, 25th September 1788

B EWITCHING FEMININITY is once again Burns's subject in this
letter to William Dunbar (d.1807), intended as a compliment
regarding his young (rather than 'little' – they are grown tall)
nieces. Dunbar was a fellow member of the Crochallan Fencibles;
a gentleman's club of which Burns was a member during his time
in Edinburgh from 1787 to 1788, and for whom it is believed he
collected and composed bawdy song. This may go some way towards
explaining why Burns felt comfortable writing to Dunbar in the way
that he does, having obviously exerted his keen male gaze.

[Accept] of my best wishes for your welfare, and the welfare of Mrs
Fordyce and your two little Nieces.— I was going to call them two
little Angels; but when I consider, though their looks have all that
celestial Sweetness, guileless Sprightliness and ingenuous Modesty
that one would expect in a young Inhabitant of Heaven, a seraph
newly entered on existence, nay, their air, their manner, their figure
(for whatever Milton had, I have no idea of a Cherub six feet high)
are quite Angelic; yet there is a Something, and not a little Something
neither, about their eyes, as well as in the *enchanting* shape and colours
of the organs themselves, as in their *fascinating* way of using them —
in short, for I hate to dwell on so disagreeable a subject as accusing
a fellow-creature, I am positively of opinion that there is more
bewitching destructive mischief in one of their GLANCES, than in the
worst half of "Satan's invisible world discovered:" now witchcraft can
never make a part in the character, at least of a GOOD Angel.— I am
sorry for the young ladies' sakes that I am forced to bear this witness
against them; but however I may deal in fiction, under my Poetic

Licence, I sacredly stick to truth in Prose.— To say no more on this unlucky business I give the young Ladies notice, that, married man as I am, and consequently out of the field of Danger, still I have so much regard for the welfare of the world I lately left, that I have half a thought of advertising them in RHYME to put mankind on their guard against such a dangerous and still *growing* mischief.—

14TH OCTOBER

Inscription on a Goblet

T ODAY'S BURNSIAN WORDS convey another ominous warning. However, this time the 'snare' is not woman, but a generous host and the 'demon drink'. Allan Cunningham, in his 1834 edition of Burns's works, suggests that the host in question was the bard's good friend John Syme (1755–1831). According to anecdote:

> One day after dinner at Ryedale, Burns wrote these lines on a goblet with his diamond. Syme would seem to have been less affected with the compliment than with defacing his crystal service, for he threw the goblet behind the fire. We are not told what the Poet thought; but it is said that Brown, the clerk of "Stamp-office Johnny" snatched the goblet out of the fire uninjured, and kept it as a relique till his death.

Might the lines on this flame-defying goblet prove appropriate for a Halloween party?

> There's death in the cup — sae beware!
>   Nay, more — there is danger in touching;
> But wha can avoid the fell snare?
>   The man and his wine's sae bewitching!

15TH OCTOBER

On Fortune and Apathy
from a letter to Crauford Tait, Esq., 15th October 1790

ON THIS DAY IN OCTOBER 1790, Burns wrote to Crauford Tait, Writer to the Signet in Edinburgh, flattering his generosity in seeking employment for the aspiring young apprentice, William Duncan. Of particular note are Burns's comments on the inherent selfishness of those wealthy individuals who fail to make their fortune a force for good. Whether or not Burns was successful in this bold approach is unknown.

You, my good Sir, were born under kinder stars; but your fraternal sympathy, I well know, can enter fully into the feelings of the young man who enters life with the laudable ambition to do something and to be something among his fellow creatures; but whom the consciousness of friendless obscurity presses to the earth and wounds to the soul!—

Even the fairest of his virtues are against him.— That independent spirit, and that ingenuous modesty, qualities inseparable from a noble mind, are, with the Million, circumstances not a little disqualifying.— What pleasure is in the power of the Fortunate and the Happy, to glad the heart of such depressed Youth by their notice and patronage!— I am not angry with mankind at their deaf economy of the purse.— The goods of this world cannot be divided without being lessened.— But why be a niggard of that which bestows bliss on a fellow-creature, yet takes nothing from their own means of enjoyment?— We wrap ourselves up in the cloak of our own better fortune, and turn away our eyes, lest the wants and woes of our brother-mortals should disturb the selfish apathy of our souls.—

16TH OCTOBER

On Robert Fergusson

THE POET ROBERT FERGUSSON, one of Burns's most important literary influences, died on this day in 1774. In this poetical tribute, Burns refers to Fergusson as 'Heaven-taught', echoing Henry Mackenzie's review of Burns's own poetry in a clear indication of the affinity he felt for his 'elder brother in the muse'. Burns laments Fergusson's tragic and premature death – he was just twenty-four when he died, impoverished, in Edinburgh's Darien Asylum – and condemns society's elevation of wealth and status, over 'Worth' and 'Genius'. For more on Burns's commemoration of Fergusson, see the entry for the sixth of February.

Ill-fated Genius! Heaven-taught Fergusson,
   What heart that feels and will not yield a tear,
To think Life's sun did set e'er well begun
   To shed its influence on thy bright career.

O why should truest Worth and Genius pine
   Beneath the iron grasp of Want and Woe,
While titled knaves and idiot-greatness shine
   In all the splendour Fortune can bestow?

17TH OCTOBER

On Superstition and Imagination
from Burns's autobiographical letter to Dr John Moore,
2nd August 1787

M ANY OF BURNS'S POEMS, songs and letters are infused with the
superstition and supernatural imagery that is so prominent in
Scottish folk culture. Here the bard describes the influence upon his
vivid imagination of supernatural tales and legends passed on by his
mother's maid.

In my infant and boyish days too, I owed much to an old Maid of my
Mother's, remarkable for her ignorance, credulity, and superstition.—
She had, I suppose, the largest collection in the county of tales and
songs concerning devils, ghosts, fairies, brownies, witches, warlocks,
spunkies, kelpies, elf-candles, dead-lights, wraiths, apparitions,
cantraips, giants, enchanted towers, dragons and other trumpery.—
This cultivated the latent seeds of Poesy; but had so strong an effect
on my imagination, that to this hour, in my nocturnal rambles, I
sometimes keep a sharp look-out in suspicious places; and though
nobody can be more sceptical in these matters than I, yet it often
takes an effort of Philosophy to shake off these idle terrors.—

18TH OCTOBER

from Tam Lin

G ROWING UP IN RURAL AYRSHIRE, Burns would have heard
this traditional Scottish ballad often. Many different versions
exist – and Burns appears to have collected several, amalgamating
them in the production of his own version for James Johnson's *Scots
Musical Museum*.

According to folk legend, Tam Lin was a mortal who was bewitched
and captured by the Queen of the Fairies. He encounters Janet, who
mysteriously falls pregnant and resolves to rescue the father of her
child lest he be offered as a 'tiend' to hell in the fairies' seven-year
sacrifice at Halloween. In this extract, Tam Lin explains the stages
of transformation that he and Janet must survive before he can be
freed of his captor. We might also recognise several important super-
natural motifs, among these recurring mention of the number seven,
the midnight (or 'witching') hour when the supernatural world was
thought to be at its most vibrant, and the colour green; ambiguous in
its representation of the duplicity of the fairy realm, but also indica-
tive of Janet's burgeoning life, fertility and protection.

And ance it fell upon a day
  That wae did me betide.
And ance it fell upon a day,
  A cauld day and a snell.

When we were frae the hunting come
  That frae my horse I fell.
The queen o' Fairies she caught me,
  In yon green hill to dwell.

And pleasant is the fairy-land;
 But, an eerie tale to tell!
Ay at the end of seven years,
 They pay a tiend to hell.

I am sae fair and fu' o' flesh
 I'm fear'd it be mysel.
But the night is Halloween, lady,
 The morn is Hallowday;

Then win me, win me, an ye will,
 For weel I wat ye may.
Just at the mirk and midnight hour
 The fairie folk will ride:

And they that wad their true love win,
 At Milescross they maun bide.
But how shall I thee ken, Tam-lin,
 O how my true love know.

Amang sae mony unco knights,
 The like I never saw.
O first let pass the black Lady,
 And syne let pass the brown;

But quickly run to the milk-white steed,
 Pu ye his rider down.
For I'll ride on the milk-white steed,
 And ay nearest the town.

Because I was an earthly knight
 They gie me that renown.
My right hand will be glov'd, lady,
 My left hand will be bare;

Cockt up shall my bonnet be,
    And kaim'd down shall my hair,
And thae's the takens I gie thee,
    Nae doubt I will be there.

They'll turn me in your arms, lady,
    Into an esk and adder,
But hald me fast and fear me not,
    I am your bairn's father.

They'll turn me to a bear sae grim,
    And then a lion bold,
But hold me fast and fear me not,
    As ye shall love your child.

Again they'll turn me in your arms
    To a red het gaud of airn;
But hold me fast and fear me not,
    I'll do to you nae harm.

And last they'll turn me, in your arms,
    Into the burning lead;
Then throw me into well-water,
    O throw me in wi' speed.

And then I'll be your ain true love,
    I'll turn a naked knight:
Then cover me wi' your green mantle,
    And cover me out o' sight.

19TH OCTOBER

On the Supernatural
from a letter to Alexander Cunningham, 10th September 1792

IN TODAY'S SELECTION, Burns claims to have writer's block. This does not, however, prevent the bard from accessing that part of his imagination described in the entry for the 17th of October, and it takes full flight in this prose passage which is replete with superstition and references to supernatural creatures.

Among these are a bogle, which was a menacing phantom, or a goblin. Brownies were fairies or hobgoblins that occupied people's homes, rearranging them to varying degrees of chaos, and Kelpies were shapeshifting water spirits – menacing creatures that often took the form of water horses to lure humans to a watery death. The cultural importance of the kelpie in Scotland is reflected in the installation (in 2013) of Andy Scott's sculptural representation of these mythical creatures at Falkirk, where two imposing horses' heads are positioned at a key turning pool on the Forth and Clyde Canal. At thirty feet in height, these dramatic feats of art and engineering are the largest equine sculptures in the world.

Here, Burns's quote is from *Hamlet*, one of Shakespeare's more supernatural plays.

But what shall I write to you?—"The voice said, cry! and I said, What shall I cry?"— O, thou Spirit! whatever thou art, or wherever thou makest thyself visible! Be thou a Bogle by the eerie side of an auld thorn, in the dreary glen through which the herd-callan maun bicker in his gloamin route frae the fauld!— Be thou a Brownie, set, at dead of night, to thy task by the blazing ingle, or in the solitary barn where the repercussions of thy iron flail half affright thyself, as thou performest the work of twenty of the sons of men, ere the cock-crowing summon thee to thy ample cog of substantial Brose!— Be thou a Kelpie, haunting the ford, or ferry, in the starless night, mixing thy laughing yell with the howling of the storm and the roaring of the flood, as thou viewest the perils and miseries of Man on the foundering horse, or in the tumbling boat!— Or, lastly, be thou a Ghost, paying thy nocturnal visits to the hoary ruins of decayed grandeur; or performing thy mystic rites in the shadow of the time-worn Church while the Moon looks, without a cloud, on the silent ghastly dwellings of the dead around thee; or, taking thy stand by the bedside of the Villain, or the Murderer, portraying on his dreaming fancy, pictures, dreadful as the horrors of unveiled Hell, and terrible as the wrath of incensed Deity!!!— Come, thou Spirit, but not in these horrid forms; come with the milder, gentle, easy inspirations which thou breathest round the wig of a prating Advocate, or the tête of a tea-bibbing Gossip, while their tongues run at the light-horse gallop of clishmaclaiver for ever and ever — come, and assist a poor devil who is quite jaded in the attempt to share half an idea among half a hundred words; to fill up four quarto pages, while he has not got one single sentence of recollection, information, or remark worth putting pen to paper for!—

20TH OCTOBER

Ca' the Yowes

T HIS ALTERNATIVE, SECOND VERSION of Burns's famous song is
infused with supernatural imagery. But note how Burns's 'Dearie'
needn't fear 'ghaists' or 'bogles'… not when they have their love to
protect them – in this life and the next.

Ca' the yowes to the knowes,
Ca' them where the heather grows,
Ca' them where the burnie rowes,
      My bonie Dearie.

Hark, the mavis' evening sang,
Sounding Clouden's woods amang;
Then a faulding let us gang,
      My bonie Dearie.
         Ca' the &c.

We'll gae down by Clouden side,
Through the hazels, spreading wide,
O'er the waves that sweetly glide
      To the moon sae clearly.
         Ca' the &c.

Yonder Clouden's silent towers,
Where at moonshine's midnight hours,
O'er the dewy bending flowers,
      Fairies dance sae cheery.
         Ca' the &c.

Ghaist nor bogle shalt thou fear;
Thou'rt to Love and Heav'n sae dear,
Nocht of ill may come thee near;
 My bonie Dearie.
  Ca' the &c.

Fair and lovely as thou art,
Thou hast stown my very heart;
I can die — but canna part,
 My bonie Dearie.
  Ca' the &c.

21st OCTOBER

from Epistle to Blacklock

B URNS'S VERSE EPISTLE TO the Rev. Dr Thomas Blacklock
(1721–1791) was dated on this day in 1789. It was composed in
response to Blacklock's verse epistle of the 24th of August, in which
he enquired warmly after the bard and his family.

Blacklock, also a skilled writer, was ordained by the presbytery
of Dumfries in 1759. In 1762 he became minister of Kirkcudbright.
However, unfortunately, his impaired vision proved an insurmount-
able challenge and he was forced to retire to Edinburgh in 1765. From
Burns's dealings with him, and from this comic and irreverent epistle,
it appears that Blacklock was a liberal clergyman with a keen sense
of humour.

But what d'ye think, my trusty fier,
I'm turn'd a gauger — Peace be here!

Parnassian queens I fear, I fear,
   Ye'll now disdain me,
And then my fifty pounds a year
   Will little gain me.

Ye glaiket, gleesome, dainty damies,
Wha by Castalia's wimplin streamies,
Lowp, sing, and lave your pretty limbies,
   Ye ken, ye ken,
That strang necessity supreme is
   'Mang sons o' Men.

I hae a wife and twa wee laddies,
They maun hae brose and brats o' duddies;
Ye ken yoursels my heart right proud is,
   I need na vaunt;
But I'll sned bosoms and thraw saught-woodies
   Before they want.

Lord help me thro' this warld o' care!
I'm weary sick o't late and air!
Not but I hae a richer share
   Than mony ithers;
But why should ae man better fare,
   And a' Men brithers!

Come, Firm Resolve, take thou the van,
Thou stalk o' carl-hemp in man!
And let us mind, faint heart ne'er wan
   A lady fair:
Wha does the utmost that he can,
   Will whyles do mair.

But to conclude my silly rhyme
(I'm scant o' verse and scant o' time),
To make a happy fireside clime

> To weans and wife,
> That's the true Pathos and Sublime
> Of Human life.

22ND OCTOBER

Tam Glen
to the tune of **The Merry Beggars**

F OR TODAY WE HAVE ANOTHER SONG that conflates superstition
and matters of the heart, in which a young woman is set upon
marrying her beloved Tam Glen, despite his lack of riches and her
parents' protestations. She naïvely looks for signs, declaring that at
the 'Valentine's dealing' – when men and women pulled names from
a hat to determine their true love – she drew Tam's name not once,
but three times. Likewise, at Halloween it was customary to hang a
wet shirt sleeve in front of the fire and wait patiently until midnight,
by which time a future lover should have come to turn the sleeve.
Of course, Burns's enthusiastic young woman sees what she wants
to see – the 'likeness' or spectre of Tam Glen. That Burns is mocking
this enamoured female and the superstitions to which she so firmly
holds is made clear in the final stanza where she bargains with her
sister to tell her only what she wants to hear.

> My heart is a breaking, dear Tittie,
> Some counsel unto me come len',
> To anger them a' is a pity,
> But what will I do wi' Tam Glen?

I'm thinking, wi' sic a braw fellow,
  In poortith I might mak a fen:
What care I in riches to wallow,
  If I mauna marry Tam Glen.

There's Lowrie the laird o' Dumeller,
  'Gude day to you brute' he comes ben:
He brags and blaws o' his siller,
  But when will he dance like Tam Glen.

My Minnie does constantly deave me,
  And bids me beware o' young men;
They flatter, she says, to deceive me,
  But wha can think sae o' Tam Glen.

My Daddie says, gin I'll forsake him,
  He'll gie me gude hunder marks ten:
But, if it's ordain'd I maun take him,
  O wha will I get but Tam Glen.

Yestreen at the Valentine's dealing,
  My heart to my mou gied a sten;
For thrice I drew ane without failing,
  And thrice it was written, Tam Glen.

The last Halloween I was waukin
  My droukit sark-sleeve, as ya ken;
His likeness cam up the house staukin,
  And the very grey breeks o' Tam Glen.

Come counsel, dear Tittie, don't Tarry;
  I'll gie you my bonie black hen,
Gif ye will advise me to Marry
  The lad I lo'e dearly, Tam Glen.

23rd OCTOBER

On Alloway Kirk (i)
from a letter to Captain Francis Grose, c. June 1790

BURNS MET WITH Captain Francis Grose (1731–1791) in July of
1789 when he lodged with Burns's friend and neighbour, Robert
Riddell, at Friars Carse. Grose was an accomplished antiquarian
and the author of *Antiquities of England and Wales* (1773–1787).
Antiquarianism refers to the study of things of the past, encompassing
history, folklore, historical sites and artefacts.

Burns convinced Grose, who had a keen interest in the occult,
to feature a drawing of Alloway Kirk in the second volume of *The
Antiquities of Scotland* (1791). Burns supplied him with three prose
accounts and one poem – 'Tam o' Shanter' – about the supernatural
goings-on in that place of local legend. Today's extract is the first of
Burns's 'Witch Stories' about Alloway Kirk.

Upon a stormy night, amid whirling squalls of wind and bitter blasts
of hail, in short, on such a night as the devil would chuse to take
the air in, a farmer or farmer's servant was plodding and plashing
homeward with his plough-irons on his shoulder, having been
getting some repairs on them at a neighbouring smithy. His way lay
by the Kirk of Alloway, and being rather on the anxious look-out
in approaching a place so well known to be a favourite haunt of the
devil and the devil's friends and emissaries, he was struck aghast by
discovering through the horrors of the storm and stormy night, a
light, which on his nearer approach, plainly shewed itself to proceed
from the haunted edifice. Whether he had been fortified from above
on his devout supplication, as is customary with people when they

suspect the immediate presence of Satan; or whether, according to another custom, he had got courageously drunk at the smithy, I will not pretend to determine; but so it was that he ventured to go up to, nay into the very kirk. As good luck would have it, his temerity came off unpunished. The members of the infernal junto were all out on some midnight business or other, and he saw nothing but a kind of kettle or caldron, depending from the roof, over the fire, simmering some heads of unchristened children, limbs of executed malefactors, &c. for the business of the night. It was, in for a penny, in for a pound, with the honest ploughman: so without ceremony he unhooked the caldron from off the fire, and pouring out the damnable ingredients, inverted it on his head, and carried it fairly home where it remained long in the family a living evidence of the truth of the story.

24TH OCTOBER

On the Late Captain Grose's Peregrinations Thro' Scotland, Collecting the Antiquities of That Kingdom

BURNS'S FONDNESS FOR Francis Grose is apparent from this warmly light-hearted survey of the antiquarian's enthusiasm, his voracious appetite for macabre relics and curious stories, and, of course, his interest in witchcraft; an interest that would inspire one of Burns's most famous works, 'Tam o' Shanter'.

Grose died suddenly just months after he published the second volume of *The Antiquities of Scotland* (1791), which featured Burns's poem as an accompaniment to Grose's drawing of Alloway Kirk – albeit in a very long footnote!

Hear, Land o' Cakes, and brither Scots,
Frae Maidenkirk to Johny Groat's!—
If there's a hole in a' your coats,
    I rede you tent it:
A chield's amang you takin notes,
    And, faith, he'll prent it.

If in your bounds ye chance to light
Upon a fine, fat, fodgel wight,
O' stature short, but genius bright,
    That's he, mark weel —
And wow! he has an unco slight
    O' cauk and keel.

By some auld, houlet-haunted biggin,
Or kirk deserted by its riggin,
It's ten to ane ye'll find him snug in
    Some eldritch part,
Wi' deils, they say, Lord safe's! colleaguin
    At some black art.—

Ilk ghaist that haunts auld ha' or chamer,
Ye gipsy-gang that deal in glamour,
And you, deep-read in hell's black grammar,
    Warlocks and witches;
Ye'll quake at his conjuring hammer,
    Ye midnight bitches.

It's tauld he was a sodger bred,
And ane wad rather fa'n than fled;
But now he's quat the spurtle-blade,
    And dog-skin wallet,
And taen the — *Antiquarian trade*,
    I think they call it.

He has a fouth o' auld nick-nackets:
Rusty airn caps and jinglin jackets,
Wad haud the Lothians three in tackets,
      A towmont gude;
And parritch-pats and auld saut-backets,
      Before the Flood.

Of Eve's first fire he has a cinder;
Auld Tubalcain's fire-shool and fender;
That which distinguished the gender
      O' Balaam's ass;
A broom-stick o' the witch of Endor,
      Weel shod wi' brass.

Forbye, he'll shape you aff fu' gleg
The cut of Adam's philibeg;
The knife that nickit Abel's craig
      He'll prove you fully,
It was a faulding jocteleg,
      Or lang-kail gullie.—

But wad ye see him in his glee,
For meikle glee and fun has he,
Then set him down, and twa or three
      Gude fellows wi' him;
And *port, O port*! shine thou a wee,
      And THEN ye'll see him!

25TH OCTOBER

On Bawdry
from a letter to Robert Cleghorn, 25th October 1793

O N THIS DAY IN 1793, Burns wrote to his male crony and fellow
Crochallan Fencible, Robert Cleghorn, that he intended to
give him the 'maidenhead' of an unmarked batch of paper. As we saw
on the 13th of October, the Crochallan Fencibles was an Edinburgh
gentleman's club, to which Burns belonged during his time in
Edinburgh and for whom he collected and composed bawdy song.

Following Burns's departure from Edinburgh in 1788, he forwarded
a significant number of bawdy songs (both collected and original)
to Cleghorn, perhaps for the club's further enjoyment. Indeed, it
is possible that Cleghorn was at one time in possession of Burns's
entire 'collection' of bawdry; an elusive manuscript that is thought to
have been the basis for the privately printed volume, *The Merry Muses
of Caledonia* (1799). In a letter dated 29th August 1790, Burns writes
rather urgently, 'I am in a hurry, a d-mn'd hurry; so take this scrawl.
– Why don't you return me my collection of [*word missing*] Songs?'

There is no doubt that Burns revelled in bawdy verse. However,
knowing that it was potentially litigious, he maintained a tight grip
on his association with the genre during his lifetime.

I have just now bought a quire of Post, and I am determined, my
Dear Cleghorn, to give you the maidenhead of it.— Indeed, that is
all my reason for, and all that I can propose to give you by this present
scrawl.— From my late hours last night, and the dripping fogs and
damn'd east-wind of this stupid day, I have left me as little soul as an
oyster.— "Sir John, you are so fretful, you cannot live long."— "Why,
there is it! Come, sing me a BAUDY-SONG to make me merry!!!—

Act Sederunt of the Session [...]

Well! The Law is good for something, since we can make a B—dy song out of it.— (N.B. I never made anything of it any other way— There is, there must be, some truth in original sin.— My violent propensity to B—dy convinces me of it.— Lack a day if that species of Composition be the Sin against "the Haly Ghaist," "I am the most offending soul alive."—

26TH OCTOBER

Act Sederunt o' the Session
to the tune of O'er the Muir Amang the Heather

AND HERE IS THE BAWDY SONG that was enclosed with yesterday's letter, in which Burns deliberately mocks official concern with the public's sexual affairs in humorous and defiantly explicit terms. The phallic imagery of the refrain, 'standing pr-cks are fauteors a' / And guilty of a high transgression', points to the ironic notion that it is the state's attempted suppression of the human body and sexuality that contravenes basic humanity, or rather, nature's law.

In Edinburgh town they've made a law,
    In Edinburgh at the Court o' Session;
That standing pr-cks are fauteors a',
    And guilty of a high transgression.—

Act Sederunt o' the Session,
    Decreet o' the Court o' Session,
That standing pr-cks are fauteors a',
    And guilty of a high transgression.—

And they've provided dungeons deep,
   Ilk lass has ane in her possession;
Untill the wretches wail and weep,
   They there shall lie for their transgression.—

Act Sederunt o' the Session,
   Decreet o' the Court o' Session,
The rogues in pouring tears shall weep,
   By act Sederunt o' the Session.—

27TH OCTOBER

On Alloway Kirk (ii)
from a letter to Captain Francis Grose, c. June 1790

TODAY WE READ Burns's second haunting tale of Alloway Kirk, a prose account of what would become 'Tam o' Shanter' and which, the bard declared, he could 'prove to be equally authentic' to the first.

On a market day in the town of Ayr, a farmer from Carrick, and consequently whose way lay by the very gate of Alloway kirk-yard, in order to cross the river Doon at the old bridge, which is about two or three hundred yards further on than the said gate, had been detained by his business 'till by the time he reached Alloway, it was the wizard hour, between night and morning. Though he was terrified, with a blaze streaming from the kirk, yet as it is a well known fact that to turn back on these occasions is running by far the greatest risk of mischief, he prudently advanced on his road. When he had reached the gate of the kirk yard, he was surprised and entertained, through the ribs and arches of an old gothic window which still faces the highway, to see a dance of witches merrily footing it round their old sooty blackguard master, who was keeping them all alive with the powers of his bag-pipe. The farmer, stopping his horse to observe them a little, could plainly descry the faces of many old women of his acquaintance and neighbourhood. How the gentleman was dressed, tradition does not say; but the ladies were all in their smocks: and one of them happening unluckily to have a smock which was considerably too short to answer all the purpose of that piece of dress, our farmer was so tickled that he involuntarily burst out, with a loud laugh, "Weel luppen Maggy wi' the short sark!" and recollecting himself, instantly spurred his horse to the top of his speed. I need not mention the universally known fact, that no diabolical power can pursue you beyond the middle of a running stream. Lucky it was for the poor farmer that the river Doon was so near, for notwithstanding the speed of his horse, which was a good one, against he reached the middle of the arch of the bridge, and consequently the middle of the stream, the pursuing, vengeful, hags, were so close at his heels, that one of them actually sprung to seize him; but it was too late, nothing was on her side of the stream but the horse's tail, which immediately gave way at her infernal grip, as if blasted by a stroke of lightning; but the farmer was beyond her reach.

However, the unsightly, tail-less condition of the vigorous steed was to the last hour of the noble creature's life, an awful warning to the Carrick farmers, not to stay too late in Ayr markets.

from Address to the Deil

BURNS'S EPITAPH FOR 'Address to the Deil' is from John Milton's epic poem *Paradise Lost* (1667); a text much admired by the bard, not least for Milton's delineation of Satan. Burns's treatment of the ubiquitous, shapeshifting devil is considerably lighter in tone and more humorous than Milton's. In these opening stanzas the bard addresses 'Auld Hornie' directly, and he describes the various haunts and forms that the devil takes, in keeping with local folklore.

> *O Prince, O chief of many throned powers,*
> *That led th'embattl'd Seraphim to war—*
> MILTON.

O Thou, whatever title suit thee!
Auld Hornie, Satan, Nick, or Clootie,
Wha in yon cavern grim an' sooty
   Clos'd under hatches,
Spairges about the brunstane cootie,
   To scaud poor wretches!

Hear me, *auld Hangie*, for a wee,
An' let poor, *damned bodies* be;
I'm sure sma' pleasure it can gie,
   Ev'n to a *deil*,
To skelp an' scaud poor dogs like me,
   An' hear us squeel!

Great is thy pow'r, an' great thy fame;
Far ken'd an' noted is thy name;
An' tho' yon *lowan' heugh's* thy hame,
        Thou travels far;
An' faith! thou's neither lag nor lame,
        Nor blate nor scaur.

Whyles, ranging like a roaran lion,
For prey, a' holes an' corners tryin;
Whyles, on the strong-wing'd Tempest flyin,
        Tirlan the *kirks*;
Whyles, in the human bosom pryin,
        Unseen thou lurks.

I've heard my rev'rend *Graunie* say,
In lanely glens ye like to stray;
Or where auld, ruin'd castles, grey,
        Nod to the moon,
Ye fright the nightly wand'rer's way,
        Wi' eldritch croon.

When twilight did my *Graunie* summon,
To say her pray'rs, douse, honest woman!
Aft 'yont the dyke she's heard you bumman,
        Wi' eerie drone;
Or, rustlin, thro' the boortrees coman,
        Wi' heavy groan.

Ae dreary, windy, winter night,
The stars shot down wi' sklentan light,
Wi' you, *myself*, I gat a fright,
        Ayont the lough;
Ye, like a *rash-buss*, stood in sight,
        Wi' wavin' sugh.

The cudgel in my nieve did shake,
Each brist'ld hair stood like a stake,
When wi' an eldritch, stoor *quaick, quaick,*
      Amang the springs,
Awa ye squatter'd like a *drake,*
      On whistling wings.

Let *Warlocks* grim, an' wither'd *Hags,*
Tell how wi' you on ragweed nags,
They skim the muirs an' dizzy crags,
      Wi' wicked speed;
And in kirk-yards renew their leagues,
      Owre howket dead.

29TH OCTOBER

On Alloway Kirk (iii)
from a letter to Captain Francis Grose, c. June 1790

BURNS'S THIRD AND FINAL curious tale of Alloway Kirk, according to the bard, 'though equally true, is not so well identified as the two former, with regard to the scene: but as the best authorities give it for Alloway, I shall relate it'.

Burns's emphasis on the authenticity of these stories would have appealed to Grose's antiquarian bent. Here we are reminded, not only of the threat of the supernatural, but also of the dangers of drink.

On a summer's evening, about the time that Nature puts on her sables to mourn the expiry of the chearful day, a shepherd boy belonging to a farmer in the immediate neighbourhood of Alloway Kirk, had just folded his charge, and was returning home. As he passed the kirk, in the adjoining field, he fell in with a crew of men and women, who were busy pulling stems of the plant ragwort. He observed that as each person pulled a ragwort, he or she got astride of it and called out, "Up horsie!" on which the ragwort flew off, like Pegasus, through the air with its rider. The foolish boy likewise pulled his ragwort and cried with the rest "Up horsie!" and, strange to tell, away he flew with the company. The first stage at which the cavalcade stopt, was a merchant's wine cellar in Bordeaux, where, without saying by your leave, they quaffed away at the best the cellar could afford, until the morning, foe to the imps and works of darkness, threatened to throw light on the matter, and frightened them from their carousals. The poor shepherd lad, being equally a stranger to the scene and the liquor, heedlessly got himself drunk; and when the rest took horse, he fell asleep, and was found so next day by some of the people belonging to the merchant. Somebody that understood Scotch, asking him what he was, he said he was such-a-one's herd in Alloway; and by some means or other getting home again, he lived long to tell the world the wondrous tale.

30TH OCTOBER

from Tam o' Shanter

A ND HERE IT IS, on the eve of Halloween – Tam o' Shanter's infamous encounter with an orgy of witches at Alloway Kirk, played on by Satan himself. The iconic imagery of this poem, alongside its captivating story, are qualities that have ensured it has become one of Burns's most famous works. Beyond this, however, it is a skilful and multifaceted performance that scrutinises male sociability, stereotypical gender roles, appetite, sex, alcohol and the danger of an imagination fuelled by drunkenness.

The wind blew as 'twad blawn its last;
The rattling showers rose on the blast;
The speedy gleams the darkness swallow'd;
Loud, deep, and lang, the thunder bellow'd:
That night, a child might understand,
The Deil had business on his hand.

Weel mounted on his grey mare, *Meg*,
A better never lifted leg,
Tam skelpit on thro' dub and mire,
Despising wind, and rain, and fire;
Whiles holding fast his gude blue bonnet;
Whiles crooning o'er some auld Scots sonnet;
Whiles glowring round wi' prudent cares,
Lest bogles catch him unawares:
Kirk-Alloway was drawing nigh,
Where ghaists and houlets nightly cry.—

By this time he was cross the ford,
Where, in the snaw, the chapman smoor'd;
And past the birks and meikle stane,
Where drunken *Charlie* brak's neck-bane;
And thro' the whins, and by the cairn,
Where hunters fand the murder'd bairn;
And near the thorn, aboon the well,
Where *Mungo's* mither hang'd hersel.—
Before him *Doon* pours all his floods;
The doubling storm roars thro' the woods;
The lightnings flash from pole to pole;
Near and more near the thunders roll:
When, glimmering thro' the groaning trees,
Kirk-Alloway seem'd in a bleeze;
Thro' ilka bore the beams were glancing;
And loud resounded mirth and dancing.—

   Inspiring bold *John Barleycorn*!
What dangers thou canst make us scorn!
Wi' tippeny, we fear nae evil;
Wi' usquabae, we'll face the devil!—
The swats sae ream'd in *Tammie's* noddle,
Fair play, he car'd na deils a boddle.
But *Maggie* stood right sair astonish'd,
Till, by the heel and hand admonish'd,
She ventured forward on the light;
And, wow! *Tam* saw an unco sight!

Warlocks and witches in a dance;
Nae cotillion brent new frae *France*,
But hornpipes, jigs, strathspeys, and reels,
Put life and mettle in their heels.
A winnock-bunker in the east,
There sat auld Nick, in shape o' beast;

A towzie tyke, black, grim, and large,
To gie them music was his charge:
He screw'd the pipes and gart them skirl,
Till roof and rafters a' did dirl.—
Coffins stood round, like open presses,
That shaw'd the dead in their last dresses:
And by some devilish cantraip sleight
Each in its cauld hand held a light.—
By which heroic *Tam* was able
To note upon the haly table,
A murderer's banes, in gibbet airns;
Twa span-lang, wee, unchristen'd bairns;
A thief, new-cutted frae a rape,
Wi' his last gasp his gab did gape;
Five tomahawks, wi' blude red-rusted:
Five scimitars, wi' murder crusted;
A garter, which a babe had strangled;
A knife, a father's throat had mangled,
Whom his ain son o' life bereft,
The grey hairs yet stack to the heft;
Wi' mair o' horrible and awefu',
Which even to name wad be unlawfu'.
Three lawyers tongues, turned inside oot,
Wi' lies, seamed like a beggars clout,
Three priests hearts, rotten, black as muck,
Lay stinkin, vile in every neuk.

  As *Tammie* glowr'd, amaz'd, and curious,
The mirth and fun grew fast and furious:
The piper loud and louder blew;
The dancers quick and quicker flew;
They reel'd, they set, they cross'd, they cleekit,
Till ilka carlin swat and reekit,
And coost her duddies to the wark,
And linket at it in her sark!

Now *Tam, O Tam*! had thae been queans,
A' plump and strapping in their teens,
Their sarks, instead o' creeshie flannen,
Been snaw-white seventeen hunder linnen!
Thir breeks o' mine, my only pair,
That ance were plush, o' gude blue hair.
I wad hae gi'en them off my hurdies,
For ae blink o' the bonie burdies!
   But wither'd beldams, auld and droll,
Rigwoodie hags wad spean a foal,
Louping an' flinging on a crummock,
I wonder didna turn thy stomach.

But *Tam* kent what was what fu' brawlie:
There was ae winsome wench and wawlie,
That night enlisted in the core,
(Lang after ken'd on *Carrick* shore;
For mony a beast to dead she shot,
And perish'd mony a bonie boat,
And shook baith meikle corn and bear,
And kept the country-side in fear.)
Her cutty sark, o' Paisley harn,
That while a lassie she had worn,
In longitude tho' sorely scanty,
It was her best, and she was vauntie.—
Ah! little ken'd thy reverend grannie,
That sark she coft for her wee Nannie,
Wi twa pund Scots, ('twas a' her riches),
Wad ever grac'd a dance of witches!

   But here my Muse her wing maun cour,
Sic flights are far beyond her pow'r;
To sing how Nannie lap and flang,
(A souple jade she was, and strang),
And how *Tam* stood, like ane bewithc'd,
And thought his very een enrich'd;

491

Even Satan glowr'd, and fidg'd fu' fain,
And hotch'd and blew wi' might and main:
Till first ae caper, syne anither,
Tam tint his reason a' thegither,
And roars out, "Weel done, Cutty-sark!"
And in an instant all was dark:
And scarcely had he Maggie rallied,
When out the hellish legion sallied.

   As bees bizz out wi' angry fyke,
When plundering herds assail their byke;
As open pussie's mortal foes,
When, pop! she starts before their nose;
As eager runs the market-crowd,
When "Catch the thief!" resounds aloud,
So Maggie runs, the witches follow,
Wi' mony an eldritch skreech and hollow.

   Ah, *Tam*! Ah, *Tam*! thou'll get thy fairin!
In hell, they'll roast thee like a herrin!
In vain thy *Kate* awaits thy comin!
Kate soon will be a woefu' woman!
   Now, do thy speedy-utmost, Meg,
And win the key-stone o' the brig;
There, at them thou thy tail may toss,
A running stream they dare na cross.
But ere the keystane she could make,
The fient a tail she had to shake!
For Nannie, far before the rest,
Hard upon noble Maggie prest,
And flew at Tam wi' furious ettle;
But little wist she Maggie's mettle!
Ae spring brought off her master hale,
But left behind her ain grey tail:
The carlin claught her by the rump,
And left poor Maggie scarce a stump.

Now, wha this tale o' truth shall read,
Ilk man and mother's son, take heed:
Whene'er to Drink you are inclin'd,
Or Cutty-sarks rin in your mind,
Think ye may buy the joys o'er dear;
Remember Tam o' Shanter's mare.

31st OCTOBER

from Halloween

THERE COULD ONLY BE ONE CHOICE for today's poem. In a note
to 'Halloween' in the Kilmarnock edition of *Poems, Chiefly in the
Scottish Dialect* (1786), Burns explains that Halloween 'is thought to
be a night when Witches, Devils, and other mischief-making beings,
are all abroad on their baneful, midnight errands: particularly, those
aerial people, the Fairies, are said, on that night, to hold a grand
Anniversary'.

Burns's account of Halloween is no horror story, however, but a
survey of superstition and Halloween rituals in eighteenth-century
rural Scotland. This extract relates the high jinks and illicit sexual
encounters of a group of young men and women as they 'pou their
stalks of corn' to predict their future partner, and burn their 'nits' (or
nuts) to determine the nature of their relationship. Either the nuts
will burn brightly side by side, or spark and jump away from one
another. Whatever the case, this is all really just an excuse for 'kiutlin'
(or cuddling) in the recently harvested hay!

Upon that *night*, when Fairies light
    On *Cassilis Downans* dance,
Or owre the lays, in splendid blaze,
    On sprightly coursers prance;
Or for *Colean* the rout is taen,
    Beneath the moon's pale beams;
There, up the *Cove*, to stray an' rove,
    Amang the rocks and streams
              To sport that night.

Amang the bonie, winding banks,
    Where *Doon* rins, wimplin, clear;
Where BRUCE ance rul'd the martial ranks,
    An' shook his *Carrick* spear;
Some merry, friendly, countra folks,
    Together did convene,
To *burn* their nits, an' *pou* their stocks,
    An' haud their *Halloween*
              Fu' blythe that night.

The lasses feat, an' cleanly neat,
    Mair braw than when they're fine;
Their faces blythe, fu' sweetly kythe,
    Hearts leal, an' warm, an' kin':
The lads sae trig, wi' wooer-babs,
    Weel-knotted on their garten,
Some unco blate, an' some wi' gabs,
    Gar lasses hearts gang startin
              Whyles fast at night.

Then, first an' foremost, thro' the kail,
    Their *stocks* maun a' be sought ance;
They steek their een, an' grape an' wale,
    For muckle anes, an' straught anes.
Poor hav'rel *Will* fell aff the drift,
    An' wandered thro' the *Bow-kail*,

An' pow't for want o' better shift
   A *runt* was like a sow-tail
           Sae bow't that night.

Then, straught or crooked, yird or nane,
   They roar an' cry a' throw'ther;
The vera *wee-things*, toddlin, rin,
   Wi' stocks out owre their shouther:
An' gif the *custock's* sweet or sour,
   Wi' joctelegs they taste them;
Syne coziely, aboon the door,
   Wi' cannie care, they've plac'd them
           To lye that night.

The lasses staw frae 'mang them a',
   To pou their *stalks o' corn*;
But *Rab* slips out, an' jinks about,
   Behint the muckle thorn:
He grippit *Nelly* hard and fast:
   Loud skirl'd a' the lasses;
But her *tap-pickle* maist was lost,
   When kiutlin in the *Fause-house*
           Wi' him that night.

The auld Guidwife's weel-hoordet *nits*
   Are round an' round divided,
An' monie lads an' lasses fates
   Are there that night decided:
Some kindle, couthie, side by side,
   And *burn* thegither trimly;
Some start awa, wi' saucy pride,
   An' jump out owre the chimlie
           Fu' high that night.

NOVEMBER

Edina! Scotia's darling seat!
   All hail thy palaces and tow'rs,
Where once beneath a Monarch's feet,
   Sat Legislation's sov'reign pow'rs!
From marking wildly-scatt'red flow'rs,
   As on the banks of Ayr I stray'd,
And singing, lone, the ling'ring hours,
   I shelter in thy honor'd shade.

from Address to Edinburgh

1st NOVEMBER

Cauld Frosty Morning

WE OFTEN GREET NOVEMBER on a dark and 'cauld frosty morning'. This song about an ardent lover, his breast 'fired' into 'madness', might go some way towards warming us up. The pursuer's 'innocent maiden' takes pity on him and is 'undone', but this tale has a happy ending, with the promise of cosy mornings forever after.

'Twas past ane o'clock in a cauld frosty morning,
   When cankert November blaws over the plain,
I heard the kirk bell repeat the loud warning,
   As, restless, I sought for sweet slumber in vain:
Then up I arose, the silver moon shining bright;
   Mountains and valleys appearing all hoary white;
Forth I would go, amid the pale, silent night,
   To seek the fair one, the cause of my pain.

Sae gently I staw to my lovely Maid's chamber,
   And rapp'd at her window, low down on my knee;
Begging that she would awauk from sweet slumber,
   Awauk from sweet slumber and pity me.
For, that a stranger to a' pleasure, peace and rest,
   Love into madness had fired my tortur'd breast;
And that I should be of a' men the maist unblest,
   Unless she would pity my sad miserie!

My True-love arose and whispered to me,
   (The moon looked in, and envy'd my love's charms;)
'An innocent Maiden, ah, would you undo me!'
   I made no reply, but leapt into her arms:
Bright Phebus peep'd over the hills and found me there;
   As he has done, now, seven lang years and mair:
A faithfuller, constanter, kinder, more loving Pair,
   His sweet-chearing beam nor enlightens nor warms.

2ND NOVEMBER

On the Loss of His Daughter
from a letter to Maria Riddell, October / November 1795

I N THE AUTUMN OF 1795, Burns lost his three-year-old daughter, Elizabeth Riddell Burns. Elizabeth was his only daughter with Jean who had survived infancy. The frankness and brevity of today's letter is a reflection of the poet's grief.

By the end of January 1796, he seemed better able to express himself on the subject, writing to Frances Dunlop, 'I have lately drank deep of the cup of affliction.— The Autumn robbed me of my only daughter and darling child, and that at a distance too, and so rapidly as to put it out of my power to pay the last duties to her.'

It is arguable whether Burns ever recovered from the shock of this very great loss. Elizabeth's death was immediately followed by the serious rheumatic illness that marked the beginning of the bard's own rapid decline.

A severe domestic misfortune has put all literary business out of my head for some time past.— Now I begin to resume my wonted studies.— I am much correspondence in your debt: I shall pay it soon.— [...]

That you, my friend, may never experience such a loss as mine, sincerely prays —

R.B.

3RD NOVEMBER

On Maria Riddell
from a letter to William Smellie, January 1792

M ARIA RIDDELL (1772–1808) was the sister-in-law of Burns's friend and patron, Robert Riddell. It is likely that the poet first met her at Robert Riddell's home, Friars Carse. They became firm friends and it is clear from Burns's letters that his regard for her was not merely due to romantic attraction (although, unsurprisingly, there seems to have been an element of that), but the consequence of her keen intellect and wit. As such, when Maria asked to be introduced to William Smellie (1740–1795), printer in Edinburgh and the first editor of *Encyclopaedia Britannica* (1768–1771), Burns was only too happy to make the introduction. Smellie, too, was impressed by Maria and published her travel book, *Voyages to Madeira and the Leeward Caribbean Isles* (1792).

I sit down, my dear Sir, to introduce a young lady to you, and a lady in the first ranks of fashion too.— What a task! You, who care no more for the herd of animals called, "Young Ladies," than for the herd of animals called — "Young Gentlemen"; You, who despise and detest the groupings and combinations of Fashion — an idiot Painter! who seems industrious to place staring Fools, and unprincipled Knaves in the fore-ground of his Picture, while Men of Sense and Honesty are too often thrown into the dimmest shades.— Mrs. Riddell who takes this letter to town with her, is a Character that even in your own way, as a Naturalist and a Philosopher, would be an acquisition to your acquaintance.— The Lady too, is a votary of the Muses; and as I think I am somewhat of a judge in my own trade, I assure you that her verses, always correct, and often elegant, are very much beyond the common run of the Lady Poetesses of the day.— She is a great admirer of your Book; and hearing me say that I was acquainted with you, she begged to be known to you, as she is just going to pay her first visit to our Caledonian Capital.— I told her that her best way was, to desire your intimate friend and her near relation, Craigdarroch, to have you at his house while she was there; and lest you should think of a lively West-Indian girl of eighteen, as girls of eighteen too often deserve to be thought of, I should take care to remove that prejudice — To be impartial, however, the Lady has one unlucky failing; a failing which you will easily discover, as she seems rather pleased with indulging it; and a failing that you will as easily pardon, as it is a sin that very much besets yourself:— where she dislikes, or despises, she is apt to make no more a secret of it — than where she esteems and respects.

4TH NOVEMBER

Impromptu on Mrs Riddell's Birthday, 4th November 1793

THIS POEM WAS WRITTEN as a compliment to Maria Riddell on her birthday. The personified 'Old Winter' laments the dark, cold reality of the season and asks Jove – or Jupiter – what he has done to merit such dismal features. In Roman mythology, Jove – king of gods and the god of sky and thunder – was honoured with ritual feasts in September and November, referred to as 'Epulum Jovis'. Happily, 'Winter' is granted his own special day, the birth of Maria Riddell, and 'rejoices' that her 'brilliance' is no match for the typically more celebrated of the seasons.

Old Winter, with his frosty beard,
Thus once to Jove his prayer preferred;
What have I done of all the year,
To bear this hated doom severe?
My cheerless suns no pleasure know;
Night's horrid car drags, dreary, slow:
My dismal months no joys are crowning,
But spleeny English, hanging, drowning.

Now Jove for once be mighty civil,
To counterbalance all this evil;
Give me, and I've no more to say,
Give me Maria's natal day!
That brilliant gift will so enrich me,
Spring, Summer, Autumn, cannot match me;
'Tis done! says Jove; so ends my story,
And Winter once rejoic'd in glory.

5TH NOVEMBER

My Peggy's Face

THIS WAS AMONG the first songs composed by Burns for inclusion in James Johnson's *Scots Musical Museum*. It was inspired by the poet's romantic interest in Margaret Chalmers (1763–1843). Some months earlier, Burns declared to Margaret in a letter, 'your pianoforte and you together have play'd the deuce somehow about my heart'. Burns spent several days with Margaret at Harvieston as part of his autumn tour of the Scottish Highlands. She later recalled that he had proposed to her, but she refused him as she was secretly engaged to another man.

Burns's correspondence of November 1787 makes clear that he was keen to publish these verses, along with 'Where Braving Angry Winter's Storms' (see the 8th of November), in the second volume of the *Scots Musical Museum*. To Johnson he wrote, 'I have a very strong private reason for wishing them in the 2d volume.' However, as will become clear from tomorrow's entry, Margaret was reluctant to see them in print.

My Peggy's face, my Peggy's form,
The frost of hermit age might warm;
My Peggy's worth, my Peggy's mind,
Might charm the first of human kind.
I love my Peggy's angel air,
Her face so truly heav'nly fair,
Her native grace so void of art,
But I adore my Peggy's heart.

The lily's hue, the rose's die,
The kindling lustre of an eye;
Who but owns their magic sway,
Who but knows they all decay!
The tender thrill, the pitying tear,
The generous purpose nobly dear,
The gentle look that Rage disarms,
These are all Immortal charms.

6TH NOVEMBER

On Poetic Compliments
from a letter to Margaret Chalmers, c. November 1787

FROM TODAY'S EXCERPT it is apparent that Margaret Chalmers, who inspired the selections for the 5th and 8th of November, was concerned that she might be identified as the object of Burns's poetic reveries. Her account some years later of a secret engagement may go some way towards explaining this. Despite Burns's forthright flattery and his somewhat unconvincing assurances that he had complimented her 'almost solely' on her 'mental charms', either she was unrelenting, or the poet was deterred from publishing the song by his disappointment at her refusal of his proposal.

'My Peggy's Face' did not appear in print until 1803, some sixteen years later and six years after the bard's death. 'Where Braving Angry Winter's Storms', however, was 'already set' when Burns wrote this letter and thus it appeared in the *Scots Musical Museum* in 1788 as originally planned.

I just now have read yours. The poetic compliments I pay cannot be misunderstood. They are neither of them so particular as to point *you* out to the world at large; and the circle of your acquaintances will allow all I have said. Besides I have complimented you chiefly, almost solely, on your mental charms. Shall I be plain with you? I will; so look to it. Personal attractions, madam, you have much above par; wit, understanding, and worth, you possess in the first class. This is a cursed flat way of telling you these truths, but let me hear no more of your sheepish timidity. I know the world a little. I know what they will say of my poems; by second sight I suppose; for I am seldom out in my conjectures; and you may believe me, my dear madam, I would not run any risk of hurting you by an ill-judged compliment. I wish to show to the world the odds between a poet's friends and those of simple prosemen.

7TH NOVEMBER

The Seventh of November

TODAY'S APTLY NAMED SONG was written in 1788 to mark the wedding anniversary of Robert Riddell and his wife Elizabeth. Burns presented it to Riddell some time in advance of the occasion (on the 16th of September) with the following account of its composition:

> As I was busy behind my harvest-folks this forenoon, and musing on a proper theme for your "Seventh of November," some of the conversation before me accidentally suggested a suspicion that this said Seventh of Nov, is a Matrimonial Anniversary with a certain very worthy neighbour of mine.— I have seen very few who owe so much to a Wedding-day as Mrs Riddell and you; and my imagination took the hint accordingly, as you will see on the next page.— A little gratitude too, had a pretty large share in firing my Muse; as amidst all the enjoyment I have in your hospitable Mansion, there

is nothing gives me more pleasure than to see the minute, cordial attentions and the sparkling glances of the Lover, while in so many Conjugal scenes in the World, a third person is hourly hurt with the insipid yawn of Satiety or the malignant squint of Disgust.—

Burns's song makes much of the perceived strength of the couple's marriage which, it is suggested, might only be compromised by the 'iron hand' of death.

The day returns, my bosom burns,
    The blissful day we twa did meet,
Tho' winter wild, in tempest toil'd,
    Ne'er summer sun was half sae sweet.
Than a' the pride that loads the tide,
    And crosses o'er the sultry line;
Than kingly robes, than crowns and globes,
    Heav'n gave me more – it made thee mine.

While day and night can bring delight,
    Or nature aught of pleasure give;
While joys above, my mind can move,
    For thee, and thee alone, I live!
When that grim foe of life below
    Comes in between to make us part;
The iron hand that breaks our band,
    It breaks my bliss – it breaks my heart!

8TH NOVEMBER

Where Braving Angry Winter's Storms
to the tune of Neil Gow's Lament for Abercairny

T ODAY'S SONG IS THE SECOND COMPOSITION inspired by
Margaret Chalmers and referred to by Burns in the letter for
the sixth of November. Burns's language captures the turbulent
weather and striking scenery at Harvieston, a small town at the foot
of the Ochil Hills in Perthshire where the bard spent several days
with Margaret in 1787. The imagery of the final stanza is a dramatic
expression of the depth of Burns's feelings for his 'Peggy'.

Where braving angry winter's storms
　　The lofty Ochels rise,
Far in their shade, my Peggy's charms
　　First blest my wondering eyes.

As one who by some savage stream
　　A lonely gem surveys,
Astonish'd, doubly marks it beam
　　With art's most polish'd blaze.

Blest be the wild, sequester'd shade,
　　And blest the day and hour,
Where Peggy's charms I first survey'd,
　　When first I felt their pow'r!

The tyrant death with grim controul,
　　May seize my fleeting breath,
But tearing Peggy from my soul
　　Must be a stronger death.

9TH NOVEMBER

from Rules and Regulations to be Observed in the Bachelors' Club

T HE TARBOLTON BACHELORS, a debating club founded by Burns, his brother Gilbert and several local men, held its first meeting in November of 1780. The prerequisite for membership is outlined in these extracts from the club's 'rules and regulations', which celebrate honesty, loyalty, equality, a healthy attitude towards the opposite sex, and a generally light-hearted approach to life. Most significant is the requirement that members 'must be a professed lover of one or more of the female sex', and so women emerge as the foremost mutual interest of the club's members.

According to records of the club, the Tarbolton Bachelors' contemplation of women and relationships was more lofty (at least on paper) than that of the bawdy Crochallan Fencibles, not least because, 'All swearing and profane language, and particularly all obscene and indecent conversation' was 'strictly prohibited'. Instead, the Bachelors debated sentimental issues such as, 'Whether do we derive more happiness from Love or Friendship?' and sought to advance their interests in the movement of the Scottish Enlightenment towards intellectual improvement.

7th. No member, on any pretence whatever, shall mention any of the club's affairs to any other person but a brother member, under the pain of being excluded; and particularly if any member shall reveal any of the speeches or affairs of the club with a view to ridicule or laugh at any of the rest of the members, he shall be for ever excommunicated from the society; and the rest of the members are desired, as much as possible, to avoid, and have no communication with him as a friend or comrade. [...]

10th. Every man proper for a member of this Society, must have a frank, honest, open heart; above any thing dirty or mean; and must be a professed lover of one or more of the female sex. No haughty, self-conceited person, who looks upon himself as superior to the rest of the Club, and especially no mean-spirited, worldly mortal, whose only will is to heap up money, shall upon any pretence whatever be admitted. In short, the proper person for this Society is, a cheerful, honest-hearted lad; who, if he has a friend that is true, and a mistress that is kind, and as much wealth as genteely to make both ends meet—is just as happy as this world can make him.

10TH NOVEMBER

The Ronalds of the Bennals

TODAY'S SONG WAS INSPIRED by the family of William Ronald, who was the wealthy owner of a large local farm near Tarbolton. Composed in the early 1780s, it refers to Tarbolton's 'proper young men's' dealings with Ronald's daughters and, somewhat satirically, to their extravagant 'tochers'. Given the interests of the Tarbolton Bachelors' Club outlined in yesterday's selection, and given that the club are known to have debated whether it was best to marry for love or money, 'the Ronalds of the Bennals' would have been a likely topic of conversation among club members. Ironically, and unfortunately for William Ronald, he was bankrupt by 1789.

In Tarbolton, ye ken, there are proper young men,
    And proper young lasses and a', man:
But ken ye the Ronalds that live in the Bennals,
    They carry the gree frae them a', man.

Their father's a laird, and weel he can spare't,
  Braid money to tocher them a', man,
To proper young men, he'll clink in the hand
  Gowd guineas a hunder or twa, man.

There's ane they ca' Jean, I'll warrant ye've seen
  As bonie a lass or as braw, man,
But for sense and guid taste she'll vie wi' the best,
  And a conduct that beautifies a', man.

The charms o' the min', the langer they shine,
  The mair admiration they draw, man;
While peaches and cherries, and roses and lilies,
  They fade and they wither awa, man,

If ye be for Miss Jean, tak this frae a frien',
  A hint o' a rival or twa, man,
The Laird o' Blackbyre wad gang through the fire,
  If that wad entice her awa, man.

The Laird o' Braehead has been on his speed,
  For mair than a towmond or twa, man;
The Laird o' the Ford will straught on a board,
  If he canna get her at a', man.

Then Anna comes in, the pride o' her kin,
  The boast of our bachelors a', man:
Sae sonsy and sweet, sae fully complete,
  She steals our affections awa, man.

If I should detail the pick and the wale
  O' lasses that live here awa, man,
The faut wad be mine, if she didna shine
  The sweetest and best o' them a', man.

I lo'e her mysel, but darena weel tell,
  My poverty keeps me in awe, man,
For making o' rhymes, and working at times,
  Does little or naething at a', man.

Yet I wadna choose to let her refuse,
  Nor hae't in her power to say na, man,
For though I be poor, unnoticed, obscure,
  My stomach's as proud as them a', man.

Though I canna ride in weel-booted pride,
  And flee o'er the hills like a craw, man,
I can haud up my head wi' the best o' the breed,
  Though fluttering ever so braw, man.

My coat and my vest, they are Scotch o' the best,
  O' pairs o' guid breeks I hae twa, man:
And stockings and pumps to put on my stumps,
  And ne'er a wrang steek in them a', man.

My sarks they are few, but five o' them new,
  Twal'-hundred, as white as the snaw, man,
A ten-shillings hat, a Holland cravat;
  There are no mony poets sae braw, man.

I never had freens weel stockit in means,
  To leave me a hundred or twa, man,
Nae weel-tocher'd aunts, to wait on their drants
  And wish them in hell for it a', man.

I never was cannie for hoarding o' money,
  Or claughtin't together at a', man,
I've little to spend and naething to lend,
  But devil a shilling I awe, man.

11TH NOVEMBER

When Wild War's Deadly Blast Was Blown
to the tune of The Mill, Mill O

TODAY IS ARMISTICE DAY, when we commemorate the commitment of the Allied and German forces to the cessation of hostilities in the First World War. The ceasefire commenced at the eleventh hour, of the eleventh day, of the eleventh month in 1918. We mark this solemn occasion with Burns's song about a soldier returning to his love in the 'gentle peace' that follows 'wild war's deadly blast'. And we remember, as Burns does, that the soldier was 'his country's stay, In day and hour of danger'. There is evidence that this song, as well as Burns's 'I'll Go and Be a Sodger', was used in First World War recruitment posters.

When wild war's deadly blast was blawn,
    And gentle peace returning,
Wi' mony a sweet babe fatherless,
    And mony a widow mourning;
I left the lines and tented field,
    Where lang I'd been a lodger,
My humble knapsack a' my wealth,
    A poor and honest sodger.

A leal, light heart was in my breast,
    My hand unstain'd wi' plunder;
And for fair Scotia hame again,
    I cheery on did wander:
I thought upon the banks o' Coil,

I thought upon my Nancy,
And ay I mind't the witching smile
   That caught my youthful fancy.

At length I reach'd the bonie glen,
   Where early life I sported;
I pass'd the mill and trysting thorn,
   Where Nancy aft I courted:
Wha spied I but my ain dear maid,
   Down by her mother's dwelling!
And turn'd me round to hide the flood
   That in my een was swelling.

Wi' alter'd voice, quoth I, Sweet lass,
   Sweet as yon hawthorn's blossom,
O! happy, happy may he be,
   That's dearest to thy bosom:
My purse is light, I've far to gang,
   And fain wad be thy lodger;
I've serv'd my king and country lang,
   Take pity on a sodger!

Sae wistfully she gaz'd on me,
   And lovelier was than ever;
Quo' she, a sodger ance I lo'ed,
   Forget him shall I never:
Our humble cot, and hamely fare,
   Ye freely shall partake it;
That gallant badge, the dear cockade,
   Ye're welcome for the sake o't.

She gaz'd – she redden'd like a rose –
   Syne pale like only lily;
She sank within my arms, and cried,
   Art thou my ain dear Willie?
By him who made yon sun and sky!

By whom true love's regarded,
I am the man – and thus may still
   True lovers be rewarded.

The wars are o'er, and I'm come hame,
   And find thee still true-hearted;
Tho' poor in gear, we're rich in love,
   And mair, we'se ne'er be parted!
Quo' she, My grandsire left me gowd,
   A mailen plenish'd fairly;
And come, my faithfu' sodger lad,
   Thou'rt welcome to it dearly!

For gold the merchant ploughs the main,
   The farmer ploughs the manor;
But glory is the sodger's prize,
   The sodger's wealth is honour:
The brave poor sodger ne'er despise,
   Nor count him as a stranger;
Remember, he's his country's stay,
   In day and hour of danger.

12TH NOVEMBER

from Lines Written on a Window at the Globe Tavern, Dumfries

BURNS, AS AN OFFICER of the Dumfries Volunteers, was prepared to defend his country and locale in the event of a military invasion (see 16th July). However, the following lines make clear that the bard's strong preference was to make love rather than wage war, and to create rather than take lives. In this, as a man who fathered at least twelve children, he certainly succeeded.

I Murder hate by field or flood,
　　Tho' glory's name may screen us;
In wars at home I'll spend my blood,
　　Life-giving wars of Venus:
The deities that I adore
　　Are social Peace and Plenty;
I'm better pleased *to make one more*,
　　Than be the death of twenty.—

13TH NOVEMBER

The Battle of Sherra-moor
to the tune of Cameronian Rant

O N THIS DAY IN 1715, Jacobite forces under the command of
John Erskine, 6th Earl of Mar (1675–1732), met the Hanoverian
army, led by John Campbell, 2nd Duke of Argyle (1680–1743), in battle
at Sherrifmuir, Perthshire. Although the Jacobite forces significantly
outnumbered their opponents, their prompt retreat resulted in
confusion regarding the outcome of the clash, which was one of the
final military engagements of the failed 1715 uprising. Here is Burns's
version of a traditional song in which two men debate the outcome
of this inconclusive battle.

O cam ye here the fight to shun,
 Or herd the sheep wi' me, man,
Or were ye at the Sherra-moor,
 Or did the battle see, man,
"I saw the battle, sair and teugh;
And reekin-red ran mony a sheugh,
My heart for fear gae sough for sough,
To hear the thuds, and see the cluds
O' Clans frae woods, in tartan duds,
Wha glaum'd at kingdoms three, man.
 Chorus la la la &c.

The red-coat lads, wi' black cockauds,
 To meet them were na slaw, man,
They rush'd and push'd, and blude outgush'd
 And mony a bouk did fa', man:
The great Argyle led on his files,

I wat they glanc'd for twenty miles;
They hough'd the clans like nine-pin kyles,
They hack'd and hash'd, while braid swords clash'd,
And thro' they dash'd, and hew'd and smash'd,
Till fey men di'd awa, man.
     Chorus la la la &c.

But had ye seen the philibegs,
     And skyrin tartan trews, man,
When in the teeth they dar'd our Whigs,
     And covenant True-blues, man;
In lines extended lang and large,
When baiginets o'erpower'd the targe,
And thousands hasten'd to the charge;
Wi' Highland wrath they frae the sheath
Drew blades o' death, till out o' breath,
They fled like frighted dows, man!
     Chorus la la la &c.

"O how deil Tam can that be true,
     The chase gaed frae the north, man;
I saw mysel, they did pursue,
     The horsemen back to Forth, man;
And at Dunblane in my ain sight,
They took the brig wi' a' their might,
And straught to Stirling wing'd their flight;
But, cursed lot! the gates were shut;
And mony a huntit, poor Red-coat,
For fear amaist did swarf, man.
     Chorus la la la &c.

My sister Kate cam up the gate
     Wi' crowdie unto me, man;
She swoor she saw some rebels run
     To Perth and to Dundee, man;
Their left-hand General had nae skill;

The Angus lads had nae gude will,
That day their neebours' blude to spill;
For fear by foes, that they should lose,
Their cogs o' brose, they scar'd at blows,
And hameward fast did flee, man.
    Chorus la la la &c.

They've lost some gallant gentlemen,
    Amang the Highland clans, man!
I fear my Lord Panmure is slain,
    Or fallen in Whiggish hands, man,
Now wad ye sing this double flight,
Some fell for wrang and some for right,
And mony bade the warld gudenight;
Say pell and mell, wi' muskets knell,
How Tories fell, and Whigs to h-ll,
Flew off in frighted bands, man.
    Chorus la la la &c.

14TH NOVEMBER

Up and Warn a' Willie

IN ANOTHER VERSION OF A TRADITIONAL SONG, gathered by
Burns for Johnson's *Scots Musical Museum*, the frustrating outcome
of the Battle of Sherrifmuir is articulated by a 'canty highlander' whose
desire is to 'restore our king' – James Francis Edward Stuart, or 'the
Old Pretender' – to the throne. He is no wiser than the protagonists
in yesterday's selection regarding the outcome of the battle, declaring
in the final stanza that, 'We baith did fight and baith did beat / And
baith did rin awa, Willie.'

Up and warn a' Willie,
Warn, warn a';
To hear my canty highland sang,
Relate the thing I saw, Willie.

When we gaed to the braes o' Mar,
   And to the wapon-shaw, Willie,
Wi' true design to serve the king
   And banish whigs awa, Willie.
     Up and warn a' Willie,
      Warn, warn, a';
For Lords and lairds came there bedeen
   And wow but they were braw, Willie.

But when the standard was set up,
   Right fierce the wind did blaw, Willie;
The royal nit upon the tap
   Down to the ground did fa', Willie.
     Up and warn a' Willie,

Warn, warn, a';
Then second sighted Sandy said
  We'd do nae gude at a', Willie.

But when the army join'd at Perth,
  The bravest ere ye saw, Willie,
We didna doubt the rogues to rout,
  Restore our king and a', Willie.
    Up and warn a' Willie,
      Warn, warn, a';
The pipers play'd frae right to left
  O whirry whigs awa, Willie.

But when we march'd to Sherra-muir
  And there the rebels saw, Willie;
Brave Argyle attack'd our right,
  Our flank and front and a', Willie.
    Up and warn a', Willie,
      Warn, warn a';
Traitor Huntly soon gave way
  Seaforth, St Clair and a' Willie.

But brave Glengarry on our right
  The rebel's left did claw, Willie,
He there the greatest slaughter made
  That ever Donald saw, Willie.
    Up and warn a', Willie,
      Warn, warn a',
And Whittam s--t his breeks for fear
  And fast did rin awa', Willie.

For he ca'd us a Highland mob
  And soon he'd slay us a' Willie;
But we chas'd him back to Stirling brig
  Dragoons and foot and a', Willie.
    Up and warn a' Willie,

Warn, warn a',
At length we rallied on a hill
And briskly up did draw, Willie.

But when Argyle did view our line,
And them in order saw Willie,
He streight gaed to Dumblane again
And back his left did draw, Willie.
Up and warn a' Willie,
Warn, warn a',
Then we to Auchterairder march'd
To wait a better fa' Willie.

Now if ye spier wha wan the day,
I've tell'd you what I saw Willie,
We baith did fight and baith did beat
And baith did rin awa, Willie.
Up and warn a', Willie,
Warn, warn a', Willie,
For second sighted Sandie said
We'd do nae gude at a', Willie.

15TH NOVEMBER

The Lazy Mist

O N THIS DAY IN 1788, Burns sent 'The Lazy Mist' to the poet
and clergyman Rev. Dr Thomas Blacklock. With nature fully
transitioned to winter and little remaining of the calendar year,
Burns's mood is one of profound reflection as he contemplates life
and the 'something' that must surely lie beyond.

The lazy mist hangs from the brow of the hill,
Concealing the course of the dark winding rill;
How languid the scenes, late so sprightly, appear,
As Autumn to Winter resigns the pale year.
The forests are leafless, the meadows are brown,
And all the gay foppery of summer is flown:
Apart let me wander, apart let me muse,
How quick Time is flying, how keen Fate pursues.

How long I have liv'd – but how much liv'd in vain;
How little of life's scanty span may remain:
What aspects, old Time, in his progress, has worn;
What ties, cruel Fate, in my bosom has torn.
How foolish, or worse, till our summit is gain'd!
And downward, how weaken'd, how darken'd, how pain'd!
Life is not worth having with all it can give,
For something beyond it poor man sure must live.

16th NOVEMBER

Whistle O'er the Lave O't

BURNS SENT THIS SONG to James Johnson in November 1788 for inclusion in the *Scots Musical Museum*. The song is not, seemingly, a reflection of Burns's own circumstances – the bard wrote to Blacklock around the same time that he was 'more and more pleased' with his marriage to Jean. This humorous account of a tumultuous marriage is instead based upon a model of traditional song that can be dated back to medieval *Chansons de mal–mariée* (songs of an unhappy wife). Several eighteenth-century inversions of this motif depict an unhappy, complaining husband and cast 'Meg' as the disagreeable spouse.

First when Maggy was my care,
Heaven, I thought, was in her air;
Now we're married, speir nae mair,
   But Whistle o'er the lave o't.

Meg was meek and Meg was mild,
Sweet and harmless as a child;
Wiser men than me's beguil'd,
   So Whistle o'er the lave o't.

How we live, my Meg and me,
How we love and how we gree;
I carena by how few may see,
   Whistle o'er the lave o't.

Wha I wish were maggots meat,
Dish'd up in her winding-sheet;
I could write – but Meg maun see't,
    Whistle o'er the lave o't.

17TH NOVEMBER

I'm O'er Young to Marry Yet

THE YOUNG WOMAN in this song resists marriage, expressing her concern that, given the long winter nights following 'Hallowmass', she 'dare na venture' into a 'man's bed' just yet. She invites her suitor to call again in the summer, but there is, nonetheless, a lingering sense that the winter has brought with it the 'frosty wind' of change.

I am my mammy's ae bairn,
    Wi' unco folk I weary, Sir,
And lying in a man's bed,
    I'm fley'd it mak me irie, Sir.

I'm o'er young, I'm o'er young,
    I'm o'er young to marry yet;
I'm o'er young, 'twad be a sin
    To tak me frae my mammy yet.

Hallowmass is come and gane,
    The nights are lang in winter, Sir,
And you an' I in ae bed,
    In trowth, I dare na venture, Sir.
        I'm o'er young &c.

Fu' loud and shill the frosty wind
 Blaws thro' the leafless timmer, Sir;
But if ye come this gate again,
 I'll aulder be gin simmer, Sir.
  I'm o'er young &c.

18TH NOVEMBER

On 'The Bonie Lass o' Ballochmyle'
from a letter to Miss Wilhelmina Alexander of Ballochmyle, inclosing a song I had composed on her, 18th November 1786

O N THIS DAY IN 1786, Burns wrote an overblown letter to Wilhelmina Alexander (1756–1843) – the daughter of the Laird of Ballochmyle – enclosing a song. The bard explained that – having admired Wilhelmina from a distance on a country walk – he was inspired to compose 'The Bonie Lass o' Ballochmyle', and he requested permission to publish it in his forthcoming Edinburgh edition of *Poems, Chiefly in the Scottish Dialect* (1787).

However, it seems that Burns's reputation had possibly gone before him. In his postscript to a copy of the letter in the 'Glenriddell Manuscript' Burns writes, 'Well Mr Burns, and did the Lady give you the desired "permission?"— No! She was too fine a lady *to notice* so plain a compliment.' It was likely much too forthright and inappropriate a compliment for the sensibilities of an eighteenth-century lady.

Poets are such outré Beings, so much the children of wayward Fancy and capricious Whim, that I believe the world generally allows them a larger latitude in the rules of Propriety, than the sober Sons of

Judgment and Prudence.— I mention this as an apology all at once for the liberties which a nameless Stranger has taken with you in the inclosed; and which he begs leave to present you with.—

Whether it has poetical merit any way worthy of the THEME, I am not the proper judge; but it is the best my abilities can produce; and, what to a good heart will perhaps be a superiour grace, it is equally sincere.—

The Scenery was nearly taken from real life; though I dare say, Madam, you don't recollect it: as I believe you scarcely noticed the poetic Reveur, as he wandered by you.— I had roved out as Chance directed, on the favourite haunts of my Muse, the banks of Ayr; to view nature in all the gaiety of the vernal year.—

The Sun was flaming o'er the distant, western hills; not a breath stirred the crimson opening blossom, or the verdant spreading leaf. 'Twas a golden moment for a poetic heart.—[...]

Such was the scene, and such the hour, when in a corner of my Prospect I spyed one of the fairest pieces of Nature's workmanship that ever crowned a poetic Landscape; those visionary Bards excepted, who hold commerce with aërial beings.—

Had CALUMNY and VILLAINY taken my walk, they had at that moment sworn eternal peace with such an Object.—

What an hour of inspiration for a Poet! It would have raised plain, dull, historic Prose to Metaphor and Measure!

The inclosed song was the work of my return home: and perhaps it but poorly answers what might have been expected from such a scene.— I am going to print a second Edition of my Poems, but cannot insert these verses without your permission.—

19TH NOVEMBER

The Bonie Lass o' Ballochmyle
to the tune of Ettrick Banks

A ND HERE IS BURNS'S COMPLIMENT to Wilhelmina Alexander. Burns conveys the imagery of his walk as described in his letter, but he goes somewhat further in his fantasy of what might have occurred had she been a 'country maid' and he had the opportunity to 'strain' her to his 'bosom'.

The bard wrote to Gavin Hamilton in March of the following year that the song was among two that were 'tried yesterday by a jury of Literati and found defamatory libels against the fastidious Powers of Poesy and Taste, and the Author forbid to print them under pain of forfeiture of character'. He goes on, 'My poor unfortunate songs come again across my memory — Damn the pedant, frigid soul of Criticism for ever and ever!'

'Twas even – the dewy fields were green,
    On every blade the pearls hang;
The zephyr wantoned round the bean,
    And bore its fragrant sweets alang:
In every glen the mavis sang,
    All Nature listening seemed the while,
Except where green-wood echoes rang
    Amang the braes o' Ballochmyle.

With careless step I onward strayed,
    My heart rejoiced in nature's joy,
When musing in a lonely glade,

A maiden fair I chanced to spy;
Her look was like the morning's eye,
    Her air like nature's vernal smile,
Perfection whispered passing by,
    Behold the lass o' Ballochmyle!

Fair is the morn in flowery May,
    And sweet is night in Autumn mild;
When roving thro' the garden gay,
    Or wandering in the lonely wild:
But woman, nature's darling child!
    There all her charms she does compile;
Even there her other works are foil'd
    By the bonie lass o' Ballochmyle.

O had she been a country maid,
    And I the happy country swain,
Tho' sheltered in the lowest shed
    That ever rose on Scotia's plain!
Thro' weary winter's wind and rain
    With joy, with rapture, I would toil;
And nightly to my bosom strain
    The bonie lass o' Ballochmyle.

Then pride might climb the slipp'ry steep;
    Where fame and honours lofty shine;
And thirst of gold might tempt the deep,
    Or downward seek the Indian mine;
Give me the cot below the pine,
    To tend the flocks or till the soil,
And every day have joys divine,
    With the bonie lass o' Ballochmyle.

20TH NOVEMBER

On a Wicked SONG
from a letter to William Chalmers and John McAdam,
20th November 1786

O N THIS DAY IN 1786, Burns sent a mock legal 'mandate' to his
cronies, Chalmers and McAdam, enclosing a bawdy song with
instructions that it should be taken to Ayr Cross and dramatically
burned after reading for its wickedness. It is clear that there was an
ample audience for bawdy song among Burns's acquaintances, and
that the poet himself revelled in the genre's comic and subversive
potential.

In the Name of the NINE. *Amen*
    We, ROBERT BURNS, by virtue of a Warrant from NATURE, bearing
date the twenty-fifth day of January, Anno Domini one thousand
seven hundred and fifty-nine, POET-LAUREAT, and BARD IN CHIEF
in and over the Districts and Countries of Kyle, Cunningham, and
Carrick, of old extent, To our trusty and well-beloved WILLIAM
CHALMERS and JOHN M'ADAM, Students and Practitioners in
the ancient and mysterious science of CONFOUNDING RIGHT and
WRONG.
    RIGHT TRUSTY,
    Be it known unto you, that whereas, in the course of our care
and watchings over the Order and Police of all and sundry the
MANUFACTURERS, RETAINERS, and VENDERS of POESY; Bards,
Poets, Poetasters, Rhymers, Songsters, Ballad-singers, &c. &c. &c. &c.
&c. male and female — We have discovered a certain ***, nefarious,
abominable, and wicked SONG or BALLAD, a copy whereof We have

here inclosed; Our WILL THEREFORE IS, that YE pitch upon and appoint the most execrable Individual of that most execrable Species known by the appellation, phrase, and nickname of THE DEIL'S YELL NOWTE; and, after having caused him to kindle a fire at the CROSS OF AYR, ye shall, at noontide of the day, put into the said wretch's merciless hands the said copy of the said nefarious and wicked Song, to be consumed by fire in presence of all Beholders, in abhorrence of, and terrorem to, all such COMPOSITIONS and COMPOSERS. And this in nowise ye leave undone, but have it executed in every point as this OUR MANDATE bears, before the twenty-fourth current, when IN PERSON We hope to applaud your faithfulness and zeal. GIVEN AT MAUCHLINE, this twentieth day of November, Anno Domini one thousand seven hundred and eighty-six.

GOD SAVE THE BARD!

21ST NOVEMBER

Epitaph on John Dove, Innkeeper

JOHN DOVE (ALSO REFERRED TO AS JOHN DOW) was the publican of the Whiteford Arms in Mauchline. Burns's irreverent epitaph conflates religious language and alcohol in sardonic reference to the eighteenth-century kirk's disapproval of drinking and public houses.

Here lies Johnny Pidgeon,
What was his religion,
Whae'er desires to ken,
To some other warl
Maun follow the carl,
For here Johnny Pidgeon had nane.

Strong ale was ablution,
Small beer persecution,
A dram was *memento mori*;
But a full flowing bowl,
Was the saving his soul,
And Port was celestial glory.

22ND NOVEMBER

On a Hangover
from a letter to Robert Ainslie, November 1791

NINETEENTH-CENTURY BIOGRAPHERS made much of Burns's association with alcohol, but on the basis of little evidence. It has been suggested that exaggerated accounts of the bard's drinking enabled nineteenth-century commentators to account for his perceived sexual indiscretions and any controversial poems and songs. There can be no doubt that Burns enjoyed male conviviality and a sociable dram. However, in the twenty-first century, we might contemplate whether a man who suffered hangovers to the extent that Burns describes in this letter to Robert Ainslie would have derived any pleasure from making a habit of it!

My dear Ainslie,

Can you minister to a mind diseased? Can you, amid the horrors of penitence, regret, remorse, head-ache, nausea, and all the rest of the d—d hounds of hell that beset a poor wretch who has been guilty of the sin of drunkenness — can you speak peace to a troubled soul?

Miserable perdu that I am! I have tried every thing that used to amuse me, but in vain: here must I sit, a monument of the vengeance laid up in store for the wicked, slowly counting every chick of the clock as it slowly — slowly numbers over these lazy scoundrels of hours, who, d—n them, are ranked up before me, every one at his neighbour's backside, and every one with a burden of anguish on his back, to pour on my devoted head — and there is none to pity me. My wife scolds me! my business torments me, and my sins come staring me in the face, every one telling a more bitter tale than his fellow.— When I tell you even *** has lost its power to please, you will guess something of my hell within, and all around me.—

23RD NOVEMBER

O Phely, Happy Be That Day
to the tune of **The Sow's Tail**

TODAY'S SONG WAS SENT to George Thomson in November 1794 when it was 'not an hour old'. Burns wrote, 'This morning, through a keen blowing frost, in my walk before breakfast, I finished my Duet which you were pleased to praise so much.' Burns adopts a series of natural metaphors to convey the couple's love for one another and finishes with the typically Burnsian notion that wealth is irrelevant when it comes to matters of the heart.

O Phely, happy be that day,
When roving through the gather'd hay,
My youthful heart was stown away,
And by thy charms, my Phely.

O Willy, ay I bless the grove
Where first I own'd my maiden love,
Whilst thou did pledge the Powers above,
To be my ain dear Willy.

As songsters of the early year,
Are ilka day mair sweet to hear,
So ilka day to me mair dear
And charming is my Phely.

As on the brier the budding rose
Still richer breathes and fairer blows,
So in my tender bosom grows,
The love I bear my Willy.

The milder sun and bluer sky
That crown my harvest cares wi' joy,
Were ne'er sae welcome to my eye,
As is a sight o' Phely.

The little swallow's wanton wing,
Tho' wafting o'er the flowery Spring,
Did ne'er to me sic tydings bring,
As meeting o' my Willy.

The bee that thro' the sunny hour
Sips nectar in the op'ning flower,
Compar'd wi' my delight is poor,
Upon the lips o' Phely.

The woodbine in the dewy weet,
When evening shades in silence meet,
Is nought sae fragrant or sae sweet
As is a kiss o' Willy.

Let fortune's wheel at random rin,
And fools may tyne, and knaves may win;
My thoughts are a' bound up in ane,
And that's my ain dear Phely.

What's a' the joys that gowd can gi'e?
I care na wealth a single flie;
The lad I love's the lad for me,
And that's my ain dear Willy.

24TH NOVEMBER

On the Birth of a Posthumous Child, Born in Peculiar Circumstance of Family Distress

TODAY'S VERSES WERE COMPOSED in November 1790 to celebrate the birth of Frances Dunlop's grandson; the son of her daughter Susan Henri, born shortly after his father's death (see 9th October). Upon hearing news of the child's arrival Burns wrote:

> I literally jumped for joy— How could such a mercurial creature as a Poet lumpishly keep his seat on the receipt of the best news from his best Friend — I siezed my gilt-headed Wangee rod, an instrument indispensably necessary in my left hand, in the moment of Inspiration and rapture — and stride — stride — quick and quicker out skipt I among the broomy banks of Nith to muse over my joy by retail.— To keep within the bounds of Prose was impossible.

In the poem, Burns makes explicit reference to the absence of the child's father; the 'shelt'ring tree' who should 'shield thee frae the storm'. He prays, however, that God will protect him from the bitter November weather; a metaphor, also, for his family's lingering grief.

Sweet flow'ret, pledge o' meikle love,
    And ward o' mony a prayer,
What heart o' stane wad thou na move,
    Sae helpless, sweet, and fair.

November hirples o'er the lea,
    Chill, on thy lovely form:
And gane, alas! the shelt'ring tree,
    Should shield thee frae the storm.

May He who gives the rain to pour,
　And wings the blast to blaw,
Protect thee frae the driving show'r,
　The bitter frost and snaw.

May He, the friend o' Woe and Want,
　Who heals life's various stounds,
Protect and guard the mother plant,
　And heal her cruel wounds.

But late she flourish'd, rooted fast,
　Fair on the summer morn:
Now, feebly bends she, in the blast,
　Unshelter'd and forlorn.

Blest be thy bloom, thou lovely gem,
　Unscath'd by ruffian hand!
And from thee many a parent stem
　Arise to deck our land.

25TH NOVEMBER

Behold My Love, How Green the Groves
to the tune of My Lodging Is on the Cold Ground

BURNS WROTE TO THOMSON in November 1794 that this was another song inspired by 'Chloris' (or Jean Lorimer) and, on this occasion, it seems she was even Burns's collaborator:

> On my visit the other day to my fair Chloris (that is the poetic name of the lovely goddess of my inspiration) she suggested an idea, which I, in my return from the visit, wrought into the following song [...] How do you like the simplicity and tenderness of this pastoral? I think it pretty well.

Several changes were made before the below version appeared in print. In this song, the overblown romance of a courtier's 'tale' is no match for the more innocent, simplistic, and yet sincere 'shepherd's phrase'.

Behold my love, how green the groves,
    The primrose banks how fair;
The balmy gales awake the flowers,
    And wave thy flaxen hair.
The lavrock shuns the palace gay,
    And o'er the cottage sings;
For nature smiles as sweet, I ween,
    To shepherds as to kings.

Let minstrels sweep the skilful string,
    In lordly, lighted ha':
The shepherd stops his simple reed,

Blythe in the birken shaw.
The princely revel may survey
    Our rustic dance wi' scorn;
But art their hearts as light as ours
    Beneath the milkwhite thorn?

The shepherd in the flowery glen,
    In shepherd's phrase will woo:
The courtier tells a finer tale,
    But is his heart as true?
These wild-wood flowers I've pu'd to deck,
    That spotless breast o' thine;
The courtier's gems may witness love—
    But 'tis na love like mine.

26TH NOVEMBER

O Bonie Was Yon Rosy Brier
to the tune of I Wish My Love Was in a Mire

ANOTHER YEAR, ANOTHER LOVE SONG to 'Chloris'! This
one was sent to Maria Riddell in November 1795. In keeping
with yesterday's song, natural imagery conveys notions of beauty,
innocence and the 'purity' of true love.

O bonie was yon rosy brier,
    That blooms sae far frae haunt o' man;
And bonie she, and ah how dear!
    It shaded frae the ev'ning sun.
Yon rose-buds in the morning dew,
    How pure, amang the leaves sae green;
But purer was the lover's vow
    They witness'd in their shade yestreen.

All in its rude and prickly bower,
    That crimson rose how sweet and fair;
But love is far a sweeter flow'r
    Amid life's thorny path o' care.
The pathless wild, and wimpling burn,
    Wi' Chloris in my arms, be mine;
And I the warld nor wish nor scorn,
    Its joys and griefs alike resign.

27TH NOVEMBER

from The Cotter's Saturday Night

T HIS EXTRACT FROM ONE OF BURNS'S most well-received poems
    may open with the 'angry', 'chill' November wind, but it goes on to
depict an idyllic and cosy family gathering in the home of an eighteenth-
century cotter. Rustic scenes such as these, taken at face value, captured
the attention and imagination of Burns's eighteenth- and nineteenth-
century readers, who perceived an autobiographical element in Burns's
description of a pious, rural family, and they thus went a long way
towards cementing his status as Scotland's national bard.

November chill blaws loud wi' angry sugh;
    The short'ning winter-day is near a close;
The miry beasts retreating frae the pleugh;
    The black'ning trains o' craws to their repose:
The toil-worn COTTER frae his labour goes,
    This night his weekly moil is at an end,
Collects his *spades*, his *mattocks*, and his *hoes*,
    Hoping the *morn* in ease and rest to spend,
And weary, o'er the moor, his course does hameward bend.

At length his lonely *Cot* appears in view,
    Beneath the shelter of an aged tree;
Th' expectant *wee-things*, toddlan, stacher through
    To meet their *Dad*, wi' flichterin noise and glee.
His wee bit ingle, blinkan bonilie,
    His clean hearth-stane, his thrifty *Wifie's* smile,
The *lisping infant*, prattling on his knee,
    Does a' his weary *kiaugh* and care beguile,
And makes him quite forget his labor and his toil.

Belyve, the *elder bairns* come drapping in,
    At *Service* out, amang the Farmers roun';
Some ca' the pleugh, some herd, some tentie rin
    A cannie errand to a neebor town:
Their eldest hope, their *Jenny*, woman-grown,
    In youthfu' bloom, Love sparkling in her e'e,
Comes hame, perhaps, to shew a braw new gown,
    Or deposite her sair-won penny-fee,
To help her *Parents* dear, if they in hardship be.

With joy unfeign'd, *brothers* and *sisters* meet,
    And each for other's weelfare kindly speirs:
The social hours, swift-wing'd, unnotic'd fleet;
    Each tells the uncos that he sees or hears.
The parents, partial, eye their hopeful years;
    Anticipation forward points the view;
The *Mother*, wi' her needle and her sheers,
    Gars auld claes look amaist as weel's the new;
The *Father* mixes a' wi' admonition due.

28TH NOVEMBER

Address to Edinburgh

BURNS LEFT THE COUNTRYSIDE to make his name as a poet in the capital – '*Scotia's* darling seat!' – late in November 1786. Today's poem, written especially for inclusion in the second Edinburgh edition of Burns's *Poems, Chiefly in the Scottish Dialect* (1787), expresses his 'awe' at the landscape and industry of this bustling city, its history and the kindness and beauty of its inhabitants. We might consider that this tribute to the capital's charms was, to an extent, a poetic exercise in ingratiating himself with Edinburgh society – and with its many potential patrons.

Edina! *Scotia's* darling seat!
　　All hail thy palaces and tow'rs,
Where once beneath a Monarch's feet,
　　Sat Legislation's sov'reign pow'rs!
From marking wildly-scatt'red flow'rs,
　　As on the banks of *Ayr* I stray'd,
And singing, lone, the ling'ring hours,
　　I shelter in thy honor'd shade.

Here Wealth still swells the golden tide,
　　As busy Trade his labours plies;
There Architecture's noble pride
　　Bids elegance and splendour rise:
Here Justice, from her native skies,
　　High wields her balance and her rod;
There Learning, with his eagle eyes,
　　Seeks Science in her coy abode.

Thy sons, *Edina*, social, kind,
  With open arms the stranger hail;
Their views enlarg'd, their lib'ral mind,
  Above the narrow, rural vale:
Attentive still to Sorrow's wail,
  Or modest Merit's silent claim;
And never may their sources fail!
  And never envy blot their name!

Thy Daughters bright thy walks adorn,
  Gay as the gilded summer sky,
Sweet as the dewy, milk-white thorn,
  Dear as the raptur'd thrill of joy!
Fair Burnet strikes th' adoring eye,
  Heav'n's beauties on my fancy shine;
I see the *Sire of Love* on high,
  And own his work indeed divine!

There, watching high the least alarms,
  Thy rough, rude Fortress gleams afar;
Like some bold Vet'ran, grey in arms,
  And mark'd with many a seamy scar:
The pond'rous wall and massy bar,
  Grim-rising o'er the rugged rock,
Have oft withstood assailing War,
  And oft repell'd th' Invader's shock.

With awe-struck thought, and pitying tears,
  I view that noble, stately Dome,
Where *Scotia's* kings of other years,
  Fam'd heroes! had their royal home:
Alas, how chang'd the times to come!
  Their royal Name low in the dust!
Their hapless Race wild-wand'ring roam!
  Tho' rigid Law cries out 'twas just!

Wild beats my heart to trace your steps,
   Whose ancestors, in days of yore,
Thro' hostile ranks and ruin'd gaps
   Old *Scotia's* bloody lion bore:
Ev'n *I* who sing in rustic lore,
   Haply *my Sires* have left their shed,
And fac'd grim Danger's loudest roar,
   Bold – following where your Fathers led!

Edina! Scotia's darling seat!
   All hail thy palaces and tow'rs,
Where once, beneath a Monarch's feet,
   Sat Legislation's sov'reign pow'rs!
From marking wildly-scatt'red flow'rs,
   As on the banks of *Ayr* I stray'd,
And singing, lone, the ling'ring hours,
   I shelter in thy honor'd shade.

29TH NOVEMBER

My Heart's in the Highlands
to the tune of Failte Na Miosg

KEEPING WITH THE THEME OF SCOTLAND and her various
landscapes, this famous song transports us from Edinburgh as a
densely populated and bustling capital to the spectacular scenery of
the idyllic-seeming Scottish Highlands.

My heart's in the Highlands, my heart is not here;
My heart's in the Highlands, a-chasing the deer;
Chasing the wild-deer, and following the roe,
My heart's in the Highlands, wherever I go.

Farewell to the Highlands, farewell to the North,
The birth-place of Valour, the country of Worth;
Wherever I wander, wherever I rove,
The hills of the Highlands for ever I love.

Farewell to the mountains, high-cover'd with snow,
Farewell to the straths and green vallies below;
Farewell to the forests and wild-hanging woods,
Farewell to the torrents and loud-pouring floods.

My heart's in the Highlands, my heart is not here,
My heart's in the Highlands, a-chasing the deer;
Chasing the wild-deer, and following the roe,
My heart's in the Highlands, wherever I go.

30th NOVEMBER

Caledonia
to the tune of Caledonian Hunt's Delight

T ODAY MARKS THE FEAST OF ST ANDREW, the patron saint of
Scotland, when Scotland – its history and culture – is celebrated
far and wide, from Ayrshire to Edinburgh and by Scottish diaspora
all over the world. It marks one of three such cultural celebrations
which have come to be known as 'Scotland's Winter Festivals'. These
are St Andrew's Day, Hogmanay and, of course, Burns Night! Our
Burnsian words for this occasion are a rousing account of 'brave',
'unconquered' Caledonia's ancient battles with Roman and Norse
invaders.

There was once a day, but old Time was then young,
    That brave Caledonia, the chief of her line,
From some of your northern deities sprung,
    (Who knows not that brave Caledonia's divine?)
From Tweed to the Orcades was her domain,
    To hunt, or to pasture, or do what she would:
Her heav'nly relations there fixed her reign,
    And pledg'd her their godheads to warrant it good.

A lambkin in peace, but a lion in war,
    The pride of her kindred, the heroine grew:
Her grandsire, old Odin, triumphantly swore,—
    "Whoe'er shall provoke thee, th' encounter shall rue!"
With tillage or pasture at times she would sport,
    To feed her fair flocks by her green rustling corn;
But chiefly the woods were her fav'rite resort,
    Her darling amusement, the hounds and the horn.

Long quiet she reigned; till thitherward steers
    A flight of bold eagles from Adria's strand:
Repeated, successive, for many long years,
    They darken'd the air, and they plunder'd the land:
Their pounces were murder, and horror their cry,
    They'd conquer'd and ruin'd a world beside;
She took to her hills, and her arrows let fly,
    The daring invaders they fled or they died.

The Cameleon-Savage disturb'd her repose,
    With tumult, disquiet, rebellion, and strife;
Provok'd beyond bearing, at last she arose,
    And robb'd him at once of his hopes and his life:
The Anglian lion, the terror of France,
    Oft prowling, ensanguin'd the Tweed's silver flood;
But, taught by the bright Caledonian lance,
    He learned to fear in his own native wood.

The fell Harpy-raven took wing from the north,
    The scourge of the seas, and the dread of the shore;
The wild Scandinavian boar issued forth
    To wanton in carnage and wallow in gore:
O'er countries and kingdoms their fury prevail'd,
    No arts could appease them, no arms could repel;
But brave Caledonia in vain they assail'd,
    As Largs well can witness, and Loncartie tell.

Thus bold, independent, unconquer'd, and free,
    Her bright course of glory for ever shall run:
For brave Caledonia immortal must be;
    I'll prove it from Euclid as clear as the sun:
Rectangle-triangle, the figure we'll chuse:
    The upright is Chance, and old Time is the base;
But brave Caledonia's the hypothenuse;
    Then, ergo, she'll match them, and match them always.

DECEMBER

And there's a hand, my trusty fiere!
And gie's a hand o' thine!
And we'll tak a right gude-willie-waught,
For auld lang syne.

from Auld Lang Syne

1st DECEMBER

Thou Gloomy December
to the tune of Thro' the Long Mair I Follow'd Him Home

WE BEGIN DECEMBER with a song inspired by Burns's relationship with Agnes McLehose, or 'Clarinda', who he met in December 1787, and from whom he parted for the last time in December 1791. The bard sent her 'Thou Gloomy December' along with 'Ae Fond Kiss' (see 14th February) and 'Behold the Hour the Boat Arrive' (see 19th February) shortly after he visited her in Edinburgh for the very last time, and a matter of weeks before she travelled to the West Indies to attempt reconciliation with her estranged husband. As in 'Ae Fond Kiss', Burns here uses powerful natural imagery to express the notion of despair in the face of inevitable – and permanent – separation.

It is worth pointing out that Burns's works inspired by the month of December, or 'Yule', can be 'gloomy'. The season's stormy weather and the long nights around the winter solstice are difficult for many and would have presented a particular challenge to Burns in his farming and excise occupations. As we move through December, these morose pieces have been tempered with works that celebrate the opportunities for friendship, conviviality and festivity that can provide a sense of warmth at this time of year, despite the cold and dark outside.

Ance mair I hail thee, thou gloomy December!
    Ance mair I hail thee wi' sorrow and care;
Sad was the parting thou makes me remember,
    Parting wi' Nancy, Oh! ne'er to meet mair.
Fond lovers parting is sweet, painful pleasure,
    Hope beaming mild on the soft parting hour,
But the dire feeling, O farewell for ever!
    Anguish unmingl'd and agony pure.

Wild as the winter now tearing the forest,
  Till the last leaf o' the summer is flown,
Such is the tempest has shaken my bosom,
  Till my last hope and last comfort is gone:
Still as I hail thee, thou gloomy December,
  Still shall I hail thee wi' sorrow and care;
For sad was the parting thou makes me remember,
  Parting wi' Nancy, Oh, ne'er to meet mair.

2ND DECEMBER

On Song and Melody
from a letter to George Thomson, September 1793

TODAY'S BURNSIAN WORDS give valuable insight into the bard's workings as a songwriter. Writing to George Thomson, Burns emphasises that music forms an essential inspirational component of his poetic process, as do his leisurely walks and the attention he gives to the natural world around him. The bard conveys a simple, oddly appealing image of him swinging on his chair by the fire as he completes the final part of his creative process and commits his song to paper. Burns then grounds his reader – and himself – with a light-hearted reference to his 'damned Egotism' – or self-absorption.

Laddie lie near me — must *lie by me*, for some time.— I do not know the air; and untill I am compleat master of a tune, in my own singing, (such as it is) I never can compose for it.— My way is: I consider the poetic Sentiment, correspondent to my idea of the musical expression; then chuse my theme; begin one Stanza; when that is composed, which is generally the most difficult part of the business, I walk out, sit down now and then, look out for objects in Nature around me that are in unison or harmony with the cogitations of my fancy and workings of my bosom; humming every now and then the air with the verses I have framed: when I feel my Muse beginning to jade, I retire to the solitary fireside of my study, and there commit my effusions to paper; swinging, at intervals, on the hind-legs of my elbow-chair, by way of calling forth my own critical strictures, as my pen goes on.—

Seriously, this, at home, is almost invariably my way!— What damn'd Egotism!

3RD DECEMBER

O May Thy Morn

T HE TITLE OF THIS SONG is perhaps misleading, since it is not about a glorious spring morning. Instead, Burns describes a lovers' tryst in a 'mirk night' of December. Darkness, here, offers a cloak for intimacy with a forbidden love. The second stanza reads as a toast to friends, appropriate for this time of year, but it also remembers those 'private' loves 'we dare na tell'.

O May thy morn was ne'er sae sweet,
    As the mirk night o' December;
For sparkling was the rosy wine,
    And private was the chamber:
And dear was she, I dare na name,
    But I will ay remember.
And dear was she, I dare na name,
    But I will ay remember.

And here's to them, that, like oursel,
    Can push about the jorum;
And here's to them that wish us weel,
    May a' that's gude watch o'er them:
And here's to them, we dare na tell,
    The dearest o' the quorum.
And here's to them, we dare na tell,
    The dearest o' the quorum.

4TH DECEMBER

On Self-Knowledge
from Burns's autobiographical letter to Dr John Moore,
2nd August 1787

BURNS OFTEN REFERS to the importance of self-knowledge. He places great emphasis upon a rational understanding of his own mind, his talents and shortcomings, here referred to as 'the various LIGHTS and SHADES in [his] character'. Today's extract is Burns's account of the soul-searching that he carried out before deciding to publish the Kilmarnock edition of *Poems, Chiefly in the Scottish Dialect* (1786), taking his first steps towards a career as a poet. And, ultimately, those initial steps have led to generations of readers sharing a fascination with the many complex 'shades' of Burns's character, conveyed through his poetry and song.

It is ever my opinion that the great, unhappy mistakes and blunders, both in a rational and religious point of view, of which we see thousands daily guilty, are owing to their ignorance or mistaken notions of themselves.— To know myself had been all along my constant study.— I weighed myself alone; I balanced myself with others; I watched every means of information how much ground I occupied both as a Man and as a Poet: I studied assiduously Nature's DESIGN where she seem'd to have intended the various LIGHTS and SHADES in my character.— I was pretty sure my Poems would meet with some applause; but at the worst, the roar of the Atlantic would deafen the voice of Censure, and the novelty of West-Indian scenes make me forget neglect.—

5TH DECEMBER

To a Louse, On Seeing One on a Lady's Bonnet at Church

TODAY'S POEM, one of Burns's best-known and oft-quoted works, is thought to have been written towards the end of 1785. In keeping with 'To a Mouse' (see 22nd January), it refers to one of nature's more maligned creatures in another perceptive survey of humanity. The poem opens with mock incredulity that an 'impudent' head louse has breached social decorum by setting foot on Jenny, a fine '*Lady*', rather than 'some poor body'. The louse's endeavour to reach the 'tapmost towerin' height' of her fashionable 'Lunardi' hat shows scant concern for Jenny's 'airs' and 'foolish notions', undermining her respectability and exposing her ignorance and conceit. Burns's final stanza begins with that most famous couplet, 'O wad some Pow'r the giftie gie us / *To see oursels as others see us!*' Burns's appeal for increased self-awareness also gestures towards the Enlightenment notion of sympathy that he encountered – and admired – in Adam Smith's *Theory of Moral Sentiments* (1759).

Ha! whare ye gaun, ye crowlan ferlie!
Your impudence protects you sairly:
I canna say but ye strunt rarely,
      Owre *gauze* and *lace*;
Tho', faith, I fear ye dine but sparely
      On sic a place.

Ye ugly, creepan, blastet wonner,
Detested, shunn'd by saunt an' sinner;
How daur ye set your fit upon her,
        Sae fine a *Lady*!
Gae somewhere else and seek your dinner,
        On some poor body.

Swith, in some beggar's haffet squattle;
There ye may creep, and sprawl, and sprattle,
Wi' ither kindred, jumping cattle,
        In shoals and nations;
Whaur *horn* nor *bane* ne'er daur unsettle
        Your thick plantations.

Now haud you there, ye're out o' sight,
Below the fatt'rels, snug and tight,
Na faith ye yet! ye'll no be right,
        Till ye've got on it,
The vera tapmost, towrin height
        O' *Miss's bonnet*.

My sooth! right bauld ye set your nose out,
As plump an' grey as onie grozet:
O for some rank, mercurial rozet,
        Or fell, red smeddum,
I'd gie you sic a hearty dose o't,
        Wad dress your droddum!

I wad na been surpriz'd to spy
You on an auld wife's *flainen* toy;
Or aiblins some bit dubbie boy,
        On's *wylecoat*;
But Miss' fine *Lunardi*, fye!
        How daur ye do't?

O *Jenny*, dinna toss your head,
An' set your beauties a' abread!
Ye little ken what cursed speed
        The blastie's makin!
Thae *winks* and *finger-ends*, I dread,
        Are notice takin!

O wad some Pow'r the giftie gie us
To see oursels as others see us!
It wad frae monie a blunder free us
        An' foolish notion:
What airs in dress an' gait wad lea'e us,
        And ev'n Devotion!

6TH DECEMBER

On Letter-Writing
from Burns's autobiographical letter to Dr John Moore,
2nd August 1787

O N THIS DAY IN 1787, Burns wrote to Agnes McLehose for the
first time. In doing so he commenced one of his most renowned,
and certainly his most sensational, epistolary relationships. Some
months earlier, the bard had written to Dr John Moore explaining
the means by which he became such an accomplished letter writer.
Noteworthy here is the pride that Burns took in his prose as well as
his poetry, and the fact that he 'kept copies' of some of the letters
written to others – in effect, acting as his own archivist – without
which a considerable portion of his correspondence might otherwise
have been lost.

My reading was enlarged with the very important addition of
Thomson's and Shenstone's works; I had seen mankind in a new
phasis; and I engaged several of my schoolfellows to keep up a
literary correspondence with me.— This last helped me much on in
composition.— I had met with a collection of letters by the Wits of
Queen Ann's reign, and I pored over them most devoutly.— I kept
copies of any of my own letters that pleased me, and a comparison
between them and the composition of most of my correspondents
flattered my vanity.— I carried this whim so far that though I had
not three farthings worth of business in the world, yet every post
brought me as many letters as if I had been a broad, plodding son of
Day-book and Ledger.—

7TH DECEMBER

On Fame
from a letter to Gavin Hamilton, 7th December 1786

O N THIS DAY IN 1786, Burns, recently arrived in Edinburgh, was beginning to realise – and articulate – the extent of his popularity among the literati. The bard's ironic, somewhat irreverent, reference to his 'eminence' in this letter, and his wry suggestion that his birthday might be remembered alongside other infamous events in history, might be considered remarkable in light of the fact that the celebration of his birthday has indeed significantly eclipsed the commemoration of these events in terms of both global reach and popular reception. The authors to whom he refers are Thomas a Kempis (c.1380–1471), a German whose devotional book, *The Imitation of Christ*, remained a popular Christian text over a number of centuries, and John Bunyan (1628–1688) who produced that ubiquitous work of Christian fiction, *The Pilgrim's Progress* (1678).

For my own affairs, I am in a fair way of becoming as eminent as Thomas a Kempis or John Bunyan; and you may expect henceforth to see my birthday inserted among the wonderful events, in the Poor Robin's and Aberdeen Almanacks, along with the black Monday, and the battle of Bothwel bridge.—

8TH DECEMBER

Musing on the Roaring Ocean
to the tune of **Druimionn Dubh**

B URNS WAS INSPIRED to compose today's song 'out of compliment
to a Mrs McLachlan whose husband is an officer in the East
Indies'. Here day and night are juxtaposed as the longing female
persona invites sleep to 'draw the curtain' on her fear and sorrow, so
that she might dream of her lover.

Musing on the roaring ocean,
  Which divides my love and me;
Wearying Heav'n in warm devotion,
  For his weal where'er he be.

Hope and Fear's alternate billow
  Yielding late to Nature's law,
Whispering spirits round my pillow
  Talk of him that's far awa.

Ye whom sorrow never wounded,
  Ye who never shed a tear,
Care-untroubled, joy-surrounded,
  Gaudy Day to you is dear.

Gentle Night, do thou befriend me;
  Downy sleep, the curtain draw;
Spirits kind, again attend me,
  Talk of him that's far awa!

9TH DECEMBER

O Were I on Parnassus Hill
to the tune of My Love Is Lost to Me

TODAY'S SONG WAS COMPOSED as a 'tribute' to Burns's wife, Jean Armour Burns. The bard invokes classical imagery to convey the notion that his immediate surroundings, and his Jean, are all the inspiration that he requires to express his deep, everlasting love in words, and with 'poetic skill'.

O were I on Parnassus hill;
Or had o' Helicon my fill;
That I might catch poetic skill,
To sing how dear I love thee.
But Nith maun be my Muses well,
My Muse maun be thy bonie sell;
On Corsincon I'll glowr and spell,
    And write how dear I love thee.

Then come, sweet Muse, inspire my lay!
For a' the lee-lang simmer's day,
I coudna sing, I coudna say,
How much, how dear, I love thee.
I see thee dancing o'er the green,
Thy waist sae jimp, thy limbs sae clean,
Thy tempting lips, thy roguish een –
    By Heaven and Earth I love thee.

By night, by day, a-field, at hame,
The thoughts o' thee my breast inflame;
And ay I muse and sing thy name,
I only live to love thee.
Tho' I were doom'd to wander on,
Beyond the sea, beyond the sun,
Till my last, weary sand was run;
  Till then – and then I love thee.

10TH DECEMBER

from The Vision

I N THE CONCLUDING STANZAS of Burns's 'The Vision', his muse
Coila encourages the poet to value and take inspiration from his
status as a *'rustic Bard'*, and to do the best he can in his 'humble
sphere', with dignity and good faith. Coila then crowns the poet with
a wreath of holly – a natural, 'rustic' symbol of his heaven-inspired
talent and creativity.

Holly, ubiquitous at this time of year, is a winter shrub with an
abundance of classical, pagan and religious associations. It has been
suggested that holly's evergreen leaves with its red berries possess
magical qualities and the ability to ward off evil spirits. The green
leaves might also be considered a symbol of fertility and the red berries
representative of hope for the return of spring. In Christianity, holly is
a symbol for Christ's crown of thorns, whereby the berries represent
the blood of Christ and the green leaves symbolise life after death.

'Then never murmur nor repine;
Strive in thy *humble sphere* to shine;
And trust me, not *Potosi's mine*,
            Nor *King's regard*,

Can give a bliss o'ermatching thine,
        A *rustic Bard*.

To give my counsels all in one,
Thy *tuneful flame* still careful fan;
Preserve *the dignity of Man*,
               With soul erect;
And trust, the UNIVERSAL PLAN,
               Will all protect.

'*And wear thou this*' – She solemn said,
And bound the *Holly* round my head:
The polish'd leaves, and berries red
               Did rustling play;
And, like a passing thought, she fled,
               In light away.

11TH DECEMBER

On Being Toasted as Caledonia's Bard
from a letter to John Ballantine, 14th January 1787

IN KEEPING WITH OUR THEME of the bard's increasing fame, today's passage records Burns's 'thunderstruck' reaction in the moment that he, the ploughman poet, was publicly lauded as 'Caledonia's Bard' by the distinguished company of the Grand Lodge of Scotland.

I went to a Mason-lodge yesternight where the Most Worshipful Grand Master Charters, and all the Grand lodge of Scotland visited.— The meeting was most numerous and elegant; all the different Lodges about town were present, in all their pomp.— The Grand Master who presided with great solemnity, and honor to himself as a Gentleman and Mason, among other general toasts gave, "Caledonia, and Caledonia's Bard, brother B—," which rung through the whole Assembly with multiplied honors and repeated acclamations.— As I had no idea such a thing would happen, I was downright thunderstruck, and trembling in every nerve made the best return in my power.— Just as I finished, some of the Grand Officers said so loud as I could hear, with a most comforting accent, "Very well indeed!" which set me something to rights again.—

12TH DECEMBER

See the Smoking Bowl Before Us
from Love and Liberty – A Cantata
to the tune of Jolly Mortals Fill Your Glasses

TODAY WE READ the provocative final song of Burns's remarkable cantata (see 10th January, and 1st and 2nd March), in which the bard undermines 'TITLE', 'TREASURE' and 'REPUTATION' and rejects the authority of 'COURTS' and 'CHURCHES' in favour of the 'VARIORUM' of human experience unrestrained by DECORUM. The song's flagrant rejection of both kirk and state and its espousal of 'LIBERTY' would have been particularly contentious around the time of the French Revolution, which partly explains the fact that Burns never published 'Love and Liberty' during his lifetime.

See the smoking bowl before us,
  Mark our jovial, ragged ring!
Round and round take up the Chorus,
  And in raptures let us sing.

A fig for those by law protected!
　　Liberty's a glorious feast!
Courts for Cowards were erected,
　　Churches built to please the Priest.

What is TITLE, what is TREASURE,
　　What is REPUTATION's care?
If we lead a life of pleasure,
　　'Tis no matter HOW or WHERE.

With the ready trick and fable
　　Round we wander all the day;
And at night, in barn or stable,
　　Hug our doxies on the hay.

Does the train-attended CARRIAGE
　　Thro' the country lighter rove?
Does the sober bed of MARRIAGE
　　Witness brighter scenes of love?

Life is all a VARIORUM,
　　We regard not how it goes;
Let them cant about DECORUM,
　　Who have character to lose.

Here's to BUDGETS, BAGS and WALLETS!
　　Here's to all the wandering train!
Here's our ragged BRATS and CALLETS!
　　One and all cry out, AMEN!

A fig for those by law protected,
　　LIBERTY's a glorious feast!
COURTS for Cowards were erected,
　　CHURCHES built to please the Priest.

13TH DECEMBER

To Clarinda

THE FESTIVE SEASON IN DECEMBER is associated with gift-giving in many cultures. And, in Burns's case, he often wrote poems to accompany presents. The following verses were presented to Agnes McLehose, or 'Clarinda', along with two glasses as a parting gift when Burns left Edinburgh in the March of 1788. This light-hearted poem is devoid of the longing that permeates his final songs for Clarinda – 'Ae Fond Kiss' and 'Thou Gloomy December'. Indeed, it is difficult to comprehend the bard's mindset at this stage in his life, not least because he married Jean Armour in the weeks that followed the giving of this gift. Interestingly, the glasses that Burns presented to Agnes – a remarkable material relic of their relationship – are now held in the collection of the National Trust for Scotland.

Fair Empress of the Poet's soul,
 And Queen of Poetesses;
Clarinda, take this little boon,
 This humble pair of Glasses:

And fill them high with generous juice,
 As generous as your mind;
And pledge me in the generous toast,
 'The whole of Humankind!'

'To those who love us!' second fill;
 But not to those whom we love,
Lest we love those who love not us:
 A third – 'To thee and me, Love!'

Long may we live! Long may we love!
   And long may we be happy!!!
And may we never want a Glass,
   Well charg'd with generous Nappy!!!!

14TH DECEMBER

Farewell Thou Stream
to the tune of **Nancy's to the Green-Wood Gane**

A VERSION OF TODAY'S SONG was included in a letter to Frances Dunlop in December 1793. Burns went through several names for his 'heroine' – and his initial choice, 'Mary', may have been a reference to Mary Campbell. The song's depiction of a hopeless lover, doomed to despair, is certainly in keeping with other works inspired by the famed and tragic 'Highland Mary'. However, Burns later altered the heroine's name to 'Maria' in honour of Maria Riddell, whose name, according to the poet, was 'infinitely more musical'. Following a brief estrangement from Maria, Burns appears to have settled upon 'Eliza'. And so, this song is an excellent example of why the names of Burns's heroines can't always be taken at face value.

Farewell, thou stream that winding flows
Around Eliza's dwelling;
O mem'ry, spare the cruel thoes
Within my bosom swelling:
Condemn'd to drag a hopeless chain,
And yet in secret languish;
To feel a fire in every vein,
Nor dare disclose my anguish.

Love's veriest wretch, unseen, unknown
I fain my griefs would cover;
The bursting sigh, th' unweeting groan,
Betray the hapless lover:
I know thou doom'st me to despair,
Nor wilt, nor canst relieve me;
But, Oh Eliza, hear one prayer,
For pity's sake forgive me!

The music of thy voice I heard,
Nor wist while it enslav'd me;
I saw thine eyes, yet nothing fear'd,
Till fears no more had sav'd me:
Th' unwary Sailor thus, aghast,
The wheeling torrent viewing,
Mid circling horrors sinks at last,
In overwhelming ruin.

15TH DECEMBER

On his Daughter Elizabeth's Illness
from a letter to Frances Dunlop, 15th December 1793

HERE WE ENCOUNTER BURNS in a sullen 'Decemberish' mood, one which the bard explains by providing an account of his young daughter Elizabeth's illness. Elizabeth was just one year old at the time. Burns's distress is palpable, as is the anxiety that he feels when he contemplates the gravity of his responsibilities as a husband and father. Elizabeth survived this period of illness, but sadly died two years later. Tragically, Burns's worst fears were further realised when he himself became fatally ill in the months following her death.

As I am in a compleat Decemberish humour, gloomy, sullen, stupid, as even the deity of Dullness herself could wish, I will not drawl out a heavy letter with a number of heavier apologies for my late silence.— Only one I shall mention, because I know you will sympathise in it: these four months, a sweet little girl, my youngest child, has been so ill, that every day, a week or less threatened to terminate her existence.

[…]

There had much need be many pleasures annexed to the states of husband and father, for God knows, they have many peculiar cares.— I cannot describe to you, the anxious, sleepless hours these ties frequently give me. I see a train of helpless little folks; me, and my exertions, all their stay; and on what a brittle thread does the life of man hang! If I am nipt off, at the command of Fate; even in all the vigour of manhood as I am, such things happen every day — Gracious God! What would become of my little flock!— 'Tis here that I envy your people of fortune.— A Father on his death-bed, taking an everlasting leave of his children, is indeed woe enough; but the man of competent fortune leaves his sons and daughters, independency and friends; while I — but, my God, I shall run distracted if I think any longer on the Subject!—

16TH DECEMBER

Lying at a Reverend Friend's House One Night, the Author Left the Following Verses in the Room Where He Slept

THE CARE AND RESPONSIBILITY of family obligations was something that weighed heavily on Burns's mind, and he often referred to this in his letters. Today's selection is a poetic variation on that same theme, in which the bard prays that death – 'the hoary Sire' – spares his family, enabling them to lead a long, fulfilled life until, 'soon or late', they are reunited in heaven.

O Thou dread Pow'r, who reign'st above,
　　I know Thou wilt me hear;
When for this scene of peace and love,
　　I make this pray'r sincere.

The hoary Sire — the mortal stroke,
　　Long, long be pleas'd to spare;
To bless his little filial flock,
　　And show what good men are.

She, who her lovely Offspring eyes
　　With tender hopes and fears,
O bless her with a Mother's joys,
　　But spare a Mother's tears!

Their hope, their stay, their darling youth,
　　In manhood's dawning blush,
Bless him, Thou God of love and truth,
　　Up to a Parent's wish.

The beauteous, seraph Sister-band,
    With earnest tears I pray,
Thou know'st the snares on ev'ry hand,
    Guide Thou their steps alway.

When, soon or late, they reach that coast,
    O'er life's rough ocean driven,
May they rejoice, no wand'rer lost,
    A Family in Heaven!

17TH DECEMBER

To John Syme
On Refusing to Dine with Him, After Having Been Promised the First of Company, and the First of Cookery, 17th December 1795

ON THIS DAY IN 1795, Burns, recovering from a lingering illness, simply could not rise to the occasion of his friend John Syme's dinner party, and declined in the following complimentary terms. If Syme's own 'converse and wit' weren't enough to rouse the poet, then unfortunately nothing would tempt him.

No more of your guests, be they titled or not,
    And cook'ry the first in the nation:
Who is proof to thy personal converse and wit,
    Is proof to all other temptation.

18TH DECEMBER

Sonnet

A THRUSH SINGING in the bleak winter landscape is the focus of Burns's pensive observation here. The bard is grateful for the relief offered by the 'blythe carol' of this 'sweet bird', as he takes comfort in contemplating joys that cannot be bought, despite the threat of 'poverty' and 'care'.

Sing on, sweet thrush, upon the leafless bough,
Sing on, sweet bird, I listen to thy strain,
See aged winter, 'mid his surly reign,
At thy blythe carol clears his furrowed brow.

So in lone poverty's dominion drear,
Sits meek content with light, unanxious heart,
Welcomes the rapid moments, bids them part,
Nor asks if they bring ought to hope or fear.

I thank thee, author of this opening day!
Thou whose bright sun now gilds yon orient skies!
Riches denied, thy boon was purer joys,
What wealth could never give nor take away!

Yet come thou child of poverty and care,
The mite high heaven bestow'd, that mite with thee I'll share.

19TH DECEMBER

On Burns's State of Perpetual Warfare
from a letter to Margaret Chalmers, 19th December 1787

O N THIS DAY IN 1787, Burns referred again to the very real dread he felt at the prospect of 'poverty'. We might consider that the state of 'perpetual warfare' that the bard so eloquently explains is reflected in the complexities and contradictions that arise from a broader understanding of his life and work.

I can't say I am altogether at my ease when I see any where in my path that meagre, squalid, famine-faced spectre, poverty; attended as he always is, by iron-fisted oppression, and leering contempt; but I have sturdily withstood his buffetings many a hard-labored day already, and still my motto is — I DARE! My worst enemy is *Moimême,* I lie so miserably open to the inroads and incursions of a mischievous, light-armed, well-mounted banditti, under the banners of imagination, whim, caprice, and passion; and the heavy armed veteran regulars of wisdom, prudence, and fore-thought move so very, very slow, that I am almost in a state of perpetual warfare, and, alas! frequent defeat. There are just two creatures I would envy, a horse in his wild state traversing the forests of Asia, or an oyster on some of the desert shores of Europe. The one has not a wish without enjoyment, the other has neither wish nor fear.

20TH DECEMBER

To Daunton Me

THE IMAGE OF 'YULE' – or Christmas time – in this song is rendered somewhat strange by the presence of the 'blude-red rose' and 'simmer lillies' blooming in snow. The conflation of summer and winter represents an uneasy disturbance in the natural order of the seasons and acts as a metaphor for the young female protagonist's prospective marriage to a 'fause' – or false – and grotesque 'auld man'.

The blude-red rose at Yule may blaw,
The simmer lilies bloom in snaw,
The frost may freeze the deepest sea,
But an auld man shall never daunton me.

To daunton me, and me sae young,
Wi' his fause heart and flatt'ring tongue,
That is the thing you ne'er shall see,
For an auld man shall never daunton me.

For a' his meal and a' his maut,
For a' his fresh beef and his saut,
For a' his gold and white monie,
An auld man shall never daunton me.
   To daunton me, &c.

His gear may buy him kye and yowes,
His gear may buy him glens and knowes,
But me he shall not buy nor free,
For an auld man shall never daunton me.
   To daunton me, &c.

He hirples twa-fauld as he dow,
Wi' his teethless gab and his auld beld pow,
And the rain rins down frae his red blear'd e'e,
That auld man shall never daunton me.
    To daunton me, &c.

21st DECEMBER

Raving Winds Around Her Blowing
to the tune of McGrigor of Roro's Lament

WE ARE NOW AT THE TIME OF YEAR when the winter solstice – the shortest day of the year, or the longest night – occurs. Today's song is replete with references to never-ending night and 'dark Oblivion'. Burns recorded in his notes to the 'interleaved' *Scots Musical Museum* that these verses were inspired by Miss Isabella M'Leod of Raza, 'alluding to her feelings on the death of her sister, and the still more melancholy death of her sister's husband, the late Earl of Loudon who shot himself out of sheer heart-break at some mortifications he suffered, owing to the deranged state of his finances'. In keeping with its dire context, there is little light to be found in this song's expression of hopeless suffering.

Raving winds around her blowing,
Yellow leaves the woodlands strowing,
By a river hoarsely roaring
Isabella stray'd deploring.
Farewell, hours that late did measure
Sunshine days of joy and pleasure;

Hail, thou gloomy night of sorrow,
Cheerless night that knows no morrow.

O'er the Past too fondly wandering,
On the hopeless Future pondering,
Chilly Grief my life-blood freezes,
Fell Despair my fancy seizes.
Life, thou soul of every blessing,
Load to Misery most distressing,
Gladly how would I resign thee,
And to dark Oblivion join thee!

22ND DECEMBER

On Whisky
from a letter to John Tennant, 22nd December 1788

O N THIS DAY IN 1788, Burns 'broke open' a cask of whisky from an old family friend – the farmer, John Tennant (1725–1810). The bard clearly had a palate for that most celebrated of Scottish drinks and, as an excise man and 'gauger', he knew only too well the value of a good dram compared with cheap 'rascally liquor'. The latter being a phrase of such quality that we might all adopt it when the occasion arises …

I yesterday tried my cask of whiskey for the first time, and I assure you it does you great credit.— It will bear five waters, strong; or six, ordinary Toddy.— The Whisky of this country is a most rascally liquor; and, by consequence, only drunk by the most rascally part of the inhabitants.— I am persuaded, if you once got a footing here, you might do a great deal of business; both in the way of consumpt, and should you commence Distiller again, this is the native barley-country.

I am ignorant if, in your present way of dealing, you would think it worth while to extend your business so far as this country-side.— I write you this on the account of an accident which I must take the merit of having partly designed too.— A neighbour of mine, a John Currie, miller in Carse-mill, a man who is in a word, "a good man," a "very" good man, even for a £500 bargain, he and his wife were in my house at the time I broke open the cask.— They keep a country Publick-house and sell a great deal of foreign spirits but all along thought that Whisky would have degraded their house.— They were perfectly astonished at my whisky, both for its taste and strength, and by their desire I write you to know if you could supply them with liquor of an equal quality, and at what price.—

23RD DECEMBER

On Burns's Profession(s)
from a letter to Lady Elizabeth Cunningham, 23rd December 1789

B Y DECEMBER 1789, Burns was able to take into full consideration his lot as an excise man. From the following passage it is clear that, on balance, he thought the 'ignominy', or shame, of working for the excise – in a job akin to a modern-day taxman – a small price to pay for the financial security and wellbeing of his family. Burns is at pains to emphasise any benefits for what he perceives to be his primary 'trade as a poet', and he makes clear that his duties as an excise men in no way detract from his poetic 'ambition'.

People may talk as they please, of the ignominy of the excise, but what will support my family and keep me independent of the world is to me a very important matter; and I had much rather that my Profession borrowed credit from me, than that I borrowed credit from my Profession.— Another advantage I have in this business is the knowledge it gives me of the various shades of Human Character; and consequently assisting me in my trade as a Poet.— Not that I am in haste for the press; as my Lord has been told: had it been so, I would have been highly wanting to myself, not to have consulted my noble, generous Patron, but still, to be Poet, is my highest ambition, my dearest wish, and my unwearied study.—

24TH DECEMBER

To John Syme

WHISKY – IN ALL ITS VARIETIES AND VINTAGES – is perhaps one of the most commonly gifted of all spirits. Millions of drams will be raised all over the world during the festive season, and certainly in the run-up to New Year. Today's complimentary lines, presented to John Syme with a gift of '*a dozen of Porter*', are easily adapted. If you have chosen whisky as a gift, why not substitute Syme's name for that of your own friend or loved one?

O had the malt thy strength of mind,
　　Or hops the flavour of thy wit;
'Twere drink for first of human kind,
　　A gift that e'en for Syme were fit.

25TH DECEMBER

On Christ
from a letter to Frances Dunlop, 13th December 1789

O N CHRISTMAS DAY – which we are marking here on the 25th, although many celebrate the 24th, and Orthodox Christians the seventh of January – Christians mark the birth of Jesus Christ, son of God. In the twenty-first century this wintertime festival is celebrated with special religious services, an international holiday, by the giving of gifts, and through the sharing of food and drink in convivial merriments. However, in the eighteenth century, Christmas was not celebrated to nearly the same extent. In fact, following the Scottish reformation – when Scotland severed ties with the Roman Catholic church and established a protestant, predominantly Calvinist kirk, Christmas celebrations were discouraged. An 'Act discharging the Yule vacance' passed in 1640 declared that 'the kirke within this kingdome is now purged of all superstitious observatione of dayes'. It is perhaps unsurprising, then, that Burns makes no mention of Christmas in his poetry or correspondence, and only a handful of fleeting references to Yule. He did, however, express profound belief in Jesus Christ. The bard's prayer to Christ in today's selection emphasises togetherness and aspires to 'a better world', making it entirely appropriate for a day that has become synonymous with peace and joy.

Jesus Christ, thou amiablest of characters, I trust thou art no Impostor, and that thy revelation of blissful scenes of existence beyond death and the grave, is not one of the many impositions which time after time have been palmed on credulous mankind.— I trust that in Thee "shall all the Families of the earth be blessed" by being yet connected together in a better world, where every tie that bound heart to heart in this state of existence shall be, far beyond our present conceptions, more endearing.—

26TH DECEMBER

The Whistle

THE FESTIVE SEASON can be a time of excess and frivolity, and so today we read Burns's account of a raucous drinking contest at Friars Carse in October of 1789. The bard notes in his introduction to this song that:

> In the train of Anne of Denmark, when she came to Scotland with our James the Sixth, there came over also a Danish gentleman of gigantic stature and great prowess, and a matchless champion of Bacchus. He had a little ebony Whistle, which, at the commencement of the orgies, he laid on the table; and whoever was last able to blow it, every body else being disabled by the potency of the bottle, was to carry off the Whistle as a trophy of victory.

According to Burns's anecdote, the previously undefeated Dane was – of course – eventually drunk 'under the table' by a Scot, and in time the whistle passed to the Riddell family. In this contest between Robert Riddell of Glenriddell, Robert Lowrie of Maxwelton and Alexander Ferguson of Craigdarroch, the latter is the victor. Burns himself is not a contestant, but the referee!

I sing of a Whistle, a Whistle of worth,
   I sing of a Whistle, the pride of the North,
Was brought to the court of our good Scottish King,
   And long with this Whistle all Scotland shall ring.

Old Loda, still rueing the arm of Fingal,
    The god of the bottle sends down from his hall —
'This Whistle's your challenge, to Scotland get o'er,
    And drink them to hell, Sir! or ne'er see me more!'

Old poets have sung, and old chronicles tell,
    What champions ventur'd, what champions fell;
The son of great Loda was conqueror still,
    And blew on the Whistle their requiem shrill.

Till Robert, the lord of the Cairn and the Scaur,
    Unmatched at the bottle, unconquered in war,
He drank his poor god-ship as deep as the sea,
    No tide of the Baltic e'er drunker than he.

Thus Robert, victorious, the trophy has gained,
    Which now in his house has for ages remained;
Till three noble chieftains, and all of his blood,
    The jovial contest again have renewed.

Three joyous good fellows with hearts clear of flaw;
    Craigdarroch, so famous for wit, worth, and law;
And trusty Glenriddel, so skilled in old coins;
    And gallant Sir Robert, deep-read in old wines.

Craigdarroch began, with a tongue smooth as oil,
    Desiring Glenriddel to yield up the spoil;
Or else he would muster the heads of the clan,
    And once more, in claret, try which was the man.

'By the gods of the ancients!' Glenriddel replies,
    'Before I surrender so glorious a prize,
I'll conjure the ghost of the great Rorie More,
    And bumper his horn with him twenty times o'er.'

Sir Robert, a soldier, no speech would pretend,
   But he ne'er turn'd his back on his foe — or his friend,
Said, toss down the Whistle, the prize of the field,
   And knee-deep in claret he'd die ere he'd yield.

To the board of Glenriddel our heroes repair,
   So noted for drowning of sorrow and care;
But for wine and for welcome not more known to fame,
   Than the sense, wit, and taste of a sweet lovely dame.

A bard was selected to witness the fray,
   And tell future ages the feats of the day;
A bard who detested all sadness and spleen,
   And wish'd that Parnassus a vineyard had been.

The dinner being over, the claret they ply,
   And every new cork is a new spring of joy;
In the bands of old friendship and kindred so set,
   And the bands grew the tighter the more they were wet.

Gay Pleasure ran riot as bumpers ran o'er;
   Bright Phoebus ne'er witness'd so joyous a corps,
And vowed that to leave them he was quite forlorn,
   Till Cynthia hinted he'd see them next morn.

Six bottles a-piece had well wore out the night,
   When gallant Sir Robert, to finish the fight,
Turn'd o'er in one bumper a bottle of red,
   And swore 'twas the way that their ancestor did.

Then worthy Glenriddel, so cautious and sage,
   No longer the warfare, ungodly, would wage;
A high ruling elder to wallow in wine!
   He left the foul business to folks less divine.

The gallant Sir Robert fought hard to the end;
    But who can with Fate and Quart Bumpers contend?
Though Fate said, a hero should perish in light;
    So uprose bright Phoebus — and down fell the knight.

Next uprose our Bard, like a prophet in drink:—
    'Craigdarroch, thou'lt soar when creation shall sink!
But if thou would flourish immortal in rhyme,
    Come — one bottle more — and have at the sublime!

'Thy line, that have struggled for freedom with Bruce,
    Shall heroes and patriots ever produce:
So thine be the laurel, and mine be the bay;
    The field thou hast won, by yon bright god of day!'

27TH DECEMBER

Rattlin, Roarin Willie

IN TODAY'S VERSE, the clubbable, sociable poet immortalises one of his boon companions from the Crochallan Fencibles, William Dunbar (d.1807). In the interleaved *Scots Musical Museum*, Burns has the following to say of this adaptation of a traditional song: 'The last stanza is mine and out of compliment to one of the worthiest fellows in the world, William Dunbar, Esq: Writer to the signet, Edinr, and Colonel of the Crochallan Corps, a club of wits who took that title at the time of raising the fencible regiments.'

O Rattlin, roarin Willie,
    O he held to the fair,
An' for to sell his fiddle
    And buy some other ware;

But parting wi' his fiddle,
　The saut tear blin't his e'e;
And Rattlin, roarin Willie,
　Ye're welcome hame to me.

O Willie, come sell your fiddle,
　O sell your fiddle sae fine;
O Willie, come sell your fiddle,
　And buy a pint o' wine;
If I should sell my fiddle,
　The warl' would think I was mad,
For mony a rantin day
　My fiddle and I hae had.

As I cam by Crochallan,
　I cannilie keekit ben;
Rattlin, roarin Willie
　Was sitting at yon boord-en',
Sitting at yon boord-en',
　And amang gude companie;
Rattlin, roarin Willie,
　Ye're welcome hame to me!

28TH DECEMBER

On Pride and Passion
from a letter to Agnes McLehose, 28th December 1787

A S WE DRAW TOWARDS the end of our daily exploration of Burns's life and works, the following extract, in which the bard describes his 'great constituent elements' seems appropriate. Certainly, this journey through the year with Burns as our companion has sought to show the poet *as he is*, taking full account of the intricacies of his character and conveying his many – and at times competing – 'enthusiasms'.

I don't know if you have a just idea of my character, but I wish you to see me *as I am*.— I am, as most people of my trade are, a strange will o' wisp being; the victim too frequently of much imprudence and many follies.— My great constituent elements are Pride and Passion: the first I have endeavoured to humanise into integrity and honour; the last makes me a Devotee to the warmest degree of enthusiasm, in Love, Religion, or Friendship; either of them or all together as I happen to be inspired.—

29TH DECEMBER

Elegy on the Year 1788

W E ARE COMING FULL CIRCLE in our 360-degree discovery of Robert Burns through the changing seasons, and so we turn our attention once again to the New Year. Certainly, the bard seemed to be meaningfully invested in the notion of New Year as a time to take stock and look to the future. In today's poem, written for publication in the *Edinburgh Evening Courant* newspaper, the bard hopes that the 'bairn', 1789, will learn from the 'dire events' and political turbulence of the previous year. It was the malady of George III in November 1788 that triggered such upheaval, leading to a battle between parliamentary power (embodied in a reversal of his usual Tory values by Pitt) and royal prerogative (championed by the Whig peer, Fox), which became known as the Regency Crisis.

For Lords or kings I dinna mourn,
E'en let them die — for that they're born!
But oh! prodigious to reflect,
A Towmont, Sirs, is gane to wreck!
O Eighty-eight, in thy sma' space
What dire events ha'e taken place!
Of what enjoyments thou hast reft us!
In what a pickle thou has left us!

   The Spanish empire's tint a head,
And my auld teethless Bawtie's dead;
The toolzie's teugh 'tween Pitt and Fox,
An' our gudewife's wee birdy cocks;

The tane is game, a bluidy devil,
But to the hen-birds unco civil;
The tither's dour, has nae sic breedin',
But better stuff ne'er claw'd a middin!

Ye ministers, come mount the pupit,
An' cry till ye be haerse an' rupit;
For Eighty-eight he wished you weel,
An' gied ye a' baith gear an' meal;
E'en mony a plack, an' mony a peck,
Ye ken yoursels, for little feck!

Ye bonny lasses, dight your een,
For some o' you hae tint a frien';
In Eighty-eight, ye ken, was ta'en,
What ye'll ne'er hae to gi'e again.

Observe the very nowt an' sheep,
How dowff an' dowie now they creep;
Nay, even the yirth itsel' does cry,
For Embro' wells are grutten dry.

O Eighty-nine, thou's but a bairn,
An' no owre auld, I hope, to learn!
Thou beardless boy, I pray tak' care,
Thou now hast got thy Daddy's chair,
Nae handcuff'd, mizl'd, hap-shackl'd Regent,
But, like himsel', a full free agent,
Be sure ye follow out the plan
Nae waur than he did, honest man!
As muckle better as you can.

30TH DECEMBER

from Poem Addressed to Mr Mitchell, Collector of Excise

AS MANY OF US TURN OUR ATTENTION to tomorrow's festivities and make preparations to bring in 'the bells' with family and friends, to reflect on the past year, and to anticipate the future with renewed resolution, Burns's words from a verse epistle composed on 'Hogmanai eve: 1795' perfectly capture the sentiment of the occasion.

So may the auld year gang out moaning,
To see the new come, laden, groaning,
Wi' double plenty o'er the loanin
       To thee and thine;
Domestic peace and comforts crowning
       The hail design.

31st DECEMBER

Auld Lang Syne
to the tune of Sir Alexander Don's Strathspey

S URELY THERE CAN BE only one way to finish *Burns for Every Day of the Year*, or *any* year for that matter! Wherever you are in the world, the likelihood is that when the clock strikes midnight, the notes and sentiments of 'Auld Lang Syne' will ring out to welcome in the New Year. Burns's version of this traditional Scottish song has become one of the world's most famous, instantly recognisable songs; a renown it rightfully enjoys as a consequence of its universally felt sentiments of memory, friendship and kindness.

'Hogmanay' – or New Year's Eve – has always been an important occasion in Scotland marked with its own distinct rituals. After midnight, the tradition of 'first footing' will commence. This is when the first person to cross the threshold of a home – ideally a tall, dark stranger, or at the very least someone who wasn't present before midnight! – brings with them luck for the New Year and a symbolic gift. Traditionally these might be a 'black bun' (a rich fruit cake), a dram of whisky, some shortbread or a lump of coal (signifying warmth for the year ahead).

With their ancient, meaningful roots, these Scottish traditions are now practised on an international scale. And, indeed, Scotland and Scotland's national bard have become synonymous with this special time of year to the extent that, in the twenty-first century, people from all over the world visit Scotland to take part in our Hogmanay festivities.

Should auld acquaintance be forgot,
   And never brought to mind?
Should auld acquaintance be forgot,
   And auld lang syne!

For auld lang syne, my jo,
   For auld lang syne,
We'll tak a cup o'kindness yet,
   For auld lang syne.

And surely ye'll be your pint stowp!
   And surely I'll be mine!
And we'll take a cup o'kindness yet,
   For auld lang syne.
      For auld &c.

We twa hae run about the braes,
   And pou'd the gowans fine;
But we've wander'd mony a weary fitt,
   Sin' auld lang syne.
      For auld &c.

We twa hae paidl'd in the burn,
   Frae morning sun till dine;
But seas between us braid hae roar'd
   Sin' auld lang syne.
      For auld &c.

And there's a hand, my trusty fiere!
   And gie's a hand o' thine!
And we'll tak a right gude-willie-waught,
   For auld lang syne.
      For auld &c.

'And fare thee weel awhile!'

AND, SO HERE WE ARE, at the end of our journey through the year with Robert Burns. It is my sincere hope that exploring these 366 selections from his poetry, song and prose has given you a sense of the bard's vast and wide-ranging oeuvre. His is a body of work generated by a monumental creativity and a remarkable complexity of character – a complexity that Lord Byron captures as only a poet could:

> What an antithetical mind! – tenderness, roughness – delicacy, coarseness – sentiment, sensuality – soaring and grovelling, dirt and deity – all mixed up in that one compound of inspired clay!
>
> LORD BYRON ON ROBERT BURNS, 13TH DECEMBER 1813

Ultimately, what is so wonderful about Burns is how he resists being put in a box. And so, these daily glimpses into his life, his times and his works bring us as close to a fully dimensional view of the Scottish National Bard as we are likely to get. Whatever perspective we might take, there's truly something in Burns for everyone.

Thank You

I OWE A DEBT OF GRATITUDE to a great many friends, family and colleagues for helping me to complete this book during the 'unprecedented times' of 2020, and for their encouragement in all of my Burns-related endeavours.

For fostering my interest in Burns from an early stage, and for a great deal of kind mentorship over the years, Professor Gerard Carruthers. To my friends and colleagues at the University of Glasgow's Centre for Robert Burns Studies – Dr Rhona Brown, Professor Nigel Leask, Professor Kirsteen McCue, Professor Murray Pittock and Dr Ronnie Young – for their scholarly insight, friendship, professional support, and the team spirit that I have come to value so much. I have had many informative and helpful conversations about Burns with Dr David Hopes, Dr Craig Lamont, Dr Ralph McLean, Professor Patrick Scott, and Chris Waddell.

To the partners of Burns Scotland (the National Burns Collection) for their backing in the various Burns-related activities that have contributed to my knowledge of his legacy and cultural hinterland, and for access to their remarkable collections. For her energy in promoting Burns and sharing an abridged version of *Burns for Every Day of the Year* through Wee Box, Amy McCusker.

For their vision and enthusiasm in commissioning this project, my sincere thanks to Ali McBride and Campbell Brown at Black & White Publishing, and to their team including Alice Latchford, Thomas Ross, and most of all Emma Hargrave, without whose ongoing positivity, encouragement and remarkable expertise this book would have been infinitely more difficult to realise. I am grateful, also, for the stunning cover design by Helen Crawford-White that perfectly captures the essence and variety of Burns's writings.

For their unwavering support and inspiration, and for doing everything they could to help create much-needed time for me to work on this project, my parents Peter and Agnes Gray, my sister and brother-in-law Geraldine and Liam McFall, my parents-in-law Calum Iain and Barbara Mackay and my brother-in-law Iain Mackay.

Finally, my heartfelt thanks go to my husband Dòmhnall and my children Eimhir and Calum Peter without whose love, reassurance and forbearance the completion of *Burns for Every Day of the Year* would simply not have been possible.

Glossary

aboon above
acquent acquainted, or familiar
aft often
agley astray
aiblins perhaps
airn iron
airts directions
aith oath
a-jee ajar
alane alone
alang along
amaist almost
amang among
anathem curse
anither another
asklent askew
auld old
awa away
aye always, or yes

baggie belly
bairan baring or uncovering
bairn(s) child(ren)
baith both
banes bones
bauld bold
beastie small creature
beld bald
ben within
bent hillock

bickering scurrying
bide remain, or stay
biel shelter
biggin building
birkie lively person
blate bashful
blaudin' beating
blaw blow
bleezan blazing
bleeze blaze
blellum blusterer
blinkit blinked
blins blinds
bludie/bludy bloody
bluid blood
boddle coin
bouk body
braid broad, or wide
brankie well-dressed
brany brandy
brattle noise or clatter
braw fine or handsome
brawlie admirably
breastie breast
brent smooth
brig bridge
brock badger
brunstane brimstone
buirdly stalwart
bummle bungler

burnie burn or stream
buskit prepared
byke crowd or swarm

caller fresh
canie/cannie shrewd
cankert ill-natured
cantie pleasant
carlin old woman
cauld cold
cell nest
chiel lad or young fellow
chimla lug fireplace
clamb climbed
clankie knock
clarkit written
claught clutched
clavers talk or chatter
cloots/clouts clothes
coof fool
coost cast off, or threw off
coulter plough blade
cour lower
cow'rin cowering
crack gossip, or talk
cranreuch frost
crock old ewe
crummock crook

daimen occasional or infrequent
daudin thrashing
daur('t) dare(d)
daurk labour
deave deafen
deil devil
dight make ready
dinna do not
dint occasion

dirl shake
dockies backsides
doited blundered
dool sorrow
dought be able to
douse sober or prudent
dowie melancholy
dub mud
duddies clothes

e'e eye
eild old age
eldritch eerie, or other-worldly
ettle aim, or intention

faem foam
fain content
fand found
fash bother
faulding slap fold gate
faut fault
fauteor wrong-doer
fechtin' fighting
fen defend or support
fidgin fain twitching with excitement
fient the devil, or fiend
fier hearty
fiere comrade or friend
foggage grass
fou drunk
frae from
frater brotherhood
furder further, or progress
furr furrow
fyke agitation, or fuss

gab mouth
gaed went

gang go
gars makes
garten garter
gat got
gaun going
gawsie fine
gear money, or possessions
ghaist ghost
gies gives
giz wig
glaikit foolish
glaizie glittering
glaum'd grabbed, or snatched
gled kite (bird)
gleg sharp, or quick
glowran glowering or gazing
gowd(en) gold(en)
gowk cuckoo, or fool
gree social standing
greet(in) cry(ing)
grun ground
grutten cried
gude-willie-waught convivial drink
guid good
gullie large knife
gulravage romp

hae have
haerse hoarse
hain'd preserved or spared
hairst harvest
hald dwelling
hale whole
hamely homely
harkit listened
harn cloth
haud hold

havins behaviour or manners
heapit heaped
hellim helm
heugh crag, or ridge
heuk hook or sickle
hizzie wench
hoordet hoarded
houghmagandy/ie fornication
houlet owl
howe hollow or deep
hurdies buttocks

icker ear of corn
ilk each
ilka every
ingle burning fire

jad wench
Janwar January
jaups splashes
jink dodge or dart
jocteleg small knife
jundie jostle

kintra country
kittle unsafe or inflammatory
kiutlin cuddling
knaggie knobbly or knotted
knappin-hammer hammer for stones
knowes hillocks
kythe tell

lades loads
laik lack
laith loath
lane(ly) lone(ly)
lang long

599

lave remainder
lay pasture or unploughed ground
lea'e leave
lear learning, or education
leesome delightful, or tender
leeze delight
leugh laughed
liein lying
lo'es loves
loof palm
loupin(g) leaping
lowe flame
lowse loose
lug ear

mailen/mailin smallholding
mair more
maist most
manna must not
maukin hare
maun must
maut malt
mense sense
minnie mother
mirkest darkest
mischanter misadventure
mony many
moodewurk mole
mools clods of earth
mottie speckled or spotted
mowe to have sexual intercourse
muckle much

neebor neighbour
neist next
neuk corner
nieve fist

nits nuts
noddle brain, or head

onie any
owre over

paidl'd paddled
painch paunch or belly
pattle spade
peghan stomach
phiz facial expression, or face
plack small coin
pleugh plough
pou pull
pow head
powther powder
prie try or taste
puir poor

raep rope
rair roar
raize provoke or rouse
raploch homely
raxan stretched, or stretching
reck care for
reek smoke
reekit smoked
reif plunder or thieve
remead remedy
rickles piled sheaves of corn
riggin roof or ridge
rin run
ripp handful of corn
roos'd roused
rout road, or way
routhie abundant, or plentiful
rowe wrap or roll
rupit hoarse

sae so
sair sore
sang song
sark skirt
sarket clothes
saut salt
scaur afraid
sconner disgust or revulsion
scrievin striding or gliding
shavie trick
sheugh ditch
shiel hut, or shed
shools shovels
shouther shoulder
shure sheared
sic such
siller silver
skaith harm
skellum scoundrel
skelpin thrashing
skinking watery
skirl shriek
skouth scope
skyrin brightly coloured
slee sly or wise
sleekit sleek or sneaky
sma' small
smeek smoke
smoor'd smothered
snaw snow
sned cut off
snell harsh
snick latch
snowket nosed
sonsie buxom or good-natured
sough deep breath
sowth try a tune

spairges spatters
spavie lump on a horse's shank
spean wean
spier enquire
sprattle scramble or struggle
spunk spark
staggie stag
stane stone
stang sting
staw crept or stole away
steekit enclosed
steeve strong
steghan eating
sten leap
stibble stubble
stimpart measure of grain
stirks young bullocks
stoupe/stowpe tankard
stoure battle or storm
stoyte lurch or stagger
strang strong
streekit stretched
stroan't pissed
sugh deep breath
suthron southern
swank agile
swarf swoon
swat sweated
swith quickly
syne since

taen taken
tap-pickle grain at the tip of a
    stalk of wheat
tapsalteerie upside down
targe light shield
tent care, or heed
tentie watchful or attentive

tentless careless, or heedless
thairm intestine
theckit thatched
thole endure
thrang a crowd
thrave a measure of straw/grain
thraw a turn
thretty thirty
thrissle thistle
thummart polecat
tim'rous timorous or shy
tint lost
tirl'd turned
tither the other
tittie sister
tod toad
toofa' falling-to
toolzie brawl, or quarrel
towmond/towmont a year
towzie unkempt
toyte totter
trashtrie rubbish
trow to believe
tulzie brawl, or quarrel
tyke dog, or mongrel

ulzie oil
unco very or strange
usquabae whisky

vauntie proud
vittle grain

wad would
waefu' woeful

wale choice, or to choose
wame stomach
wan won
wanrestfu' restless
warl' world
warly worldly
wa's walls
wauket thickened
waukin awake, or waking
wauks wakens
waur worse
wawlie fine, or handsome
wee little
weel well
weet wet
westlin' westerly
whatt whetted
whigmaleerie ornament
whiles sometimes
whittle knife
willcat wildcat
wimplin meandering
winna will not
winnocks windows
win's winds
wit know

wooer-bab garter worn by a suitor
wordy worthy
wrang wrong

yerd/yird yard
yestreen yesterday evening
yett gate
yowes ewes

Index of Titles

Awa Whigs Awa **10th June**
Ay Waukin O **6th June**
Behold My Love, How Green the Groves **25th November**
Behold the Hour the Boat Arrive **19th February**
Beware o' Bonie Ann **7th October**
Blythe Hae I Been on Yon Hill **29th May**
Bonie Bell **20th March**
Braw Lads o Galla Water **24th May**
Ca' the Yowes to the Knowes **27th February / 20th October**
Caledonia **30th November**
Castle Gordon **7th September**
Cauld Frosty Morning **1st November**
Charlie He's My Darling **15th April**
Clarinda, Mistress of My Soul **16th February**
Come, Let Me Take Thee to My Breast **28th August**
Comin Thro' the Rye **8th September**
Contented Wi' Little **23rd January**
Country Lassie **15th June**
Dainty Davie **2nd May**
Deed of Assignment, July 1786 **23rd July**
Elegy on the Death of Robert Ruisseaux **26th July**
Elegy on Peg Nicholson **13th March**
Elegy on the Year 1788 **29th December**
Epigram **28th June**
Epigram – Under the Portrait of Miss Burns **11th October**
Epistle to a Young Friend **15th May**
Epistle to Blacklock **21st October**
Epistle to Davie, A Brother Poet **16th January / 27th May**
Epistle to John Goldie in Kilmarnock **20th August**
Epistle to John Lapraik **7th January / 1st April**
Epitaph – For the Author's Father **13th February**
Epitaph on Holy Willie **10th February**
Epitaph on John Dove, Innkeeper **21st November**
Fair Jenny **19th September**
Farewell Thou Stream **14th December**
Green Grow the Rashes **1st February**
Had I a Cave on Some Wild, Distant Shore **18th August**

Halloween **31st October**

Here's a Bottle and an Honest Friend **31st January**

Here's a Health to Ane I Loe Dear **12th July**

Hey for a Lass wi' a Tocher **18th March**

Highland Lassie, O **10th May**

Highland Mary **14th May**

Holy Willie's Prayer **9th February / 7th August**

How Lang and Dreary Is the Night **1st October**

Hunting Song **28th September**

I Dream'd I Lay **8th April**

I Love My Jean **25th February**

I'm O'er Young to Marry Yet **17th November**

I Reign in Jeanie's Bosom **23rd February**

Impromptu on Mrs Riddell's Birthday **4th November**

In the Character of a Ruined Farmer **13th June**

Inconstancy in Love **26th February**

Inscription on a Goblet **14th October**

It Is Na, Jean, Thy Bonie Face **26th March**

It Was A' For Our Rightfu' King **29th April**

It Was Upon a Lammas Night **1st August**

Jessie – A New Scots Song **10th April**

John Anderson My Jo **20th June**

John Barleycorn – A Ballad **11th September**

John Come Kiss Me Now **29th February**

Johnie Cope **21st September**

Killiecrankie **27th July**

Lament for James, Earl of Glencairn **30th January**

Lament of Mary Queen of Scots on the Approach of Spring **8th February**

Lassie wi' the Lintwhite Locks **16th March**

Libel Summons **4th June / 3rd July**

Lines on the Fall of Fyers, Near Loch Ness **5th September**

Lines Written by SOMEBODY on the Window of an Inn **27th August**

Lines Written on a Window at the Globe Tavern **12th November**

Logan Braes **25th May**

Love and Liberty – A Cantata *I Am a Bard of No Regard* **10th January /**
I Am a Son of Mars **1st March /** *I Once Was a Maid* **2nd March /** *See the Smoking Bowl Before Us* **12th December**

Lying at a Reverend Friend's House One Night **16th December**
Musing on the Roaring Ocean **8th December**
My Father Was a Farmer **6th January**
My Girl She's Airy **20th May**
My Heart's in the Highlands **29th November**
My Nanie's Awa **29th September**
My Peggy's Face **5th November**
My Wife's a Winsome Wee Thing **18th June**
Nature's Law **3rd September**
O Bonie Was Yon Rosy Brier **26th November**
O Lassie, Art Thou Sleeping Yet **20th January**
O Leave Novels, Ye Mauchline Belles **24th February**
O May Thy Morn **3rd December**
O My Luve's Like a Red, Red Rose **1st June**
O Once I Lov'd **12th January**
O Phely, Happy Be That Day **23rd November**
O Poortith Cauld and Restless Love **5th February**
O Saw Ye Bonie Lesley **22nd August**
O' Saw Ye My Maggie **15th March**
O Were I on Parnassus Hill **9th December**
O Were My Love Yon Lilac Fair **31st May**
O Whistle, and I'll Come to Ye **27th April**
Ode for General Washington's Birthday **22nd February**
On a Bank of Flowers **5th June**
On a Scotch Bard Gone to the West Indies **14th August**
On Marriage **19th June**
On Robert Fergusson **16th October**
On Seeing a Wounded Hare Limp by Me **19th April**
On the Birth of a Posthumous Child **24th November**
On the Late Captain Grose's Peregrinations Thro' Scotland **24th October**
Poem Addressed to Mr Mitchell, Collector of Excise **30th December**
Poor Mailie's Elegy **12th March**
Postscript to The Author's Earnest Cry & Prayer **27th March**
Rantin' Rovin' Robin **24th January**
Rattlin, Roarin Willie **27th December**
Raving Winds Around Her Blowing **21st December**
Remorse **20th July**

Robin Shure in Hairst **10th September**
Sandy and Jockie **17th June**
Scotch Drink **27th January**
Scots Wha Hae **24th June**
Second Epistle to Davie **29th June**
Sensibility How Charming **19th July**
She Says She Lo'es Me Best Of A' **5th October**
Sketch. New Year's Day. To Mrs Dunlop **1st January**
Song – Composed in August **15th August**
Sonnet **18th December**
Sonnet on the Death of Robert Riddell Esq. of Glenriddell, April 1794
    22nd April
Stanzas on the Same Occasion **22nd July**
Such a Parcel of Rogues in a Nation **1st May**
Tam Glen **22nd October**
Tam Lin **18th October**
Tam o' Shanter **29th January / 30th October**
Tam Samson's Elegy **21st August**
The Auld Farmer's New-Year Morning Salutation **3rd January**
The Battle of Sherra-moor **13th November**
The Birks of Aberfeldy **30th August**
The Bonie Lass o' Ballochmyle **19th November**
The Bonie Wee Thing **7th April**
The Braw Wooer **8th May**
The Brigs of Ayr (i) **22nd September**
The Brigs of Ayr (ii) **23rd September**
The Charming Month of May **16th May**
The Cotter's Saturday Night **7th May / 13th August / 27th November**
The Death and Dying Words of Poor Mailie **11th March**
The Deil's Awa wi' th' Exciseman **11th July**
The Dumfries Volunteers **16th July**
The Farewell. To the Brethren of St James's Lodge, Tarbolton **1st July**
The Farewell **5th April**
The First Psalm **17th May**
The Fornicator **21st May**
The Heron Ballads: John Bushby's Lamentation **23rd March**
The Highland Widow's Lament **17th April**

The Holy Fair **6th August**

The Holy Tulzie **3rd August**

The Hue and Cry of John Lewars **12th October**

The Humble Petition of Bruar Water to the Noble Duke of Atholе **31st August**

The Inventory **23rd May**

The Kirk of Scotland's Garland – A New Song **11th August**

The Lazy Mist **15th November**

The Lea-rig **12th September**

The Lovely Lass o' Inverness **16th April**

The Lover's Morning Salute to His Mistress **3rd October**

The Posie **3rd February**

The Rantin Dog the Daddie O't **2nd April**

The Rights of Women *spoken by* Miss Fontenelle **8th March**

The Ronalds of the Bennals **10th November**

The Selkirk Grace **26th January**

The Seventh of November **7th November**

The Slave's Lament **25th March**

The Small Birds Rejoice **30th April**

The Solemn League and Covenant **17th August**

The Song of Death **24th July**

The Twa Dogs, A Tale **8th June**

The Vision **8th January / 13th January / 10th December**

The Whistle **26th December**

Their Groves o' Sweet Myrtle **17th March**

There Was a Lass, and She Was Fair **10th March**

There'll Never Be Peace Till Jamie Comes Hame **13th April**

Thou Fair Eliza **7th June**

Thou Gloomy December **1st December**

Third Epistle to Lapraik **13th September**

Tibbie, I Hae Seen the Day **30th September**

To a Haggis **25th January**

To a Louse **5th December**

To a Mountain Daisy **20th April**

To a Mouse **22nd January**

To Alexander Cunningham **28th July**

To Alexander Findlater **14th March**

To Clarinda **13th December**

To Daunton Me **20th December**
To Dr John Mackenzie **2nd July**
To Hugh Parker **11th June**
To John Syme **17th December / 24th December**
To Mary in Heaven **13th May**
To Miss Ainslie in Church **6th May**
To Miss Cruickshank, a Very Young Lady **3rd May**
To Miss Jessy Lewars **27th June**
To Miss Logan **4th January**
To Mr Tytler of Woodhouselee **7th February**
To the Rev. John McMath **18th September**
To W. Simpson, Ochiltree **18th May / 23rd August**
Up and Warn a' Willie **14th November**
Up in the Morning Early **17th January**
Wha'll M-w Me Now **9th September**
When Wild War's Deadly Blast Was Blown **11th November**
Where Braving Angry Winter's Storms **8th November**
Whistle O'er the Lave O't **16th November**
Why Should Na Poor Folk Mowe **15th July**
Will Ye Go to the Indies, My Mary **12th May**
Willie Brew'd a Peck o' Maut **28th January**
Wilt Thou Be My Dearie **11th February**
Winter, A Dirge **19th January**
Written in Friar's Carse Hermitage **2nd June**
Written with a Pencil Over the Chimney-Piece **29th August**
Ye Jacobites by Name **18th April**
Yestreen I Had a Pint o' Wine **31st March**
Yon Wild Mossy Mountains **15th September**
Young Peggy **25th April**
You're Welcome, Willie Stewart **19th May**

Letters

To Robert Ainslie
> On Marriage **26th May**
> On Responsibility **14th June** / 8th June 1788
> On a Hangover **22nd November** / November 1791

To Miss Wilhelmina Alexander of Ballochmyle
> On The Bonie Lass o' Ballochmyle **18th November** / 18th November 1786

To James Armour
> Burns's Last Written Words **18th July** / 18th July 1796

To John Arnot
> On the Houghmagandie Pack **4th April** / April 1786

To Miss Lesley Baillie of Mayville
> On Blythe Hae I Been on Yon Hill **28th May** / May 1793

To John Ballantine
> On Being Toasted as Caledonia's Bard **11th December** / 14th January 1787

To David Blair
> On Lord Balmerino's Durk **24th August** / 25th August 1795

To Captain Richard Brown
> On Life **28th February** / February 1788

To James Burness
> On Religion and Moral Sense **10th August** / 3rd August 1784

To Gilbert Burns
> On the Highland Tour **17th September** / 17th September 1787

To Margaret Chalmers
> On the Prospect of Ellisland **9th June** / 14th March 1788
> On the Excise **7th July** / 17th February 1788
> On Burns's State of Perpetual Warfare **19th December** / 19th December 1787
> On Poetic Compliments **6th November** / circa November 1787

To William Chalmers and John McAdam
> On a Wicked SONG **20th November** / 20th November 1786

610

To James Clarke
On Burns's Final Illness **26th June** / 26th June 1796
To Robert Cleghorn
On Quitting Ellisland **2nd October** / October 1791
On Bawdry **25th October** / 25th October 1793
To William Corbet
On Conscience **20th September** / September 1792
To Miss Helen Craik
On Poetry **22nd March** / 9th August 1790
On Poets **9th August** / 9th August 1790
To Crauford Tait, Esq.
On Fortune and Apathy **15th October** / 15th October 1790
To Alexander Cunningham
On Love **4th February** / 24th January 1789
On Politics **20th February** / 20th February 1793
On Marriage **21st June** / 10th September 1792
On Being Busy **8th August** / 8th August 1790
On Moral Sense **16th August** / 25th February 1794
On the Supernatural **19th October** / 10th September 1792
To Lady Elizabeth Cunningham
On Burns's Profession(s) **23rd December** / 23rd December 1789
To Mr William Dunbar
On Two Bewitching Young Ladies **13th October** / 25th September 1788
To Mrs Frances Dunlop
On New Year **2nd January** / New Year's Day morning 1789
On New Year **5th January** / 1st Jan 1795
On Fame **15th January** / 15th January 1787
On Poetic Ability **4th May** / 4th May 1788
On Ellisland **12th June** / 13th June 1788
On Henry Mackenzie **14th January** / 10th April 1790
In Anticipation of Another Child **22nd June** / 22nd June 1789
On William Wallace **23rd June** / 15th November 1786
On the French Revolution **17th July** / 12th January 1795
On the Harvest **4th September** / 5th September 1788
On Children **24th September** / 24th September 1792
On Religion **6th October** / 6th October 1790
On the Death of Mrs Susan Henri **9th October** / October 1792

On Anguish and Low Spirits **10th October** / 21st January 1788

On his Daughter Elizabeth's Illness **15th December** / 15th December 1793

On Christ **25th December** / 13th December 1789

To 'E'

On Marriage and Friendship **16th June** / c.1781

To the Earl of Buchan

On Bannockburn **25th June** / 12th January 1794

To James, Earl of Glencairn

On the Excise **6th July** / 1st February 1788

To the *Edinburgh Evening Courant*

On the Stuarts **14th April** / 8th November 1788

On America **5th July** / 8th November 1788

To David Erskine, Lord Buchan

On the Prospect of Touring Scotland **25th August** / 7th February 1787

To Mr Graham of Fintry / Robert Graham Esq. of Fintry

On the Excise **8th July** / 10th September 1788

On Adam Smith's *The Wealth of Nations* **9th March** / 13th May 1789

On Being Appointed to My Excise Division **9th July**

On the Excise **10th July** / 9th December 1789

On the French Revolution **13th July** / 5th January 1793

To Mr Fyfe

On Leaving Edinburgh **5th May** / 5th May 1787

To Captain Francis Grose

On Alloway Kirk (i) **23rd October** / c. June 1790

On Alloway Kirk (ii) **27th October** / c. June 1790

On Alloway Kirk (iii) **29th October** / c. June 1790

To Gavin Hamilton

On That Unlucky Paper **3rd April** / 15th April 1786

On Fame **7th December** / 7th December 1786

To John Kennedy

On the Human Heart **26th September** / 26th September 1786

To John McMurdo

On Poets and Beggars **9th January** / 9th January 1789

To Agnes McLehose

On That Delicious Passion **15th February** / December 1787

On Boundaries **17th February** / 25th January 1788

On Clarinda's Contempt **18th February** / February 1790

On Pride and Passion **28th December** / 28th December 1787

On Religion **12th August** / 8th January 1788

To John Mitchell Esq

On the Excise **6th September** / c. September 1790

To Dr John Moore

On Burns's First Poetic Composition **11th January**

On Reading **4th March**

On Mossgiel Farm **7th March**

On the Religious Satires **2nd August**

On Superstition and Imagination **17th October**

On Self-Knowledge **4th December**

On Letter Writing **6th December**

To Robert Muir

On Visiting Stirlingshire **26th August** / 26th August 1787

To John Richmond

On Emigration **30th July** / 30th July 1786

On Women **2nd September** / 1st September 1786

To Maria Riddell

On the Loss of His Daughter **2nd November** / October/November
1795

To James Sibbald

On Expressing Gratitude **23rd April** / January 1787

To David Sillar

On Poetry and Marriage **5th August** / 5th August 1789

To Sir John Sinclair

On the Monkland Friendly Society **5th March**

To Rev. John Skinner

On the *Scots Musical Museum* **8th October** / 25th October 1787

To William Smellie

On Maria Riddell **3rd November** / January 1792

To James Smith

On Marrying Jean **28th April** / April 1788

On Burns's West Highland Tour **30th June** / 30th June 1787

To John Tennant

On Whisky **22nd December** / 22nd December 1788

Bibliography

By Robert Burns

Commonplace Books, Tour Journals and Miscellaneous Prose, ed. Nigel Leask (Oxford: Oxford University Press, 2014).

Facsimile of Burns's Celebrated Poem, entitled The Jolly Beggars. From the Original Manuscript, in the possession of Thomas Stewart, Esq. Greenock. (Glasgow: James Lumsden & Son; Edinburgh: William Blackwood; London: Longman and Co., 1823).

Poems Ascribed to Robert Burns, the Ayrshire Bard, (Glasgow: Thomas Stewart, 1801).

Poems, Chiefly in the Scottish Dialect, (Kilmarnock: John Wilson, 1786).

Poems, Chiefly in the Scottish Dialect, (Edinburgh: William Creech, 1787).

Poems, Chiefly in the Scottish Dialect, 2 Vols, (Edinburgh: William Creech, 1793).

Robert Burns's Commonplace Book 1783–1785. Reproduced in Facsimile from the Poet's Manuscript in the Possession of Sir Alfred Joseph Law, M.P. With Transcript Introduction and Notes by James Cameron Ewing and Davidson Cook (1938), 2nd edn ed. David Daiches (London: Centor Press, 1965).

The Fornicators Court, ed. Gerard Carruthers & Pauline Gray, (Edinburgh: Abbotsford Library Research Project, 2009).

The Letters of Robert Burns (1931) ed. J. De Lancey Ferguson; 2nd edn ed. G. Ross Roy, 2 Vols (Oxford: Clarendon Press, 1985).

The Merry Muses of Caledonia, introduced by G. Ross Roy, (1799; facsimile repr. Columbia: University of South Carolina Press for the Thomas Cooper Library, 1999).

The Poems and Songs of Robert Burns, ed. James Kinsley, 3 Vols, (Oxford: Clarendon Press, 1968).

The Works of Robert Burns; with an account of his life, and a criticism on his writings. To which are prefixed some observations on the character and condition of the Scottish peasantry, ed. James Currie, 4 Vols, (London: Cadell & Davis, 1800).

The Works of Robert Burns, with his Life, ed. Allan Cunningham, 8 Vols, (London: Cochrane & Co., 1834).

*

Burns, Robert & Johnson, James, *The Scots Musical Museum*, ed. Murray Pittock, (Oxford: Oxford University Press, 2018).

Cromek, R.H. (ed.), *Reliques of Robert Burns; Consisting Chiefly of Original Letters, Poems, and Critical Observations on Scottish Songs*, (London, 1808).

Thomson, George (ed.), *A Select Collection of Original Scottish Airs*, (Edinburgh, 1793–1802).

Secondary Sources

Carruthers, Gerard, *Robert Burns*, (Tavistock: Northcote, 2006).

Carruthers, Gerard (ed.), *The Edinburgh Companion to Robert Burns*, (Edinburgh: Edinburgh University Press, 2009).

Crawford, Robert, *The Bard*, (London: Pimlico, 2009).

Leask, Nigel, *Robert Burns and Pastoral: Poetry and Improvement in Late Eighteenth-Century Scotland*, (Oxford: Oxford University Press, 2010).

Low, Donald A. (ed.), *Robert Burns: The Critical Heritage*, (London: Routledge & Kegan Paul, 1974).

McGuirk, Carol, *Robert Burns and the Sentimental Era*, (Georgia: University of Georgia Press, 1985).

O'Rourke, Donny (ed.), *Ae Fond Kiss: The Love Letters of Robert Burns and Clarinda*, (Edinburgh: Mercat Press, 2000).

Pittock, Murray (ed.), *Robert Burns in Global Culture*, (Lewisburg, PA: Bucknell University Press, 2011).

Purdie, D., Carruthers, G. & McCue, K. (eds), *The Burns Encyclopedia* (London: Robert Hale, 2013).